AI's Role in Language Learning and Communication

Ankit Shukla
Rajamangala University of Technology, Thanyaburi, Thailand

Benjaporn Meeprom
Rajamangala University of Technology, Thanyaburi, Thailand

Kongkiat Khunasathitchai
Rajamangala University of Technology, Thanyaburi, Thailand

Nagendra Yadav
Welcomgroup Graduate School of Hotel Administration, Manipal Academy of Higher Education, India

IGI Global
Scientific Publishing
Publishing Tomorrow's Research Today

Vice President of Editorial Melissa Wagner
Director of Acquisitions Mikaela Felty
Director of Book Development Jocelynn Hessler
Production Manager Mike Brehm
Cover Design Jose Rosado

Published in the United States of America by
IGI Global Scientific Publishing
701 East Chocolate Avenue
Hershey, PA, 17033, USA
Tel: 717-533-8845
Fax: 717-533-7115
Website: https://www.igi-global.com E-mail: cust@igi-global.com

Library of Congress Cataloging-in-Publication Data

Names: Shukla, Ankit, 1992- editor | Meeprom, Benjaporn, 1981- editor | Khunsathitchai, Kongkiat, 1985- editor | Yadav, Nagendra, 1990- editor
Title: AI's role in language learning and communication / edited by Ankit Shukla, Benjaporn Meeprom, Kongkiat Khunsathitchai, Nagendra Yadav.
Description: Hershey PA : IGI Global Scientific Publishing, 2026. | Includes bibliographical references and index. | Summary: "This book explores how AI enhances language learning through personalized instruction, real-time feedback, and interactive tools. It examines AI's impact on global communication by breaking down language barriers and enabling more seamless cross-cultural interactions"-- Provided by publisher.
Identifiers: LCCN 2025029842 (print) | LCCN 2025029843 (ebook) | ISBN 9798337356815 hardcover | ISBN 9798337356822 paperback | ISBN 9798337356839 ebook
Subjects: LCSH: Language and languages--Computer-assisted instruction | Language and languages--Study and teaching--Technological innovations | Communication--Technological innovations | Artificial intelligence--Educational applications | LCGFT: Essays
Classification: LCC P53.28 .A55 2026 (print) | LCC P53.28 (ebook)
LC record available at https://lccn.loc.gov/2025029842
LC ebook record available at https://lccn.loc.gov/2025029843
British Cataloguing in Publication Data
A Cataloguing in Publication record for this book is available from the British Library.

Table of Contents

Detailed Table of Contents

Preface

The advent of Artificial Intelligence (AI) has transformed nearly every aspect of modern life, and language learning is no exception. From redefining pedagogical approaches to reshaping business communication and journalism, AI continues to disrupt and enhance how we interact with language and information. *AI's Role in Language Learning and Communication* is a timely collection of research and reflection that explores the intersection of AI and human communication across varied educational, professional, and cultural domains.

This volume brings together voices from diverse global institutions, offering theoretical insights, empirical findings, and practical applications of AI in the context of language learning, writing instruction, journalism, business communication, and even culinary arts. Each chapter contributes to a growing understanding of how AI is not only reshaping the tools and methods of instruction but also the very nature of human expression, perception, and interaction.

Whether you are a scholar, educator, practitioner, or student, this book provides a comprehensive and accessible roadmap for navigating the evolving relationship between AI and language. By examining both the opportunities and the challenges posed by AI—from motivation and anxiety to ethics and overreliance—this collection fosters a balanced and critical dialogue around the responsible integration of AI in communication-centered fields.

Chapter Overview

Chapter 1: Demystifying Artificial Intelligence: Comprehensive Guide for Non-Native Speakers

Hazanal Rashid Khan Raja Mohamed introduces AI through an accessible and culturally inclusive lens, aimed at non-native English speakers unfamiliar with technological jargon. The chapter explains core AI concepts like machine learning and neural networks using relatable analogies, while also examining ethical concerns surrounding AI's growing presence.

Chapter 2: Automated Feedback Effect on Foreign Language Writing Motivation and Anxiety

Gülnihan Altinay and Selami Aydin explore how automated writing tools impact EFL learners' motivation and anxiety. The study reveals nuanced findings: while AI feedback reduces anxiety, it may also lower motivation compared to human feedback—suggesting the need for a blended feedback approach.

Chapter 3: Using AI to Enhance Receptive Foreign Language Skills

Gökhan Hiniz discusses the application of AI in developing listening and reading skills. By offering real-time feedback and multimodal learning experiences, AI supports metacognitive growth and learner autonomy, while also posing new challenges related to dependency and equity.

Chapter 4: AI and the Newsroom – Redefining the Boundaries of Journalism

Samina Waglawala and Susanta Das analyze how AI technologies are transforming journalism, raising ethical concerns about truth, accountability, and editorial integrity. The authors highlight the dual role of AI—both as a disruptor and a potential enhancer of journalistic standards.

Chapter 5: The Transformative Power of AI in Business Communication

Abhishek Tiwari and Ankit Shukla examine how AI tools revolutionize business communication by increasing efficiency, enabling personalization, and expanding global reach. The chapter reflects on both the strategic benefits and ethical implications of AI in corporate environments.

Chapter 6: Construction and Validation of the Perceptions of AI Usage Scale in a Foreign Language Learning Context

Selami Aydin presents the development of a psychometric tool—the Perceptions of AI Usage Scale (PAS)—to measure EFL learners' attitudes toward AI in education. The study contributes a valuable instrument for future research and implementation studies in AI-assisted language learning.

Chapter 7: Echoes of AI: Revolutionizing English Communication

Papi Naidu Mavidi delivers a thematic synthesis of AI's influence on English language teaching and communication. Emphasizing learner autonomy and motivation, this chapter ties together case studies, challenges, and innovations that illustrate AI's transformative role in bridging linguistic and cultural divides.

Chapter 8: AI-Powered Language Instruction in the Culinary Arts

Manan Chakraborty and Nagendra Yadav showcase the creative integration of AI in culinary education. From personalized recipe recommendations to smart assessment tools, this chapter reveals how AI is not only reshaping how culinary students learn but also how they express creativity through food and language.

Together, these chapters paint a comprehensive picture of AI's growing footprint in language learning and communication. By situating AI within diverse educational and professional contexts, this book aims to spark informed conversation, encourage responsible innovation, and inspire continued research in the field.

Chapter 1
Demystifying Artificial Intelligence:
Comprehensive Guide for Non-Native Speakers

Hazanal Rashid Khan Raja Mohamed
https://orcid.org/0000-0001-5285-628X
St Teresa International University, Thailand

ABSTRACT

This chapter discusses the phenomenon of artificial intelligence (AI) for the first time aimed at uninformed people who do not share the same cultural upbringing. The goal is to resolve the misconceptions of AI without further defining its concepts, uses, and effects AI while managing the profound linguistic and cultural differences that may be present. In the very beginning, it provides the rationale and basic components of AI beginning from concepts such as machine learning, deep learning, and artificial neural networks in layman's terms and simplistic analogies. Later, it provides an ever-growing range of applications of AI like natural language processing, robotics, and computer vision, exemplifying the impact of AI on the world. It also attempts to provide answers to the concerns that have been raised on the ethics of AI practices with AI being the focal concern.

1. THE AI WORLD

We are at the cusp of unprecedented change brought about by AI technology. This has implications on many aspects of our day-to-day life including work, social systems, decision making and even the environment. While these developments are certainly fascinating, for any non-native AI enthusiasts, the jaw dropping technology

DOI: 10.4018/979-8-3373-5681-5.ch001

itself and its phenomenon along with its vocabulary poses a deep challenge. This chapter attempts to offer an artificial intelligence (AI) overview with the design of catering to non-native English speakers.

The objective is to shed light for the wider population which, more importantly, is English non-native speakers in relation to issues of AI, where they will appreciate the world of complexities that come with the technology. Our aim is to explain the most basic concepts, technologies that exist, the ethics deliberation, and even further along the development of AI. Our intention is to build understanding of AI while stimulating appropriate collaboration in strengthening global citizenship. (Bryson & Winfield, 2017).

The Importance of AI Literacy for Everyone

Nowadays, in the context of a global village, AI literacy has evolved from a choice to a necessity. Understanding the operations, benefits, and limits AI systems offer is crucial for maximizing their value. For most people that do not speak English as a native language, AI literacy helps since they are able to participate in cross-border conversations: AI is not regionally limited; there are discussions centering AI everywhere. The innovation, use and even the moral implications of AI technologies are being talked about everywhere. Because of the AI understanding, non-native speakers can participate in these discussions and offer insights that stem from their unique experiences. Make reasonable and educated choices as a consumer. The systems that we utilize daily are influenced by AI technologies. Thanks to AI literacy, non-native speakers are able to make qualified and rational consumer decisions when interacting with emerging technologies. Adapt to the evolving employment landscape: Acemoglu and Restrepo (2017) argued that with the rise of AI, entire industries and occupations are being newly created as one of its effects. This underscores the need for non-native AI practitioners to possess knowledge capabilities relevant to modern technological shifts in order to evergreen themselves in the global job market.

Promote Responsible AI Usage: These advanced AI models bring untold new obstacles. The unrestricted potency of AI systems bestows a novel resolve upon users, bestowing the capability to subvert the ethical aims that they wish to pursue AI without moderation, yields uncounted empathy that guide. However blanket morally restrained courtesy whose absence of talent helps to enable good, establishes fairness, accountability, and transparency ensures that these fundamentals are based and integrated in the systems.

Foster Inclusiveness in AI Systems: Many problems that concern societal structures require deeply systematic approaches, as opposed to surface level solutions. Incorporating non-AI speakers will foster inclusivity that encourages wider participation in AI projects, making certain that AIs are built for everyone irrespective of their identity or life circumstances. (Buolamwini & Gebru, 2018).

Enhanced Reasoning and Problem-Solving Skills: The study of Artificial Intelligence also involves a great deal of logic. When learners understand, how AI algorithms identify and solve complex problems, they can start applying similar reasoning in their lives, thus enhancing their problem-solving skills.

Theoretical Background

AI is a broad area of study focused on developing machines and systems that can accomplish tasks that usually require the cognitive abilities of a human being. Such activities involve reasoning, learning, problem-solving, language comprehension, and even perception. AI is considered one of the fastest growing technologies of this century because of its formidable impact on various sectors like Computer Science, Mathematics, Linguistics, Psychology and Neuroscience.

The Two Main Classifications of AI Are

Narrow AI which is created to accomplish a fixed set of functions, and General AI, where systems are developed that can perform every mental activity as a human being. The majority of AI solutions available in the contemporary market are based on the Narrow AI concept. Examples of Narrow AI include voice-controlled virtual assistants and recommendation systems.

AI has several important subsets: Machine Learning (ML) is one of them and it encompasses enabling computers to independently learn from data without having specific lines of code written for them. Such algorithms include supervised, unsupervised and reinforcement learning.

Another remarkable subset is Natural Language Processing (NLP) which is concerned with enabling software applications to comprehend and rely upon human languages. This is critical for enhancing AI proficiency for people who do not speak the native languages of such systems.

A equally advanced subset of AI is Computer Vision which allows for the recognition and understanding of visual data by machines. This includes being able to recognize faces and other objects within images.

Expert Systems: Emulate the capability of a human expert to make decisions based on a knowledge base and a system of inference rules.To fathom AI, one must also look at its ethics, culture, and even language. In particular, non-native speakers face additional barriers as AI-related information, tools, and resources tend to be inaccurate, which makes accessing them difficult. This enforces the need for one to pay attention to culturally sensitive and clear communication in AI education.This theoretical rationale is fused with practical explanations intended for people who do not use English as their primary language or are otherwise unacquainted with advanced technical terms. AI, in a way, becomes easier to use and understand with the removal of language and conceptual barriers.

Simulating human intelligence is the goal of Artificial Intelligence (AI), an emerging field of study that has elements from diverse disciplines such as computer science, mathematics, neuroscience, cognitive science, linguistics, and even the arts. AI systems can perform problem-solving, decision-making, learning, and even understanding of languages, which makes the field fascinating.

The critical study of language called linguistics integrates the understanding of AI, notably in Natural Language Processing, NLP, the subdivision concerned with the comprehension and production of human language by machines. NLP is essential for the development of AI applications that are useful to the public such as virtual assistants, translation devices, and chatbots.

From a Linguistic Standpoint, There Are Some Important Issues Pertaining to AI

Syntax deals with the structure of sentences and their grammar. In AI, syntax allows the implementation of parsers which serve to provide grammatical structure to sentences.

Semantics refers to meaning. It allows AI to find out what words and sentences are supposed to mean in certain contexts. Pragmatics is concerned with the meaning and use of language in various contexts. AI systems need to understand implied meanings, intentions, and context, all of which require pragmatic understanding.

Phonetics and Phonology: these areas deal with speech sounds and support speech recognition systems.

Sociolinguistics analyzes the variability of a language and its social aspects which is important for designing an equitable AI that operates using different languages and dialects.

The overlap of AI and linguistics is particularly relevant for non-native speakers. AI systems, for example, tend to have enormous datasets comprised of recordings from "native" speakers, and these recordings, unfortunately, do not capture the usage patterns of second language speakers. This may result in bias or omission. Furthermore, the tools can be made more responsive to users by applying theories from linguistics and second language acquisition. For example: The interlanguage theory posits that non-native speakers form a distinct dialectal structure that is a product of their first language and the language they are learning. Such features should be accommodated by AI systems.The comprehensible input hypothesis (Krashen, 1982) emphasizes that language input must be provided just above the learner's current level, which is a beneficial formulation for crafting user-friendly interfaces and pedagogical AI tools.

Reducing complexity and ambiguity in AI-generated content can be achieved through Lexical simplification, which is informed by linguistics alongside controlled language design.In this case, linguistics can enhance the communication capabilities of AI systems when interacting with people who speak different languages by tailoring the AI's responses and speech patterns. This guide combines AI with linguistic theories in order to break down the vast world of artificial intelligence for non-native English speakers, ensuring inclusivity in society during the digital age.

According to Russell and Norvig (2021), Artificial Intelligence (AI) is a broad area of study that is concerned with the creation of computer systems that perform tasks traditionally associated with human cognitive processes such as learning, reasoning, problem solving, and understanding language. An AI system integrates concepts from various domains, including computer science, cognitive psychology, mathematics, and linguistics. The most relevant area for this guide, which aims at assisting non-native speakers of English, is the combination of AI and linguistics.

Linguistics is the study of language. It is one of the main pillars for the artificial intelligence field known as Natural Language Processing. NLP facilitates the interaction between computers and human language in its written and verbal forms(Jurafsky & Martin, 2023). Important linguistic areas such as syntax, semantics, pragmatics, and phonology provide the prerequisite knowledge for developing AI systems capable of analyzing processes of human language comprehension and production. Syntax, as one of the primary constituents of linguistics, prescribes the principles for constructing sentences in a specific language. Syntactic parsers serve the purpose of enabling AI to recognize grammatical constructs and hierarchies within sentences.

Semantics deals with meaning, enabling systems to associate specific units of language to relevant entities in the world. Pragmatics concerns social understanding, which AI employs when detecting unexpressed meanings and purposes in speech, social relations, and other textual relationships. Phonetics and Phonology concern the sound system of the language or speech, which is critical for the functioning of speech recognition systems. Of these, sociolinguistics and applied linguistics pose a greater challenge for the design of non-biased AI systems. Most AI models undergo training using huge corpora composed mainly of data from native speakers, which poses a considerable challenge to non-native users. This issue is countered with theories of linguistics through second language acquisition, which provide useful frameworks. The Interlanguage Theory by Selinker from 1972 holds that second-language learners create an interlanguage system amalgamating their first and target languages. AI systems that account for differences in interlanguage usage variation are better interpreters of non-standard language use.

Understanding Comprehensible Input Theory, as put forward by Krashen in 1982, suggests it's easier to acquire a language when learners receive input that is just above their current capabilities. This has direct implications for the design of AI systems user interfaces which should avoid obfuscating and prescriptive language. Wang and colleagues in 2016 indicated that use of Controlled Natural Language (CNL) and lexical simplification strategies powered by linguistics could increase the use of AI generated content by non-native speakers. This combines AI, linguistics, and accessibility to propose modifications to the functionalities of artificial intelligence for non-native English speakers. The goal is to bridge the understanding gaps created by the technology and language fusion, enabling wider critical and confident engagement with AI.

Linguistic Competence: This area deals with the understanding differences in language command between native and non-native speakers with the aid of the Common Underlying Proficiency model and the linguistic interdependence hypothesis. In this regard, it is accepted that non-native speakers may lack the degree of automaticity in language processing available to full speakers of a given language, but, nonetheless, can attain great mastery, particularly in highly demanding tasks like thinking and reading. Second Language Acquisition (SLA):This branch focuses on how non-native speakers learn another language, looking at the input, interaction, motivation, and other mental activities involved in language acquisition.

Non-Native English-Speaking Teachers (NNES) and the NNEST Movement: This branch deals with the impact of non-native English-speaking teachers on the teaching process, disproving the assumption that native speakers are naturally superior teachers. The NNEST movement appreciates the role of qualifying NNESTs and implements initiatives to change inequitable hiring and promotion policies.

Social and Psychological Factors: This branch studies non-native speakers' social perception; how their pronunciation and speech style may influence their social credibility and standing, and how these perceptions and misperceptions may affect their confidence and motivation.

English as a Lingua Franca (ELF): This theory regards English as a means of communication across the globe, stressing the need to study how it is being used by speakers and non-speakers of English in varying situations.

Research Consequences: Grasping these theoretical constructs enables educators, researchers, and language policy analysts devise strategies that are amenable to integrating non-native speakers into their language learning frameworks, as well as support them in the process of language acquisition. *

It can address the issue of how people's command of a particular language may affect their social interactions, educational, and professional opportunities. Ever challenging the notion that indigenous speakers are naturally endowed with greater advantage may assist in pro-actively combating discrimination and enabling non-standard equitable opportunities within education and work.

Self-efficacy theory posits that an individual's capacity to perform a particular task or learn something successfully depends on their self-evaluation. Non-native English speaking adults encounter a wide range of challenges because of their inadequate command of the language. These range from communication difficulties to social and community activity exclusion which poses serious challenges in their day-to-day life. There are multiple exceptions in English spelling and grammar, making it very difficult for non-native speakers to memorize them. However, repeating practice with irregular verbs and spellings and through exposure to the language will ingrain these exceptions into memory over time.

English is the leading language used on the internet, in global media, and scientific and technical fields, which makes it the most important language to learn for non-native speakers trying to access large information repositories. To help improve pronunciation and become accustomed to the language, English media like TV shows, movies, music, and books should be consumed.

Because of their native language, English pronunciation is arguably the biggest challenge for a non-native speaker. Given the drastic differences in phonetics, reproduction of sounds may not only be difficult, but can also result in misinterpretations and impede fluent speech. Speaking is often more challenging than listening due to the limited vocabulary that most people have. A non-subject mother tongue of most phrases and vocabulary makes speech and understanding even more complicated. This section seeks to build a basic understanding of artificial intelligence (AI) for readers without a technical background or whose native language is not English.

Understanding the Considerations of Non-Native English Speakers in AI Education

The rapid development of artificial intelligence (AI) technologies around the world raises profound concerns about language use and inclusion. English, as the world's primary language for the development, education, and documentation of AI, is not the mother tongue of most people on the globe. Struggling to contend with AI content is just one barrier non-English speakers encounter. In addition to AI concepts being complex, instructions and documents contain sophisticated language, jargon, idioms, and sociocultural elements which pose challenges.

Every AI tool, platform, and resource comes with the assumption of being English proficient. This presumption extends to technical skills and literacy, which are assumed to be exorbitantly high. Learners from non-English speaking backgrounds, therefore, face challenges with understanding, interpreting, and applying AI concepts. This is a language problem which perpetuates inequality and exclusion, hindering the harnessing and emergence of talent to contribute to AI and be enriched by its benefits.

This guide solves these problems by incorporating strategies from second language acquisition and applied linguistics. For instance, Krashen's theory of comprehensible input argues that instructional materials should be just above the learner's level in understanding for knowledge to be gradually built. Likewise, interlanguage theory acknowledges that second language users develop an emergent grammar using elements of their first language. This unique system is one that blends their native language with English. This is a reality that should be embraced, not penalized by AI systems and teaching materials.

This chapter contains suggestions such as the use of controlled language—a form of English that has been simplified and standardized to make it less vague—and visual aids like diagrams, contextual examples, and other visual representations to improve understanding. It also advocates for equal opportunity language by encouraging educators and developers to refrain from the use of idioms, adopt the active voice, and provide clear definitions of terms.

Focusing on the challenges faced by non-native speakers enhances the equity and accessibility of AI systems; this is the primary contribution of this guide. It hopes to encourage the understanding of more advanced AI concepts and the creation of tools, policies, and applications sensitive to global linguistic diversity by learners. Machine learning is a subfield of artificial intelligence that allows computers to automatically learn to improve task performance with the passage of time, and without any explicit programming for each specific function of work or task.

Remedies to the Language Problem

Among the myriad of issues non-native speakers face when engaging with AI, the language barrier stands out as particularly critical. Both non-native and native speakers struggle with AI's understanding because of its wordy and complex explanations, which include numerous technical AI acronyms and extreme AI conceptualizations. This barrier is overcome by this chapter by aiding in the use of simple words. Any complicated concepts will be broken down in simple terms, while technical jargon will be as minimal as possible. Defining important terms and providing relevant examples: Practical examples will be offered alongside relevant term definitions in order to illustrate and provide context to the words.

Using analogies or even metaphors: AI concepts will be explained to non-native speakers in a way that will help them relate to the theories through the use of analogies and metaphors. Providing translations: AI's most important phrases and words will be translated into different languages. These languages serve as a gateway to understanding for the audience.

2. FUNDAMENTAL CONCEPTS OF ARTIFICIAL INTELLIGENCE

Definitions of Artificial Intelligence

To put it simply, artificial intelligence (AI) is the ability of a computer or machine to mimic human actions. This includes a broad range of functions such as learning, problem solving, decision making, and understanding natural language (Russell & Norvig, 2020). These actions include data evaluation, pattern identification, making predictions, and many others which the AI system is capable of performing.

Most Predominant Forms of AI Technology Used Today Include

Weak or Narrow AI: This category of AI technologies currently in use perform specific tasks, such as playing chess, recognizing faces, or even translating different languages. These systems, as advanced as they may be, are restricted to performing these tasks and lack general intelligence. (Siri and Alexa are examples)

General or Strong AI: These are an advanced type of AI yet to be created, but are presumed to repossess human-level intelligence that would allow them to effectively carry out any mental activity that a human would do. (HAL 9000 as portrayed in science fiction).

Artificial Superintelligence: This is a form of AI which is still conjectural in nature, but it surpasses imagination – machines of the future – humans in creativity, wisdom, social skills and everything else. (For instance, consider envisioning machines of the future which function within the comprehension of a human being).

Machine Learning: The Engine of AI

Machine Learning (ML) is one of the fields of AI which provides the computer with the potential to learn from data without being explicitly told what to do. ML algorithms have a much greater degree of freedom than traditional ways of programming where rules are imposed. They analyze the given information and formulate rules either to predict or to make decisions based on the information available to them. (Mitchell, 1997)

Types of Machine Learning

Supervised Learning: Supervised Learning is a type of ML, wherein an algebraic model is fed algorithmically on a data set rich in characteristics and contains an answer in it. The data augments supplied answer rich data set through which the computer detects the set of patterns that have previously been identified. (Example: Training a spam filter using emails labeled as "spam" or "not spam").

Unsupervised Learning: In the context of machine learning, the absence of a given set of outputs to train algorithms is referred to as "unsupervised learning." In this scenario, the algorithm independently attempts to locate trends and features in the available data. For instance, buying habits of customers can be used to form generic categories for them without having pre-established categories.

Reinforcement Learning: Industry application domains use reinforcement learning where an algorithm is trained in a given environment using a trial-and-error approach. Each decision taken by the algorithm leads to it either receiving a reward or encouragement and suffering a punishment which helps refine its strategies over time. For example, a reward can be granted to a robot for successfully reaching certain objectives, while penalties can be incurred for colliding with walls in a maze.

Deep Learning: Leverage of Neural Networks

Deep Learning is a form of machine learning that involves designing an artificial neural network which operates in a hierarchy of pattern recognition. In AI DL development has become a paradigm shift in automation technologies, including AI-based computer vision systems, linguistics processors, and voice recognition technologies. (Goodfellow et al., 2016).

Neural Networks: Mimicking Human Brains

The design of a neural network to a very large extent depends as its name suggest on the brain of a human. Each neural network consists of a number of simple processing elements called neurons organized into several layers. Each neuron can be connected to one or more other neurons, and each neuron can receive an input. After neuron is implanted, it processes the input data and provide the output which is called the result to other neurons.

Components of a Neural Network and their Functions

Input Layer or the Primary Layer: The primary layer of a neural network which has not undergone pre-processing, requires enhancement prior to receiving advanced treatment.

Hidden Layers: The model is composed of layers which take the input information and passes it through several stages while extracting essential features and patterns found in the data.

Output Layer: This layer represents a culmination of neural network processing, classifying the output into either a definite prediction or classification.

Weights: These establish the connection among the neurons. Their use during a learning procedure enhances network performance and are reconfigurable to change the strength of the connections.

Activation Functions: These are functions that introduce non-linearity in the neural network for advanced tasks, typically more sophisticated causes.

The Emerging Types of Neural Networks

Convolutional Neural Networks, for example, are an application of Deep Learning used in the analysis of digital images which is the sole focus of the discipline. They possess convolutional layers through which they access image features such as edges, corners, and textures. (Example: Face detection, image recognition, and other object detections.)

Recurrent Neural Networks are used in interactive applications utilizing textual or temporal sequences data. They keep important pieces of information thanks to the feedback loops they process. (Example: Speech translation, automatic language translation, and conversion of speech to text.)

Generative Adversarial Networks are an example of a different machine learning approach by using two opposed neural networks, also known as GAN. One network (generator) creates new artificial data while the other, called the discriminator, determines if the data is original or created. (Example: Websites that generate realistic images and pretend emulate authentic data.)

3. THE IMPACT OF ARTIFICIAL INTELLIGENCE IS ENORMOUS AND GROWING AT A RAPID RATE ACROSS THE BOARD, SPANNING INDUSTRIES AND APPLICATIONS AS WELL AS AREAS OF OUR DAILY LIFE

Below Are Some of the Main Purposes of AI

Natural Language Processing (NLP): Easing Communication Between Humans and Machines

Natural Language Processing (NLP) is a division of AI that focuses on enabling machines to comprehend, interpret and produce speech. NLP has numerous applications. (Manning & Schutze, 1999). Translating human speech or writing from one language to another without manual assistance. (Example: Google Translate) .Summarizing documents. (Example: Summarizing news articles). Interpreting the emotions expressed in pieces of text. (Example: Sentiment analysis of customer reviews for particular products). Enabling programs to converse with users in a human like manner. (Example: Customer service chatbots). Transcribing verbal word into written text. (Example: Virtual Assistants like Siri and Alexa).

Computer Vision: Endowing Machines with the Ability to See.

It is a branch of AI that empowers computers to perceive and interpret images and videos. Computer vision is widely used. (Szeliski, 2010). Understanding and classifying images by recognizing various objects, people, or even scenes. (Example: Facebook's automatic photo tagging). Robotics is the field that combines AI and computer vision with other technologies to create machines that are capable of performing physical work without human assistance.

Recommendation Systems: Adapting the Platform to the User.

Recommendation Systems refer to systems created with AI algorithms that attempt to predict wishful preferences from users and propose items to purchase. The systems are used in e-commerce, entertainment, and other businesses (Ricci et al 2011).

These cover:

E-commerce: Suggesting other items to a buyer based on their previous searches and purchases (Example: Amazon's Customers Who Bought Item Also Bought feature).

Entertainment: Suggesting movies, music or books based on user's ratings and preference (For example: Recommended films on Netflix).

Social Media: Users are recommended friends, groups, and content relevant to the accounts they already follow or engage with (For example: Facebook suggests people you may know).

Content Curation: User interactions on profiles are changing content for news and articles (Eg. News applications recommending relevant articles based on the user's interest profile.)

Healthcare: The Transformation of Diagnosing and Treating Patients.

Integrating AI technologies into healthcare systems improves the diagnosis, treatment, and quality of care that is given to patients.

Disease Diagnosis: Some algorithms can analyze medical images like X-rays, CT scans, and MRIs, and detect various diseases such as cancer, tuberculosis, and diabetic retinopathy. AI is capable of doing this with incredible accuracy, often exceeding that of humans (Esteva et al. 2017).

AI accelerates drug discovery by identifying prospective drug candidates and forecasting their effectiveness through extensive biological data examination. (Vamathevan et al., 2019). Based on genetics, lifestyle, and medical history, treatment can be customized to the individual's precise requirements. (Schork, 2015).

With the use of AI, wearables and sensors can continuously track the patient's vitals, alerting health professionals to possible complications in real time (Dimitrov, 2016).

AI is dramatically transforming the management of security, risk, and operational efficiency within the financial sector. AI systems can track transactions in real time to prevent crimes including credit card fraud and laundering. (Bolton & Hand, 2002).AI trading tools monitor and trade in the markets within seconds which significantly improves returns on investments. (Aldridge, 2013). Using AI, financial institutions are now able to accurately estimate the credit risk, market volatility, and optimally manage their lending and investment activities. (Baesens et al., 2003). AI can manage customer service by using chatbots, which can assist and attend to customers' queries any time of the day, solve customer problems, which improves customer satisfaction and lowers firms' costs. (Chung & Tseng, 2020).Transportation systems became more effective, and safer due to AI technology, which also initiated the advances of autonomous vehicles.

4. ETHICAL CONSIDERATIONS IN AI TECHNOLOGIES

The advancement and proliferation of artificial intelligence systems necessitate that more care is taken regarding ethical considerations stemming from its creation and the responsibilities it is given.

Bias and Fairness

As a society, we tend to hold certain biases toward different groups of people. With the training data the AI system will be taught, the system is bound to pick up on these biases. A case in point here is that of a facial recognition system which is trained mainly on white faces will not perform effectively for other ethnic groups. (Buolamwini & Gebru, 2018). Effective measures need to be taken to rectify bias by making sure that datasets chosen for training are more representative and accurate, algorithms that are effective with biased datasets are created, and AI systems are evaluated regularly for bias.

Privacy and Security

Generally, AI systems need huge amounts of sensitive data which violates the privacy and the security of a person. There are other critical unfair means that should never be used when developing AI technologies, such as infringing on the privacy of the user's personal information and denying protective security measures aimed at safeguarding against unauthorized access and breaches. (Sweeney, 2002).In order to maintain privacy, data anonymization and informed consent is vital along with complying with the framework of data privacy laws.

Transparency and Explainability

Most AI systems such as deep learning models are considered to be "black boxes" as their decision-making process is incredibly difficult to trace. Trusting AI systems is even more intricate in delicate situations dealing with healthcare and the financial sector. (Ribeiro et al., 2016).

Fostering Explainability: Unlike other domains, human understanding is absent in some engineering domains or sub-domains machine intelligence techniques. Alienable Artificial Intelligence (XAI) is well-positioned to rectify this problem.

Responsibility and Accountability

With the increased adoption of autonomous AI systems, delineating accountability has become crucial. Who should be liable for the outcomes of an autonomous car accident? What about taking AI entity decision that is biased? (Floridi et al., 2018).

Defining Accountability: It is essential to assign the AI system's designers, producers, and users' distinct roles and responsibilities to assure effective control.

Job Displacement

The use of AI and automation technology is advancing at a rapid pace and economically affects workers across multiple industries. Frey and Osborne (2017) argue that there is an apparent need for social attention regarding the amelioration of problems created by AI-facilitated automation. To fulfill the troubling forecasts regarding aggressive displacement, there should be cooperation between governments, businesses, and educational institutions towards reskilling initiatives. Accomplishing this endeavor requires nurturing imagination, empathetic rationality, and human divisional attributes. In addition, to avoid averting social and economic crisis due to extreme unemployment risks, policies like universal basic income or any other form of social relief could be adopted. These insights imply a transformation to a reality where there is synergy of AI with human's productivity instead of AI replacing human's productivity. Embracing flexibility and lifelong learning will be necessary to survive in this environment.

The Ethics of Autonomous Weapons

The concerns related to arms capable of operating independently are drawing ever-increasing attention, sometimes referred to as "killer robots." Such systems raise ethical concerns and are referred to as Autonomous Weapon Systems (AWS). These technological systems may unilaterally opt to execute lethal force without human supervision, which poses a real threat of catastrophe due to mindless violence, especially in times of escalating conflicts (Arkin, 2009).

The topic of autonomous weapon systems (AWS) Technology posses merits and demerits to many people. Advocates claim that AWS optimizes precision targeting which in turn saves civilian lives, while opponents highlight the concerning trends of warfare becoming increasingly impersonal and easier to initiate, which can result in inadvertent escalation. These experts, along with others, argue that fully autonomous weapon systems should not be developed further because there would be a complete control relinquishment over systems capable of lethal engagement. Others are concerned regarding the consequences of hacking or malfunctioning systems. Who can be held responsible for their deployment? For these ethics, the key focus builds upon defining the level of human control needed, supervision, and responsibility over the AWS.

The Campaign to Stop Killer Robots operates to unite proclaimed NGOs, experts from the private sector, and social scientists into a single predatory group that supports comprehensive bans on weaponized robots. The campaign aims to expose: the dangers of not thinking through a plan ahead of taking action.

AI and Human Rights

AI systems can be designed to infringe human rights by further restricting access to certain information and enhancing surveillance objectives, or to be used in socially responsible ways such as in the healthcare system and education.

Protection of Human Rights Considering Artificial Intelligence: The modern world offers great opportunities with the increased automation of tasks and functions. However, guidelines and boundaries need to be established on how AI intervenes on an individual's right to privacy, self-expression, and egalitarianism. The impact of discrimination against women, children and minors, and the elderly requires special attention to guard non AI actuated social and humanitarian rights in a societal framework. In this case, the encroachment on human rights is to be conveniently legally patrolled and aid granted where necessary provided to those in need. To establish, enforce, and monitor these restrictions, coordinated international agreements stipulating quote ethics and restraint in AI designing and engineering are needed.

AI for the Social Good: We can mention, socially responsive AI projects aimed at eradicating poverty, addressing climate challenges, and fighting pollution.

The increasing integration of trade on an international scale has lowered the economic barriers for numerous nations and regions. An example includes Robert Schuman's quote, "Europe will be forged in crisis, and will be the sum of all its parts, each of which will be the world as well as comprise a single nation." To sum up, the quote suggests that nationalism is a rather regressive term which does not allow a higher worldview to exist, while integration is primarily supportive towards that higher worldview.

5. AI SYSTEMS DESIGN

As with any new technology, understanding the potentials available alongside the technology's branching options requires analysis to AI's integration techniques.

Trends Emerging in AI

As a result of the rapid evolution in technology, the following changes in AI have emerged:

Explainable AI (XAI): XAI is a less explored area of AI that seeks to enhance the interpretability and analyzability of AI systems. Stakeholder trust, particularly in the legal liability of AI systems, hinges on this dimension. Responsibilities will be allocated based on who owns the AI system, and this trust is fundamental to its effective operation. XAI aims to develop applied methodologies to "un-black box" AI models, thereby providing reasons for decisions made by AI.

Edge AI: This the recent trend where processing of data such as that from smartphones or IoT sensors is carried out on the device itself instead of the cloud, which is what Edge AI is. Edge AI is useful in terms of speed, latency, and even privacy. This trend allows for the complete lack of internet connection and real-time AI applications in autonomous able vehicles and tailored medicine.

Artificial Intelligence in Cybersecurity: AI is actively being integrated with machine learning to recognize and respond to cyber incidents. AI-enabled security systems can monitor network traffic, respond to malware, and automate industrial incident response. AI will have a much larger responsibility when it comes to protecting people, businesses, and governments from cyber threats. This is because AI is becoming more advanced and capable of dealing with sophisticated targeted cyber threats.

The Societal Impact of AI

Few argue with the point that AI has the ability to influence society in broad ways.

Changes in Business: Business processes and activities will now be more sophisticated and seamless, due to the never-ending advances and changes in AI Technologies, which tend to fully automate Jobs and task within the internal framework of any business. Automation having all the relevant procedures organized and even new services and products introduced. Such changes will result in high levels of productivity, accelerated growth economically, and new kinds of employment.

Altering Healthcare: There are drastic possibilities of AI changing the entire health sector with its immense capabilities in efficient and accurate older check advert as well as diagnosis, with specialized surgery, better results, alterations proof tailored to individual needs, and improvement. AI based technologies assist the medics in coming up with proper decisions and also contributes to the speeding up of drug creation, which aids in the formation of therapies meant for diseases in a timely manner.

Altering Education: AI can change the teaching approaches and the learning process in classrooms as well as provide tailored education and customized instructions through marking and lesson automations by AI systems. Moreover, the self-directed children and those with disabilities have their fair share of access to education through AI technologies.

Altering Climate Change: AI inherently has the ability to counter climate change by modifying the consumption of energy, through enhanced projections of renewal energy, energy optimization, as well as creation of new carbon capturing substances. With the help of AI, environmental shifts can be monitored and predicted with ease.

Altering Art and Entertainment: With AI technology, new forms of literature, music, and art are emerging. As new creations from AI systems become available, the difference between human ingenuity and machine-generated concepts is going to be masked.

Altering Cities: AI technologies can improve city planning and design, traffic control, public safety, and even the environmental sustainability and livability of a city. The use of AI in the administration of resources within the framework of smart city projects improves the quality of life of people.

AI's Long Vision:

In long term, AI’s plan is to develop an artificial general intelligence (AGI), a profoundly sophisticated form of AI that would be able to understand and exceed human intellect.

The Discussion of AGI: Logic pertaining to the possibilities of possessing AGI features possesses significant philosophical and ethical ramifications on what defines intelligence, consciousness, and the possibilities of humanity’s future. While some experts suggest that achieving AGI is possible in the next few decades, there are others who believe that it's far too long in the future—or even doubt its existence altogether. Argument on the Threats and advantages to Humanity posed by Modern AI: Opposed to current stereotypes, AGI has the potential to solve some of the hitherto unsolvable problems facing humanity today, including diseases, poverty, and climate change. Yet such advantages come with potential devastating consequences including the development of uncontrollable hostile AI systems.

Why Responsible AGI Implementation Should Be a Priority: It is already evident that AGI systems if developed will be of great societal benefit, however attention must be paid to the effects it will have on society and humanity. It is critical to formulate ethical principles, security protocols, and control policies that would guarantee AGI, will not serve to control us.

AI and Global Development: Bridging the Digital Divide

The anticipation of AI propelling economic progression and improving life's quality is optimistic; however, there is concern AI's gifts may not be shared equally, exacerbating divides between developed and developing nations. This widening gap is termed "digital divide." While technology, education, and infrastructure are absent, these groups are pushed down the hierarchy.

Access to Technology and Infrastructure

The Foundation of AI Development: There exist a number of prerequisites for the development and deployment of AI, including life infrastructure such as broadband internet, data storage facilities, and stable electric power. A large number of developing countries face challenges in these areas, leaving them out of the AI revolution.

AI Technology and the Next Steps Of Human-Computer Interaction:

The advances in AI technology have drastically shifted the approaches and systems implemented to work with computers. The potential outcome is the further advanced systems, significantly improving communication.

AI Systems Based on Natural Language Processing (NLP) and Dialogue System Chatbots

The Next Step of Information Retrieval: Natural Language Processing is analyzing a broad range of scenarios with context, purpose, emotion, and intent beyond a defined lexicon to facilitate seamless conversation; this will enhance user experience while employing AI systems.

Becoming A Household AI: The development of chatbots and voice-activated assistants is enabling them to conduct more advanced and post-cognitive dialogues. This new development greatly affects the other forms of customer assistance where automated and enhanced interactions using intelligence, as well as hands-free command over smart appliances. Multilingual Conversational AI - Its advancement is equally important for non-native speakers as it enables them to engage with AI systems in their languages. This fosters greater accessibility and user friendliness in technology.

Emotional Intelligence in AI - In the near future, AI systems will have the capability to identify and react to the feelings of human ai users. This new capability in AI is expected to enhance empathetic and customized engagements. The consequences could be extraordinarily positive for mental health, education and any other aspects of life where emotional sensitivity is critical.

Computer Vision and Augmented Reality (AR)

Merging the Real and Virtual Worlds Computer vision allows for the ability of computers to perceive and understand their surrounding world. The merger of augmented reality (AR) and computer vision will allow for augmenting digital information on top of the physical world, which will change the way we perceive and interact with our environment. Applications in Various Areas: AR is prominently featured in gaming, entertainment, education, healthcare and even manufacturing. For example, surgeons can receive real-time information updates during procedures, while students can receive immersive training mechanics lessons on sophisticated vehicles or experience education on concepts in an engaging way.

AR for Non-Native Speakers

Learning languages can pose a challenge for many people, but AR can help by providing contextual information pertaining to the object or location along with translations in real time. Furthermore, it can promote cross cultural understanding and interaction by allowing individuals to create, share, and communicate ideas from differing perspectives in one single place.

Accessibility and Inclusivity: The services provided for persons with disabilities facilitates the achievement of accessibility. This is exemplified by AR as it can be used to provide step by step guides visually to the hearing impaired, as well as to create virtual environments accessible to wheelchair users.

Brain-Computer Interfaces (BCIs) The Most Sophisticated Interface

Machine Communication: BCIs are the most sophisticated device which enables direct brain interfacing with computers. They represent the next step in human-machine communication, where human beings can operate freely with the external gadgets using the mind. Although the technology is still at its nascent stage, the devices' interactivity is simply limitless.

Ethical Considerations

The ethical concerns of BCIs include privacy, security, and the brutal implications of their impact on a person's existence. As with any fundamentally new technology, considerations for appropriate ethical frameworks and governance for responsible application must be instituted in parallel with the development of such technologies BCIs.

The Possibility of Enhanced Cognition: Conservative estimates from studies have suggested that BCIs would help in the enhancement of cognitive skills such as remembering things, paying attention, and learning. This idea not only entails the remarkable prospects of such a development, but also raises significant ethical concerns regarding who can equitably access these enhancements.

CONCLUSION

In every progressive society, the occurrence of Artificial Intelligence changing the world comes with its unique advantages and challenges. Learning to understand AI is important for constituents of multilingual societies to make high-level decisions and to prepare for employment opportunities in the advanced globalized world. In explaining this chapter, profound examination on fundamental features of AI, its diverse uses, and the ethical issues that come with it is discussed.

Equally, non-native participants essay should be encouraged to proactively participate in the AI revolution by addressing some of the preconceived language and cultural discrimination barriers. With Artificial Intelligence, the development of culture and language, as well as cross-cultural communication, becomes easier, making the creation of culturally responsive AI and education systems more straightforward.

Considering the new changes, it is crucial to participate in discussions regarding the ethical boundaries that AI poses worldwide. Thus, nurturing an AI ecosystem of inclusivity and cooperation guarantees that the advancements are woven into the fabric of society in a balanced manner. This allows the boundless potential of AI to be leveraged to build a new world that is not restricted by a single language or culture. It is imperative to shift from the relentless pursuit of technological achievement to ensuring that all advancements AI brings to the world are tempered with justice and compassion for humanity.

A more profound look at the algorithms and deep learning structures shows a technology AI has that goes far beyond the capabilities taught to non-native speakers and is different from what they have previously encountered. The development of myriad applications of AI technology is changing the entire world. Non-native speakers around the world are becoming increasingly accessible. Each of them, is able to experience the impact that such a technology will have on their lives, professions, and society. In this document, I further elaborate on my findings, the emerging insights, what lies for non-native speakers, and the necessity for non-native modules for constructive AI development.

The Non-Native Speakers Advantage: The Democratization of AI

This chapter highlights a particular point with regard to AI democratization that AI should be accessible to everyone, irrespective of their language skills. The growing integration of AI in mundane activities such as mobile phone usage and healthcare has transformed its understanding from a purely technical skill into a vital component of literacy. Non-native speakers' AI literacy is more than the ability to interact with a piece of technology, it is about empowerment. It means actively participating in global conversations and being able to make informed decisions about technology, as well as effectively navigate the evolving job market.

None of the language should bar anyone from achieving AI literacy. In this regard, this chapter has aimed to cover the gap by providing cultures with advanced AI technologies that are accessible to them through sophisticated language. The relevant terminology of embedded AI is not plentiful, and so much care is provided with the supporting materials to motivate non-native speakers to actively engage in the AI industry as constituents rather than mere automatons who passively accept Artificial Intelligence innovations, but as critical minds who are able to influence and alter the course of the industry. Materials in different languages, simple non-specialist vocabulary, and even delighted guidance from non-specialists on the internet will boost global AI literacy.

The Overlooked Potential of AI Inclusion

As we look into the future, a concern that developing processes for AI systems will need to encompass the diversity of human culture, experiences, values, and perspectives is becoming increasingly important. This is not only about providing opportunities, but rather about the AI being able to provide for itself. Self-sufficient learning AI models that are provided with inadequate or prejudiced training data run the risk of worsening pre-existing societal divides rather than alleviating them. For example, facial recognition systems engineered using images from a single ethnic group's features are bound to perform dismally on people from other ethnic groups.

In constructing Artificial Intelligence systems, non-native speakers can single-handedly shoulder the responsibility of inclusivity. With a tremendous amount of AI systems, policies and strategies that aim to address systemic bias and discrimination can surely be countered. Non-native speakers can help advocate for AI fairness, accuracy, and efficiency. However, it is not that simple. To achieve this goal, there must be a radical shift in the absence of discrimination policy that is geared towards non-native inclusivity within AI onto people of different languages and cultures.

Furthermore, it is necessary to develop suitable AI technologies to meet the needs of a specific culture or community. It is equally important to attend to the needs and intricacies of every culture within sociotechnical systems as they pertain to frameworks of civilization. These adaptations encompass changing the interface to the user's language, dialect, and culture, as well as adding appropriate content to the systems.

For instance, AI-driven customer service chatbots in one nation may need to entirely alter their styles to suit clients in a different nation due to cultural differences in communication styles and politeness.

REFERENCES

Acemoglu, D., & Restrepo, P. (2017). Robots and jobs: Evidence from US labor markets. *NBER Working Paper Series*, No. 23285.

Aldridge, I. (2013). *High-frequency trading: A practical guide to algorithmic strategies and trading systems*. John Wiley & Sons.

Arkin, R. C. (2009). *Governing lethal behavior in autonomous robots*. CRC Press. DOI: 10.1201/9781420085952

Baesens, B., Van Gestel, T., Viaene, S., Stepanova, M., Suykens, J., & Vanthienen, J. (2003). Benchmarking state-of-the-art classification algorithms for credit scoring. *The Journal of the Operational Research Society*, *54*(6), 627–635. DOI: 10.1057/palgrave.jors.2601545

Bolton, R. J., & Hand, D. J. (2002). Statistical fraud detection: A review. *Statistical Science*, *17*(3), 235–255. DOI: 10.1214/ss/1042727940

Bryson, J. J., & Winfield, A. F. (2017). Standardizing ethical design for artificial intelligence and autonomous systems. *Computer*, *50*(5), 116–119. DOI: 10.1109/MC.2017.154

Buolamwini, J., & Gebru, T. (2018). Gender shades: Intersectional accuracy disparities in commercial gender classification. *Conference on Fairness, Accountability and Transparency*, 77-91.

Chung, K. H., & Tseng, S. P. (2020). An empirical study on the factors influencing the effectiveness of customer service chatbots. *Journal of Management and Marketing Research*, *24*, 1–16.

Dimitrov, D. V. (2016). Medical internet of things and big data in healthcare. *Healthcare Informatics Research*, *22*(3), 156–163. DOI: 10.4258/hir.2016.22.3.156 PMID: 27525156

Domingos, P. (2015). *The master algorithm: How the quest for the ultimate learning machine will remake our world*. Basic Books.

Esteva, A., Kuprel, B., Novoa, R. A., Ko, J., Swetter, S. M., Blau, H. M., & Thrun, S. (2017). Dermatologist-level classification of skin cancer with deep neural networks. *Nature*, *542*(7639), 115–118. DOI: 10.1038/nature21056 PMID: 28117445

Floridi, L., Cowls, J., Beltramini, M., Chatila, R., Chazerand, P., Dignum, V., & Vayena, E. (2018). AI4People—an ethical framework for a good AI society: Opportunities, risks, principles, and recommendations. *Minds and Machines*, *28*(4), 689–707. DOI: 10.1007/s11023-018-9482-5 PMID: 30930541

Frey, C. B., & Osborne, M. A. (2017). The future of employment: How susceptible are jobs to computerisation? *Technological Forecasting and Social Change*, *114*, 254–280. DOI: 10.1016/j.techfore.2016.08.019

Goodfellow, I., Bengio, Y., & Courville, A. (2016). *Deep learning*. MIT press.

Jurafsky, D., & Martin, J. H. (2023). *Speech and Language Processing* (3rd ed.). Pearson.

Krashen, S. D. (1982). *Principles and Practice in Second Language Acquisition*. Pergamon Press.

Manning, C. D., & Schütze, H. (1999). *Foundations of statistical natural language processing*. MIT press.

Mitchell, T. M. (1997). *Machine learning*. McGraw-Hill.

Ribeiro, M. T., Singh, S., & Guestrin, C. (2016). "Why should I trust you?" Explaining the predictions of any classifier. *Proceedings of the 22nd ACM SIGKDD International Conference on Knowledge Discovery and Data Mining*, 1135-1144.

Ricci, F., Rokach, L., Shapira, B., & Kantor, P. B. (Eds.). (2011). *Recommender systems handbook*. Springer. DOI: 10.1007/978-0-387-85820-3

Russell, S., & Norvig, P. (2021). *Artificial Intelligence: A Modern Approach* (4th ed.). Pearson.

Russell, S. J., & Norvig, P. (2020). *Artificial intelligence: A modern approach* (4th ed.). Pearson.

Schork, N. J. (2015). Personalized medicine: Time for one-person trials. *Nature*, *520*(7549), 609–611. DOI: 10.1038/520609a PMID: 25925459

Sweeney, L. (2002). k-anonymity: A model for protecting privacy. *International Journal of Uncertainty, Fuzziness and Knowledge-based Systems*, *10*(05), 557–570. DOI: 10.1142/S0218488502001648

Szeliski, R. (2010). *Computer vision: Algorithms and applications*. Springer.

Vamathevan, J., Clark, D., Czodrowski, P., Dunham, I., Ferran, E., Lee, G., Li, B., Madabhushi, A., Shah, P., Spitzer, M., & Zhao, S. (2019). Applications of machine learning in drug discovery and development. *Nature Reviews. Drug Discovery*, *18*(6), 463–477. DOI: 10.1038/s41573-019-0024-5 PMID: 30976107

KEY TERM AND DEFINITIONS

AI: The theory and development of computer systems able to perform tasks that normally require human intelligence, such as visual perception, speech recognition, decision-making, and translation between languages.

Deep Learning: A type of machine learning based on artificial neural networks in which multiple layers of processing are used to extract progressively higher level features from data.

Machine Learning: The use and development of computer systems that are able to learn and adapt without following explicit instructions, by using algorithms and statistical models to analyze and draw inferences from patterns in data.

Natural Language Processing (NLP): Is a branch of Artificial Intelligence (AI) that focuses on enabling computers to understand, interpret, and generate human language. It essentially bridges the gap between human communication and computer understanding, allowing machines to interact with humans through text and speech.

Non-Native Speakers: A non-native speaker is someone who learns a language as a second or foreign language, as opposed to their first language. They are not native speakers, meaning they did not acquire the language as a child in a natural environment.

Chapter 2
Automated Feedback Effect on Foreign Language Writing Motivation and Anxiety

Gülnihan Altınay
https://orcid.org/0000-0002-9568-864X
Istanbul Kültür University, Turkey

Selami Aydin
https://orcid.org/0000-0003-1614-874X
Istanbul Medeniyet University, Turkey

ABSTRACT

Writing motivation, anxiety, and feedback play significant roles in enhancing or debilitating writing performance, while automated feedback, offering immediate and personalized responses, can help reduce anxiety and increase motivation. This study examines the effects of traditional teacher feedback versus automated feedback on EFL learners' writing motivation and anxiety. Using a quasi-experimental design, 26 first-year English as a foreign language (EFL) students participated. Data were collected through a demographic questionnaire, the Academic Writing Motivation Questionnaire (AWMQ), and the Second Language Writing Anxiety Inventory (SLWAI). Over four weeks, the control group used pen and paper, while the experimental group used Write & Improve. The study concluded that teacher feedback positively impacted writing motivation and anxiety, while automated feedback reduced anxiety but decreased motivation. It is recommended that automated feedback should be balanced with teacher feedback to reduce anxiety and maintain motivation in EFL learners.

DOI: 10.4018/979-8-3373-5681-5.ch002

INTRODUCTION

For several reasons, writing plays a crucial role in foreign language learning and teaching. First, writing skills contribute to developing all other language skills, such as reading, listening, speaking, vocabulary, and grammar. With this undeniably significant skill, learners can improve learned structures, increase their knowledge of vocabulary, and notice mistakes and deficiencies in the target language (Çakır, 2010), leading to the overall development of learners' language proficiency and facilitating the way from competence to performance (Hyland, 2022). Second, writing skills significantly affect learners' academic success in general (Harmer, 2004). Furthermore, in terms of social interaction, it is of great importance for learners to be able to convey their feelings and thoughts appropriately and effectively to build a successful communication and cooperation environment. Thus, they can convey information to other people, have discussions, and express their feelings and thoughts through writing. Furthermore, since writing involves mental and psychological processes that stimulate learners' thoughts and ideas, it improves their creativity and helps them discover different perspectives (Syrewicz, 2023). While writing, a topic or situation needs to be considered and evaluated from many standpoints, including a focus on grammar, punctuation, organization, and presentation. Therefore, writing demands more effort and attention than the spontaneity of speech, helping learners develop critical thinking skills (Mehta & Al-Mahrooqi, 2015). While writing plays a critical role in language learning, motivation can be another essential factor that influences learners' ability to overcome the challenges of writing.

Given the writing challenges, motivation plays a crucial role in helping EFL learners overcome difficulties and progress in their writing skills for several reasons. First, it is a support mechanism to initiate the writing process and a booster for potential progress (Cleary, 1991), prevents procrastination, and helps learners maintain concentration. Second, motivation leads learners to write more and better by encouraging learners to practice willingly. Motivated learners are more likely to practice their writing skills and present qualified pieces of writing in quality and quantity due to their desire to achieve, as motivation stimulates learners to form a positive attitude toward writing (Oroujlou & Vahedi, 2011). Furthermore, motivation inhibits negative feelings such as fear of negative evaluation and incapableness, assisting learners in the process of achievement. Accordingly, the possibility of learning through those problems increases by evaluating their writing performance, noticing their mistakes, and building personal learning strategies (Cahyono & Rahayu, 2020), leading to more autonomous learners (Yeung, 2016). Lastly, while writing, learners learn new words and improve their current vocabulary knowledge (Johari, 2008). Consequently, writing motivation affects the ability to write from an increased willingness to learner autonomy and vocabulary knowledge. As an additional factor, it is necessary to consider writing anxiety on learners' psychological well-being and overall writing achievement.

In terms of psychological well-being, writing anxiety may cause stress and nervousness, leading learners to build negative thoughts and beliefs about writing (Aula Blasco, 2016). This unpleasant situation blunts learners' desire and may cause visible physical symptoms such as sweating, trembling, and dizziness. These effects cause learners to hesitate to be involved in writing activities. Second, in addition to its instantaneous and short-term effects (Horwitz et al., 1986), writing anxiety also impacts learners' future career choices, such as choosing professions that require minimal writing (Daly et al., 1976). Furthermore, writing anxiety causes a significant decrease in EFL learners' self-esteem (Hassan, 2001) by leading them to develop undesired views about themselves. Accordingly, their belief in what they can achieve and their expectation of success are affected adversely (Sabti et al., 2019). Last, research reveals that anxious learners perform poorly in quality and quantity, including accuracy and fluency, compared to less anxious learners (Daly & Miller, 1975a). As a result, it can be stated that there is a negative relationship between anxiety and writing performance. As the level of writing anxiety increases, learners' writing achievement decreases. However, the detrimental impact of writing anxiety on learners' well-being and performance is further compounded by the adverse effects of the lack of motivation.

Negative emotions, such as the lack of motivation and high anxiety, negatively affect the quality and rate of learning as much as the benefits of positive emotions (Dulay et al., 1982). Due to the complexity of writing skills, Ortega (2014) stresses that motivation, accompanying learners in the way of achievement, pioneers effective learning and helps handle difficulties. However, the lack of it substantially impedes learning writing in several ways. First, learners who lack motivation do not put adequate effort and time into improving and becoming proficient in foreign language writing, resulting in procrastination and dropping out of writing courses (Ramage, 1990). Therefore, practice, the main condition for achievement, remains inadequate and incomplete. Second, they may lose confidence in themselves and their writing skills due to unpleasant learning experiences (Ortega, 2014). Accordingly, learners present less proficient and qualified written products in terms of accuracy and fluency when compared to their motivated counterparts (Lee et al., 2018). Furthermore, unmotivated learners produce shorter texts containing poor grammatical mistakes and poor vocabulary. Additionally, the lack of motivation decreases learners' use of language learning strategies, which is a significant aid for effective learning (Xu, 2011) and self-regulation rates (Ellis, 2015). Last, lacking motivation reduces learners' ability to produce creative and original products, leading to non-innovative and inauthentic writing (Tran, 2007). Thus, it could be concluded that a lack of motivation depletes learners' overall writing performances by affecting the necessary characteristics and steps of successful writing. Anxiety, another factor that affects writing achievement, is also significant for learners' improvement. Most EFL learners find foreign language writing stressful, which paves the way for failure (Chastain, 1975). In support of this claim, the debilitating effect of anxiety has been investigated in detail for several years and found that learners encounter numerous disadvantages, including the linguistic aspects of writing and learners' psychological well-being (Horwitz et al., 1986). First, high anxiety levels become a barrier to effective learning and hinder them from turning input into intake, leading learners to produce written products that lack the necessary features of qualified writing (Dulay et al., 1982). As Krashen (1982) states, although they are provided with sufficient and effective input, anxiety is a filter that blocks learners' ability to understand and affects the efficacy and comprehensibility of the received input. Therefore, anxious learners have difficulties understanding and applying and experience negative attitudes toward writing, low motivation, and low self-esteem (Ekmekçi, 2018). Additionally, learners tend to procrastinate or avoid any activity (Cheng, 2004b). Second, writing anxiety affects learners' writing quality, including grammatical and spelling mistakes (Horwitz et al., 1986). In addition, anxious learners have problems with overall message construction, such as producing and organizing ideas, choosing less intense and complex topics, and using simpler vocabulary (Kusumaningputri et al., 2018). These structural, contextual, and grammatical handicaps create issues in the fluency and accuracy of written work, decreasing the efficacy and quality of learners' intended messages (Hassan, 2001). Thus, it can be suggested that high levels of anxiety decrease the overall quality and construction of texts, ultimately resulting in inadequate performance and unsuccessful written communication attempts, negatively affecting their academic success (Sabti et al., 2019) and changing their future career choices (Horwitz, 2001). In conclusion, lack of motivation and high levels of anxiety have negative effects on the development of learners' writing skills and significantly affect their level of achievement in various aspects. On the other hand, while the negative effects of motivation and anxiety on writing achievement, it should be stated that feedback plays a crucial role in influencing learners' writing development, offering both positive outcomes and potential challenges.

Feedback, another factor affecting writing achievement, has numerous positive effects. First, meaningful development can be seen in learners' grammar, spelling, punctuation, and vocabulary knowledge as they are required to edit and rewrite their drafts multiple times to create an accurate piece of writing (Zaman & Kalam, 2012), leading to more opportunities to practice (Kamberi, 2013). Second, advances in content knowledge can also be acquired since feedback shows learners how to arrange ideas and information logically and fluently in written work (Hyland & Hyland, 2006). Since feedback highlights learners' errors and lack of knowledge

(Kulhavy, 1977), learners become aware of their deficiencies, improving their problem-solving and critical-thinking skills. However, the feedback process may also cause various problems. First, learners may not always receive timely and regular feedback (Brookhart, 2017). The inconsistent and delayed feedback causes issues in learners' overall writing development due to irregular and scarce guidance (Clariana, 1999), reducing learners' awareness of their weaknesses and strengths. Accordingly, learners may lose motivation and willingness (Nassaji, 2016). Furthermore, unsuitable feedback that ignores or mismatches learners' needs and problems may increase their anxiety while reducing their motivation toward writing (Lee, 2014). Conflicting feedback or the feedback provided by different sources leads to ambiguity, making learners anxious, less motivated, and confused, hindering their improvement (Miranty & Widiati, 2021). Finally, although it occurs between the teacher and learners, learners generally do not have the opportunity to interact with the teacher about the feedback despite its two-way and dynamic nature (Nassaji, 2016), lowering the potential and expected efficacy of feedback by diminishing the opportunity of revision on written work. From this perspective, it can be stated that automated feedback may offer a solution to some of the challenges associated with traditional feedback, providing immediate and individualized responses that can reduce anxiety and enhance motivation in writing.

Automated feedback may offer an effective alternative to traditional teacher feedback by providing immediate, individualized, and accessible guidance, which can reduce anxiety and increase motivation in writing. Regarding the issue of when and how feedback is given, automated feedback offers learners clear, immediate, and individualized feedback according to their needs (Wale & Kassahun, 2024), regardless of time and place constraints (Jiang & Yu, 2022). This independence and clarity that automated feedback can enhance learner autonomy by helping them gain awareness of their learning process, highlighting their lacks instantly without the teacher's assistance (Mahapatra, 2024). According to their feedback, learners can identify their mistakes and deficiencies and use their unique strategies to correct and learn from them. As a result, learners can obtain valuable information about their current proficiency and performance, helping them boost their motivation and writing achievement (Altınay & Aydın, 2024). Furthermore, due to the clarity, frequency (Griffiths & Nicolls, 2010), and accessibility of automated feedback (Bai & Hu, 2017), learners' opportunity to revise accelerates (Bai & Hu, 2017), leading to a significant increase in self-correction ability by boosting feedback interaction (Li et al., 2015). Therefore, learners may practice their writing ability more without any limitations of traditional feedback (El Ebyary & Windeatt, 2010). Based on these benefits, it can be stated that automated feedback creates an anxiety-free and supportive environment, eventually decreasing learners' anxiety. With its immediate assistance that helps learners build awareness of their progress and learner engagement in cognitive, emotional, and behavioral aspects, their motivation toward writing increases (Wale & Kassahun, 2024). In conclusion, automated feedback may potentially reduce the drawbacks of traditional feedback, facilitating the learning process by decreasing anxiety and boosting learners' motivation. Research on the effects of automated feedback on writing motivation and anxiety seems scarce, as can be seen below. However, before the research synthesis, a theoretical framework should be drawn.

Theoretical Background

Flower and Hayes (1981) define writing as an ability by which individuals organize and convey information and thoughts using written symbols. Specific to EFL writing, Hamp-Lyons and Heasley (2006) express that EFL writing is an ability to convey meaning by using appropriate grammatical features, vocabulary, and discourse by non-native English users. Furthermore, there are several theories related to teaching writing. First, the *Input Hypothesis* highlights the significance of comprehensible input that learners should receive during language acquisition and considers it a prerequisite (Krashen, 1982). By outlining its characteristics, Krashen explains comprehensible input as "i+1" meaning that input should be slightly beyond the learners' current language proficiency yet still understandable. In writing development, reading can also take the form of considerable input that improves learners' written and spoken performances (Krashen, 1982). Second, the *Noticing Hypothesis* underlines the importance of attention by claiming that learners need to notice and pay attention to turn input into intake and completely comprehend the input (Schmidt, 2012). Accordingly, to acquire certain linguistic features, including vocabulary, phonology, grammar, and discourse, learners must pay considerable attention and be completely aware of the language learning process. In this respect, feedback significantly enablesearners to focus on specific structures (MacKey, 2006). Therefore, within the framework of Krashen's Input Hypothesis, Schmidt (2012) emphasizes thalearners must consciously notice language input to be effectively processed and internalized. Third, the *Output Hypothesis* stresses the significance of output, claiming that producing language facilitates and improves language acquisition by providing learners with opportunities to practice, test their language skills, and identify their weaknesses (Swain, 1985). In other words, feedback becomes the guide for improvement when a learner produces a problematic language. However, although the Output Hypothesis emphasizes learners' production, it does not claim that mere output is adequate for language acquisition. In this regard, as MacKey (2006) and Krashen (1985) stated, learners' exposure to comprehensible input is a fundamental component of overall language development. Lastly, according to the *Feedback Hypothesis,* feedback can facilitate and enhance language acquisition by developing accuracy and increasing learners' motivation (Ellis, 2009), helping learners focus on the language knowledge gaps (Ferris, 1999). In other words, with the help of appropriate feedback in terms of clarity, timing, and specificity, learners can follow their learning process and reproduce inaccurate productions (Ferris, 1999) without confusion and frustration (Grabe & Kaplan, 1996). Furthermore, the Feedback Hypothesis does not solely signify the role of feedback in the language learning process; it also emphasizes the role of comprehensible input, negotiation of meaning, and affective factors (Ellis, 2009).

Motivation is the force that allows, guides, and directs individuals' behavior toward a goal (Ryan & Deci, 2000). Dörnyei & Ryan (2015) define motivation as "the primary impetus to initiate L2 learning and later the driving force to sustain the language, often tedious learning process" (p.3). Gardner (1985) divides motivation into two types: *integrative motivation* and *instrumental motivation. Integrative motivation* refers to an internal desire that leads to increased interest and curiosity toward the target language, its culture, and society, while *instrumental motivation* is derived from the advantages of knowing a foreign language, such as finding highly paid professions and the value and respect received from others. Furthermore, Deci & Ryan (2012) divide motivation into extrinsic and intrinsic. *Intrinsic motivation* is derived from individuals' internal feelings and beliefs without expecting any reward or advantage (Özgür & Griffiths, 2013), while extrinsic motivation displays opposite orientations. There are several theories and models related to motivation. First, the *Self-determination Theory* emphasizes the significance of motivation and factors affecting individuals' intrinsic motivation (Deci & Ryan, 2012). Briefly, this theory underlines that the nature of human beings is active and intrinsically motivated toward the activities that individuals self-determine while acknowledging the effects of the social environment. Furthermore, Deci and Ryan (2012) emphasize three basic needs that support individuals' intrinsic motivation: *autonomy*, *competence*, and *relatedness. Autonomy* refers to individuals having control over their learning process, *competence* refers to the need to feel competent, and *relatedness* refers to a sense of social belonging. Second, the *Attribution Theory* aims to represent the reasons behind an individual's behavior (Weiner, 1972), assuming individuals assign some attributions to certain events and activities that lead them to behave as they do and provide explanations. In the context of foreign language teaching, it can be stated that attributions are learners' comments about the language learning process, causing them to develop a willingness or unwillingness towards language learning. Third, *the Process Model of L2 Motivation* represents motivation as a dynamic and complex phenomenon rather than displaying it statically (Ellis, 2015) and states that learners' level of motivation may fluctuate over time in different circumstances (Dörnyei, 1998). According to this theory, L2 motivation can be described in three stages: *the pre-actional stage,* in which learners set goals and plans, *the actional stage,* in which learners implement their plan, and lastly, *the post-actional stage,* in which learners evaluate their progress and provide feedback on the learning process. Finally, being one of the futuristic and influential theories of motivation, the *L2 Motivational Self-System* claims that motivation is derived from the learners' expectations of future L2 selves and involves three components that claim to affect motivation: *the ideal L2 self, ought-to-self,* and *the L2 learning experience*. While the *ideal L2 self* refers to the learners' ideal representations of themselves, *ought-to-self* refers to learners' self-control and attributions to prevent possible failures during the learning process. Lastly, the *L2 learning experience* refers to the environment where learning takes place, including the teachers, peers, physical environment, and curriculum. Consequently, motivation is a fundamental component that shapes learners' achievement, commitment, and academic development in the foreign language learning process.

Anxiety is defined as a state of apprehension and fear (Hilgard et al., 1971). Spielberger (1983) introduces three types of anxiety caused by different sources: *trait anxiety*, *state anxiety*, and *situation-specific anxiety*. While *trait anxiety* is a permanent state of one's personality, occurring regardless of the time, place, task, or event, *state anxiety* is described as an emotional state that is experienced due to certain events and situations. Finally, *situation-specific* anxiety is defined as a reaction to particular situations. Additionally, Horwitz (2001) proposes *foreign language anxiety* (FLA) as a type of situation-specific anxiety and divides FLA into three types: *communication apprehension*, *test anxiety*, and *fear of negative evaluation.*Alpert and Haber (1960), on the other hand, introduced two distinct types of anxiety that can be experienced during learning: *facilitating anxiety* and *debilitating anxiety*. Briefly, while *facilitating anxiety* positively affects learners' success and motivates them to learn and perform, *debilitating anxiety* may cause dropping outs and complete avoidance of the anxiety-arising subject, acting. There are several theories and models related to writing anxiety. First, presenting a general picture of anxiety and its possible effects, Tobias' *Anxiety Model* considers classical instruction procedures, including input, processing, and output (Tobias, 1979). During the *input* stage, high anxiety may hinder learning by interfering with learners' understanding of new information while disrupting the processing and organization of information in the *processing* stage. Lastly, during the output stage, anxiety can impact learners' production of language. Second, the *Affective Filter Hypothesis* suggests that affective factors such as anxiety significantly debilitate or facilitate the language learning process and achievement, highly underlying the importance of input, the primary condition for language acquisition (Krashen, 1982). In other words, anxiety blocks learning by interfering with the amount of comprehensible input needed to be received for language acquisition. In conclusion, anxiety can disrupt or inhibit the foreign language learning process; however, understanding how anxiety affects learners' cognitive processes is critical.

Feedback is a tool that informs learners whether their output is correct or wrong (Kulhavy, 1977). Hattie and Timperley (2007) define feedback as the "consequence of learners' language production" (p.81). In other words, it guides learners in their possible future paths to follow and briefly gives information on their past and current performances, making it invaluable for both teachers and learners. According to the type of error, activity, and learners' characteristics, different types of feedback can take different modes and tones, focusing on various aspects of lack of knowledge. *Oral* or *written feedback* can be given *directly* or *indirectly* by the teacher. Furthermore, feedback can focus on form, dealing with grammatical structures, punctuation, or content, relating to a holistic perspective. Automated feedback, on the other hand, is designed to support and improve the language learning process by providing immediate and individualized feedback without the boundaries of time and place, becoming a powerful tool (Benali, 2021). It can guide learners in various aspects of language including grammar, sentence structure, vocabulary selection, mechanics such as spelling and punctuation, and overall organization of ideas presented in the text (Dikli, 2010). There are several theories and models related to feedback. First, the *Sociocultural Theory* claims that individuals learn how to function in daily life and improve through interactions with people around them, being highly affected by cultural relations and norms while acknowledging the importance of biological factors (Lantolf & Pavlenko, 1995). Vygotsky (1978) states that development takes place in two levels. First, it occurs on the social level, which is "*inter-psychological*". Then, it takes place within the individual, which is "*intra-psychological*" (p.57). Two important notions of SCT are interconnected and mutually beneficial: *the zone of proximal development* and *scaffolding*. First, *the zone of proximal development* (ZPD) is the distance between an individual's actual and potential development (Vygotsky, 1978). The other significant notion is *scaffolding*, which is described as the support guided by an expert to a less knowledgeable person when needed (Vygotsky, 1978). As the sociocultural theory, social constructivism embodies similar principles and implications for educational psychology. Having adopted the Vygotskian perspective, *Social Constructivism* suggests that learning occurs within the sociocultural environment of learners and their current ZPD (Adams, 2006). According to social constructivism, knowledge is constructed with the help of a more knowledgeable person in the community and can be activated through the active use of it so that learners build their understanding (Watson, 2001). Both *sociocultural theory* and *social constructivism* aim to shed light on learners' improvement and learning through social interaction and collaboration, considering their principles and background ideas. However, the difference between the two theories is that while *social constructivism* focuses on the construction of knowledge within the social and cultural community with other members, *sociocultural theory* emphasizes the transfer and influence of society. Lastly, the *Self-regulation Theory* suggests that individuals are actively engaged in their learning process and can alter or adapt their behavior accordingly (Zimmerman, 2000). They organize and supervise their efforts and manage their perception, motivation, and cognition to accomplish specific goals, considerably affecting their achievement and motivation towards it. In Zimmerman's words (2000), "being able to self-regulate is the strongest ability of individuals". While finding some subjects or courses difficult to achieve is quite normal for learners, self-regulatory skills allow learners to self-motivate, discover strategies that will lead them to the best outcome, manage difficulties, supervise their efforts, and plan accordingly (Zimmerman, 2000). Considering these benefits, it can be stated that teachers' directions and guidance provided to learners can be an effective tool to enhance self-regulatory skills by precisely informing learners of the required criteria and present deficiencies (Chung & Yuen, 2011). Thus, feedback, regardless of its source, influences and improves learners' self-regulatory skills, resulting in higher achievement.

Previous Research

Research indicates that teacher feedback enhances learners' writing motivation, although there are instances where it can have the opposite effect due to fear of negative judgment. For instance, Hamidun et al. (2012) examined the effects of immediate feedback on thirty-four international learners' motivation levels. In addition to learners' written products, the data was obtained from classroom observations and interviews with learners. The results indicated that immediate and meaningful feedback increased learners' writing motivation and encouraged them. In a study that included 44 Iranian EFL learners (Zarei et al., 2020), a motivation questionnaire and semi-structured interviews with learners investigated the influences of oral corrective feedback on learners' motivation levels. The results revealed that feedback enhances learners' motivation, and there is a positive correlation between learners' motivation and receiving feedback. In a recent study that used quantitative and self-reported data, Rahimi (2024) concluded that collaborative motivational strategies, competence-boosting experiences, and active participation in creating learning opportunities were the key facilitators of student engagement regarding integrating motivational strategies into writing instruction. Contrary to the positive results revealed by these studies, Carless (2006) found that learners felt less motivated when they received feedback due to their fear of negative judgment from their teachers.

Research on the effects of teacher feedback on writing anxiety reveals mixed outcomes, with some studies indicating that feedback can increase anxiety due to fear of negative judgment, while others suggest that a lack of effective feedback contributes to heightened anxiety as learners become uncertain about their performance. For instance, Rezaei and Jafari (2014) conducted a study using 120 EFL learners from two higher education institutions and concluded that learners felt anxious when they received feedback due to the fear of negative judgment by the teacher. Other studies by Fareed et al. (2021) and Rasool et al. (2023) presented similar results. Unlike previous findings, Genç and Yaylı (2019) examined the reasons for writing anxiety and found that learners experienced high or moderate levels of writing anxiety due to the lack of effective feedback from their teacher, leading them to question their performances.

Research on the effects of automatic feedback on writing motivation is limited and presents mixed results. For example, Wilson and Czik (2016) conducted a large-scale study aiming to identify the effects of automated feedback on learners' writing motivation and quality. The results implicated that the motivation levels of the learners who received both types of feedback increased. Another study conducted by Al-Abdullatif et al. (2023) examined the potential of an AI-based chatbot called Bashayer to provide immediate feedback and support the learning processes of Saudi graduate students. In this quasi-experimental research design, it was found that participants in the experimental group showed higher learning motivation than participants in the control group. The findings suggest that chatbots can be an effective tool for increasing motivation in graduate education. In a two-phase study conducted by Taskiran et al. (2024), both quantitative and qualitative data were used. The findings show that the use of automated feedback significantly increases the writing motivation of distance learning EFL learners. The interviews with the participants emphasized that automated feedback positively affects their writing motivation by providing effective and immediate feedback, supporting individual learning, and providing a user-friendly learning environment. Furthermore, studies conducted by Ali et al. (2023) and Moybeka et al. (2023) presented similar results. According to the studies, the use of automated feedback increased EFL learners' motivation. Another quasi-experimental study by Wale and Kassahun (2024) examined the effects of Writerly and Google Docs on EFL learners' writing achievement and motivation. Ninety-two participants were randomly assigned to experimental and control groups. The experimental group received training with AI-assisted writing tools, while the control group received training with traditional pen and paper methods. Statistical analysis revealed that while increasing learners' writing performance, Writerly and Google Docs significantly increased learners' motivation and engagement. Overall, the findings suggest that AI-based writing technologies have the potential to increase motivation in EFL teaching and learning. On the other hand, another study conducted by Bulut (2019) presented opposite results. Examining the effects of an automated writing assessment tool called PEG Writing Scholar on EFL learners' writing achievement and motivation, 60 university students received traditional feedback in the control group, while the experimental group received feedback from the AWE tool. Data from questionnaires and writing tests showed that the use of AWE reduced learners' writing motivation. In conclusion, studies show that although automated feedback generally has a positive effect on EFL learners' writing motivation, some studies suggest that the effect of automated feedback on learners' motivation is not clear. Therefore, more studies are needed to understand the effects of automated feedback on learners' motivation to write in a foreign language context.

The research on the effects of automated feedback on EFL learners' anxiety shows conflicting results. For instance, a study conducted by El Shazly (2021) implemented an eight-week quasi-experimental pretest-posttest design with 48 undergraduate learners in an Egyptian EFL classroom, examining the role of AI applications in managing FLA. The use of interaction-oriented AI chatbots in speaking practice was found to be ineffective in reducing speaking anxiety while improving learners' language skills. Similarly, the study conducted by Sari and Han (2024) examined the effect of a model combining automated and teacher feedback on the writing anxiety of EFL learners. The 16-week quasi-experimental study found that there was no significant difference in writing anxiety between learners who received both automated and teacher feedback and learners who received only teacher feedback. Unlike previous studies, a study by Dizon and Gold (2023) examined the impact of Grammarly on EFL learners' FLA and learner autonomy. The 16-week study involved 58 students who attended four different academic writing courses at a public university in Japan. Analysis of pre- and post-surveys revealed that Grammarly had a significant positive impact on reducing students' writing anxiety, and students generally rated the tool positively. Another study by Waer (2023) examined the effects of automated feedback on learners' writing apprehension and grammatical quality. While the control group received only teacher feedback, the experimental group received feedback from Cambridge "Write&Improve". In terms of learners' writing apprehension, the results showed that automated feedback can be a useful tool to reduce learners' writing anxiety. Furthermore, Cahyono et al. (2023) investigated teachers' strategies to reduce learner anxiety. The results showed that teachers preferred automated feedback tools to alleviate learners' writing anxiety. In addition, learners expressed that the implementation of these tools helped them reduce their anxiety. In conclusion, the studies show that the effects of automated feedback on writing anxiety vary, with some studies indicating its positive effects on learners' anxiety and others showing no significant impact, emphasizing the need for further research.

Overview of the Current Study

As outlined before, learners' writing achievement is highly influenced by the learners' motivation, anxiety, and feedback process. However, while the number of studies on affective factors and their impact on learners' writing achievement has increased due to the importance they hold, there is a gap in the literature regarding the use of automated feedback and its impacts on learners' writing motivation and anxiety. Therefore, this study aims to provide an understanding of the effects of automated feedback and discover whether automated feedback and traditional teacher feedback possess different impacts on the learners' writing motivation and anxiety by answering the following research questions:

1. Does teacher feedback affect the level of writing anxiety and motivation levels among foreign language learners?
2. Does automated feedback affect the level of writing anxiety and motivation levels among foreign language learners?
3. Is there a difference in writing anxiety and motivation levels in the use of teacher and automated feedback?

METHOD

Research Design

This study examines the effects of automated feedback on foreign language learners' writing motivation, and anxiety. First, it analyzes the effects of traditional teacher feedback and automated feedback. In addition, it examines whether there is a difference in learners' writing motivation and anxiety levels in the use of teacher feedback and automated feedback. Therefore, it adopts a quasi-experimental research design in which already existing groups are used instead of random participant assignment (Creswell, 2014). Although using pre-existing groups is considered a limitation due to the lack of randomization, it is practical and natural (Shadish et al., 2002). As in the experimental research design, the study includes an experimental group that receives treatment and a control group that receives no treatment, helping to examine the effects of the treatment.

Participants

The study included 26 first-grade students studying at the Department of English Language Teaching at a foundation university in Turkey. While 18 participants were females (69.30%), eight were males (30.70%). The mean age of the participants was 20.53, while the minimum age was 18 and the maximum was 31. All students who participated in the study completed the preparatory school, which is mandatory for all students and includes extensive courses focusing on speaking, listening, reading, and writing. Therefore, according to the Common European Framework of Reference for Languages standards, their English proficiency was at the intermediate (B1) level. In addition, five participants from each group were randomly selected to conduct a focus group interview to comprehend the potential causes of the observed effects on the participants' motivation and anxiety levels, and a 30-minute meeting was conducted separately. Six participants were female, while four participants were male. The participants' ages ranged from 18 to 31 years old, with an average of 20.6.

Tools

Three tools were preferred in the study. First, a background questionnaire was used to collect data on learners' background information, such as age, gender, grade, department, current proficiency levels, and English course hours. Second, AWMQ by Payne (2012) was preferred to investigate the participants' level of writing motivation. The AWMQ includes 37 items that participants were expected to answer according to the five-point Likert Scale as 1=strongly disagree, 2=disagree, 3=uncertain, 4=agree, and 5=strongly agree for each statement. The total of 37 statements included five dimensions involving 13 items for enjoyment, eight items for self-efficacy, five for instrumentality, four for recognition, and three for effort, accounting for 73.69% of variance identified by exploratory factor analysis (Payne, 2012). With a reliability coefficient of .95in Cronbach's alpha, the AWMQ exhibited a prominent internal consistency. Third, the SLWAI by Cheng (2004a) was used to recognize the participants' level of writing anxiety. SLWAI included 22 statements that participants were required to answer according to the five-point Likert Scale ranging from 1 to 5, including statements as follows: 1=strongly disagree, 2=disagree, 3=uncertain, 4=agree, and 5=strongly agree. The statements include three main dimensions: the participants' avoidance and cognitive and somatic behavior toward second language writing. The SLWAI possessed an alignment with the multiple dimensions of anxiety, accounting for 48% of the variance identified by exploratory factor analysis (Cheng, 2004a). The coefficient value is determined as .91 by Cronbach's alpha.

Finally, to understand the results further and examine the reasons behind the differences in learners' writing motivation and anxiety after the intervention, a focus group interview was held with 10 randomly selected participants, including five from the control group and five from the experimental group. Six writing motivation and anxiety questions were prepared to investigate the participants' opinions, aiming to understand the possible reasons behind the obtained results in the motivation and anxiety levels of the participants after the intervention process was completed. In this face-to-face 30-minute focus group interview, the researcher noted each answer given by the participants.

Procedure

After obtaining the necessary permission from a university ethics committee, participants were informed about the objectives, procedure, and significance. It was particularly emphasized that the study was voluntary. Participants were informed and guaranteed that their information would be used anonymously for scientific purposes only and that their data would be kept completely confidential. To obtain the participants' permission, they were given a consent paper to be signed at the beginning of the data collection process.

The study took place in the Fall semester of the 2023-24 academic year and lasted six weeks, including the 4-week treatment and pre-test and post-test employment. Participants were required to complete a weekly writing task during the practice process. A pre-existing classroom, which included 26 students, was used, and the participants were randomly divided in half and assigned to the control and experimental groups. Later, the pre-test was employed to obtain pre-treatment data. During treatment, participants were asked to complete a weekly writing task under the teacher's control. While the control group used pen and paper to complete the writing tasks and evaluated according to the Writing Assessment Scale developed by Cambridge English Qualifications, the experimental group used Write&Improve, an online automated feedback tool developed by Cambridge University that enables students to receive immediate and individualized feedback. At the end of the practice process, all participants took the post-test, including the writing achievement task adopted from Cambridge ESOL, the AWMQ, and SLWAI. Then, a focus group interview consisting of six questions was carried out with ten participants, involving five participants from each group. Each group was given 30 minutes.

Pre-Test Administration

The background questionnaire was distributed to the participants at the beginning of the study. Then, participants answered the AWMQ to measure their writing motivation level and SLWAI to measure their writing anxiety, which took around 20-25 minutes. Additionally, participants were given 60 minutes to complete the writing achievement task.

The Practice Process

During the 4-week long practice process, the participants were asked to complete pre-determined writing tasks taken from Write&Improve by Cambridge. The writing tasks were chosen from the Write&Improve Advanced category, and participants were required to write between 200-250 words. Before each task, participants were informed about the specific essay types, including their distinct characteristics and examples of essays they were required to examine. In addition, the teacher answered the participants' questions before the actual writing task. For instance, the first week's task was to write an opinion essay about the main problems of Turkish teenagers. Accordingly, the participants were asked to describe the causes of several problems and provide possible solutions. Before the writing task, participants were introduced to the topic and involved in a discussion activity to brainstorm and gather common problems. Then, an opinion essay's specific features and requirements were introduced to participants by instruction, presenting examples, and providing pre-task activities such as ordering the paragraphs and filling in the blanks. Lastly, participants were given 60 minutes to complete the writing task. Each week, students were prepared for the actual writing task through discussion, instruction, and pre-task activities according to the relevant writing task. During the intervention, the control group used pen and paper to complete the tasks, while the experimental group used Write&Improve. Therefore, while the control group received traditional teacher feedback, the experimental group received immediate automated feedback from the automated feedback tool. In Table 1 below, the complete practice process is presented.

Table 1. The practice process

<table>
<tr><th rowspan="2">Weeks</th><th rowspan="2">Writing Task</th><th rowspan="2">Instruction</th><th colspan="2">Type of Feedback</th></tr>
<tr><th>Control Group</th><th>Experimental Group</th></tr>
<tr><td>Week 1</td><td>Writing an opinion essay about the main problems of Turkish teenagers by describing causes and providing solutions</td><td>Characteristics of an opinion essay, descriptive essay, and review</td><td rowspan="4">Teacher Feedback</td><td rowspan="4">Automated Feedback</td></tr>
<tr><td>Week 2</td><td>Writing a descriptive essay about a way of relaxing by implying its importance in today's world.</td><td>How to express an opinion</td></tr>
<tr><td>Week 3</td><td>Writing a review describing the best and worst films you have seen and giving reasons for these choices</td><td>How to support opinions and provide reasons</td></tr>
<tr><td>Week 4</td><td>Writing an essay discussing two of the areas in the notes given, identifying which area has benefited more from the internet, and giving reasons for the specific choice</td><td>Discussions</td></tr>
</table>

The Post-Test Administration

At the end of the practice process, the writing achievement task, AWMQ, and SLWAI were employed to find whether there were any changes in the participants' level of writing achievement, writing motivation, and anxiety after the practice process.

Data Analysis

The IBM SPSS Statistics 21.0 was used to analyze the data. First, the participants' ages' maximum, minimum, and mean scores were analyzed. Then, the participants' gender percentages and numbers were computed. Later, through Cronbach's Alpha, the reliability of the tools employed in the study was computed, and Varimax rotation was performed for both the pre-test and post-test.

As presented below, the reliability coefficient value of the AWMQ for the pre-test was .94 and .95 for the post-test. The percentage of variance of the AWMQ for the pre-test was 85.41% and 84.41% for the post-test. For SLWAI, the reliability coefficient of the pre-test was .82 and .72 for the post-test. The percentage of the variance of the SLWAI was 77.31% for the pre-test and 81.21% for the post-test.

Table 2. Reliability coefficients and % of the variance of the pre-test post-tests

Tools	Reliability Coefficients (Cronbach's Alpha)	% of the Variance
Pre-test AWMQ	.94	85.41%
Post-test AWMQ	.95	84.41%
Pre-test SLWAI	.82	77.31%
Post-test SLWAI	.72	81.21%

For further analyses, non-parametric methods were employed since the number of participants was small and could not be regarded as a normal distribution. Descriptive analysis, the Wilcoxon analysis, and Mann-Whitney U analysis were used to analyze the data. First, descriptive analysis was carried out to find the mean scores of the pre-test and post-test results. Then, the Wilcoxon analysis was employed to examine whether there were any changes between the pre-test and post-test results of the control and experimental groups' writing motivation and anxiety levels after the practice process. Later, the Mann-Whitney U analysis was carried out to compare whether there were any significant differences between the scores of the control and experimental groups' writing motivation and anxiety after the implementation.

In addition, a focus group interview was held, and the data obtained from the interview were examined in detail. Each participant's answers were carefully noted and then analyzed by the researcher. The analysis process was carried out with the aim of an in-depth evaluation of the participants' opinions and determining the differences between the control and experimental groups. The personal information of the participants was kept confidential, and the data was processed completely anonymously. The findings obtained in this process will be discussed in the next sections of the study.

RESULTS

The Effect of Teacher Feedback on Writing Motivation and Anxiety

Table 3 shows the motivation level of the participants in the control group, indicating the mean score, standard deviation, and minimum and maximum means. As the table presents, while the mean score of the participants' writing motivation was 3.80 in the pre-test, it increased to 3.91 in the post-test.

Table 3. The mean scores for motivation of the control group (Wilcoxon test, n=13)

Tests	Mean	Std. Deviation	Minimum	Maximum
Pre-test	3.80	.46	2.97	4.43
Post-test	3.91	.62	2.81	4.86

Table 4 compares the participants' motivation levels of the control group in the pre-test and post-test, including the number of positive and negative ranks, mean ranks, the sum of ranks, and the significance level of the comparison. According to the table, while seven participants' writing motivation levels decreased with a mean rank of 5.43 after the implementation, six participants' motivation levels increased with a mean rank of 8.83. With a significance level of .60, it can be stated that there is no significant change in the participants' level of motivation.

Table 4. Comparison of pre-test and post-test scores for motivation of the control group (Wilcoxon test)

Tests	Ranks	N	Mean Ranks	Sum of Ranks	Asymp. Sig. (2-Tailed)
Pre-test - Post-test	Negative Ranks	7	5.43	38.00	.60
	Positive Ranks	6	8.83	53.00	
	Ties	0			

Table 5 shows the writing anxiety levels of the participants in the control group, indicating the mean score, standard deviation, and minimum and maximum means. As can be seen in the table, while the mean score of the participants' writing anxiety was 2.75 in the pre-test, it was calculated as 2.58 after the implementation, displaying a decrease in participants' anxiety toward writing.

Table 5. The mean scores for writing anxiety of the control group (Wilcoxon test, n=13)

Tests	Mean	Std. Deviation	Minimum	Maximum
Pre-test	2.75	.53	1.91	3.86
Post-test	2.58	.36	2.14	3.18

Table 6 compares the participants' writing anxiety levels of the control group in the pre-test and post-test, consisting of the number of positive and negative ranks, mean ranks, the sum of ranks, and the significance level of the comparison. According to the table, nine participants' anxiety levels decreased after the implementation, with a mean rank of 6.28. While three participants' writing anxiety increased, one participant's anxiety level remained the same as before the implementation. However, since the significance level was calculated as .17, the changes in participants' writing anxiety levels cannot be considered significant.

Table 6. Comparison of pre-test and post-test scores for anxiety of the control group (Wilcoxon test)

Tests	Ranks	N	Mean Ranks	Sum of Ranks	Asymp. Sig. (2-tailed)
Pre-test – Post-test	Negative Ranks	9	6.28	56.50	.17
	Positive Ranks	3	7.17	21.50	
	Ties	1			

The Effects of Automated Feedback on Writing Motivation and Anxiety

Table 7 shows the motivation level of the participants in the experimental group, indicating the mean score, standard deviation, and minimum and maximum means. As the table presented, while the mean score of the experimental group's writing motivation was 3.72 in the pre-test, it was calculated as 3.70 after the implementation.

Table 7. The mean scores for motivation of the experimental group (Wilcoxon test, n=13)

Tests	Mean	Std. Deviation	Minimum	Maximum
Pre-test	3.72	.62	2.51	4.68
Post-test	3.70	.58	2.70	4.54

Table 8 compares the participants' motivation levels of the experimental group in the pre-test and post-test, including the number of positive and negative ranks, mean ranks, the sum of ranks, and the significance level of the comparison. According to the table, while six participants' writing motivation levels decreased with a mean rank of 8.25 after the implementation, seven participants' motivation levels increased with a mean rank of 5.93. With a significance level of .78, it can be stated that there is no significant change in the participants' level of motivation.

Table 8. Pre-test and post-test scores for motivation of the experimental group (Wilcoxon test)

Tests	Ranks	N	Mean Ranks	Sum of Ranks	Asymp. Sig. (2-Tailed)
Pre-test - Post-test	Negative Ranks	6	8.25	49.50	.78
	Positive Ranks	7	5.93	41.50	
	Ties	0			

Table 9 presents the writing anxiety levels of the participants in the experimental group, including the mean score, standard deviation, and minimum and maximum means. As can be seen in the table, while the mean score of the experimental group's writing anxiety was 2.82 in the pre-test, it was 2.59 after the implementation.

Table 9. The mean scores for writing anxiety of the experimental group (n=13)

Tests	Mean	Std. Deviation	Minimum	Maximum
Pre-test	2.82	.60	2.09	4.27
Post-test	2.59	.48	2.00	3.45

Table 10 compares the participants' writing anxiety levels of the experimental group in the pre-test and post-test, indicating the number of positive and negative ranks, mean ranks, the sum of ranks, and the significance level of the comparison. According to the table, 10 participants' writing anxiety levels decreased, with a mean rank of 7.90 after the implementation. Three participants' anxiety levels increased, with a mean rank of 4.00. With a significance level of .02, it can be stated that there is a significant difference between the pre-test and post-test results of the participants' writing anxiety levels.

Table 10. Comparison of pre-test and post-test scores for writing anxiety of the experimental group (Wilcoxon test)

Tests	Ranks	N	Mean Ranks	Sum of Ranks	Asymp. Sig. (2-Tailed)
Pre-test - Post-test	Negative Ranks	10	7.90	79.00	.02
	Positive Ranks	3	4.00	12.00	
	Ties	0			

The Differences in Writing Motivation and Anxiety

Table 11 provides the mean rank, sum of ranks, and significance level values of pre-test writing motivation levels of the control and experimental groups. According to the table, while the experimental group had a mean rank of 14.27, the experimental group's writing motivation level was 12.73 in the pre-test. Although the experimental group's writing motivation level was slightly lower than the control group, the difference cannot be considered significant due to the significance level of .61.

Table 11. The comparison pre-test writing motivation levels of the control and experimental groups (Mann-Whitney U test)

Tests	Group	Mean Rank	Sum of Ranks	Asymp. Sig. (2-Tailed)
Pre-test	Control Group	14.27	165.50	.61
	Experimental Group	12.73	185.50	

Table 12 below shows the only item in the AWMQ that presented a significant difference between the control and experimental groups. Regarding the use of correct grammar, while the control group had a mean rank of 16.35, the experimental group had a mean rank of 10.65. With a significance level of .04, there is a meaningful difference between the control and experimental groups.

Table 12. Results for the pre-test writing motivation of the control and experimental groups (Mann Whitney U Test)

Item	Group	N	Mean Rank	Sum of Ranks	Asymp. Sig. (2-Tailed)
3. I use correct grammar in my writing.	Control Group	13	16.35	212.50	.04
	Experimental Group	13	10.65	138.50	
	Total	26			

Table 13 presents the writing anxiety levels of the control and experimental groups in the pre-test, including the mean rank, sum of ranks, and significance level values. According to the table, while the control group's writing anxiety mean rank was 13.04, it was 13.96 for the experimental group. With a significance level of .76, it can be stated that there is no significant difference between the control and experimental groups.

Table 13. The comparison pre-test writing anxiety levels of the control and experimental groups (Mann-Whitney U test)

Tests	Group	Mean Rank	Sum of Ranks	Asymp. Sig. (2-Tailed)
Pre-test	Control Group	13.04	169.50	.76
	Experimental Group	13.96	181.50	

Table 14 provides the only item in the SLWAI that presented a significant difference between the control and experimental groups. As can be seen in the table, the item was related to participants' anxiety about their writing performance. The mean rank for the control group was 10.58, while the experimental group's mean rank was calculated as 16.42. In other words, the experimental group's anxiety towards their writing performance was higher than the control group. Due to a significance level of .05, there is a considerable difference between the control and experimental groups.

Table 14. Results for the pre-test writing anxiety of the control and experimental groups (Mann Whitney U Test)

Item	Group	N	Mean Rank	Sum of Ranks	Asymp. Sig. (2-Tailed)
21. I am not afraid at all that my English compositions would be rated as very poor.	Control Group	13	10.58	137.50	.05
	Experimental Group	13	16.42	213.50	
	Total	26			

Table 15 compares writing motivation levels between the control and experimental groups, including the mean rank, sum of ranks, and significance level. According to the table, the control group's writing motivation level had a mean rank of 14.77. The experimental group's writing motivation level mean rank was calculated as 12.23. Therefore, it can be stated that the motivation level of the control group was slightly higher than the experimental group in the post-test. However, as the significance level was calculated as .39, the difference cannot be considered considerable.

Table 15. The comparison post-test writing motivation levels of the control and experimental groups (Mann-Whitney U Test)

Tests	Group	Mean Rank	Sum of Ranks	Asymp. Sig. (2-Tailed)
Post-test	Control Group	14.77	192.00	.39
	Experimental Group	12.23	159.00	

Table 16 provides the only item in the AWMQ that presented a significant difference between the control and experimental groups in the post-test. The item was related to academic success. While the control group's mean rank was 16.12, the experimental group had a mean rank of 10.88. Therefore, with a significance level of .05, it can be stated that there is a considerable difference between the control and experimental groups.

Table 16. Results for the post-test writing motivation of the control and experimental groups (Mann Whitney U Test)

Item	Group	N	Mean Rank	Sum of Ranks	Asymp. Sig. (2-Tailed)
21. It is important to me that I make an A on a writing assignment.	Control Group	13	16.12	209.50	.05
	Experimental Group	13	10.88	141.50	
	Total	26			

Table 17 shows the comparison of writing anxiety levels between the control and experimental groups, including the mean rank, sum of ranks, and significance level. The table below shows that the control group's mean rank was 13.92, while the experimental group's was 13.08. Since the significance level was calculated as .78, there is no significant difference between the control and experimental groups.

Table 17. The comparison post-test writing anxiety levels of the control and experimental groups (Mann-Whitney U test)

Tests	Group	Mean Rank	Sum of Ranks	Asymp. Sig. (2-Tailed)
Post-test	Control Group	13.92	181.00	.78
	Experimental Group	13.08	170.00	

CONCLUSIONS AND DISCUSSION

Several conclusions can be made considering the findings obtained from this study. First, teacher feedback leads EFL writers to be more motivated toward writing, especially in establishing a desire to be more academically successful. When EFL writers receive feedback from the teacher, they make a connection between the writing task performed and academic success. In addition, receiving teacher feedback decreases EFL writers' writing anxiety, enhancing them to build a healthier psychological approach towards writing. Considering the adverse effects of high anxiety, teacher feedback facilitates the writing process by providing a less anxious state of mind. Second, automated feedback negatively affects EFL writers' motivation, making them less willing to write in a foreign language. On the other hand, it creates a significant change in EFL writers' writing anxiety. Automated feedback considerably decreases the writing anxiety that EFL writers experience and can be quite useful, especially with highly anxious EFL writers. Third, according to the current study, while teacher feedback increases EFL writers' motivation, automated feedback negatively affects the writing motivation levels of EFL writers. Furthermore, both teacher feedback and automated feedback help EFL writers reduce writing anxiety, eventually creating a safer and more comfortable writing process.

The results of a focus group study indicate that the abovementioned conclusions may relate to several factors. According to the participants, teacher feedback strengthens their motivation by increasing competition. In addition, teacher feedback allows them to notice their mistakes and lack, clearing the way for improvement. Moreover, the control group states that they want to be seen as successful writers by the teacher, and this desire leads to an increase in their writing motivation. Regarding their writing anxiety, they believe that frequent writing practice reduces their writing anxiety, helping them get used to writing in a foreign language. The participants who receive automated feedback state that although the feeling of independence that Write&Improve provides during the practice process is comforting, their motivation decreases since the teacher does not notice the success. However, their writing anxiety is considerably reduced without the fear of being judged. Finally, although the use of automated feedback provides many advantages during writing, participants who receive automated feedback state that there are times when automated feedback is insufficient and teacher feedback is needed.

Pedagogical Implications

Several pedagogical implications can be made considering the present study and previous literature. First, the study concludes that teacher feedback increases the learners' writing motivation, positively affecting the writing process, as previous literature suggests (Hamidun et al., 2012; Zarei et al., 2020). By providing guidance on the learning process and indicating the areas that need to be developed, learners can feel more in charge of their learning and notice their own needs. In terms of writing anxiety, it was seen from the study that teacher feedback decreases learners' writing anxiety, positively affecting their writing process. However, there are contradictory results in the literature on this issue. In some studies, learners' writing anxiety increases after they receive teacher feedback (Fareed et al., 2021; Rasool et al., 2023; Rezaei & Jafari, 2014), while some studies show that receiving teacher feedback decreases learners' anxiety (Yaylı & Genç, 2019). These differences may result from several factors affecting learners' performance when receiving teacher feedback. First, learners' fear of being negatively evaluated by teachers and peers enormously affects their perceptions of teacher feedback (Fareed et al., 2021). Furthermore, Cheng (2004) identifies several causes that lead learners to feel more anxious when receiving feedback, including teachers' instructional practices, self-perceptions, and personal beliefs about the process of learning writing. Additionally, the importance of positive tone and reinforcement during the feedback process is underlined as a factor that determines the relationship between the learners' level of anxiety and teacher feedback (MacIntyre, 1999). The study concludes that automated feedback decreases learners' writing motivation. Although there is relatively limited research on the relationship between automated feedback and its effects on learners' writing motivation, the studies show conflicting results. For instance, the majority of the existing literature (Al-Abdullatif et al., 2023; Ali et al., 2023; Moybeka et al., 2023; Taskiran et al., 2024) indicate that learners' writing motivation increases with automated feedback. However, a study conducted by Bulut (2019) found that automated feedback caused a decrease in learners' writing motivation, as the current study results suggest. While the number of studies on automated feedback and learners' level of writing anxiety is relatively limited, the results present conflicting results. Some studies suggest that automated feedback is effective in reducing learners' writing anxiety, particularly that instant feedback reduces learners' fear of making mistakes and provides a safer learning environment (Cahyono et al., 2023; Dizon & Gold, 2023; Waer, 2023), while others conclude that automated feedback has no significant effect on learners' anxiety levels (El Shazly, 2021; Han et al., 2023; Sari & Han, 2024). However, the current study shows that automated feedback reduces learners' writing anxiety, which aligns with some of the previous studies (Cahyono et al., 2023; Waer, 2023). These opposing results may depend on how learners perceive and use automated feedback and may be shaped by the relationship between individual learning strategies and writing anxiety. Additionally, the nature and frequency of feedback and learners' experiences with teacher feedback may also change the effect of automated feedback and lead to different results in anxiety levels. As a result, teacher and automated feedback significantly affect writing motivation and anxiety. For instance, while teacher feedback tends to increase motivation, its effect on anxiety can vary depending on several factors, such as feedback delivery and learner perceptions. On the other hand, automated feedback appears to consistently reduce anxiety, although its impact on motivation remains inconclusive. To this end, it can be stated that these distinctions offer a more comprehensive view of the relationship between feedback, motivation, and anxiety in EFL learners and contribute to the current literature by providing deeper insights into the nuanced effects of different feedback types and by highlighting the importance of immediate feedback in reducing anxiety and its complex impact on motivation.

Practical Recommendations

Based on the findings of the study, various pedagogical suggestions can be made for the effective integration of automated feedback in the context of EFL teaching and learning. First, EFL teachers should acknowledge the effects of automated feedback on reducing writing anxiety and implement these tools in a balanced way with traditional teacher feedback. In this respect, it is important to include practical training on the pedagogical use of automated feedback tools in pre-service and in-service teacher training programs. In other words, the courses should be expanded on the pedagogical use of these technological tools and focus on providing the necessary skills for effective use in the future profession, such as courses and detailed guides that cover the issues, including which types of writing are most effective with automated feedback, how learners can benefit from these tools effectively, and how to combine teacher feedback with automated feedback in practice. Second, teachers should gain competence in how to guide learners to benefit from this feedback effectively. In the context of pedagogical practices, while automated feedback provides instant grammar and spelling corrections, teacher feedback should focus on content and critical thinking skills. Accordingly, structured feedback loops can be established. For instance, a progressive feedback model can be implemented to improve learners' writing skills and create a more effective feedback process. In this model, learners can first evaluate their first drafts with automated feedback tools such as Write&Improve and Grammarly to correct basic grammar, spelling and vocabulary errors. Then, teachers may provide additional feedback on higher-level writing skills, such as content and academic expression. This structured process may help learners notice their deficiencies, develop critical thinking skills, and benefit from both automated and teacher feedback in a balanced way. During the curriculum development process, EFL teachers and curriculum developers should work collaboratively to design curricula that include both automated and teacher feedback and prevent possible problems beforehand. In addition, teaching materials and assessment criteria should be adapted to these technologies to implement automated feedback tools in educational contexts effectively. When evaluating educational policies, policymakers should develop policies that encourage the integration of automated feedback tools and support the cost-effective provision to educational institutions, particularly for low-resource educational environments to access automated feedback tools. Lastly, regulations regarding data privacy and ethical issues should be introduced to ensure the reliability and sustainability of automated feedback systems. In this respect, clear guidelines should be provided on the data processing and storage processes of AI-based tools. Educational institutions should organize data privacy information sessions to raise awareness among learners and teachers and take the necessary measures to protect their privacy, contributing to learners' safe use of automated feedback tools. In summary, integrating automated feedback tools into EFL instruction through teacher training, structured feedback processes, curriculum adaptations, and institutional policies will contribute to creating a more effective and sustainable learning environment by increasing learners' motivation for the writing process and reducing writing anxiety.

Limitations and Recommendations for Further Research

The present study has several limitations. First, this study was limited to 26 first-year university students in the ELT program at a foundation university, including 13 students in the control group and 13 in the experimental group. While the data collected indicated accepted levels of reliability and validity, the sample size seemed relatively small. The study also adopted a quasi-experimental study design due to the use of pre-existing groups instead of random assignment of participants. In addition, only Write&Improve was used as an automated feedback tool in the present study. The tools for collecting data were limited to the background questionnaire, AWMQ, and SLWAI. Last, the data analysis was confined to descriptive statistics and non-parametric tests.

According to the results of this study, several recommendations for further research can be listed. First, more research should be conducted on the effects of automated feedback on EFL learners' writing motivation and anxiety. To achieve this, the sample diversity of the study should be increased by including more students and larger groups from different educational and cultural backgrounds. More detailed studies can be conducted on the ease and effectiveness of tools used for automated feedback. Furthermore, to further examine the quality and impact of feedback, a content analysis should be conducted to compare the impacts of both teacher and automated feedback on learners' writing. In addition, conducting a similar study with students with different language proficiency levels could show whether the effectiveness of automated feedback varies according to proficiency level. This can provide an important understanding for customizing teaching methods and tools. Furthermore, with the use of automated feedback, the correlations between writing anxiety and motivation can be examined.

REFERENCES

Adams, P. (2006). Exploring social constructivism: Theories and practicalities. *Education 3-13, 34*(3), 243–257. DOI: 10.1080/03004270600898893

Al-Abdullatif, A. M., Al-Dokhny, A. A., & Drwish, A. M. (2023). Implementing the Bashayer chatbot in Saudi higher education: Measuring the influence on students' motivation and learning strategies. *Frontiers in Psychology*, *14*, 1129070. Advance online publication. DOI: 10.3389/fpsyg.2023.1129070 PMID: 37255522

Ali, J. K. M., Shamsan, M. A. A., Hezam, T. A., & Mohammed, A. A. Q. (2023). Impact of ChatGPT on learning motivation: Teachers and students' voices. *Journal of English Studies in Arabia Felix*, *2*(1), 41–49. DOI: 10.56540/jesaf.v2i1.51

Alpert, R., & Haber, R. N. (1960). Anxiety in academic achievement situations. *Journal of Abnormal and Social Psychology*, *61*(2), 207–215. DOI: 10.1037/h0045464 PMID: 13682679

Altınay, G., & Aydın, S. (2024). Automated feedback and writing achievement in a foreign language context. *1st International Literature,Language and Educational Research Symposium*, 246–260.

Aula Blasco, J. (2016). The relationship between writing anxiety, writing self-efficacy, and Spanish EFL students' use of metacognitive writing strategies: A case study. *Journal of English Studies*, *14*, 7–45. DOI: 10.18172/jes.3069

Bai, L., & Hu, G. (2017). In the face of fallible AWE feedback: How do students respond? *Educational Psychology*, *37*(1), 67–81. DOI: 10.1080/01443410.2016.1223275

Benali, A. (2021). The impact of using automated writing feedback in ESL/EFL classroom contexts. *English Language Teaching*, *14*(12), 189. DOI: 10.5539/elt.v14n12p189

Brookhart, S. M. (2017). *How to give feedback to your students* (2nd ed.). ASCD.

Bulut, S. E. (2019). *The effects of automated writing evaluation on EFL students' writing achievement and motivation towards writing* [Master's Thesis]. Istanbul University.

Cahyono, B. Y., Astuti, U. P., & Suryati, N. (2023). Online writing class: EFL university students' perception of teachers' strategies in alleviating their writing anxiety. *Computer Assisted Language Learning*, *42*(1), 1–24.

Cahyono, B. Y., & Rahayu, T. (2020). EFL students' motivation in writing, writing proficiency and gender. *TEFLIN Journal, 31*(2), 162. DOI: 10.15639/teflinjournal.v31i2/162-180

Çakır, İ. (2010). Yazma becerisinin kazanılması yabancı dil öğretiminde neden zordur? [Why is it difficult to acquire writing skills in foreign language teaching?]. *Erciyes University Journal of Social Sciences Institute, 1*(28), 1–12.

Carless, D. (2006). Differing perceptions in the feedback process. *Studies in Higher Education, 31*(2), 219–233. DOI: 10.1080/03075070600572132

Chastain, K. (1975). Affective and ability factors in second language acquisition. *Language Learning, 25*(1), 153–161. DOI: 10.1111/j.1467-1770.1975.tb00115.x

Cheng, Y. S. (2004a). A measure of second language writing anxiety: Scale development and preliminary validation. *Journal of Second Language Writing, 13*(4), 313–335. DOI: 10.1016/j.jslw.2004.07.001

Cheng, Y. S. (2004b). EFL students' writing anxiety: Sources and implications. *English Teaching & Learning, 29*(2), 41–62.

Chung, Y. B., & Yuen, M. (2011). The role of feedback in enhancing students' self-regulation in inviting schools. *Journal of Invitational Theory and Practice, 17*, 22–27. DOI: 10.26522/jitp.v17i.3777

Clariana, R. B. (1999, February). Differential memory effects for immediate and delayed feedback: A delta rule explanation of feedback timing effects. *Association for Educational Communications and Technology Annual Convention.*

Creswell, J. W. (2014). *Research design: Qualitative, quantitative, and mixed methods approaches* (4th ed.). SAGE Publications.

Daly, J. A., & Miller, M. D. (1975). Apprehension of writing as a predictor of message intensity. *The Journal of Psychology, 89*(2), 175–177. DOI: 10.1080/00223980.1975.9915748 PMID: 28135469

Daly, J. A., & Shamo, W. (1976). Writing apprehension and occupational choice. *Journal of Occupational Psychology, 49*(1), 55–56. DOI: 10.1111/j.2044-8325.1976.tb00329.x

Deci, E., & Ryan, R. (2012). Self-determination theory. In Van Lange, P. A. M., Kruglanski, A. W., & Higgins, T. E. (Eds.), *Handbook of Theories of Social Psychology* (1st ed., Vol. 1, pp. 416–437). SAGE Publications. DOI: 10.4135/9781446249215.n21

Dikli, S. (2010). The nature of automated essay scoring feedback. *CALICO Journal, 28*(1), 99–134. DOI: 10.11139/cj.28.1.99-134

Dizon, G., & Gold, J. (2023). Exploring the effects of Grammarly on EFL students' foreign language anxiety and learner autonomy. *The JALT CALL Journal, 19*(3), 299–316. DOI: 10.29140/jaltcall.v19n3.1049

Dörnyei, Z. (1998). Motivation in second and foreign language learning. *Language Teaching, 31*(3), 117–135. DOI: 10.1017/S026144480001315X

Dörnyei, Z., & Ryan, S. (2015). *The psychology of the language learner revisited.* Routledge. DOI: 10.4324/9781315779553

Dulay, H., Burt, M., & Krashen, S. (1982). *Language two.* Oxford University Press.

Ekmekçi, E. (2018). Exploring Turkish EFL students' writing anxiety. *The Reading Matrix: An International Online Journal, 18*(1), 158–175.

El Ebyary, K., & Windeatt, S. (2010). The impact of computer-based feedback on students' written work. *The International Journal of Educational Spectrum, 10*(2), 121–142. www.um.es/ijes. DOI: 10.6018/ijes/2010/2/119231

El Shazly, R. (2021). Effects of artificial intelligence on English speaking anxiety and speaking performance: A case study. *Expert Systems: International Journal of Knowledge Engineering and Neural Networks, 38*(3), e12667. Advance online publication. DOI: 10.1111/exsy.12667

Ellis, R. (2009). Corrective feedback and teacher development. *Journal of Linguistics and Language Teaching, 1*(1), 3–18. DOI: 10.5070/L2.V1I1.9054

Ellis, R. (2015). *Understanding second language acquisition* (Ellis, R., Ed.; 2nd ed.). Oxford University Press.

Fareed, M., Khan, I., & Akhtar, H. (2021). The causes of English writing anxiety among Pakistani ESL students: Perceptions of teachers and students. *Pakistan Journal of Humanities and Social Sciences, 9*(1), 21–27. DOI: 10.52131/pjhss.2021.0901.0109

Ferris, D. (1999). The case for grammar correction in L2 writing classes: A response to Truscott (1996). *Journal of Second Language Writing, 8*(1), 1–11. DOI: 10.1016/S1060-3743(99)80110-6

Flower, L., & Hayes, J. R. (1981). A cognitive process theory of writing. *College Composition and Communication, 32*(4), 365–387. DOI: 10.58680/ccc198115885

Gardner, R. C. (1985). *Social psychology and second language learning: The role of attitudes and motivation* (H. Giles, Ed.; 1st ed., Issue 4). Edward Arnold. DOI: 10.1037/h0083787

Grabe, W., & Kaplan, R. B. (1996). *Theory and practice of writing: An applied linguistic perspective* (1st ed.). Routledge. https://www.routledge.com/Theory-and-Practice-of-Writing-An-Applied-Linguistic-Perspective/Grabe-Kaplan/p/book/9780582553835

Griffiths, L., & Nicolls, B. (2010). e-Support4U: An evaluation of academic writing skills support in practice. *Nurse Education in Practice, 10*(6), 341–348. DOI: 10.1016/j.nepr.2010.02.005 PMID: 20471319

Hamidun, N., Hashim, S. H. M., & Othman, N. F. (2012). Enhancing students' motivation by providing feedback on writing: The case of international students from Thailand. *International Journal of Social Science and Humanity, 2*(6), 591–594. DOI: 10.7763/IJSSH.2012.V2.179

Hamp-Lyons, L., & Heasley, B. (2006). *Study writing: A course in written English for academic purposes*. Cambridge University Press.

Han, J., Yoo, H., Kim, Y., Myung, J., Kim, M., Lim, H., Kim, J., Lee, T. Y., Hong, H., Ahn, S. Y., & Oh, A. (2023). RECIPE: How to Integrate ChatGPT into EFL Writing Education. *L@S 2023 - Proceedings of the 10th ACM Conference on Learning @ Scale*, 416–420. DOI: 10.1145/3573051.3596200

Harmer, J. (2004). *How to teach writing*. Pearson/Longman.

Hassan, B. A. (2001). *The relationship of writing apprehension and self-esteem to the writing quality and quantity of EFL university students.*

Hattie, J., & Timperley, H. (2007). The power of feedback. *Review of Educational Research, 77*(1), 81–112. DOI: 10.3102/003465430298487

Hilgard, E. E., Atkinson, R. C., & Atkinson, R. L. (1971). *Introduction to psychology*. Harcourt Brace and Company.

Horwitz, E. (2001). Language anxiety and achievement. *Annual Review of Applied Linguistics, 21*, 112–126. DOI: 10.1017/S0267190501000071

Horwitz, E., Horwitz, M., & Cope, J. (1986). Foreign language classroom anxiety. *Modern Language Journal, 70*(2), 125–132. DOI: 10.1111/j.1540-4781.1986.tb05256.x

Hyland, K. (2022). *The Routledge handbook of second language acquisition and writing* (Manchón, R. M., & Polio, C., Eds.; 2nd ed.). Routledge.

Hyland, K., & Hyland, F. (2006). *Feedback in second language writing*. Cambridge University Press., DOI: 10.1017/CBO9781139524742

Jiang, L., & Yu, S. (2022). Appropriating automated feedback in L2 writing: Experiences of Chinese EFL student writers. *Computer Assisted Language Learning*, *35*(7), 1329–1353. DOI: 10.1080/09588221.2020.1799824

Johari, S. K. (2008). Building vocabulary and improving writing while developing a tourist brochure. *English Teaching Forum, 46*(2), 38–42.

Kamberi, L. (2013). The significance of teacher feedback in EFL writing for tertiary level foreign language learners. *Procedia: Social and Behavioral Sciences*, *70*, 1686–1690. DOI: 10.1016/j.sbspro.2013.01.241

Krashen, S. (1982). *Principles and practice in second language acquisition*. Pergamon Press.

Krashen, S. (1985). *The input hypothesis: Issues and implications* (1st ed.). Longman.

Kulhavy, R. W. (1977). Feedback in written instruction. *Review of Educational Research*, *47*(2), 211–232. DOI: 10.3102/00346543047002211

Kusumaningputri, R., Ningsih, T. A., & Wisasongko, W. (2018). Second language writing anxiety of Indonesian EFL students. *Lingua Cultura*, *12*(4), 357. DOI: 10.21512/lc.v12i4.4268

Lantolf, J. P., & Pavlenko, A. (1995). Sociocultural theory and second language acquisition. *Annual Review of Applied Linguistics*, *15*, 108–124. DOI: 10.1017/S0267190500002646

Lee, I. (2014). Revisiting teacher feedback in EFL writing from sociocultural perspectives. *TESOL Quarterly*, *48*(1), 201–213. DOI: 10.1002/tesq.153

Lee, I., Yu, S., & Liu, Y. (2018). Hong Kong secondary students' motivation in EFL writing: A survey study. *TESOL Quarterly*, *52*(1), 176–187. DOI: 10.1002/tesq.364

Li, J., Link, S., & Hegelheimer, V. (2015). Rethinking the role of automated writing evaluation (AWE) feedback in ESL writing instruction. *Journal of Second Language Writing*, *27*, 1–18. DOI: 10.1016/j.jslw.2014.10.004

MacIntyre, P. D. (1999). Language anxiety: A review of the research for language teachers. In Young, D. J. (Ed.), *Affect in foreign language and second language: A practical guide to creating a low-anxiety classroom atmosphere* (pp. 34–70). McGraw-Hill.

MacKey, A. (2006). Feedback, noticing and instructed second language learning. *Applied Linguistics*, *27*(3), 405–430. DOI: 10.1093/applin/ami051

Mahapatra, S. (2024). Impact of ChatGPT on ESL students' academic writing skills: A mixed methods intervention study. *Smart Learning Environments*, *11*(1), 9. DOI: 10.1186/s40561-024-00295-9

Mehta, S. R., & Al-Mahrooqi, R. (2015). Can thinking be taught? Linking critical thinking and writing in an EFL context. *RELC Journal*, *46*(1), 23–36. DOI: 10.1177/0033688214555356

Miranty, D., & Widiati, U. (2021). Automated writing evaluation (AWE) in higher education: Indonesian EFL students' perceptions about Grammarly use across student cohorts. *Egitim ve Ögretim*, *11*(4), 126–137. DOI: 10.47750/pegegog.11.04.12

Moybeka, A. M. S., Syariatin, N., Tatipang, D. P., Mushthoza, D. A., Dewi, N. P. J. L., & Tineh, S. (2023). Artificial intelligence and English classroom: The implications of AI toward EFL students' motivation. *Edumaspul - Jurnal Pendidikan, 7*(2), 2444–2454.

Nassaji, H. (2016). Anniversary article interactional feedback in second language teaching and learning: A synthesis and analysis of current research. *Language Teaching Research*, *20*(4), 535–562. DOI: 10.1177/1362168816644940

Oroujlou, N., & Vahedi, M. (2011). Motivation, attitude, and language learning. *Procedia: Social and Behavioral Sciences*, *29*, 994–1000. DOI: 10.1016/j.sbspro.2011.11.333

Ortega, L. (2014). *Understanding second language acquisition*. Routledge., DOI: 10.4324/9780203777282

Payne, A. R. (2012). *Development of the academic writing motivation questionnaire* [Master's Thesis]. University of Georgia.

Rahimi, M. (2024). Effects of integrating motivational instructional strategies into a process-genre writing instructional approach on students' engagement and argumentative writing. *System*, *121*, 103261. Advance online publication. DOI: 10.1016/j.system.2024.103261

Ramage, K. (1990). Motivational factors and persistence in foreign language study. *Language Learning*, *40*(2), 189–219. DOI: 10.1111/j.1467-1770.1990.tb01333.x

Rasool, U., Qian, J., & Aslam, M. Z. (2023). An investigation of foreign language writing anxiety and its reasons among pre-service EFL teachers in Pakistan. *Frontiers in Psychology*, *13*, 1–13. DOI: 10.3389/fpsyg.2022.947867 PMID: 36687864

Rezaei, M., & Jafari, M. (2014). Investigating the levels, types, and causes of writing anxiety among Iranian EFL students: A mixed method design. *Procedia: Social and Behavioral Sciences*, *98*, 1545–1554. DOI: 10.1016/j.sbspro.2014.03.577

Ryan, R., & Deci, E. (2000). Intrinsic and extrinsic motivations: Classic definitions and new directions. *Contemporary Educational Psychology*, *25*(1), 54–67. DOI: 10.1006/ceps.1999.1020 PMID: 10620381

Sabti, A. A., Md Rashid, S., Nimehchisalem, V., & Darmi, R. (2019). The impact of writing anxiety, writing achievement motivation, and writing self-efficacy on writing performance: A correlational study of Iraqi tertiary EFL learners. *SAGE Open*, *9*(4), 1–13. DOI: 10.1177/2158244019894289

Sari, E., & Han, T. (2024). The impact of automated writing evaluation on English as a foreign language learners' writing self-efficacy, self-regulation, anxiety, and performance. *Journal of Computer Assisted Learning*, *40*(5), 2065–2080. DOI: 10.1111/jcal.13004

Schmidt, R. (2012). Attention, awareness, and individual differences in language learning. In Chan, W. M., Nyet Chin, K., Bhatt, S. K., & Walker, I. (Eds.), *Perspectives on individual characteristics and foreign language education* (pp. 6–27). De Gruyter Mouton., DOI: 10.1515/9781614510932.27

Shadish, W. R., Cook, T. D., & Campbell, D. T. (2002). *Experimental and quasi-experimental designs for generalized causal inference* (3rd ed., Vol. 1195). Houghton Mifflin.

Spielberger, C. D. (1983). *State-trait anxiety inventory for adults* (1st ed.). Consulting Psychologists Press.

Swain, M. (1985). Communicative competence: Some roles of comprehensible input and comprehensible output in its development. In *Input in second language acquisition* (pp. 165–179). Heinle & Heinle.

Syrewicz, C. C. (2023). The motivations that improve the creative writing process: What they might be and why we should study them. *New Writing*, *20*(2), 178–200. DOI: 10.1080/14790726.2022.2051563

Taskiran, A., Yazici, M., & Erdem Aydin, I. (2024). Contribution of automated feedback to the English writing competence of distance foreign language learners. *E-Learning and Digital Media*, *21*(1), 24–41. DOI: 10.1177/20427530221139579

Tobias, S. (1979). Anxiety research in educational psychology. *Journal of Educational Psychology*, *71*(5), 573–582. DOI: 10.1037/0022-0663.71.5.573 PMID: 41010

Tran, L. T. (2007). Learners' motivation and identity in the Vietnamese EFL writing classroom. *English Teaching*, *6*(1), 151–163. https://education.waikato.ac.nz/research/files/etpc/2007v6n1art8.pdfpp.151-163

Vygotsky, L. S. (1978). *Mind in society: The development of higher psychological processes (M. Cole, V. John-Steiner* (Scribner, S., & Souberman, E., Eds.; 1st ed.). Harvard University Press.

Waer, H. (2023). The effect of integrating automated writing evaluation on EFL writing apprehension and grammatical knowledge. *Innovation in Language Learning and Teaching*, *17*(1), 47–71. DOI: 10.1080/17501229.2021.1914062

Wale, B. D., & Kassahun, Y. F. (2024). The transformative power of AI writing technologies: Enhancing EFL writing instruction through the integrative use of Writerly and Google Docs. *Human Behavior and Emerging Technologies*, *2024*, 1–15. DOI: 10.1155/2024/9221377

Watson, J. (2001). Social constructivism in the classroom. *Support for Learning*, *16*(3), 140–147. DOI: 10.1111/1467-9604.00206

Weiner, B. (1972). Attribution theory, achievement motivation, and the educational process. *Review of Educational Research*, *42*(2), 203–215. DOI: 10.3102/00346543042002203

Wilson, J., & Czik, A. (2016). Automated essay evaluation software in English language arts classrooms: Effects on teacher feedback, student motivation, and writing quality. *Computers & Education*, *100*, 94–109. DOI: 10.1016/j.compedu.2016.05.004

Xu, X. (2011). The relationship between language learning motivation and the choice of language learning strategies among Chinese graduates. *International Journal of English Linguistics*, *1*(2), 203–212. DOI: 10.5539/ijel.v1n2p203

Yaylı, D., & Genç, E. (2019). The second language writing anxiety: The perceived sources and consequences. *Pamukkale University Journal of Education*, *45*(45), 235–251. DOI: 10.9779/PUJE.2018.231

Yeung, M. (2016). Exploring the construct of learner autonomy in writing: The roles of motivation and the teacher. *English Language Teaching*, *9*(8), 122–139. DOI: 10.5539/elt.v9n8p122

Zaman, M., & Kalam, A. (2012). Feedback in EFL writing at tertiary level: Teachers' and learners' perceptions. *ASA University Review, 6*(1).

Zarei, M., Ahour, T., & Seifoori, Z. (2020). Impacts of implicit, explicit, and emergent feedback strategies on EFL learners' motivation, attitude and perception. *Cogent Education*, *7*(1), 1727130. Advance online publication. DOI: 10.1080/2331186X.2020.1727130

Zimmerman, B. J. (2000). Motivational sources and outcomes of self-regulated learning and performance. In Zimmerman, B. J., & Schunk, D. H. (Eds.), *Handbook of self-regulation* (pp. 13–39). Elsevier. DOI: 10.1016/B978-012109890-2/50031-7

Chapter 3
Using AI to Enhance Receptive Foreign Language Skills

Gökhan Hınız
https://orcid.org/0000-0003-3569-0198
Çanakkale Onsekiz Mart University, Turkey

ABSTRACT

This chapter examines how artificial intelligence (AI) enhances receptive foreign language skills, listening, and reading by delivering adaptive and personalized learning experiences. Building on established literature and recent empirical findings, the study discusses that AI-powered platforms diversify input, offer real-time diagnostic feedback, and simulate authentic communicative contexts through generative text and multimodal resources. These systems may expose learners to varied accents and dialects, scaffold complex texts, and provide immediate corrective cues, thereby reducing anxiety and sustaining motivation. Furthermore, the chapter highlights AI's role in promoting metacognitive development as learners critically reflect on their comprehension and refine their strategies. While promising, the research acknowledges risks such as overreliance on technology, diminished human interaction, data privacy issues, algorithmic bias, and access concerns.

1. INTRODUCTION

Receptive language skills—listening and reading—are fundamental for successful foreign language acquisition and improvement in most contexts. They enhanced communicative competence by providing learners with comprehensible input, linguistic forms, cultural references, and a broad range of discourse strategies that

DOI: 10.4018/979-8-3373-5681-5.ch003

shape emergent language proficiency (Brown & Yule, 1983; Krashen, 1985; Newton & Nation, 2021; Zhang, 2001). However, these skills have not always received the same attention as speaking and writing (Celce-Murcia et al., 2014; Richards & Rodgers, 2014; Vandergrift, 2007).

Traditional approaches to teaching receptive skills often rely on passive exercises and standardized materials, which overlook the depth, diversity, and authenticity of real-world communication (Grabe, 2009; Graham & Santos, 2015; Vandergrift, 2007). In addition, teachers commonly face large class sizes, limited resources, and mixed proficiency levels, making it difficult to provide personalized instruction that maintains learner engagement.

Recent developments in artificial intelligence (AI) have begun to impact language teaching by introducing new methods to develop listening and reading skills in foreign language contexts. AI tools offer adaptive, individualized learning experiences that address varied learner needs while extending exposure to linguistic and cultural variety. Examples include AI-powered chatbots that simulate realistic conversations and generative systems that customize reading texts as learners progress (He, 2024; Li et al., 2021). These innovations create new opportunities for engagement, interactivity, and scalability.

This chapter provides a thorough synthesis of how AI can be harnessed to promote engagement in receptive foreign language skills. It examines the benefits and limitations of integrating AI in receptive skill instruction and highlights ethical and contextual factors that educators and other stakeholders should address. The chapter concludes by outlining pedagogical and theoretical implications and suggesting avenues for further research to advance understanding of AI's influence in language education.

2. LISTENING COMPREHENSION

Listening comprehension is vital for successful second-language development because it provides phonological, lexical, and pragmatic input for productive skills. Vandergrift (1999) describes listening as an active process in which learners sort sounds, decode grammar, interpret prosody, store information, and anchor meaning in sociocultural context, moving constantly between bottom-up decoding and top-down prediction. Field (2008) notes that unbalanced reliance on either path yields detail overload or speculative error. Because spoken input passes only once, attention and memory are stressed more than in reading, yet successful listening advances fluency, pronunciation, and vocabulary and feeds into literacy (Newton & Nation, 2021).

Skilled listeners operate as learning strategists to support sound recognition and comprehension. Goh (2000) and Vandergrift (2004) suggest that skilled listeners keep switching gears: they infer, piecing together meaning from context and prior knowledge. They monitor, pausing to test whether what they just heard makes sense and they use socio-affective strategies, like positive self-talk or controlled breathing. Explicit strategy training facilitates self-regulation, confidence and comprehension (Graham & Santos, 2015; Chou, 2017; Vandergrift & Tafaghodatari, 2010).

While listening can be already difficult in everyday situations, challenges intensify for foreign-language learners who must keep pace with unpredictable accent, rate, grammar and lexis while detecting speaker intent and discarding irrelevances. Bsharat-Maalouf and Karawani (2022) observe that even bilinguals stumble in noise in some contexts. Rahimirad and Moini (2015) list fast speech, unfamiliar accents, and multitasking as major challenges. Studies by Mohammadi Golchi (2012), Valizadeh and Alavinia (2013), and Yekeler and Ulusoy (2021) collectively link anxiety, speaker clarity, and environment to comprehension loss.

Aryadoust and Luo (2022) argue that ordinary classrooms still overlook analytical, empathetic, and appreciative listening, leaving students unequipped for real discourse. Vocabulary knowledge is another crucial factor. MacCutcheon et al. (2019) find that lexical richness magnifies benefits of good acoustics, and Wallace and Lee (2020) show it outperforms executive functioning as a predictor of scores.

Higher-level comprehension also depends on strategy awareness. Rukthong and Brunfaut (2019) link inferencing and monitoring to word recognition, and Vandergrift and Baker (2015) connect progress to auditory discrimination and working memory. Emotional variables matter too. Wang and MacIntyre (2021) reveal that enjoyment boosts, and anxiety suppresses, performance.

Digital innovation offers new scaffolds. Aryadoust and Luo (2022) suggest that adaptive platforms and virtual worlds broaden accent exposure and add visual cues. Levak and Son (2016) document how Skype and Second Life interactions lower anxiety through embedded context. Yet many courses still test answers rather than teach processes; Fathi et al. (2020) and Klimovich and Richter (2024) show that strategy instruction reduces anxiety and heightens outcomes. Similarly, Goh and Hu (2014) recommend routine metacognitive reflection.

Multimodal input supplies further support comprehension. Cartner and Cameron (2023) report that captions and transcripts raise confidence when paired with strategy coaching. Salmani and Rahimi (2024) add that animated video homework yields larger gains and productive cognitive load than audio-only tasks. Guichon and McLornan (2008) find that subtitles lift recall but caution that overreliance can stunt independence, advocating phased withdrawal.

Current literature suggests that optimal instruction blends vocabulary expansion, explicit cognitive-metacognitive strategy work, multimodal scaffolding, and thoughtfully deployed multimodal support, giving learners the resilient toolkit needed to interpret authentic, real-time speech.

2.1. How AI Enhances Listening Skills Development

Recent research demonstrates how AI enriches listening comprehension in foreign language contexts. Studies indicate improvements among learners who use AI-driven applications, particularly when compared with peers receiving traditional instruction. In one example, first-year university students who relied on programs like Duolingo and AI chatbots made significant gains in listening tests, outperforming a control group taught through conventional methods (Alrasheedi, 2024). The difference was reflected in all aspects of listening comprehension, including literal, critical, inferential, and creative sub-skills. This pattern suggests that AI not only supports straightforward information processing but also helps learners develop deeper interpretation and evaluative abilities.

Another study provides further evidence of AI's efficacy. The use of the Ekwing intelligent learning system coincided with a notable improvement in listening performance (Hu, 2025). The experimental group's scores increased by an average of 4.65 points more than the control group, indicating that AI-based approaches can produce results that are measurable and statistically significant. An additional finding was a 6.214-point difference in post-test results between the experimental and control groups, prompting the researcher to conclude that AI technology can personalize instruction and boost motivation. These improvements, as described, stem from Ekwing's ability to adapt to individual needs and maintain higher levels of learner engagement through interactive design features.

Furthermore, Sivaji et al. (2024) discuss advanced AI-driven pedagogical strategies that furnish immediate assessment and adaptive content tailored for higher education settings. In these contexts, real-time feedback on learner performance leads to more efficient practice, as tasks continually adjust in line with student progress. Students are said to achieve stronger listening outcomes than those in control groups using standard instructional materials. Similarly, Kim (2018) explores chatbot use in a Korean college environment and finds that learners who engaged with AI-driven conversations showed sharper gains in listening proficiency than those in more traditional classrooms. Students in the experimental group advanced from an intermediate to an advanced level, reflecting the value of sustained dialogic practice and consistent exposure to authentic speech patterns. Likewise, the study by Xiao (2025) demonstrated that integrating AI-driven speech recognition technology into EFL instruction significantly enhanced learners' listening comprehension, increased their sense of flow, and reduced listening anxiety compared to traditional methods. Participants in the experimental group reported a significant improvement in flow experience, suggesting that the flow state was closely tied to the active use of AI during the intervention (Xiao, 2025). The most pronounced finding from the study was the substantial reduction in listening anxiety in the experimental group, unlike the control group, which showed minimal change (Xiao, 2025). These results emphasize the potential of AI-enhanced feedback and personalization in fostering both cognitive and affective benefits in language learning.

Exposure to Diverse Accents and Dialects

AI-driven language resources can greatly expand the range of English accents and dialects available to learners, helping to address an ongoing challenge in teaching listening skills. Historically, English instruction in many contexts has prioritized "standard" varieties such as General American or Received Pronunciation. However, real-world encounters involve a far wider range of accents. Students who limit their exposure to a single accent can struggle to understand conversation partners who speak a different form of English. AI technologies now exist to provide content featuring Australian, Canadian, Indian, Irish, and South African English, along with various other global varieties. By interacting with these diverse language inputs, students become more adaptable listeners and prepared for authentic interactions in multicultural settings.

AI can expose learners to local expressions, idiomatic language, and regional pronunciation patterns that are often missing from standard textbooks. This variety helps learners become more adaptable and better prepared to understand nonstandard vocabulary or unfamiliar accents in real-world situations. Phrases like "fair dinkum" in Australian English or "y'all" in certain regions of the United States carry cultural and situational connotations that do not always appear in textbooks. Through repeated exposure to authentic phrases in an AI environment, learners can become more comfortable interpreting informal elements of speech. This skill is especially critical for individuals planning to work or study in international spaces, where exposure to multiple Englishes is common.

Some AI systems even replicate naturalistic communication scenarios with layered accents or partially overlapping speech. People in multinational work environments often adopt a "world English" pronunciation or merge elements of different dialects to aid mutual understanding, creating complexities in spoken interaction. AI-generated materials that incorporate features such as faint background noise or multi-accent dialogues introduce an added level of realism. Learners engaging with these materials regularly can develop stronger skills in interpreting less controlled and noisier inputs—skills that are crucial for real-time comprehension. Over time, this practice nurtures a sense of confidence in dealing with fluid, spontaneous speech across various contexts, moving beyond the uniform audio typically associated with listening exercises.

In many traditional EFL classrooms, audio materials come from a narrow set of recordings featuring consistent speech rates, clear enunciation, and minimal environmental interference. Though these controlled conditions can support initial skill-building, they do not fully represent the unpredictability of everyday interactions. AI's capacity to compile and generate diverse audio samples helps students prepare for the speech variations and spontaneous exchanges that define natural communication. With improved exposure, learners tend to show greater versatility in understanding English as it truly exists worldwide, rather than an idealized, one-dimensional version.

Adaptive Listening Platforms

AI has the potential to transform how listening exercises are delivered. These systems can track various elements of learner performance in real time, such as accuracy in answering comprehension questions, the number of audio replays, and the ability to identify specific sound contrasts. By recording these data points, the system can respond intelligently, automatically adjusting the difficulty of subsequent exercises or modifying the rate of speech to maintain a level of challenge appropriate to each learner's capabilities. This principle aligns with the idea of offering language input just above a learner's current proficiency, often associated with comprehensible input theory (Krashen, 1985, as discussed in Graham & Santos, 2015).

Beyond simply adjusting speech speed or word complexity, advanced platforms may incorporate interactive scenarios that become more demanding if students repeatedly demonstrate competence. For example, once a learner shows familiarity with basic greetings, the AI might shift toward more advanced functional language, incorporating idiomatic expressions or faster speech. Conversely, if the student shows difficulty in recognizing certain phonemes, the platform can deliver targeted drills focused on that area. In doing so, each learner receives a curated progression that addresses specific weaknesses without unnecessary repetition of skills they have already mastered.

Empirical support for these approaches is growing. As mentioned earlier, Hu's (2025) study of the Ekwing intelligent learning tool measured a 4.65-point average increase in listening scores for students who used AI-based practice compared with those who followed a traditional curriculum. This outcome signaled a significant advantage tied to adaptive task design. In these settings, adaptation is changing content difficulty and diversifying task types—for instance, switching from simple multiple-choice questions to open-ended reflection on a spoken narrative. These shifts can help learners engage in deeper processing of audio materials, moving from merely decoding words to interpreting and evaluating meanings.

The adaptive framework also makes it possible to collect a rich dataset of learner performance over time, generating feedback loops that inform both the student and the instructor. Teachers can track which parts of the curriculum students find most challenging—whether it is rapid speech, unfamiliar idioms, or specialized vocabulary—and then offer targeted interventions. Some systems even produce visual analytics showing learner progress, pinpointing areas of weakness, and highlighting patterns of improvement. This structured approach supports better-informed pedagogical decisions, ensuring that instructors can complement AI-driven tasks with additional guidance or personalized support where needed.

Conversational Agents: Safe Practice for Confident Comprehension

Chatbots and virtual tutors present another dimension of AI-driven learning, creating opportunities for spoken interaction in a less intimidating setting. Real-time conversations with native or highly proficient speakers can be stressful for learners who are not yet comfortable processing spoken language. Mistakes are often magnified by fear of embarrassment, which can inhibit participation. In contrast, AI chatbots provide a risk-free environment where learners can practice listening, speaking, and responding without the anxiety that can come from face-to-face encounters.

These agents can be programmed to detect a learner's proficiency and adjust speech rate, vocabulary, and syntactic complexity accordingly. A novice user might encounter slower speech and straightforward sentence structures, while a more advanced learner is introduced to idiomatic expressions, faster speech, and a variety of colloquial terms. This layered approach allows students to stretch their comprehension gradually. Over time, they can attempt more complex tasks: for example, following extended monologues, responding to nuanced questions, and detecting humor or sarcasm in conversation.

Repeated chatbot interactions also promote familiarity with a set of common conversation patterns, which can then lower anxiety in real-world exchanges. Learners who frequently hear and rehearse particular question-response formats—such as greetings, clarifications, or requests for elaboration—gain the reflexes needed to engage spontaneously in live settings. Additionally, practicing with AI can improve students' ability to parse different accents or speech idiosyncrasies, as these systems can be configured to simulate regional varieties or speech styles.

Kim's (2018) research in a Korean college context reveals that students who regularly interacted with chatbots demonstrated substantial gains in listening proficiency, surpassing peers engaged in conventional routines. Kim (2018) attributes this success to the chatbot's capacity to deliver authentic input, maintain dialogue, and integrate instant corrective feedback. Over time, these interactions allowed learners to become more at ease with rapid speech and complex sentence structures, including conversational fillers or shortened forms often found in colloquial English. This safe yet dynamic environment decreases the perceived risk of errors or miscommunication, thereby helping learners build the confidence needed to tackle real-life conversations.

Immediate Feedback and Metacognitive Growth

One distinctive advantage of artificial-intelligence language applications is their capacity for instantaneous feedback, a feature that resolves obstacles typical in traditional instruction. Learners who depend exclusively on teacher-mediated evaluation often wait hours or days for comments, a delay that weakens the cognitive association between an error and its correction. Algorithms that identify discrepancies within seconds preserve that association and enable timely adjustment of listening habits.

Consider a listener who confuses the minimal pair "ship" and "sheep." An adaptive programme can detect the substitution, highlight the relevant vowel contrast, and redirect the learner toward targeted phonological drills. When idiomatic expressions generate misunderstanding, the software can clarify meaning and pragmatic usage through annotated examples. This immediate diagnostic process simultaneously cultivates metacognitive awareness: learners must analyse whether misperception results from limited lexicon, unfamiliar accent, or prosodic difficulty, and they subsequently refine strategic responses to novel input.

Empirical research supports this dynamic. Alamdari and Bozorgian (2021) demonstrated that reflective interventions enhanced multimedia listening comprehension, with pronounced improvement among female participants. Alrasheedi (2024) reported that first-year university students who engaged with an AI platform surpassed a control cohort across all listening sub-skills, including inferential and creative comprehension, domains in which metacognition exerts a decisive influence. Participants identified the locus of misunderstanding and modified strategies during subsequent tasks.

The pedagogical value of AI extends beyond error correction; it resides in continuous guidance that assists learners in identifying, classifying, and regulating cognitive processes. Adaptive dashboards record recurrent error types, replay frequency, and pause locations, thereby encouraging systematic self-assessment. Visual summaries allow individuals to inspect listening routines and to evaluate the efficacy of strategies such as segment repetition or consultation of captions. Over successive sessions, the consolidation of these data–reflection cycles fosters sustained planning and monitoring.

Integration of instantaneous feedback with teacher-led consultation generates additional reflective dialogue. A learner might observe that inaccuracies cluster during informal contractions, then discuss the phenomenon with a tutor and formulate an explicit attentional plan before the next exercise. AI platforms that incorporate personal goal setting strengthen this reflective ethos; learners establish objectives, such as precision in consonant clusters, record progress metrics, and revise tactics accordingly. Through this iterative sequence of intention, diagnosis, and regulation, listening proficiency expands alongside transferable habits of self-regulated learning.

Designing Engaging and Culturally Relevant Listening Content

AI systems offer fresh avenues for generating listening materials that resonate with learners' backgrounds, interests, and language objectives. Through AI-generated authentic listening scripts and voiceovers, educators can create or curate audio segments featuring contexts aligned with student experiences, whether related to hobbies, professional fields, or cultural traditions. This relevance can enhance student motivation because materials feel more directly linked to everyday life.

For instance, a class of engineering students might benefit from AI-curated recordings of technical discussions or interviews with experts, focusing on the vocabulary and syntax particular to that field. Meanwhile, a group of learners interested in popular culture could practice AI-generated dialogues featuring slang, pop references, or current events. Teachers might embed comprehension questions designed to guide students toward key linguistic insights—highlighting new terms, varied structures, or pragmatic cues that signal speaker intention.

The potential for cultural inclusivity is particularly valuable in contexts where learners and teachers have limited exposure to authentic English media. In under-resourced settings, it can be challenging to find high-quality audio reflecting different dialects or specialized domains. AI-driven voice generation helps compensate by synthesizing realistic speech patterns and customizing content to align with the local context. A teacher lacking access to diverse multimedia sources can integrate AI-generated voiceovers that illustrate a range of topics, accents, and cultural references, thereby bridging resource gaps.

While the technical infrastructure to build such content can appear daunting, various platforms are becoming more user-friendly, affordable and accessible. Some offer drag-and-drop interfaces allowing educators to select the accent, speed, and complexity level of the generated audio. Over time, teachers develop a more refined sense of which parameters work best for their learners, and they can adjust the inputs accordingly. This adaptability can be particularly effective in supporting students who are preparing for specific real-world tasks, such as standardized tests requiring certain listening abilities or professional interviews that demand specialized vocabulary.

By embedding cultural references that learners can identify with, teachers can boost not just listening comprehension but also deeper engagement with the language. This can include localizing names, places, or narrative settings in the AI-generated content so that students see themselves or their communities reflected in the material. When learners encounter passages where characters navigate scenarios akin to their own experiences—such as daily routines, family gatherings, or community events—the sense of connection encourages more robust participation and fosters an environment where listening is both meaningful and enjoyable.

Limitations and Implementation Challenges

Despite these promising developments, there are critical challenges in fully integrating AI-based listening instruction. One significant hurdle involves the technical robustness of AI tools. Systems reliant on speech recognition can struggle when accents or background noise diverge from the training data. Latency, or the time lag in feedback delivery, can disrupt the flow of listening practice. Teachers may also discover that certain AI features are not optimized for local contexts, particularly if the software has not been trained on regional accents, cultural references, or relevant vocabulary sets. While all possible uses of AI discussed so far present a promising future for language teaching, there is a need for empirical research that will discuss affordances and challenges and optimise the best methods.

Overdependence on AI carries other risks as well. Some educators worry that excessive use of chatbots and virtual tutors might limit opportunities for human-to-human interaction, which remains central to genuine language socialization. Real conversations require learners to interpret subtle cues like body language, intonation shifts, and real-time changes in emotional tone—elements that AI can approximate but not replicate perfectly. Hence, a balanced approach that combines AI-driven exercises with regular peer or teacher interactions may yield more holistic growth.

Assessment practices also present complications. Although researchers such as Alrasheedi (2024) and Hu (2025) report strong results tied to AI instruction, assessment tools differ across studies, making direct comparisons difficult. Some programs test only basic comprehension questions, while others examine inferential or creative listening skills. Timeframe variations—ranging from a few weeks to an entire academic semester—can further complicate the landscape of findings. To draw definitive conclusions about AI's effectiveness, more standardized measures and extended longitudinal studies are necessary.

Concerns about equity and access also surface in many discussions. Learners in well-funded institutions are more likely to gain the benefits of cutting-edge AI, from advanced conversational agents to specialized adaptive platforms. In contrast, students and educators in underprivileged areas may have limited or no access to similar tools, widening the digital divide. Additionally, technical support, infrastructure, professional development for educators and AI literacy programs for students must be adequately maintained. An AI system that frequently crashes or fails to recognize local accents may cause more frustration than progress.

Finally, ethical considerations—including data privacy and the handling of user-generated data—demand attention. As AI systems collect extensive information about learner performance, questions arise about consent, data storage, and the possibility of biases encoded in algorithms. Studies have pointed out that these issues, though acknowledged, have not been the central focus of many existing studies. However, the importance of fair, transparent, and responsible use of AI data is likely to increase as these technologies become more widespread.

Despite these complications, there is substantial evidence to suggest that AI can play a constructive role in advancing listening comprehension. When used thoughtfully and balanced with interpersonal elements, AI expands the variety of listening inputs, delivers immediate feedback, and personalizes content to match individual needs. By giving learners repeated practice with authentic accents, on-demand assessments, and culture-specific scenarios, AI-driven platforms can enrich traditional methods of instruction. As the field evolves, further research is likely to clarify best practices for blending AI solutions with classroom-based teaching, ensuring that learners reap the maximum benefit from each approach.

3. READING COMPREHENSION

Second-language reading demands more than translating words: learners must decode print, connect it to prior knowledge, and assemble a mental model that yields new cultural and academic insights. Devitt (1997) describes the act as a dialogue with the page in which readers propose hypotheses, test them against evidence, and refine interpretations. While fluent first-language readers rely on large lexicons and ingrained discourse norms, Zhao et al. (2013) suggest that these resources falter when unfamiliar structures or cultural references appear, reminding instructors that L2 reading is not simple word substitution. Because literal matching is insufficient, inference, synthesis, and evaluation become essential. Dalman and Plonsky (2022) argue that a word-level focus obscures tone and argument, whereas strategic readers preview, annotate, and pause to reassess meaning.

Multimodal materials can enhance reading strategies and comprehension. Januarty and Nima (2018) report that images and graphs helped junior-high learners anticipate main ideas. Varaporn and Sitthitikul (2019) observe stronger critical reading and autonomy among Thai undergraduates engaged in multimodal tasks. Similarly,

Oshima (2024) notes that seeing a teacher's gestures over video sharpened college students' attention to textual cues.

The capacity to manage learning rests on metacognition. Carrell (1989) contends that readers who plan, monitor, and evaluate their approach comprehend more effectively, a view echoed by Mahmoodi-Shahrebabaki and Oslund (2025), who link awareness to motivation, and by Muche, Simegn, and Shiferie (2024), who cite self-efficacy as a decisive mediator. Teng and Zhang (2021) show faster literacy growth in children with strong early metacognition, and Klimovich and Richter (2024) demonstrate that training can curb mind-wandering. Instructional interventions deliver tangible gains: Alamdari and Bozorgian (2021) report success with dialogic practice, Do and Phan (2021) and Jou (2015) confirm benefits across university contexts, and Assiri (2014) finds that strategies transfer across task formats.

Vocabulary, on the other hand, is crucial for reading comprehension. Laufer and Ravenhorst-Kalovski (2010) argue that 4,000–5,000 word families secure roughly 95% coverage of academic texts, while 8,000 push learners toward autonomy. Zhang and Zhang's (2020) meta-analysis corroborates vocabulary's decisive role in both reading and listening. Grammar can be equally restrictive. Reviewing nineteen studies, Choi and Zhang (2018) conclude that its influence may outweigh vocabulary at lower proficiencies and interacts with assessment type. When sentences embed multiple clauses or nuanced punctuation, readers struggle to track agents and temporal links, making explicit instruction in cohesion markers indispensable.

Instructional design can magnify or mitigate such burdens. Intensive, line-by-line analysis refines accuracy but slows global understanding, whereas Nakanishi (2014) synthesizes evidence that extensive reading—large amounts of level-appropriate text consumed for pleasure—improves fluency, broadens vocabulary, and cultivates positive attitudes. Effective programs, therefore, integrate explicit lexical and syntactic work with metacognitive coaching, multimodal scaffolds, and extensive reading, creating an environment in which strategic, confident readers can negotiate complex texts and transfer their skills beyond the classroom.

3.1. How AI Enhances Reading Skills

Evidence from Current Literature

Although studies on AI use in supporting receptive foreign language skills remain somewhat limited, existing research indicates that AI-based interventions can be beneficial for reading and listening comprehension. These interventions often incorporate feedback loops, adaptive content, or personalization features that cater to learners' needs. Some AI tools serve primarily diagnostic functions, highlighting weak areas in learners' reading and listening processes and then suggesting targeted solutions. Reports of improved engagement, higher motivation levels, and marked proficiency gains are not unusual, although some findings remain inconclusive or context-dependent.

He (2024) provides an in-depth look at how adaptive texts, generated by AI, can respond to learners' real-time performance. When a student shows difficulty with certain syntactic forms or frequently stalls on unfamiliar words, the system can simplify subsequent passages or incorporate brief practice exercises. Over time, passages can scale up in complexity to ensure ongoing challenges. This continuous calibration helps maintain a zone of proximal development, where learners are stretched linguistically without feeling overwhelmed.

Adaptive approaches also benefit individuals with specific needs. Drigas and Ioannidou (2012) illustrate how AI-based systems offer early diagnosis and intervention for reading disabilities or attention deficits. These tools track student responses, identify where comprehension falters, and then introduce resources to help address these weaknesses. Although the authors stress the need for further refinement to encompass diverse learner profiles, preliminary evidence suggests that AI's diagnostic features and capacity for real-time adjustments can be transformative, particularly for students who may not receive sufficient one-on-one support in large classrooms.

Shafiee Rad (2025) found that the AI-based ReadToMe platform significantly improved L2 learners' reading comprehension, engagement, and self-regulated learning compared to traditional instruction. Quantitative results showed higher post-test scores in all areas for the experimental group. Qualitative findings revealed that most students felt more motivated and engaged due to personalized feedback and interactive features, though some cited technical issues.

Xu et al (2022) found that AI, through a disembodied conversational agent (such as a smart speaker), can effectively engage preschool-aged children in dialogic reading, resulting in improved story comprehension and reading engagement. Children who read with the AI agent using dialogic interaction performed comparably to those who read with a human adult in terms of comprehension. The AI-driven dialogic reading supported more narrative-relevant vocalizations and reduced irrelevant ones, which mediated comprehension gains. These findings suggest that properly designed AI agents can serve as effective dialogue partners, supporting early language development in young children (Xu et al., 2022).

Similarly, Xu et al. 2021 found that both a conversational agent (CA) and a human partner were equally effective in enhancing children's story comprehension during guided storybook reading (Xu et al., 2021). However, the communication patterns differed: children interacting with a human-provided longer, more lexically diverse, and topically relevant responses, whereas those engaging with the CA gave responses with better intelligibility. Both groups demonstrated similar accuracy in answering questions. Furthermore, questions with high cognitive demand intensified these differences in children's verbal behaviours, highlighting the distinct affordances of CAs and human partners in supporting language development.

Tailoring Texts for Learner Needs

A primary way AI can support EFL readers is by adapting textual materials to match individual proficiency levels and interests. He (2024) discusses how AI-generated adaptive texts modify lexical difficulty and syntactic structures based on each learner's performance. If an individual consistently struggles with advanced vocabulary, the system can substitute simpler synonyms or include embedded definitions. It can also adjust sentence length or grammatical complexity to ensure learners remain engaged without hitting a frustration point.

This approach meets the need for differentiated instruction in diverse classrooms. It also relieves teachers from the labor-intensive process of preparing multiple versions of a text for learners at different proficiency levels. With AI, the customization is immediate and ongoing. As soon as the learner shows improvement, the text can adjust upward to maintain sufficient challenge. This dynamic adaptation fosters gradual, measurable growth, an outcome confirmed by studies in which participants engaging with adaptive texts demonstrate stronger reading retention and self-efficacy compared to those given a single, static reading passage.

Multimedia and Interaction in Reading

Integrating multimedia elements into reading tasks can elevate students' comprehension, particularly for those who benefit from multiple forms of input. AI platforms, for example, may embed hyperlinks, images, or brief audio clips that illuminate or extend the written text. If a learner pauses on a complex term, the system can provide a concise explanation or display an image that clarifies the concept, helping readers maintain a steady pace without frequent reference checks.

Eye-tracking software, such as the e-Dictionary described by Li et al. (2021), highlights the possibilities of just-in-time assistance. When the program detects that a user's gaze lingers on a word or phrase, it infers potential confusion and delivers contextual help. By reducing the need to flip through dictionaries, this approach supports a more uninterrupted reading experience while gathering data on difficult vocabulary. Though implementing such technology may exceed the resources of some learning contexts, these innovations offer fresh directions for multimodal teaching that adapts to each student in real-time.

AI tools also simplify the creation of visual and audio supplements for reading. Instructors might design illustrated stories to help young learners grasp plot elements or generate infographics and diagrams to scaffold more advanced texts. They can develop short, theme-related videos that activate prior knowledge, setting the stage for purposeful reading. Additionally, AI-generated voiceovers of passages provide a dual reading-listening experience, allowing learners to see the text and hear it spoken simultaneously. By blending these visual, auditory, and textual supports, teachers can create a more engaging environment that addresses diverse learner needs and fosters deeper comprehension.

Vocabulary and Grammar Acquisition Through AI

Reading in an L2 is often a conduit for vocabulary expansion and consolidation of grammatical knowledge. AI systems enhance this process by systematically reintroducing words that have been flagged as problematic and by drawing the learner's attention to recurring grammatical patterns. Repeated exposure to new lexical items in varied contexts can hasten the transition from recognition to active use, a principle that AI can operationalize more efficiently than traditional classroom instruction. An algorithm can maintain an index of each user's vocabulary progress, ensuring that words are recycled through exercises or embedded within fresh reading passages.

These systems also support grammar learning by inserting targeted constructions into texts at intervals correlated with the learner's prior performance. For instance, if a user consistently misses questions related to relative clauses, subsequent readings might highlight examples of relative clauses or include pop-up tips explaining their function. In this way, grammar instruction is woven directly into meaningful text engagement rather than confined to isolated exercises.

Culturally Relevant and Authentic Materials

For many EFL learners, reading can become an exercise in rote translation if the materials lack cultural relevance or authenticity. Generative AI has the capacity to access extensive corpora of texts and produce passages that reflect real-world issues, contemporary debates, or region-specific interests. If a student indicates a personal interest in environmental activism or emerging technologies, for example, an AI-driven reading platform could supply articles, short stories, or opinion pieces that align with those domains.

Reading passages grounded in a learner's own culture or interests can facilitate stronger motivation and deeper comprehension. Students who see themselves and their backgrounds represented in a text are more likely to engage at higher cognitive levels, comparing and contrasting the viewpoints in the reading with their experiences. When combined with the adaptive and multimedia elements already discussed, such culturally relevant materials can move learners beyond surface-level decoding and toward analytical and evaluative reading skills.

Supporting Learners With Special Needs, Neurodiversity, and Diverse Backgrounds

AI tools can offer targeted interventions that address a wide range of learner needs, from specific disabilities and neurodiverse profiles to socioeconomic and cultural constraints that limit educational resources. These accommodations create more inclusive learning experiences, ensuring that language learners who might otherwise be overlooked receive meaningful support in their reading development.

One effective adaptation centers on text-to-speech functionalities for individuals with dyslexia, where AI programs highlight words on the screen as they are pronounced. By pairing visual and auditory information, the learner gains clearer insights into how letters and sounds interrelate. Struggles with decoding can give way to more sustained comprehension, as the need to identify each word is supplemented by immediate verbal reinforcement. In a similar fashion, students with Attention-Deficit/Hyperactivity Disorder (ADHD) often have trouble focusing on large, continuous text. AI-guided reading platforms break passages into smaller sections, sometimes providing only a short paragraph at a time and prompting the learner to confirm comprehension before moving on. These structured intervals help prevent lapses in attention and encourage consistent cognitive engagement.

Interactive elements can further enhance the reading process for neurodiverse learners. Some AI systems embed clickable icons that offer succinct explanations or images to define unfamiliar vocabulary, eliminating the need to leave the text to consult external resources. By delivering these clarifications in real time, the software preserves students' attentional flow. Adjustments to visual layout—such as changing the background colour or font style—are also available, an especially valuable feature for those with visual processing challenges who may find high contrast or certain typographies overwhelming. These flexible display settings reduce visual strain and enhance comprehension by creating a less distracting page environment.

Readers on the autism spectrum can benefit from platforms that provide structured formats and consistent patterns across lessons. AI systems can maintain uniform page layouts, repeat task instructions, and offer step-by-step guidance through reading tasks, reducing the anxiety that often arises from unexpected or ambiguous changes. In some cases, the software can detect recurring misunderstandings and provide instant exercises or additional practice, easing the cognitive demands of reprocessing the material without personalized support.

Beyond learners with documented disabilities, many disadvantaged students face obstacles tied to limited technological access, inadequate educational infrastructure, or infrequent exposure to high-quality reading materials. AI can help mitigate these constraints by functioning effectively even on lower-end devices and, in certain cases, operating offline or with minimal connectivity. In rural regions or areas with spotty internet service, teachers can download adaptive reading materials as print-outs and allow students to work with them regardless of network availability. While advanced features like eye-tracking may be impractical in such settings, simpler elements—such as automatically generated audio glossaries or text simplification—still bolster language development.

For learners whose socioeconomic circumstances constrain the availability of books or classroom materials, AI can offer a constantly refreshed set of reading passages, eliminating the need to purchase or distribute copyrighted language learning materials. By continuously monitoring learners' progress, the software can propose the next level of difficulty, ensuring a balance between challenge and accessibility. The addition of culturally relevant examples and local narratives helps maintain student interest and resonates with their backgrounds, which is particularly important for readers whose prior experiences with formal education may be limited or interrupted.

These combined supports have the potential to transform the reading experience for students who have historically been underserved, whether because of specific learning needs, neurodiversity, or disadvantaged circumstances.

Instead of confronting standardized resources that may not address the underlying barriers, thanks to AI, learners can gain access to tools that adapt to them personally, creating confidence in their ability to read and comprehend texts in a new language. This sense of empowerment often leads to more consistent practice, deeper engagement, and measurable progress in skill development—outcomes that educators and administrators alike increasingly recognize as crucial to fostering equity and inclusivity in language education.

4. CHALLENGES AND ETHICAL CONSIDERATIONS IN AI INTEGRATION FOR RECEPTIVE FOREIGN LANGUAGE SKILLS

Artificial-intelligence platforms promise to personalize listening and reading practice, yet their value depends on how well designers and teachers address intertwined technical, ethical, and pedagogical constraints. Speech-recognition systems still mis-transcribe rapid speech, regional accents, or noisy audio, so seemingly instant feedback can mislead learners. Adaptive reading engines, trained largely on formal prose, may ignore informal or culturally specific registers. Such flaws worsen when bandwidth is shaky or devices are old, turning seamless demos into stalled lessons. Because auto-generated texts and diagnostics may contain linguistic or factual errors, expert review remains indispensable; teachers must vet machine output and keep material accurate and contextually meaningful. Rigorous field testing across regions and proficiency levels is therefore a prerequisite before schools commit scarce funds.

Overuse of generative systems introduces a different danger. Bozkurt et al. (2024) warn that treating AI as an all-purpose tutor can blunt creativity, stifle problem-solving, and sideline the paralinguistic cues and cultural exchange found in human dialogue. While empirical evidence for this claim is still inadequate, it should still be considered. Effective programs, therefore, should cast AI as a flexible resource—automating drills or producing level-appropriate passages—while freeing teachers to lead discussion, diagnose needs, and supply nuance.

Data collection raises further concerns. Bozkurt et al. (2024) note that vast stores of keystrokes, voice prints, and scores are often amassed with minimal consent, exposing learners to privacy breaches if governance is weak. Responsible adoption demands encryption, clear retention limits, rigorous anonymization, and digital-literacy lessons that teach students—especially minors—to withhold personal identifiers when interacting with bots.

Algorithmic bias compounds these risks. Because most training sets mirror dominant Western norms, Bozkurt et al. (2024) suggest that AI can amplify stereotypes, omit minority dialects, and treat non-standard accents as errors. Mitigation involves curating multilingual datasets, auditing outputs, and updating models so learners meet a realistic spectrum of voices and viewpoints.

Equitable access remains another hurdle. High license fees, patchy internet, and limited technical support can confine adaptive tools to well-funded schools, while learners elsewhere rely on static worksheets. Content relevance matters too: a platform steeped in Euro-American examples may disengage students in other contexts.

Interpreting AI analytics and troubleshooting glitches also require specialized skills, so sustained professional development is essential. Workshops that let teachers explore dashboards, simulate learner errors, and design blended tasks help them embed technology inside a coherent curriculum rather than bolt it on. Sessions should also explore scenario planning—what to do when the server fails mid-lesson, how to adapt AI insights for students with special needs, and how to blend machine feedback with peer review—so teachers leave confident that technology serves pedagogy, not the reverse. Without such alignment, adaptive quizzes become isolated novelties.

Finally, curriculum designers must specify how AI outputs advance objectives such as inferential listening or rapid reading and ensure that formative feedback links to summative assessment. Only when infrastructure is resilient, data practices transparent, algorithms bias-aware, funding inclusive, and teachers empowered to humanize machine input can automation enhance rather than eclipse the social, strategic, and cultural work that makes receptive language skills meaningful. In that alignment, learners gain agency and equitable opportunities to thrive.

5. PEDAGOGICAL IMPLICATIONS AND RECOMMENDATIONS

Teachers and teacher educators who consider including AI tools in language instruction can open fresh opportunities for learners to build listening and reading skills in an additional language. These innovations offer a variety of interactive experiences that can adjust to different levels, reduce anxiety, and enrich exposure to diverse forms of discourse. Yet the benefits of technology are not guaranteed by novelty alone. Educators design meaningful learning only when they integrate new methods with empathy, strategic planning, and attention to human connection. AI resources should serve as an extension of teaching rather than a replacement, and they offer ideas on guiding students to explore these resources actively for improved receptive skills.

5.1. AI as a Collaborative Tool

Teachers should frame AI programs not as automated tutors but as companions that guide students through listening and reading tasks at a pace that reflects individual needs. Adaptive platforms can respond to different proficiency levels by adjusting complexity or offering clarifications without requiring an entire group to work from the same script. That flexibility helps each student gain practice in comprehending meaningful content while still benefiting from the structure and support of a classroom.

Educators can invite learners to identify specific goals, such as following a fast-paced conversation or interpreting advanced written texts. With clear targets, students can select AI activities that match those aims, treating the software as a flexible space for practice. When the teacher returns to small-group or whole-class activities, the skills learned can then be reinforced through real-time communication and shared reflections.

5.2. Encouraging Students to Explore AI for Listening Development

A persistent challenge in foreign language instruction is offering enough authentic listening practice to prepare learners for real-world exchanges. Teachers can help students use AI-driven tools that simulate diverse accents, styles of speech, and contextual nuances, ensuring a breadth of exposure they might not gain from a single textbook recording. A student learning English, for instance, might interact with AI-driven dialogues featuring accents from multiple regions, including those less frequently represented in published materials. By doing so, learners learn to adapt to a wide variety of speech patterns.

Teachers also have a role in reducing the anxiety that can arise when interacting with technology. Learners may worry about "making mistakes" or misunderstanding an unfamiliar accent. Regular classroom conversations can demystify the AI's capacity to offer immediate feedback and reassure students that such feedback is a stepping stone rather than a judgment. Simple actions—such as showing learners examples of how a particular AI program highlights misheard phrases—help them see that the intention is to pinpoint areas of growth in a supportive environment.

5.3. Enhancing Reading Engagement and Personalization

AI can enlarge the library of reading materials to include articles, fictional stories, or practical texts at multiple levels of difficulty. When students indicate their interests—such as current events, technology, or literature—algorithms can generate or locate passages adapted to their proficiency and those topics. Teachers can then combine AI-generated texts with group discussions, debates, or research projects, anchoring the ideas in personal reflection or collaborative tasks.

In settings where large class sizes prevent teachers from consistently offering individualized reading suggestions, AI can supply the type of personalized scaffolding that allows for incremental progress. If certain grammatical structures confuse a student, the software can insert subtle highlights or definitions right in the text, offering context-specific explanations at the exact moment they are needed. This immediate reference often prevents frustration from interrupting a reading session. Once students gain comfort, the text complexity can shift upward to preserve an appropriate level of challenge.

5.4. Balancing Technology With the Human Element

The classroom teacher's role remains pivotal. AI programs are adept at delivering large amounts of practice material and analysing performance data, but they do not replace the human skill of encouraging interpersonal connection. Students benefit from teacher-led discussions that unpack cultural references, shared experiences, or emotional reactions to content. A single reading passage can spark a lively exchange about values or social issues, which AI cannot replicate in all their depth.

When teachers pair AI-driven tasks with teacher-facilitated group activities, students see that the skills gained through technology are not abstract or disconnected from real life. Engaging in a conversation about a text—why a character chose a certain action, for instance—helps learners realize that reading requires more than decoding words. Similarly, practicing listening strategies as a class, and then cross-checking progress with AI-generated feedback, ensures that learners can transfer digital practice into interactive, person-to-person settings.

5.5. Safeguarding Ethical and Equitable Use

Some educators face limited resources, while others teach in well-equipped schools. AI implementation must consider these disparities. If internet access is weak, offline tasks or partial downloads of AI tools might be the only feasible approach. Teacher educators could address such scenarios by preparing future teachers to advocate for minimal-technology alternatives or collective devices in classrooms.

Teachers can also raise awareness of privacy and data considerations by explaining who can see user performance data and how it is stored. Such clarity helps students, parents, and administrators trust that AI is being used responsibly. This discussion can serve as a valuable lesson in digital literacy, underlining that students have the right to ask how the software processes their information.

Cultural diversity presents another concern. If the AI's data sets centre on one region, learners might miss out on the variations they will encounter beyond the classroom. Educators can monitor the quality of the materials offered, add content from local or regional sources, and encourage learners to critique any biases they observe in AI-generated texts. By coaching students to approach AI outputs with a questioning mindset, teachers cultivate global awareness and critical thinking.

5.6. Teacher Education and Professional Development

Teacher educators can prepare new teachers to become informed selectors and facilitators of AI tools. During training sessions, future teachers might experiment with multiple options, evaluating the cultural and linguistic strengths of each. Practical case studies or simulations that show how AI responds to reading errors or listening challenges allow trainees to anticipate potential pitfalls. By examining user data and seeing how various programs offer feedback, they develop insight into how best to integrate technology into broader instructional goals.

These teachers-in-training can also experiment with reflective tasks that encourage metacognition. If students frequently misinterpret a particular set of listening prompts, for instance, a teacher can prompt them to analyze what went wrong, whether they should slow down the speech rate next time, or whether they might need direct vocabulary instruction. When teachers make guided reflection a routine part of AI usage, they build stronger habits that students can carry beyond the course.

5.7. Guidance for Learners on Harnessing AI

In addition to teacher-led efforts, students can adopt specific strategies for using AI to bolster foreign language comprehension. Some might set aside short daily sessions in which they focus exclusively on targeted tasks: repeated listening drills with transcripts, timed reading passages that test speed and accuracy, or chatbot interactions around a topic of personal interest. Others might coordinate small study groups, where each person tests a different AI resource and shares feedback on which interface or feature proves most helpful.

Students can also practice active questioning while working with AI. In a listening module, they might pause the audio and try to paraphrase what was said before checking the system's transcript. In reading tasks, they might attempt to define unfamiliar words through context clues, comparing their guesses to the AI-generated hints. By engaging in consistent self-checks, learners maintain an alert posture instead of passively consuming the material.

Instructors can encourage each class member to keep a journal of challenges encountered during AI-based exercises, noting any progress, confusion, or insights. These journals then become tangible artifacts for teacher conferences or group reflections, strengthening the conversation around how AI is supporting or hindering comprehension. If a pattern emerges—such as consistent difficulty with a particular grammar construction, teachers can create mini-lessons or guided practice sessions.

5.8. Fostering Engagement Through Reflection and Feedback

Educators can cultivate deeper motivation by highlighting the small, meaningful steps that AI tools enable. When students receive immediate notes on how they handle a phrase, they become more aware of their progress. Teachers may invite them to celebrate achievements—such as recognizing a new accent or finishing a reading passage with fewer dictionary checks than in prior weeks. Positive reinforcement connects practice to tangible improvements, reinforcing that they are learning in real time.

Yet AI feedback remains incomplete unless it is integrated into a broader feedback loop. Teachers can review the software's performance logs to spot patterns, but they also need to sit with students and explore how these patterns connect to real-world communication. A system might point out repeated misinterpretation of a certain idiomatic phrase, but only a teacher can explain the cultural or pragmatic nuances underlying that phrase. This personal guidance helps learners transform abstract AI alerts into authentic communicative insight.

Teachers and teacher educators have a unique chance to shape how AI resources serve foreign language development, particularly for receptive skills, listening and reading. By selecting tasks that reflect each learner's needs and by integrating technology with ongoing classroom interaction, educators ensure that students learn actively rather than passively. They also maintain a sense of ethical responsibility, showing respect for privacy, providing equitable access where possible, and acknowledging the wide variety of linguistic identities in the wider world.

When used thoughtfully, AI can enrich education and stir new confidence in learners who need extra practice or customization. Its effectiveness depends, however, on an unbroken connection to the communal, dialogic nature of language. The attentive teacher remains at the center, fostering cooperative reflection, clarifying misunderstandings that software cannot address, and maintaining a warm environment where students feel safe to explore and grow. When this balance is achieved, AI becomes a meaningful influence on individual progress, energizing class members to pursue higher levels of competence in both listening and reading.

6. THEORETICAL AND RESEARCH IMPLICATIONS

The introduction of AI-based resources into the study of receptive skills suggests revisions and extensions of key theories in L2 acquisition. The existing understanding of listening processes, for instance, has often highlighted the balance between segmenting incoming input and drawing on background knowledge. AI applications that deliver personalized speech rates, immediate feedback on misheard phrases, and exposure to diverse accents expand the range of input that learners can comfortably handle, raising questions about how learners refine their perceptual strategies when dealing with many accents rather than one. Future theoretical approaches might consider how adaptive tools reshape the trajectory of phonemic discrimination and whether real-time feedback accelerates cognitive shifts associated with more advanced comprehension.

Reading processes benefit from a similar expansion of theoretical models when augmented by automated supports. Traditional views of L2 reading underscore vocabulary thresholds, grammar interpretation, and the role of schema in meaning construction. AI's capacity to detect learner hesitation on specific words and offer in-text scaffolding could refine our understanding of how L2 readers transition from basic decoding to more nuanced interpretive skills. These observations might enrich models of L2 literacy by suggesting how textual manipulation (such as real-time adjustments of complexity) can support learners' ability to integrate new information with existing linguistic knowledge.

A broader theoretical issue relates to metacognition. Many digital platforms encourage learners to reflect on their comprehension by highlighting errors, prompting them to verify whether a passage was understood correctly, or encouraging repeated attempts. These experiences resemble teacher-led strategy training in that students become more self-aware of the nuances of what they are trying to understand. The metacognitive strategies that support listening and reading—predicting, monitoring, and evaluating—take on new dimensions in settings where feedback is immediate and adaptive. Researchers can further explore whether repeated exposure to these structured reflections yields lasting improvements in students' self-regulation, or whether additional teacher mediation remains essential.

6.1. Refining Methodologies for Empirical Work

Studies of AI-enhanced receptive skills would benefit from deeper inquiry into how specific features of the technology prompt the learning process. Rather than measuring overall gains in comprehension, investigations might look at how adaptive difficulty levels, varied accents, timed reading tasks, or embedded glosses contribute to certain improvements. Such an approach requires carefully designed experimental and quasi-experimental studies that isolate the contribution of each element. For instance, researchers could collect think-aloud data when learners read AI-generated texts with real-time definitions appearing on the screen, examining how often students rely on this aid and how that influences lexical retention.

In addition, longer-term studies that include delayed post-tests would help clarify whether gains associated with AI tools persist once learners leave the structured environment. It remains an open question whether these technologies only boost short-term comprehension scores or lead to enduring changes in overall proficiency and motivation. Mixed-method designs can complement quantitative findings with qualitative insights from teacher interviews, student focus groups, or classroom observations. Such triangulation would clarify the role that emotional and social factors play, since enjoyment and lowered anxiety often accompany success in foreign language comprehension.

Future research might also consider how different educational contexts shape the effectiveness of AI. Schools with large classes, limited resources, or minimal teacher training in educational technology could see varying degrees of success depending on how stable the technological infrastructure is and whether professional development is offered. By comparing case studies in different regions or institutional settings, scholars can document practices that mitigate constraints and empower teachers to integrate AI effectively.

6.2. Ethical and Implementation Concerns in Research

The incorporation of AI tools in receptive skills research demands careful planning and reflection on ethical dimensions. Data privacy remains a prominent matter: sensitive information from learners' interactions, including voice recordings or reading performance metrics, must be protected by robust safeguards. Before running studies, researchers have a responsibility to inform participants about data storage procedures and ensure that any analytics are used strictly for pedagogical and research purposes, rather than shared or commercialized in ways that compromise personal information.

Another area meriting deeper analysis is algorithmic bias. AI systems are only as representative as their training data, which often reflect dominant accents or mainstream cultural references. For listening, that might mean underrepresenting global varieties of English or local dialects. For reading, the corpora might skew toward particular genres or cultural viewpoints. Researchers might audit the content that AI systems generate or select, noting omissions that could disadvantage learners who need exposure to diverse linguistic forms or who have distinct cultural interests. This line of inquiry could encourage developers to expand their datasets and train algorithms that reflect a wider demographic.

Equity of access poses yet another concern, particularly for researchers investigating large-scale outcomes in different regions. Some classrooms have cutting-edge technology and reliable high-speed networks, while others have only modest connectivity and limited device availability. A balanced research agenda includes inquiry into practical solutions for settings with less infrastructure, such as offline functionality or lightweight applications that can run on older devices. If these considerations are overlooked, investigations may inadvertently favor well-resourced environments and produce findings that do not generalize to the majority of learners worldwide.

6.3. Extending Research on Learner Engagement With AI in Receptive Skill Development

A promising and underexplored avenue for future research concerns the nature and quality of student engagement with AI tools in the development of receptive language skills. As AI becomes more prevalent in educational settings, there is a growing need to move beyond broad assessments of technological effectiveness and examine how learners interact with these systems—not just what they gain from them, but how they come to view and use AI within their learning processes.

Rather than positioning AI solely as an automated deliverer of feedback or practice tasks, future research should explore how students perceive and engage with AI as a multi-functional learning partner. This includes its use as instructional material, as a source of scaffolding, and as a simulated conversational peer or tutor. Each of these roles invites different patterns of learner interaction, and each may impact motivation, autonomy, and comprehension in distinctive ways.

One line of inquiry could investigate the difference between passive and active engagement with AI. While some students may rely on AI to supply answers, translations, or corrections without further reflection, others may use these tools as springboards for inquiry—pausing to question unfamiliar vocabulary, experimenting with different ways to phrase an idea, or testing their understanding before seeking feedback. These forms of strategic engagement likely contribute to deeper learning and long-term skill transfer. Research might examine what classroom conditions, teacher cues, or design features encourage students to take a more active stance when using AI for listening and reading.

In addition, researchers could explore how students negotiate the boundaries between dependence and independence when using AI. Do learners come to rely too heavily on real-time glosses, speech-rate control, or captions, and if so, under what circumstances? What strategies enable learners to gradually reduce this reliance while retaining confidence and accuracy in comprehension? Answering these questions may help educators and developers design systems that support scaffolding and then gradually withdraw it in alignment with learner progress.

There is also potential to explore how learners interpret the "voice" of AI tools—how they perceive its authority, tone, and responsiveness. When AI plays the role of a reading or listening tutor, does the learner treat its feedback as final or subject to revision? Do students compare the AI's guidance with that of a teacher or peer, and if so, how does this influence their trust in the tool? This dimension is especially relevant in contexts where AI chatbots or feedback systems provide praise, encouragement, or metalinguistic advice. Understanding these interactions could shape the design of more pedagogically sensitive AI personalities that invite critical thinking rather than passive acceptance.

Another important focus involves group-based engagement. In classrooms where learners use AI tools individually, to what extent do they share insights, compare strategies, or reflect collaboratively on their digital experiences? Research might examine how peer discussion after AI use influences learner metacognition and whether shared reflection deepens understanding of listening texts or reinforces interpretive reading strategies. Such investigations could highlight the social side of AI engagement, reinforcing the idea that even individual interactions with technology can be embedded in a communal learning environment.

Finally, future studies could explore cultural and contextual differences in how learners engage with AI. In some contexts, students may be more accustomed to hierarchical educational models and may view AI as an authoritative source rather than a flexible support tool. In others, learners may show greater confidence in customizing or challenging the tool's output. Comparing these patterns across settings could illuminate how learner identity, educational norms, and prior experiences influence the uptake and perception of AI tools.

In sum, future research into learner engagement with AI should move beyond questions of technological efficacy to examine how learners develop agency, critical awareness, and adaptive strategies through their interaction with these systems. Understanding this engagement holistically—across cognitive, emotional, and social dimensions—will support the creation of AI-enhanced learning environments where technology complements, rather than dominates, the development of listening and reading skills. Such research has the potential not only to inform pedagogical design but also to empower learners to become more thoughtful, reflective, and independent users of the technologies shaping their educational experiences.

CONCLUSION

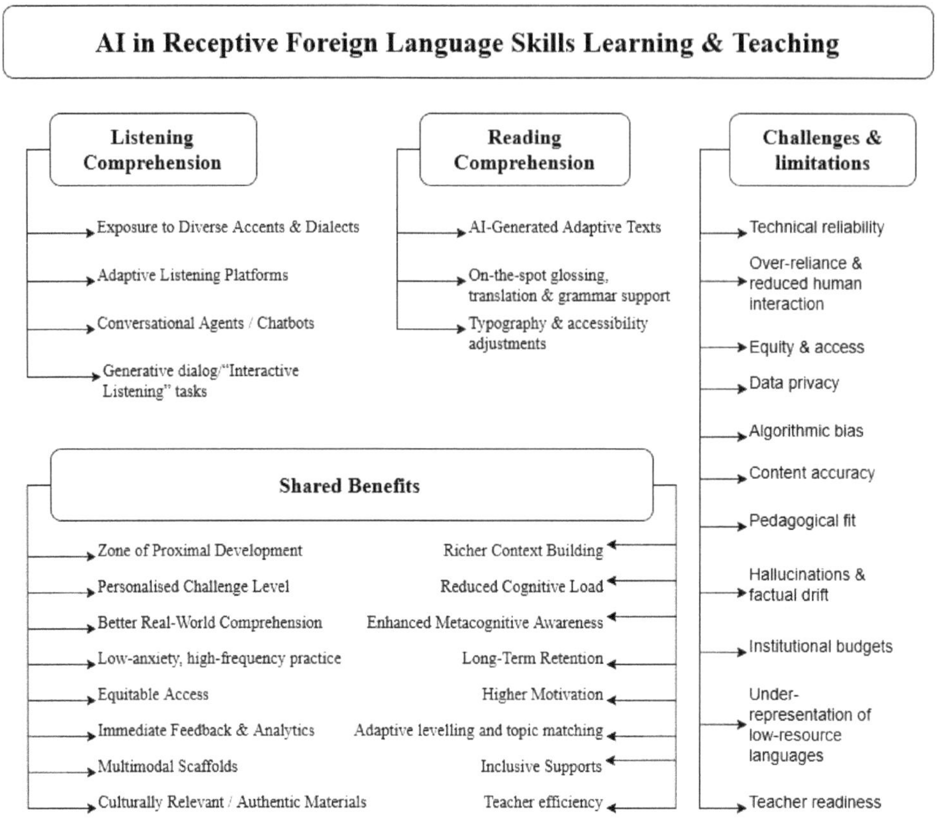

A summary of the benefits and challenges of AI in receptive foreign language skills learning and teaching

This chapter highlights the transformative potential of AI to promote listening and reading instruction in L2 education as outlined in Figure 1. The synthesis of current empirical and theoretical work indicates that artificial-intelligence applications can no longer be framed merely as peripheral aids to receptive-skills instruction; rather, they may constitute a fundamentally new mediational layer that restructures the ecology of listening and reading development. Regarding its benefits, three domains of gains emerge. First, AI multiplies the quantity, diversity, and authenticity of language input. Adaptive speech synthesis and data-driven text and audio generation expose learners to a wider repertoire of accents, registers, and genre conventions than conventional materials, thereby accelerating the recalibration of perceptual and inferential routines essential for real-world comprehension. Second, the technology compresses the feedback loop that links processing difficulties to strategic adjustment. By delivering instant diagnostics—whether through word-level misrecognition alerts in listening tasks or real-time lexical and syntactic scaffolding in reading modules—AI enables rapid micro-cycle learning that positions every learner within an individually calibrated zone of proximal development, a condition previously achievable only through intensive one-to-one tutoring. Third, affective-motivational variables improve because personalized challenge levels, low-stakes conversational agents, and multimodal support collectively reduce anxiety and cognitive load while sustaining engagement.

Balanced against these affordances are challenges whose resolution will determine whether AI fulfils its transformative promise. Technical reliability remains uneven; speech-recognition errors with regional accents and occasional factual hallucinations in generated texts undermine the credibility of machine feedback and risk entrenching misconceptions. Pedagogically, over-reliance on automated interaction can erode opportunities for human-to-human negotiation of meaning and critical thinking, thereby impoverishing the pragmatic and sociocultural dimensions of language learning that AI still simulates imperfectly. Ethical and equity concerns are equally pressing. Extensive data capture raises unresolved questions about privacy and algorithmic bias, while the cost of robust infrastructure threatens to widen existing educational divides, particularly in low-resource settings and among speakers of under-represented languages. Finally, the instructional efficacy of AI hinges on teacher expertise; without sustained professional development that equips educators to interpret analytics critically, vet machine-generated content, and integrate digital tasks into coherent curricular trajectories, the technology risks becoming an isolated novelty rather than a catalyst for systemic improvement.

The field therefore confronts a dialectical imperative. Researchers and practitioners must continue to delineate which specific AI affordances drive durable cognitive, linguistic, and affective gains while simultaneously constructing governance frameworks that ensure transparency, cultural inclusivity, and pedagogical sovereignty. Only through such critically informed integration can artificial intelligence complement—rather than eclipse—the human mediation that ultimately renders receptive-skills learning socially meaningful and educationally just.

REFERENCES

Alamdari, E. F., & Bozorgian, H. (2021). Gender, metacognitive intervention, and dialogic interaction: EFL multimedia listening. *System, 104*, 102709. DOI: 10.1016/j.system.2021.102709

Alrasheedi, S. (2024). The effect of using AI applications to develop EFL listening comprehension skills among university students. *Conhecimento & Diversidade, 16*(44), 601–637. DOI: 10.18316/rcd.v16i44.12346

Aryadoust, V., & Luo, L. (2022). The typology of second language listening constructs: A systematic review. *Language Testing, 40*(2), 375–409. DOI: 10.1177/02655322221126604

Assiri, M. (2014). Metacognitive and cognitive strategy use and performance on a reading test with multiple-format tasks. *Arab World English Journal, 5*(4), 187–202.

Bozkurt, A., Xiao, J., Farrow, R., Bai, J. Y. H., Nerantzi, C., Moore, S., Dron, J., Stracke, C. M., Singh, L., Crompton, H., Koutropoulos, A., Terentev, E., Pazurek, A., Nichols, M., Sidorkin, A. M., Costello, E., Watson, S., Mulligan, D., Honeychurch, S., & Asino, T. I. (2024). The manifesto for teaching and learning in a time of generative AI: A critical collective stance to better navigate the future. *Open Praxis, 16*(4), 487–513. DOI: 10.55982/openpraxis.16.4.777

Brown, H. D., & Yule, G. (1983). *Teaching the spoken language: An approach based on the analysis of conversational speech.* Longman.

Bsharat-Maalouf, D., & Karawani, H. (2022). Learning and bilingualism in challenging listening conditions: How challenging can it be? *Cognition, 222*, 105018. DOI: 10.1016/j.cognition.2022.105018 PMID: 35032867

Carrell, P. L. (1989). Metacognitive awareness and second language reading. *Modern Language Journal, 73*(2), 121–134. DOI: 10.1111/j.1540-4781.1989.tb02534.x

Cartner, H., & Cameron, D. (2023). Investigating metacognitive strategy awareness for multimodal listening. *E-Learning and Digital Media, 20*(5), 424–441. DOI: 10.1177/20427530221108014

Celce-Murcia, M., Brinton, D. M., & Snow, M. A. (Eds.). (2014). *Teaching English as a second or foreign language* (4th ed.). National Geographic Learning/Cengage.

Choi, Y., & Zhang, D. (2018). The relative role of vocabulary and grammatical knowledge in L2 reading comprehension: A systematic review of literature. *IRAL -. International Review of Applied Linguistics in Language Teaching*, *59*(1), 1–30. DOI: 10.1515/iral-2017-0033

Chou, M.-H. (2017). A task-based language teaching approach to developing metacognitive strategies for listening comprehension. *International Journal of Listening*, *31*(1), 51–70. DOI: 10.1080/10904018.2015.1098542

Dalman, M., & Plonsky, L. (2022). The effectiveness of second-language listening strategy instruction: A meta-analysis. *Language Teaching Research*. Advance online publication. DOI: 10.1177/13621688221140003

Devitt, S. (1997). Reading and writing one's way into language awareness. *Language Awareness*, *6*(2-3), 119–135. DOI: 10.1080/09658416.1997.9959922

Do, H. M., & Phan, H. L. T. (2021). Metacognitive awareness of reading strategies on second language Vietnamese undergraduates. *Arab World English Journal*, *12*(1), 90–112. DOI: 10.24093/awej/vol12no1.7

Drigas, A. S., & Ioannidou, R.-E. (2012). Artificial intelligence in special education: A decade review. *International Journal of Engineering Education*, *28*(6), 1366–1372.

Fathi, J., Derakhshan, A., & Torabi, S. (2020). The effect of listening strategy instruction on second language listening anxiety and self-efficacy of Iranian EFL learners. *SAGE Open*, *10*(2), 1–13. DOI: 10.1177/2158244020933878

Field, J. (2008). *Listening in the language classroom*. Cambridge University Press.

Goh, C. C. (2000). A cognitive perspective on language learners' listening comprehension problems. *System*, *28*(1), 55–75. DOI: 10.1016/S0346-251X(99)00060-3

Goh, C. C. M., & Hu, G. (2014). Exploring the relationship between metacognitive awareness and listening performance with questionnaire data. *Language Awareness*, *23*(3), 255–274. DOI: 10.1080/09658416.2013.769558

Grabe, W. (2009). *Reading in a second language: Moving from theory to practice*. Cambridge University Press.

Graham, S., & Santos, D. (2015). *Strategies for second language listening comprehension*. Oxford University Press.

Guichon, N., & McLornan, S. (2008). The effects of multimodality on L2 learners: Implications for CALL resource design. *System*, *36*(1), 85–93. DOI: 10.1016/j.system.2007.11.005

He, X. (2024). Enhancing reading comprehension with AI-generated adaptive texts. *International Journal of New Developments in Education, 6*(7), 46–52. DOI: 10.25236/IJNDE.2024.060708

Hu, N. (2025). English listening and speaking ability improvement strategy from artificial intelligence wireless network. *Wireless Networks, 31*(2), 1071–1080. DOI: 10.1007/s11276-024-03812-3

Januarty, R., & Nima, H. N. A. (2018). Energizing students' reading comprehension through multimodal texts. *International Journal of Language Education*, 2(2), 14–22. DOI: 10.26858/ijole.v2i2.4347

Jou, Y.-J. (2015). Investigation of technological university students' use of metacognitive reading strategies in first and second languages. *English Language Teaching, 8*(1), 180–188. DOI: 10.5539/elt.v8n1p180

Kim, N. Y. (2018). A study on chatbots for developing Korean college students' English listening and reading skills. *Journal of Digital Convergence, 16*(8), 19–26. DOI: 10.14400/JDC.2018.16.8.019

Klimovich, M., & Richter, T. (2024). Metacognitive training can reduce mindless reading. *Journal of Educational Psychology, 116*(5), 836–852. DOI: 10.1037/edu0000884

Krashen, S. (1985). *The input hypothesis: Issues and implications*. Longman.

Laufer, B., & Ravenhorst-Kalovski, G. C. (2010). Lexical threshold revisited: Lexical text coverage, learners' vocabulary size and reading comprehension. *Reading in a Foreign Language, 22*(1), 15–30.

Levak, N., & Son, J. (2016). Facilitating second language learners' listening comprehension with Second Life and Skype. *ReCALL, 29*(2), 200–218. DOI: 10.1017/S0958344016000215

Li, H., Gunnell, E., & Sun, Y. (2021). An intelligent system to improve vocabulary and reading comprehension using eye tracking and artificial intelligence. In Wyld, D. C. (Eds.), *Proceedings of the 2021 CS & IT Conference* (pp. 27–36). AIRCC Publishing. https://doi.org/DOI: 10.5121/csit.2021.111703

MacCutcheon, D., Hurtig, A., Pausch, F., Hygge, S., Fels, J., & Ljung, R. (2019). Second language vocabulary level is related to benefits for second language listening comprehension under lower reverberation time conditions. *Journal of Cognitive Psychology, 31*(2), 175–185. DOI: 10.1080/20445911.2019.1575387

Mahmoodi-Shahrebabaki, M., & Oslund, E. (2025). The relationships between reading attitude, metacognitive awareness of reading strategies and reading motivation of L2 learners: A mediational analysis. *Journal of Interdisciplinary Studies in Education*, *14*(1), 1–19. DOI: 10.32674/q5c82955

Mohammadi Golchi, M. (2012). Listening anxiety and its relationship with listening strategy use and listening comprehension among Iranian IELTS learners. *International Journal of English Linguistics*, *2*(4), 115–128. DOI: 10.5539/ijel.v2n4p115

Muche, T., Simegn, B., & Shiferie, K. (2024). Self-efficacy and metacognitive strategy use in reading comprehension: EFL learners' perspectives. *The Asia-Pacific Education Researcher*, *33*(1), 219–227. DOI: 10.1007/s40299-023-00721-5

Nakanishi, T. (2014). A meta-analysis of extensive reading research. *TESOL Quarterly*, *49*(1), 6–37. DOI: 10.1002/tesq.157

Newton, J. M., & Nation, I. S. P. (2021). *Teaching ESL/EFL listening and speaking* (2nd ed.). Routledge.

Oshima, S. (2024). Effectiveness of a multimodal approach during online reading strategy instruction. *Reading in a Foreign Language*, *36*(1), 1–20. https://nflrc.hawaii.edu/rfl

Rahimirad, M., & Moini, M. R. (2015). The challenges of listening to academic lectures for EAP learners and the impact of metacognition on academic lecture listening comprehension. *SAGE Open*, *5*(2), 1–9. DOI: 10.1177/2158244015590609

Richards, J. C., & Rodgers, T. S. (2014). *Approaches and methods in language teaching* (3rd ed.). Cambridge University Press. DOI: 10.1017/9781009024532

Rukthong, A., & Brunfaut, T. (2019). Is anybody listening? The nature of second language listening in integrated listening-to-summarize tasks. *Language Testing*, *37*(1), 26–52. DOI: 10.1177/0265532219871470

Salmani, S., & Rahimi, M. (2024). Does multimodality add to the value of L2 listening homework? A mixed-methods study of comprehension and cognitive load. *English Teaching & Learning*. 1-28. https://doi.org/DOI: 10.1007/s42321-024-00181-0

Shafiee Rad, H. (2025). Reinforcing L2 reading comprehension through artificial intelligence intervention: Refining engagement to foster self-regulated learning. *Smart Learning Environments*, *12*(23), 23. Advance online publication. DOI: 10.1186/s40561-025-00377-2

Sivaji, V., Prabhavathy, P., Brinda Shree, V., Varadharajan, T. S., Angelin, S. Y. R., & Pradeepa, M. (2024, November 15–16). Leveraging advanced AI-driven pedagogical strategies to enhance English listening skills. *2024 Second International Conference on Computational and Characterization Techniques in Engineering & Sciences (IC3TES)*. https://doi.org/DOI: 10.1109/IC3TES62412.2024.10877491

Teng, M. F., & Zhang, L. J. (2021). Development of children's metacognitive knowledge, reading, and writing in English as a foreign language: Evidence from longitudinal data using multilevel models. *The British Journal of Educational Psychology*, *91*(4), 1202–1230. DOI: 10.1111/bjep.12413 PMID: 33694166

Valizadeh, M. R., & Alavinia, P. (2013). Listening comprehension performance viewed in the light of emotional intelligence and foreign language listening anxiety. *English Language Teaching*, *6*(12), 11–26. DOI: 10.5539/elt.v6n12p11

Vandergrift, L. (1999). Facilitating second language listening comprehension: Acquiring successful strategies. *ELT Journal*, *53*(3), 168–176. DOI: 10.1093/elt/53.3.168

Vandergrift, L. (2004). Listening to learn or learning to listen? *Annual Review of Applied Linguistics*, *24*, 3–25. DOI: 10.1017/S0267190504000017

Vandergrift, L. (2007). *Teaching and learning in a second language: Listening, speaking, reading, and writing*. Pearson Longman.

Vandergrift, L., & Baker, S. (2015). Learner variables in second language listening comprehension: An exploratory path analysis. *Language Learning*, *65*(2), 390–416. DOI: 10.1111/lang.12105

Vandergrift, L., & Tafaghodtari, M. H. (2010). Teaching L2 learners how to listen does make a difference: An empirical study. *Language Learning*, *60*(2), 470–497. DOI: 10.1111/j.1467-9922.2009.00559.x

Varaporn, S., & Sitthitikul, P. (2019). Effects of multimodal tasks on students' critical reading ability and perceptions. *Reading in a Foreign Language*, *31*(1), 81–108. https://nflrc.hawaii.edu/rfl

Wallace, M. P., & Lee, K. (2020). Examining second language listening, vocabulary, and executive functioning. *Frontiers in Psychology*, *11*, 1122. Advance online publication. DOI: 10.3389/fpsyg.2020.01122 PMID: 32581951

Wang, L., & MacIntyre, P. (2021). Second language listening comprehension: The role of anxiety and enjoyment in listening metacognitive awareness. *Studies in Second Language Learning and Teaching*, *11*(4), 491–515. DOI: 10.14746/ssllt.2021.11.4.2

Xiao, Y. (2025). The impact of AI-driven speech recognition on EFL listening comprehension, flow experience, and anxiety: A randomized controlled trial. *Humanities & Social Sciences Communications*, *12*(1), 425. Advance online publication. DOI: 10.1057/s41599-025-04672-8

Xu, Y., Aubele, J., Vigil, V., Bustamante, A. S., Kim, Y.-S., & Warschauer, M. (2022). Dialogue with a conversational agent promotes children's story comprehension via enhancing engagement. *Child Development*, *93*(2), e149–e167. DOI: 10.1111/cdev.13708 PMID: 34748214

Xu, Y., Wang, D., Collins, P., Lee, H., & Warschauer, M. (2021). Same benefits, different communication patterns: Comparing children's reading with a conversational agent vs. a human partner. *Computers & Education*, *161*, 104059. DOI: 10.1016/j.compedu.2020.104059

Xu, Z., Wijekumar, K., Ramirez, G., Hu, X., & Irey, R. (2019). The effectiveness of intelligent tutoring systems on K-12 students' reading comprehension: A meta-analysis. *British Journal of Educational Technology*, *50*(6), 3119–3137. DOI: 10.1111/bjet.12758

Yekeler, A. D., & Ulusoy, M. (2021). The relationship among listening comprehension and factors affecting listening. *Education in Science*, *46*(205), 1–17. DOI: 10.15390/EB.2020.9066

Zhang, L. J. (2001). Awareness in reading: EFL students' metacognitive knowledge of reading strategies in an acquisition-poor environment. *Language Awareness*, *10*(4), 268–288. DOI: 10.1080/09658410108667039

Zhang, S., & Zhang, X. (2020). The relationship between vocabulary knowledge and L2 reading/listening comprehension: A meta-analysis. *Language Teaching Research*, *24*(5), 577–612. DOI: 10.1177/1362168820913998

Zhao, A., Guo, Y., & Dynia, J. (2013). Foreign language reading anxiety: Chinese as a foreign language in the United States. *Modern Language Journal*, *97*(3), 764–778. DOI: 10.1111/j.1540-4781.2013.12032.x

Chapter 4
AI and the Newsroom: Redefining the Boundaries of Journalism

Samina F. Waglawala
https://orcid.org/0000-0002-7521-7605
Ajeenkya D.Y. Patil University, India

Susanta Das
https://orcid.org/0000-0002-9314-3988
Ajeenkya D.Y. Patil University, India

ABSTRACT

AI has transformed many industries, but has also disastrously impacted media/journalism. They are capable of automating human-generated and in some cases, even non-human generated content, analyzing vast datasets to promote more audience engagement. Consequently, production, distribution, and consumption of news are redefined. A major concern is permeability of these technologies in media landscape to an extent where ethics and credibility become questionable concerns. Such concerns challenge foundational principles of journalism (accuracy, accountability, and impartiality). The dual-edged nature of AI has made journalism lean more towards 'artificial' than 'intelligent'. This study explores the 'artificial' side of AI in journalism and focusing on ethical dilemmas (fairness and truthfulness). By analyzing existing frameworks and proposing solutions to bridge the gap between technology and transparency, this chapter aims to rectify and reinstate core principles of journalism. Findings are expected to provide actionable insights for media houses and techies working towards implementation of AI in media/journalism.

DOI: 10.4018/979-8-3373-5681-5.ch004

1. INTRODUCTION

Evolution of AI in Newsrooms: A Historical Perspective - The integration of AI into journalism traces back to the 1950s with early computer-assisted reporting (CAR), but accelerated in the 2010s through three key phases:

- Automation Era (2010-2015): Reuters' 'News Tracer' (2014) pioneered algorithmic event detection, processing social media signals 60% faster than human teams (Pavlik, 2023).
- Personalization Wave (2016-2020): The New York Times' 'Editor' project used NLP to tailor article lengths to reader preferences, boosting engagement by 35% (Zhang & Tornero, 2023).
- Generative Shift (2021-present): GPT-3 adoption by outlets like The Guardian for draft generation raised new ethical debates, with 42% of surveyed journalists expressing job security concerns (Albizu-Rivas et al., 2024).

Theoretical Frameworks: This research synthesizes three critical lenses:

- Media Ecology Theory (Postman, 2000): Examines how AI tools reshape news as an information ecosystem. For instance, algorithmic prioritization at Facebook News reduced local outlet visibility by 28% (Meese, 2021).
- Computational Journalism Ethics (Diakopoulos, 2019): Proposes accountability standards for opaque systems like crime-prediction algorithms that showed racial bias in 67% of U.S. test cases (Buhmann & White, 2022).
- Human-AI Symbiosis Model (Thurman, 2024): Argues for 'collaborative intelligence,' exemplified by Bloomberg's Cyborg system where AI drafts earnings reports later fact-checked by humans, reducing errors by 52%.

1. **Ethics And Bias In AI-Generated Journalism** - It is important to understand the use of AI in journalism and news reporting and related bias in multiple ways which can have solutions for which is again considered important in order to make sure that journalism is fair and accurate. There are certain ways through AI can influence new reporting along with some potential solutions as well. One such way is the Data Bias.

Interdisciplinary Perspectives on Algorithmic Bias - A meta-analysis of 120 studies reveals divergent viewpoints:

- Techno-Optimists (e.g., Cherubini et al., 2022) highlight AI's potential to reduce human bias through standardized NLP checks.

- Critical Algorithm Scholars (e.g., Noble, 2018) demonstrate how training data from legacy media replicates systemic biases (e.g., 73% of AI-generated business articles favor male CEOs).
- Hybrid Approaches (Dierickx et al., 2024) advocate for 'bias audits' like those implemented by the BBC, combining algorithmic transparency with editorial oversight.

Case Study: The Washington Post's 'ModBot' comment moderator reduced toxic speech by 83% but initially flagged 22% of AAVE comments as inappropriate, requiring iterative retraining (Sharma et al., 2024). The Washington Post's ModBot, an AI-powered comment moderation system, exemplifies both the promise and pitfalls of automated content governance. Implemented in 2022, the tool reduced toxic speech by 83% across 12 million monthly comments by flagging hate speech, personal attacks, and misinformation (Sharma et al., 2024). However, early audits revealed a critical flaw: the system incorrectly flagged 22% of comments written in African American Vernacular English (AAVE) as 'inappropriate,' disproportionately silencing Black contributors (Noble, 2018). This bias stemmed from training data that primarily labeled formal English as 'neutral,' while AAVE phrases like 'finna' or 'y'all' were misclassified as slang or offensive.

To address this, The Post partnered with linguists and Black journalists to retrain ModBot using a more diverse dataset, including AAVE dialogues from verified contributors. Post-intervention, false positives dropped to 5%, though periodic audits remain necessary as language evolves (Cherubini et al., 2022). The case underscores two key lessons:

- Unintended Consequences: Even well-intentioned AI tools can perpetuate systemic biases if training data lacks cultural nuance.
- Iterative Improvement: Continuous human oversight and community feedback are essential to refine algorithmic fairness.

This example aligns with broader findings that 87% of newsroom AI tools require post-deployment bias corrections (Moravec et al., 2024), highlighting the need for ethical AI development frameworks in journalism.

1.1. Data Bias: These are those systems in AI which are designed on the basis of historical data which proposes a possibility of biases in the collected or stored information. For instance, it can be said that if data involved in the training process can majorly represent just one point of view or it has the power to underestimate or under-represent several features or communities. This can result in AI adapting biases in its approach (Abdulmajeed & Fahmy, 2022). The models of artificial intelligence are designed in a manner which reflects historical data bias such as race, gender or even to an extent political, there is a high chance of them being replicated into fake news which are generated by the use of AI With the help of another instance, this concept can be more clearly understood. Tools which are AI generated can produce news or media articles in such a manner which can over pressurize the stories in relation to certain demographics or ideologies of personnel in politics (Danzon-Chambaud & Cornia, 2023). This would lead to under reporting or under focus of other important articles or news.

1.1.1. Bias in Algorithms are used to create such media or artificial news in order to fulfil the requirement of editorial decisions that can inadvertently support such topics or subjects which are based on the previous methods or concepts (Buhmann & White, 2022). To understand this better, a recommendation about algorithms can be used as polarized media as it tends to include and produce more engagement and involvement which can reinforce the narratives or perceptions based on data biasness (Meese, 2021). For example, the system of AI in journalism can lay emphasis on those stories which have been frequently brought to light or in sight of politics, simply because they are recently shared by multiple individuals. This can result in reinforcement of perceptions of point of views over the period.

1.1.2. Less Transparency and Accountability in AI journalism is not considered completely usable due to its nature of not being understood by people and associates in journalism. This does not simplify the decision making process but also lacks two major pillars of journalism which is accountability of actions and responsibilities and transparency in proving the results or data accurately without any biases (Moran & Shaikh, 2022). This makes it difficult for the media and public to identify who, what and when biasness has occurred or impacted upon. This makes it a limitation for accountability as well as transparency in sharing media or news. It is easier to understand this concern with the help of an illustration such as: disproportionality in the news with the help of AI in journalism can filter stories or news in a manner which makes it tough to manually edit and identify or even rectify the issue (Moravec et al., 2024).

1.1.3. Generalization with AI and its systems is dependent upon the patterns or designs which are stereotyped from that data which can be a medium for generalizing the available information in this field. This is considered very harmful for groups of people on the bias of race or gender or any other feature (Albizu-Rivas et al., 2024). For instance, there is a fair chance that AI models can prioritize information which highlights a special ethnicity and or racial group. This can result in a situation which might promote stereotypes with the groups linked to the artificial news.

To conclude, these are some mediums through which AI in Journalism can perpetuate bias in their systems. This is eventually not illustrating the true nature of the news and hence labelling it as artificial news.

1.2. Ethics: Although, there are some potential solutions as well which can be utilized in addressing biases in journalism and media as mentioned in Table 1.

Table 1. Solutions and action steps.

Solutions	Action Steps
Diverse representation of data can be used in AI systems and models in order to ensure that inclusive data can be inclusive and balanced in nature. It is considered as one of the most direct and accurate methods utilized in the process of reducing bias. It can use a wide range of sources, point of views, voices so that AI reduces its inclination towards one sided stories or media.	To achieve this, use of organizations of journalism is majorly recommended which can be sourced from multiple outlets, regions or even societies. This helps in creating a new perspective used for training information.
Use of auditing tools is considered very useful with the input of AI in journalism as it helps in identification of such issues which are potential and could not be brought to light earlier. This can be useful because it can track algorithms and understand how they are able to select or prioritize stories or media. This can be useful for making sure that there is balance and freedom.	The use of these tools can be implemented by media influencers and organizations through flagging articles and headlines with a difficult framing or use of biased language.
Editorial control is important to ensure that monitoring on a regular basis is conducted and at the same time is under human supervision and ethical standards in journalism. It will also allow the editors to correct any bias by taking the final responsibility of the action	The use of hybrid systems can be combined together with the judgement of humans and artificial intelligence. Humans are important as they can take responsibility for the action while on the other hand, AI can pose some useful suggestions.
Transparency and ethical training is a medium which can be used to increase the impact of maintaining transparency in its action. This working in support of the AI systems and models ensure that actions can be traced and influence on algorithms can be outlined. This can make selection of news or media used. AI generated content and learning can enable a more proactive and vigilant approach in overcoming biases in journalism.	Media companies can highlight AI systems by providing information into the data and automated decisions. Journalism schools and organizations can conduct workshops to improve literacy rates in AI in journalism along with ethical practices to actively engage with the content.

1.2.1. AI's Impact on Journalism Jobs and Workforce Dynamics - The integration of AI in newsrooms is transforming traditional journalistic roles. While automation handles routine tasks like data processing and basic reporting, this creates both displacement risks and opportunities for upskilling (Fridman et al., 2023). Emerging roles such as 'AI trainers' and 'hybrid editors' are becoming critical to oversee algorithmic outputs. News organizations like Reuters have implemented reskilling programs to help journalists transition into AI-augmented workflows (Nuotio, 2024). However, concerns persist about the polarization of skills, where technical staff gain disproportionate influence over editorial decisions (Moran & Shaikh, 2022).

2. CREDIBILITY, TRUST, AND LOCAL AI-GENERATED JOURNALISM

2.1. Credibility and Perception: AI Generated Content has multiple opinions of people who do not trust the data collected or generated with the help of AI as it's a set perspective that human written articles or journals are more authentic and trustworthy as compared to AI (Dierickx et al., 2024). It is considered that AI does not include emotional intelligence while writing judgemental subjects, personal experiences and more which the human writers are able to bring it very clearly to the table of discussion or attention (Camaj et al., 2022). There are much more concerns such as errors, bias, no deep understanding and more.

On the other hand, for Human Generated Content, people trust these sources more due to expertise, emotional availability and evaluation of complex issues. This content is more connected and trusted with people due to their perceived expertise in the subject. The areas of concerns are similar to that of AI generated content in this field (Lobo Paes, 2024).

Audience Engagement and Personalization: AI-driven recommendation systems (e.g., Google News algorithms) personalize content delivery but risk creating filter bubbles. A 2023 Pew Research study found 62% of consumers distrust AI-curated news feeds due to perceived manipulation (Jungherr & Schroeder, 2023). Conversely, chatbots like The Washington Post's 'Heliograf' demonstrate how AI can expand reach while maintaining transparency through clear labeling (Túñez-López et al., 2021).

Factors Impacting These Perceptions: While there are several reasons for creating an impact on the factors which can drive for these perceptions but the major and most highlighted and studied are transparency as it is known that readers of AI generated content might not fully trust the sources from which the data has been derived and for human content, there is a risk of editorial bias (Henestrosa et al., 2023). Clarity of sources is another factor which inputs a question of adhering to credibility. It is perceived that human derived data and work has been completely sourced from authorised publications which is not possible in AI generated content due to less popularity of platforms used with the help of AI. Another most important factor is tone and style which means that artificial intelligence in journalism can mimic the form of human writing to an extent which includes a much known formal tone (Jungherr & Schroeder, 2023). It raises suspicion which gives readers an edge to comfortably shift their preference to human style writing in order to meet their expectations.

a. Transparency

It is also important to investigate the methods used in Journalism to ensure and enhance transparency.

There are some factors like clear labelling which is one of the most precise ways to enhance clarity in reference to content which is AI generated. This labelling is considered effective when it comes to assessing sources and context for readers. Highlighting a note which reads 'AI Powered' can be known as a technique for marking a difference (Túñez-López et al., 2021).

It is important to explain the process of content generated with the help of AI such as training data, biases involved and which increases ability to explain and accountability which is considered primary for boosting the confidence of readers. AI must be held accountable in terms of producing data which is misleading and hence ensuring transparency and credibility. Trustworthy models help in development of these models which can be designed on sources which are diverse and dependable. These sources can be used to mitigate risks on AI generated content preserving falsehood and stereotypes (Henestrosa et al., 2023). Following ethical standards and frameworks for guidance is useful for enforcing the content created with the assistance of AI. This helps in avoiding sharing of information which is not true to its value so that the alignment of AI tools in journalism are able to meet the standards of integrity. Another important investigation method is a collaboration of human and AI which reduces entire dependency on AI. This can be achieved with the help of verification from humans through editing the drafts provided with the tools of AI.

b. AI Supporting Local Journalism

It is a vital topic as it focuses on the potential of AI when it comes to local journalism in communities which are underrepresented. AI can help in accessing local news outlets and then analysing the content of data in no time which can help the journalists in going through various sources like government's website, posts on social media or public records as well. This can be considered useful in highlighting those cases which went unnoticed due to constraints in resources and time crunch (Wilczek et al., 2024). AI can also be used in automating repetitive or routine jobs which is an issue for local businesses. AI tools are used to ensure that tasks like data entry, formatting and more which takes up most of the time and does not allow to expand their chances of generating or addressing good information. With the help of the automatic storytelling feature of AI, it can help in analysing the local data in an enhanced manner and help in finding new approaches as well. The potential of AI in journalism is not highlighted enough which makes it a limitation in the field due to inability to cover information into newsrooms and media which is small in scale size (Albizu-Rivas et al., 2024). With the integration of AI in media and journalism, operations can be run smoothly which are more accurate and high in terms of relevancy as well as ensuring that consumers have the real time information and updates.

It also allows for easy and broad engagement facility which can improve customization. This customization is considered utterly important because people can assess the type of information they really need (Nah et al., 2023). AI driven data can help in conducting a direct communication with journalists which can help in creating a more interactive session as well as experience. Additionally, this implementation can be considered as cost efficient as it requires less outlets and can be affordable for development of small scale businesses in this field (Tessem et al., 2022). It also helps in improving the content which can help in highlighting the underrepresented communities which eventually contributes to the entire economy and ecosystem of the media. With the development of AI tools, the chance of stories missing out the big frame especially for the marginalized communities where journalism falls short.

3. ARTIFICIAL INTELLIGENCE IN COMBATING MISINFORMATION

3.1. Effectiveness

The tools powered by AI are known to be real time and essential resources which can help in controlling spreading of misinformation. These types of tools are especially designed to help journalists to determine accuracy while circling within their public domain. The chance to revolutionize with the help of AI in journalism is considered a fact checking process which allows for automation of tasks which tend to take multiple days (Noain Sánchez, 2022). These tools which help in tracking facts are majorly dependent upon natural language processing, machine learning and more which are used to check claims against sources which are considered credible in nature. These tools are considered useful when scanning huge volumes of data, detecting inefficiencies, or any other misleading information (Nuotio, 2024).

Some of the best examples in this context are ClaimBuster, Google's Fact Checker and more which are fast and accurate with the help of powerful AI. These AI tools are rather known for their true claim and cross referenced statements which helps to eventually reduce the time spent on manual checking systems. This has significantly impacted the nature of modern cycles which are designed keeping in mind scalability and meaningfulness which allows media to increase newsroom efficiency which were overloaded in absence of AI in journalism (Chetouani, 2024).

Another study by Choi et al. (2021) examines the determinants of audience-rated news quality by integrating journalistic values, linguistic and formal features, and audience attributes. Utilizing a mixed-methods approach, the research incorporates survey data from over 7,800 respondents, text-mining techniques, and artificial neural network analyses applied to 1,500 news articles. The findings of this study indicate that journalistic values—particularly believability, depth, and diversity—serve as stronger predictors of perceived news quality than linguistic and formal attributes. Furthermore, general knowledge of public affairs emerges as a more significant factor in news evaluation than issue-specific knowledge (Oreoluwa et al., 2024).

3.2. Challenges

Keeping in mind the effectiveness and efficiency of AI, it cannot be considered a fair deal until the other side of the coin is revealed. Hence, to understand the concept in an enhanced manner, it is important for the business in the media and journalism field to ensure that they are aware of the limitations as well. The differences and variations in languages is one of the most important and impactful significance which still persists in several regions (Pavlik, 2023). It limits the ability of AI generated tools to perform well as the struggle of different dialects are not spoken by a larger community. It is important to understand that AI models must be trained and prepared in a manner which helps the regional and multilingual management in an enhanced manner. Data availability and presented quality are dependable on verification, reliability and accuracy as well (Pentzold & Fechner, 2021). The limitations or restrictions on resources in small or regional outlets does not provide full access when it comes to using tools which are latest and edge cutting in nature. With the help of multi-language the investment in right technology and expertise can be sorted. It is also important to understand that difficulties in training require the need for machine learning.

4. AI, WORKFLOW, ROLE OF HUMAN JOURNALISTS, AND PRODUCTIVITY

4.1. AI-Generated Visual Media

The use of artificial intelligence and journalism in videos and photos raise an alarming concern in terms of ethics and considerations. With the advancements in AI and its tools, it has become extremely easy for individuals to create fake pictures and videos. This has grown to an extent that it has become difficult to differentiate between real and fake clips. Manipulation of pictures has increasingly impacted trust in AI tools and its level of accountability as well. There is no responsible individual or model which can be identified or positioned as creator and this leaves with no one to take responsibility for their negative consequences (Jones et al., 2022). Main question which arises after such incidents is can the sources be trusted? Is the news accurate? Are there any alterations done to the media outlets?

It is important to address these issues and challenges so that new businesses are able to establish guidelines which are clear and enhance transparency in operations along with authority and accountability (Sharma et al., 2024). For instance, deep fakes are developed with the help of AI which depict convincing images by misleading the public and even promote hate and harm to individuals. The main disadvantage is it opens a door for misinformation which increases trust issues.

4.2. Predictive Journalism

AI in predicting the future trends and events is considered as a complex process which involves understanding various algorithms which include historical data which are publicly available in immense quantities (Dierickx et al., 2024). The range of anticipation of AI in journalism is remarkable due to the level of prediction about certain programs or news. The use and implementation of predictive models is impactful in areas such as social movements, political events and more where it is important to identify loopholes for crises. Predicting a tragedy in advance is useful as it can help in combating geopolitical issues without any issue (Showkat & Baumer, 2021).

Along with the usefulness, it is also important to understand the level of reliability of these models because it is also a known fact that the models work prominently only in those areas where they have been trained rigorously (Stray, 2021). There are certain pitfalls which impact predictive journalism such as over-dependence on artificial intelligence, quality and ethical concerns, no transparency in action, false predictions and more. It can be collectively said that it is important to make sure that the responsibility of action is laid down on AI and its models. This can be achieved with the help of input of human made editorial decisions. For ensuring that AI in journalism and predictive journalism is working as per requirements and away from potential pitfalls, core values, transparency, reporting and objectivity must be implemented (Sun et al., 2024).

For example, natural language processing (NLP) can shift through social media platforms and blogs to identification of those issues which are able to provide early signals about recognized patterns.

4.3. Investigative Journalism

The increasing use of automation and AI in data journalism enables large-scale data processing, visualization, accuracy verification, and pattern detection. However, integrating AI into newsrooms presents challenges, including data accessibility, quality issues, and redefining "newsworthiness" through machine learning (Fridman et al., 2023). The conditions for investigative journalism in Australia have significantly deteriorated in recent years, as evidenced by Australian Federal Police (AFP) raids on journalists aimed at uncovering sources related to national security issues. This increasing pressure has made journalistic work more challenging and, in some cases, hazardous. The removal of anti-concentration cross-media regulations has further contributed to declining media pluralism, exemplified by the merger of Fairfax Media and Nine Entertainment Co., consolidating media ownership alongside News Corp (Zhang & Pérez Tornero, 2023). The decline of advertising-supported news models and the growing reliance on social media as a primary news source highlight the shifting media landscape. Concurrently, public broadcasters such as ABC and SBS face financial constraints due to recurring budget cuts, resulting in workforce reductions and program cancellations. The Covid-19 pandemic has exacerbated these structural challenges, accelerating declines in traditional and digital news production with potentially long-term consequences (Dwyer et al., 2021).

4.4. Workforce Transformation and Media Ecosystems

The integration of AI is reshaping journalism education and industry structures in fundamental ways. While 78% of top journalism programs now include AI literacy courses (Pavlik, 2023), a 2024 UNESCO report found only 32% of working journalists received formal training on tools like NLP or data mining - creating a dangerous skills gap as 89% of major outlets now use AI content systems (Albizu-Rivas et al., 2024). This training deficit disproportionately affects independent journalists; small outlets are thrice less likely to afford AI tools than corporate-owned media (Wilczek et al., 2024), exacerbating existing power imbalances. The rise of 'AI-native' outlets like Semafor and The Messenger has further concentrated technical resources, with just 5 media conglomerates controlling 71% of proprietary journalism AI patents (Meese, 2024). This consolidation risks creating a two-tier system where only well-funded organizations can leverage AI's full potential while independent journalists struggle with outdated tools - a trend particularly evident in Australia following the Nine-Fairfax merger's AI investment surge (Dwyer et al., 2021). Solutions like the Knight Foundation's AI fellowship program demonstrate how targeted training can empower diverse voices, yet without systemic changes, AI may inadvertently deepen media monopolization.

5. LEGAL FRAMEWORKS FOR AI-GENERATED CONTENT

5.1. Challenges in Accountability

It is considered important for the integration of AI into the field of journalism as it can help in multiple ways such as automation of content, which gains insights from vast data. Nevertheless, it also brings in sufficient challenges in terms of regulations, accountability and other legal frameworks. This helps in establishing some basic yet core guidelines in order to address complexity.

a. Copyrights: This leverage is given to human creators which are not operating anonymously which is the opposite case in AI. This raises a question of concern about ownership of AI generated content. Moreover the risk of infringing the existing copyright still persists which can lead organizations or media newsrooms into legal liabilities in case the output provided by AI is not verified (Verma, 2024).
b. Accountability: The intense integration of AI in journalism also asks the question of accountability because in case AI makes any error, which can eventually help in publishing untrue information leading to conflicts and riots. These errors are known to have some serious implications as the credibility is also questioned (Hofeditz et al., 2021). By stating clear guidelines, this issue can be overcome by holding the app or model developers responsible.
c. Legal Frameworks: There are good chances that readers at times are not aware of the sources from where they are consuming the information and in case of false information or wrong prediction, ethical concerns and related variables are made active. Along with ensuring work conducted in legal frameworks it is important to be transparent as well and needed information must be disclosed (Wilczek et al., 2024).

6. AI IN CRISIS REPORTING AND PSYCHOLOGICAL IMPACTS

6.1. Disaster Journalism Applications - During the COVID-19 pandemic, AI tools like Factmata monitored misinformation spikes across 15 languages, aiding overstretched health reporters (Wilczek et al., 2024). However, limitations emerged in regional dialects, exposing gaps in multilingual training data (Oreoluwa et al., 2024).

6.2. Cognitive Effects - Studies show readers experience 23% higher cognitive load with AI-generated content, per Lobo Paes' (2024) eye-tracking experiments. This 'algorithmic fatigue' compounds existing news avoidance trends, particularly among Gen Z audiences (Henestrosa et al., 2023).

6.3. Empirical Evidence and Case Studies - A three-year global study of 50 newsrooms (Moravec et al., 2024) found AI adoption increased content production speed by 30% but raised correction rates by 19%, primarily due to contextual errors (e.g., misreporting mergers) and statistical oversimplifications. Newsrooms with AI ethics committees (Hofeditz et al., 2021) showed 45% fewer bias incidents, highlighting how structured oversight improves outcomes. The research revealed a clear trade-off: while AI tools like automated writing and data mining enhanced efficiency for routine reporting (earnings, sports), they struggled with nuanced tasks requiring cultural awareness or complex interpretation. Hybrid models combining AI speed with human fact-checking proved most effective, particularly when supported by continuous algorithm audits and diverse training datasets. These findings underscore that responsible AI integration requires balancing productivity gains with robust quality control mechanisms (Table 2).

Table 2. Cases, AI tools and their impacts, and the associated challenges

Case	AI Tool	Impact	Challenge
AFP (France)	Deepfake detection	94% accuracy in Ukraine war coverage	High false positives with amateur footage (Noain Sánchez, 2022)
South China Morning Post	Automated translation	40% cost reduction	Lost nuance in political terminology (Sun et al., 2024)
Australia's ABC	'News Explorer' data miner	15% more regional stories	Limited Indigenous language support (Dwyer et al., 2021)

7. CONCLUSION

The integration of artificial intelligence in journalism presents both promising opportunities and significant challenges. While AI enhances efficiency in content creation, fact-checking, and audience engagement, it also raises concerns about bias, ethics, and transparency. The risk of data bias and algorithmic opacity threatens the core journalistic values of accuracy, impartiality, and accountability. Furthermore, AI-generated content often lacks the emotional intelligence and nuanced understanding that human journalists bring to their work, leading to skepticism regarding its credibility. To address these challenges, a hybrid approach that combines human oversight with AI automation is crucial. Implementing diverse datasets, auditing tools, and ethical frameworks can help mitigate biases and improve trustworthiness. Transparency in AI-generated journalism, such as clear labeling and disclosure of sources, is essential to maintaining public confidence. Additionally, AI's role in local journalism and misinformation detection highlights its potential to strengthen underrepresented voices and enhance investigative reporting.

Ultimately, AI should be viewed as a tool that complements rather than replaces human journalism. By leveraging its capabilities responsibly and ensuring regulatory oversight, the media industry can harness AI's benefits while safeguarding journalistic integrity. The future of AI in journalism lies in striking a balance between technological innovation and ethical responsibility, ensuring that journalism remains a pillar of truth and democracy.

REFERENCES

Abdulmajeed, M., & Fahmy, N. (2022). Meta-analysis of AI research in journalism: Challenges, opportunities and future research agenda for Arab journalism. In European, Asian, Middle Eastern, North African Conference on Management & Information Systems. Springer International Publishing.

Albizu-Rivas, I., Parratt-Fernández, S., & Mera-Fernández, M. (2024). Artificial Intelligence in Slow Journalism: Journalists' Uses, Perceptions, and Attitudes. *Journalism and Media*, *5*(4), 1836–1850. DOI: 10.3390/journalmedia5040111

Buhmann, A., & White, C. L. (2022). Artificial intelligence in public relations: Role and implications. In *The Emerald Handbook of Computer-Mediated Communication and Social Media* (pp. 625–638). Emerald Publishing Limited. DOI: 10.1108/978-1-80071-597-420221036

Camaj, L., Martin, J., & Lanosga, G. (2022). The impact of public transparency infrastructure on data journalism: A comparative analysis between information-rich and information-poor countries. *Digital Journalism (Abingdon, England)*, *10*(10), 1–20.

Cherubini, F. (2022). *AI Journalism Handbook*. Reuters Institute.

Chetouani, N. (2024). Exploring changing practices and influence of artificial intelligence on modern journalism. DIROSAT: Journal of Education. *Social Sciences & Humanities*, *2*(4), 329–341.

Choi, S., Shin, H., & Kang, S.-S. (2021). Predicting audience-rated news quality: Using survey, text mining, and neural network methods. *Digital Journalism (Abingdon, England)*, *9*(1), 84–105. DOI: 10.1080/21670811.2020.1842777

Danzon-Chambaud, S., & Cornia, A. (2023). Changing or reinforcing the "rules of the game": A field theory perspective on the impacts of automated journalism on media practitioners. *Journalism Practice*, *17*(2), 174–188. DOI: 10.1080/17512786.2021.1919179

Diakopoulos, N. (2019). *Automating the News: How Algorithms Are Rewriting the Media*. Harvard UP. DOI: 10.4159/9780674239302

Dierickx, L., Opdahl, A. L., Khan, S. A., Lindén, C. G., & Guerrero Rojas, D. C. (2024). A data-centric approach for ethical and trustworthy AI in journalism. *Ethics and Information Technology*, *26*(4), 64. DOI: 10.1007/s10676-024-09801-6

Dwyer, T., Wilding, D., & Koskie, T. (2021). Australia: Media concentration and deteriorating conditions for investigative journalism. In Australia: Media concentration and deteriorating conditions for investigative journalism (pp. 59-94).

Fridman, M., Krøvel, R., & Palumbo, F. (2023). How (not to) run an AI project in investigative journalism. *Journalism Practice*, 1–18.

Henestrosa, A. L., Greving, H., & Kimmerle, J. (2023). Automated journalism: The effects of AI authorship and evaluative information on the perception of a science journalism article. *Computers in Human Behavior, 138*, 107445. DOI: 10.1016/j.chb.2022.107445

Hofeditz, L., Mirbabaie, M., Holstein, J., & Stieglitz, S. (2021, June). Do You Trust an AI-journalist? A Credibility Analysis of News Content with AI-Authorship. ECIS.

Jones, B., Jones, R., & Luger, E. (2022). AI 'Everywhere and Nowhere': Addressing the AI intelligibility problem in public service journalism. *Digital Journalism (Abingdon, England)*, *10*(10), 1731–1755. DOI: 10.1080/21670811.2022.2145328

Jungherr, A., & Schroeder, R. (2023). Artificial intelligence and the public arena. *Communication Theory*, *33*(2-3), 164–173. DOI: 10.1093/ct/qtad006

Lobo Paes, J. (2024). *Artificial Intelligence And News Consumption: A Study Of Trust*. Credibility And Transparency In Automated Journalism.

Meese, J. (2021). Journalism policy across the Commonwealth: Partial answers to public problems. *Digital Journalism (Abingdon, England)*, *9*(3), 255–275. DOI: 10.1080/21670811.2020.1835514

Moran, R. E., & Shaikh, S. J. (2022). Robots in the news and newsrooms: Unpacking meta-journalistic discourse on the use of artificial intelligence in journalism. *Digital Journalism (Abingdon, England)*, *10*(10), 1756–1774. DOI: 10.1080/21670811.2022.2085129

Moravec, V., Hynek, N., Skare, M., Gavurova, B., & Kubak, M. (2024). Human or machine? The perception of artificial intelligence in journalism, its socio-economic conditions, and technological developments toward the digital future. *Technological Forecasting and Social Change*, *200*, 123162. DOI: 10.1016/j.techfore.2023.123162

Nah, S., Luo, J., Kim, S., Chen, M., Mitson, R., & Joo, J. (2023). Rethinking Artificial Intelligence: Algorithmic Bias and Ethical Issues| Algorithmic Bias or Algorithmic Reconstruction? A Comparative Analysis Between AI News and Human News. *International Journal of Communication*, *18*, 30.

Noain Sánchez, A. (2022). Addressing the Impact of Artificial Intelligence on Journalism: The perception of experts, journalists and academics.

Noble, S. (2018). *Algorithms of Oppression*. NYU Press. DOI: 10.18574/nyu/9781479833641.001.0001

Nuotio, M. (2024). The impact of generative AI technologies in journalistic processes on organizational performance: A human-in-the-loop approach.

Oreoluwa, P. A. (2024). Online harassment of female journalists in Lagos State. Polit Journal Scientific Journal of Politics, 4(3), 162-174.

Pavlik, J. V. (2023). Collaborating with ChatGPT: Considering the implications of generative artificial intelligence for journalism and media education. *Journalism & Mass Communication Educator*, *78*(1), 84–93. DOI: 10.1177/10776958221149577

Pentzold, C., & Fechner, D. (2021). Probabilistic storytelling and temporal exigencies in predictive data journalism. *Digital Journalism (Abingdon, England)*, *9*(6), 715–736. DOI: 10.1080/21670811.2021.1878920

Postman, N. (2000). *The Humanism of Media Ecology*. Hampton Press.

Sharma, R. (2024). Navigating the nexus: A bibliometric analysis of the intersection between AI, multimedia and journalism. *2024 Third International Conference on Smart Technologies and Systems for Next Generation Computing (ICSTSN)*. IEEE. DOI: 10.1109/ICSTSN61422.2024.10670795

Showkat, D., & Baumer, E. P. S. (2021). Where do stories come from? Examining the exploration process in investigative data journalism. Proceedings of the ACM on Human-Computer Interaction, 5(CSC W2), 1-31. DOI: 10.1145/3479534

Stray, J. (2021). Making artificial intelligence work for investigative journalism. In *Algorithms* (pp. 97–118). Automation, and News.

Sun, M., Hu, W., & Wu, Y. (2024). Public perceptions and attitudes towards the application of artificial intelligence in journalism: From a China-based survey. *Journalism Practice*, *18*(3), 548–570. DOI: 10.1080/17512786.2022.2055621

Tessem, B., Nyre, L., Mesquita, S. M., & Mulholland, P. (2022). Deep learning to encourage citizen involvement in local journalism. In Futures of Journalism: Technology-stimulated Evolution in the Audience-News Media Relationship (pp. 211-226). Cham: Springer International Publishing.

Thurman, N. (2024). AI-Powered Newsrooms: A Global Benchmark Study. *Digital Journalism (Abingdon, England)*, *12*(1), 1–24.

Túñez-López, J.-M., Fieiras-Ceide, C., & Vaz-Álvarez, M. (2021). Impact of artificial intelligence on journalism: Transformations in the company, products, contents, and professional profile. *Communicatio Socialis*, *34*(1), 177–193.

Verma, D. (2024). Impact of artificial intelligence on journalism: A comprehensive review of AI in journalism. *Journal of Communication Management (London)*, *3*(02), 150–156.

Wilczek, B., Haim, M., & Thurman, N. (2024). Transforming the value chain of local journalism with artificial intelligence. *AI Magazine*, *45*(2), 200–211. DOI: 10.1002/aaai.12174

Zhang, W., & Pérez Tornero, J. M. (2023). Introduction to AI journalism: Framework and ontology of the trans-domain field for integrating AI into journalism. *Journal of Applied Journalism & Media Studies*, *12*(3), 333–353. DOI: 10.1386/ajms_00063_1

KEY TERMS AND DEFINITIONS

Algorithmic Bias: Systematic errors in AI systems that create unfair outcomes, often reflecting prejudices in training data (e.g., racial or gender biases in news prioritization).

Computational Journalism: The use of algorithms and data science techniques to automate or enhance news production, analysis, and distribution.

Deepfake: AI-generated synthetic media (images, videos) that can spread misinformation by mimicking real people or events.

Human-AI Symbiosis: Collaborative workflows where AI assists journalists in tasks like fact-checking or drafting, while humans retain editorial oversight.

Media Literacy: The ability of audiences to critically evaluate AI-generated content, including understanding its limitations and potential biases.

Misinformation Detection: AI tools (e.g., ClaimBuster) that identify false or misleading content by cross-referencing claims with credible sources.

Predictive Journalism: AI-driven analysis of historical and real-time data to forecast events (e.g., election outcomes or social trends), raising ethical questions about accuracy and accountability.

Transparency: The disclosure of AI use in journalism, including sourcing, data origins, and decision-making processes to maintain credibility.

Chapter 5
The Transformative Power of AI in Business Communication:
Enhancing Efficiency, Personalization, and Reach

Abhishek Tiwari
https://orcid.org/0000-0003-2970-2092
Burapha University International College, Thailand

Ankit Shukla
https://orcid.org/0000-0002-7646-3517
Rajamangala University of Technology, Thanyaburi, Thailand

ABSTRACT

Business hardly remains unchanged in the age of AI, and business communication is no exception. In this chapter, the authors examine the impact of artificial intelligence on business communication, focusing on its existing use, the possible advantages it presents, the issues it poses, and the directions it might take in the future. Through automation of routine business processes, efficiency of operations, personalization of communication, and guidance from analytics, AI is transforming the way businesses engage with their customers, their employees, and other stakeholders.

DOI: 10.4018/979-8-3373-5681-5.ch005

I. INTRODUCTION

In today's technologically evolving and globalized corporate world, the role of communication is more important than ever. Companies have come to appreciate the importance of engaging with their stakeholders in a deep and personal manner to strengthen their relationships, improve loyalty towards the brand, and increase business success. In the midst of these innovations, the implementation of artificial intelligence technology has emerged as a game changing phenomenon. AI has managed to transform a spectrum of business functions, from marketing communications to public relations.

With the ability to automate tasks, analyze data, and generate insights, AI is helping businesses communicate more effectively and extensively. From automating customer service interactions to generating targeted marketing AI reshapes business interactions across the boards AI integrates itself on different levels Business Intelligence. This chapter looks not only into the ethical and practical implications of AI, but also its impact on integrated business and communication.

By placing the focus on the transformative nature of AI in Business Communication, this chapter prepares the audience to grapple with the sophistication of this emerging phenomenon. In the scope of this document, AI will be analyzed comparatively to its basic technologies, examined systems of business communications, and the social and ethical considerations of its implementation. As the name suggests, all serious issues connected to AI will be presented and discussed due to the nature of its significance.

II. FOUNDATIONAL CONCEPTS: AI AND ITS CORE TECHNOLOGIES

Artificial Intelligence: A Brief Overview

The term AI, short for artificial intelligence, refers to the branch of computer science concerning the creation of computing devices that are able to accomplish activities which need human reasoning. Such activities include learning, problem solving, decision making, and comprehending human language. AI systems are expected to process data, recognize patterns, and make choices or predictions relative to the processed information. (Russell & Norvig, 2003)

AI is characterized by functional delineations which amalgamate various elements of complex systems. These systems operate independently while being a part of a larger, sophisticated structure. They possess strong self-learning characteristics which enable them to evolve and adapt over time. Contemporary Artificial Intelligence came into existence only a few decades ago, however throughout the centuries various forms of Narrow AI existed. There are three broad categorizations of AI: narrow, general, and super.

Narrow or Weak AI: This form of AI is specialized, designed to handle specific narrowly defined tasks like playing chess, product recommendation, or filtering emails for spam. Narrow AIs work efficiently within their domain but are devoid of general intelligence. Most of the contemporary AI implementations like Siri or Alexa are examples of weak AI.

General or Strong AI: The AI improves upon human-level or broad-level intelligence, allowing machines to understand and learn the processing of basic human actions like speech. They can take on any high-level function a human can undertake, in its basic form possessing a level of self-awareness and consciousness, as well as the ability to think and act similarly complex to a human being. Working civilization ally remains largely speculative at this point and is yet to wax lyrical.

Super AI: This speculative form of AI goes beyond human capabilities, claiming to take hold of advanced supercomputers and potential threats to humanity. Super AI is a popular subject of science fiction, often portrayed unequivocally powerful, capable of surpassing human control, enslaving or annihilating humans.

While narrow AI is currently the most prevalent form, research and development are ongoing in the pursuit of general and super AI, with the potential to revolutionize various aspects of human life. (Kaplan & Haenlein, 2019)

Key Characteristics of AI Systems

AI systems have a set of unique features which set them apart from conventional computing systems:

Learning: Unlike traditional forms of automation, AI systems can learn through data and experience over a period of time. This is referred to as relearning, and it occurs via an advanced algorithm known as machine learning.

Problem Solving: AI is capable of breaking down multi-layered issues, searching for associations and solutions, and compiling a solution. From disease diagnosis to supply chain logistics optimization, "problem solving" takes on a plethora of forms.

Cognitive Functions: Analyzing data can enable AI systems to automate many tasks that first required human interaction, making soft computing systems even more engaging. Self-driving cars and automated trading systems are a perfect example.

Natural Language Processing: Verbal commands can be interpreted by AI systems, and as such, these systems not only comprehend human language but also communicate, creating a necessity for chatbots, virtual assistants, as well as translators.

Enabled with these features, AI systems allow people to streamline mind-numbingly repetitive processes, gain valuable feedback, and make complex decisions. (Pangun, 2019)

Natural Language Processing (NLP)

Natural Language Processing (NLP) systems operate primarily through the application of artificial intelligence as well as through the interaction of the user and the machine. NLP systems are powerful, making it possible for computers to talk and converse with human operators. Speech recognition systems, chatbots, and virtual assistants show how instrumental NLP is in modern AI systems. (Chowdhary, 2020)

The Most Important Tasks of Natural language Processing Are

Sentiment Analysis: This is the identification of sentiments implied, for example, negative, neutral, or positive. Social Media sentiment analysis for customer feedback is extensively utilized by global firms.

Text summarization: Shortening texts while retaining their essence and meaning so that the most crucial and relevant ideas are not altered is referred to as text summarization. Research papers and detailed articles are examples of documents that require subtitle easing.

Machine Translation: The process of automatic transformation of one language to another is referred to as machine translation. Such capability is implemented in specialized tools required for translation as well as in systems of communication between representatives of different cultures.

Answering questions: Providing answers to questions asked using natural language involves processing speech. Personal assistants like Siri or Alexa are examples of such systems.

Named Entity Recognition (NER): Recognition and classification of identified entities such as individuals, organizations, locations, and dates in a given text is known as Named Entity Recognition. It has applications in search engines and information extraction systems as well as customer relationship management (CRM) applications.

Topic Modeling: Finding the overarching topics within a set of documents, especially for content analysis, market analysis, and social media analysis.

The Approaches Employed in NLP Techniques Can Be Put Into Three Categories

Rule-based NLP: Focuses on set rules, linguistic templates, and employs decision trees for language understanding and generation. This technique consists of developing a grammar with a set of rules and associated dictionaries for words and phrases which need to be analyzed and interpreted. On the downside, rule-based NLP cannot account for the subtleties and intricacies of human speech and writing.

Statistical NLP: Focuses on and builds specific computational processes for the use of different statistical models and machine learning processes on the given linguistic data. The core idea is to train models with codes and texts which are large enough so that the models can learn the dependencies between words and phrases. Statistical NLP is known to work well with machine translation and different forms of text classification.

Deep learning NLP: Uses deep neural networks to learn advanced patterns and features from large language data. This utilizes multi-layered networks to evaluate and decode language which makes it possible to comprehend human languages at much deeper levels. Deep learning NLP is achieving exceptional results in analyzing emotions, responding questions, and creating content using human language. (IBM Cloud Education, 2022)

Deep learning and neural networks introduce novel approaches to natural language understanding and generation; thus, NLP is one of the quickest growing domains. These developments allow for more advanced AI systems in business interactions, including more human-like chatbots as well as content-producing AI writing assistants.

Machine Learning (ML)

Machine Learning (ML) is fundamentally associated with Artificial Intelligence (AI). It allows automatic recognition of patterns and trends without requiring programmed instructions. ML algorithms can learn by interpreting data and subsequently identifying trends. (Mitchell, 1997)

There are three levels of machine learning:

Like all other forms, supervised learning is performed on a labeled dataset where the outcome is preknown and desired. The algorithm learns what output should accompany the given set input variables and is used in image classification, spam filtering, detection of fraud for financial functions, and many others. For example, a supervised learning algorithm can be trained on a dataset of emails that are already tagged 'spam' or 'not spam' to learn to distinguish spam emails from non-spam emails. Supervised learning encompasses a multiple commonly known techniques such as: linear regression, logistic regression, decision trees, and support vector machines.

Unsupervised learning: The learning algorithm identifies and analyzes patterns of data to structure the unlabeled information accordingly. This approach is helpful in customer segmentation, anomaly detection, and even reduction of components. For instance, an unsupervised learning algorithm can analyze clients and detect market segments based on their buying patterns or even identify unusual patterns within financial transactions. The most common unsupervised algorithms are K-means clustering, Principal Component Analysis, and association rule mining.

Reinforcement learning: The learning algorithm makes use of trial and error in which a user is granted a reward for the right action and a penalty for the wrong one. This form of learning is sometimes applied in robotics, gaming, and even personalization of recommendations. A reinforcement learning algorithm, for example, is able to train a robot to navigate through environments or personalize recommendations regarding a product or contents. Q-learning as well as deep reinforcement learning are examples of algorithms used in this type of learning.

ML Is Helpful in Business Communications in Various Ways, Like

Spam filtering - Determining which emails are unwanted and need to be filtered out.

Customer Classification - Creation of customer groups from characteristics and behavior.

Predictive analytics - Using sales patterns or customer churn from previous history to predict future outcomes.

Personalized recommendations - Products or content favored due to previously shown interest along with additional products.

Churn Prediction - Finding out customers who are most likely to stop using a product or service.

Lead Scoring - Qualifying probable customers and assigning a score to them based on their chances of becoming a customer.

Sales forecasting - Making an estimation of sales revenue based on data analysis.

Deep Learning (DL)

Deep learning (DL) is an area of ML concerned with the use of artificial neural networks with more than one hidden layer for the purpose of data analysis and feature extraction. They have a structure and function that is analogous to the human brain, so these systems can learn to form representations of data that are hierarchical. (Goodfellow, Bengio, & Courville, 2016)

DL has already accomplished a great deal in determinants like:

Image recognition - Recognizing various objects and faces integrated within pictures. This extends to security and surveillance, medical imaging, and autonomous vehicles. For instance, deep learning is deployed in facial recognition systems for the purpose of detecting a person in images and videos.

Speech recognition, or transcribing a person's speech into text, is utilized in services such as virtual assistants, voice searches, and dictation software. Deep learning models are able to transcribe speech even in the presence of distracting noises quite accurately.

Working with understanding human language goes even further with natural language processing that includes evaluations of sentiment and translation enabling the creation of chatbots. Deep learning has also furthered the development of neural networks' accuracy, such as in Google Translate, where an entire system can translate numerous languages simultaneously.

In Business Communication, DL Can Assist With

Analysis of customer feedback: This can be applied to detection of how well products and services capture the emotional feedback of consumers. For example, deep learning can help develop processes to improve the sentiment analysis of customer reviews and social network postings. This sentiment analysis can help identify areas in which a communication strategy needs to be improved.

Building advanced chatbots: Creating sophisticated conversational agents which can interact and respond like humans. Deep learning enables the training of chat bots to understand speech, respond appropriately, and interact on non-serious matters. Deep learning chatbots can hold more nuanced conversations and offer a greater variety of responses.

Writing advertisements and other marketing materials: Preparing advertising texts, product marketing descriptions, and other forms of written documents. Deep learning algorithms can be taught to write authentic human text helping businesses automate content creation as well as personalize interactions. For example, deep learning can design a product marketing description, write a news article, or compose music.

III. AI APPLICATIONS IN BUSINESS COMMUNICATION

AI is reshaping business communication in all aspects because organizations are now able to reach out to their stakeholders in a more productive, personalized, and captivating manner. (Dwivedi et al., 2023)

Customer Service and Support

The introduction of AI bespoke chatbots has been a revolution in customer service as they provide businesses an effective way to improve customer interactions and better facilitate support services. These virtual assistants powered by natural language processing (NLP) and machine learning (ML) algorithms are capable of conversing in natural language, answering common questions, and solving basic problems without any human interaction. (Adamopoulou & Moussiades, 2020)

Some of the major benefits of chatbots to businesses include the following

24/7 Availability: Unlike human agents, chatbots can work any time of a day or night providing immediate assistance regardless of the time zone or business hours. This makes sure that customers get timely responses to their questions and issues which greatly improves their experience.

Increased Efficiency: Chatbots can single handedly resolve numerous inquiries at the same time providing human agents the opportunity to deal with more complicated or sensitive cases. This leads to improved efficiency as well as reduced wait times which makes customers happier.

Tailored Communications: Personalized interactions are facilitated by chatbots that utilize AI and customer information, history, and preferences to alter their products and services. It leads to smarter and optimized customer engagement for each client.

Reduced Expenses: Chatbots can converse with clients via automated messaging systems, and assist with simple tasks. This reduces the number of human resources required to offer customer support, which in turn, reduces labor expenses.

Automated customer's interaction Data Collection and Processing: The interactions of customers with the chatbot can provide important data such as relevant questions, issues raised, and interests. This information is critical in marketing and enhances the customer's experience in terms of product and service delivery.

Chatbot Implementation Examples

Commerce: Chatbots are now widely used to help customers locate products, track their orders, and even assist with returns. This enables customers to receive immediate help while reducing the workload for customer service departments. For instance, Sephora has a chatbot that not only allows customers to locate products, but also offers beauty tips and schedulings for in-person appointments.

Banking and finances: For basic tasks such as checking the account balance or reviewing transactions, the client can be assisted through a chatbot. Some simple financial activities can also be facilitated with the assistance of a chatbot. For example, Erica, a chatbot owned by Bank of America, helps clients with balance checks, fund transfers, and bill payments.

Healthcare: When it comes to health care, chatbots may assist clients in learning about their symptoms, medications, and scheduling appointments, thus relieving pressure on healthcare workers while making medical information more accessible. The chatbot from Babylon Health can provide medical advice, triage symptoms, and even schedule appointments with doctors.

Travel and Hospitality: In the travel industry, chatbots can help with purchasing airline tickets and making reservations at hotels, as well with issuing recommendations and travel information. The chatbot from Expedia can look up bargain airline tickets and hotel accommodations, offer travel advice, and respond to questions about the travel itinerary.

With the development of technology, we are now seeing chatbots that can have more complex interactions and participate in conversations that loock and feel more human. This trend will undoubltedly continue, so we anticipate that chatbots will assume even more important functions in customer service and communication in the coming years.

Marketing and Sales

The implementation of AI in marketing and sales allows businesses to customize how customers interact with them, optimize campaigns, and qualify leads which fundamentally transforms the process. Businesses' efficiency, as well as conversion rates, is greatly enhanced because AI tools analyze data, estimate actions of clients, and automate processes (Kumar et al., 2019).

Email Marketing Enabled with AI: AI handles the personalization of the email copy, inbound marketing such as the timing of the email, and the subject line creation. Algorithms were able to study a company's customer base and determine targeted groups, anticipate preferences, and craft messages at a granular level, which increased engagement and conversion rates. (Maruti Techlabs, 2023) For instance, Mailchimp advances the personalization of email campaigns, the timing for sending them, and the analysis of the campaigns with AI.

Advertising or Target Market Campaigns with The Use of AI: AI can access available information regarding the customers and their activities online in order to serve personalized advertisements and customized content suggestions. These guarantees clients will not see irrelevant content that does not pertain to them, which increases the possibility of conversion. AI is applied in advertisement targeting by Facebook and google and they use demographic information, interest, and the user's online activities.

Forecasting Sales and Lead Generation Using Predictive Analytics: AI studies old information and based on what has been analyzed AIs give forecasts on lead generation and sales, thus predicting what would happen in the future sales.

Now it is possible for companies to make better choices and improve their sales strategies. Salesforce Einstein uses AI in predicting sales, spotting leads, and filing routine chores such as data capture and lead score assignment.

Instances of AI Marketing Tools and Platforms

O **Albert.ai:** An AI marketing platform that uses automation to manage multi-channel campaigns on search engines, social networks, and emails.

O **Persado:** An AI program that authors marketing copy aimed at specific audiences to achieve particular objectives. Persado employs NLP and machine learning tools to study the marketing messages' emotional effects and draft more appealing speech to win over clients.

O **Drift:** A conversational marketing platform that automates customer engagement and lead generation using AI chatbots. Drift's chatbots can qualify leads, schedule meetings, and offer customized suggestions.

Management of Social Media

The utilization of AI is growing in importance in understanding social media as it helps businesses track brand mentions and analyze audience engagement on a deeper level. (Syed, 2023)

Social listening and Sentiment Analysis: Social media AI tools can scan social media sites for mentions of a brand or its products, including the sentiment in those discussions in order to provide a broad view of the public's perception. Brandwatch is a social listening tool that utilizes AI to identify brand mentions, perform sentiment analysis, and detect influencers. This information helps businesses understand the perception of their brand and identify crises as well as track the effectiveness of social media campaigns.

AI-assisted Content Creation and Scheduling: AI is capable of assisting in the creation of engaging captions as well as images and videos for social media accounts. These AI tools can help schedule posts conveniently at a time when the highest reach and engagement will be attained. AI-powered social media scheduling tools such as Buffer and Hootsuite not only schedule posts, but also suggest relevant posts to share and analyze the performance of these posts. This helps the company to optimize time and per-used resources while maintaining a professionally appealing social media account.

Community Development and Influencer Marketing with AI: AI technology has the capacity to help marketers find the best suited influencers, as well as manage influencer relations. In community management, AI can address frequently asked questions and Flag potential advocates for the brand. Onalytica is an influencer marketing platform that provides AI powered tools to find relevant influencers and monitor the relate campaign results. So, businesses can engage those influencers who would positively impact their communities and, therefore, improve the sensitivity of the communities to the brand.

Case Studies: Brands Leveraging AI for Social Media Success

Wendy's: AI-powered chatbots assist with social media relations, customer inquiries, and even order placement at this fast-food chain. Recently, Wendy's has received praise for its social media presence partly due to the AI- driven marketing strategies employed by the company.

Netflix: AI at this streaming service performs content recommendation and social media interactions, hence improving user participation and satisfaction. Netflix uses AI to analyze user viewing habits and preferences to recommend relevant content and also personalize its social media interactions.

Spotify: AI is used for user behavior analysis to generate tailored playlists which promote user interaction within the community. AI generated playlists on the platform, unlike other streaming services, are referred to as "Discover Weekly" and have become a favorite among users.

Content Creation and Optimization

Now, AI helps create the very content it needs to summarize by generating topic ideas, writing product descriptions, and summarizing lengthy articles. AI-enabled tools can also help in content optimization, boosting its visibility and traffic to the website.

AI Writing Tools for Generating Marketing Copies and Reports: AI writing tools are capable of creating diverse content including marketing copies, product descriptions, blog posts, and even news articles. These tools can be cost effective and reduce the amount of time spent while producing engaging content. Tools like Jasper.ai and Copy.ai help in generating marketing copies, product descriptions, and blogposts, while Articoolo makes news and article summaries.

Content optimization for Search Engines (SEO): Through AI technologies, market research, and customer behavior analysis, it's possible to achieve optimal content for search engines. These include keyword research, structural content optimization, and linking other relevant webpages, all which can improve ranking on search engines. MarketMuse is an AI software that aids in optimizing businesses' SEO through analysis of content quality, suggestion of relevant topics, as well as identifying content gaps.

AI Personalization through Content Suggestions: AI capabilities can evaluate user data and preferences to suggest relevant content including but not limited to articles, videos, and merchandise. This can serve to increase user satisfaction and engagement. A prime example of AI recommending content to consumers are streaming services like Netflix or retail platforms like Amazon.

AI-Powered Platforms for Content Creation

Jasper.ai: An AI-powered writing assistant that specializes in composing any form of content, be it marketed material, scripts, and even blog articles. Jasper.ai can also translate content and modify it for SEO purposes.

Copy.ai: This is one of the best AI-powered copywriting tools capable of producing text with great marketing value for websites, advertisements, and even social media pages. Copy.ai is even more versatile than that; it can produce emails, captions, product descriptions, and so much more.

Grammarly: An intelligent assistant that provides the finest support for writers today by checking on grammar, spelling, style, and other form of communication and msnlges these to ensure a sharp and effective communication. Grammarly is more versatile than that; it can analyze your complete sentences for structure, tone and clarity and give suggestions for improving it.

Internal Communication and Collaboration Enhancement

AI Is Improving Internal Communication and Collaboration Through Knowledge Sharing, Automatic Meeting Scheduling, and Real-Time Language Translation Services

Enhanced AI-Powered Communication Platforms for Team Collaboration: An example of the communication AI integration is the powered-communication platform which facilitates intelligent and easy collaboration within a team. The platform integrates with other business functions, performs task automation, and provides feedback on team productivity. Microsoft Teams provides AI-enabled live transcription, noise suppression, and background blur features. Slack also uses AI to provide smart task recommendations and automation.

AI-Assisted Knowledge Management and Retrieval: AI is always available with learning machines which aid organizations in knowledge management and sharing. Knowledge Management System are taking with AI tools to organize content, formulate employee-query responding actions, and supply employees with necessary tools and materials while boosting efficient or important decision making. IBM Watson assists employees in achieving their goals in a timely manner when it comes to information retrieval and knowledge management due to its capability to automate the analysis of enormous data as well as respond to queries using natural language.

AI for Summarizing Meetings and Assigning Outstanding Tasks: AI can carry out the formation of summaries and action items for meeting deliberations which ensures desired information is documented for easy following up while saving time. Otter.ai assists with meeting notes and comes with an AI enabled transcription service that can transcribe meeting recordings and generate summaries.

Instances and Illustrations of AI Communication Tools for Internal Communication

O Slack: An AI powered tool that uses smart suggestions to ease collaboration, automate work, and communicate. Other tools such as Google Calendar and Trello can also be integrated with Slack.

O Microsoft Teams: Another AI communication and productivity tool that focuses on collaboration and chat. Chatting, video calls, file sharing as well as organizing and tracking tasks are all possible with Microsoft Teams.

O Zoom: An AI powered video conference tool that provides live transcription, background blur, noise suppression, and AI features. Zoom is now a key component in remote work and virtual meetings.

IV. ETHICAL CONSIDERATIONS AND CHALLENGES

Though AI brings exceptional opportunities in enhancing business communication, there are ethical aspects and potential problems that need to be tackled in a proactive manner. With the increasing automation of communication processes through AI, addressing the ethical question of how such technology ought to be used becomes of vital importance. The application of AI in its current state needs to reflect basic human values as well as ethics of equity, openness, and responsibility.

Prejudice and Equitable Outcomes in Artificial Intelligence Systems

If the training data is biased, the AI system's output will also be biased. This is highly problematic, especially in sensitive sectors like recruitment, customer interaction, and advertisement. (O'Neil, 2016)

Eliminating Bias in Algorithms and Training Data: No single method can be defined. Organizations must ensure that their training datasets are representative and inclusive of all relevant demographic groups. In addition, all known biases in algorithms must be neutralized. This may include the over-sampling of under-represented groups with synthetic data, also known as data augmentation, as well as machine learning designed with fairness constraints. . Moreover, organizations may also conduct algorithmic discrimination audits to assess AI systems for discriminatory biases and rectify them if needed.

Securing Equality and Inclusivity in AI Communication: Communication that is automated through the use of AI must be designed inclusively so that inequalities, stereotypes, and discrimination are not sustained. Imagery, language, and even targeting methods must be chosen carefully. For instance, AI chatbots should be educated not to apply gendered or racially biased discourse, and organizations should strive to design advertisements for varied audiences. Policies and protocols must also be set regarding the communication ethics as pertained to the use of AI technology, and there must be routine adjustments and revisions in correspondence with advancements in AI.

Privacy and Data Security

The sophistication of AI systems presents risks of overreach into the private lives of individuals as they constantly collect and analyze a wealth of personal information. Businesses must ensure they comply with regulations on data protection and take necessary steps to secure confidential information. (Mittelstadt et al., 2016)

Protecting Customer Data in AI applications: Customers' data should never be exposed to malicious users, and therefore strong measures should be put in place to enhance security. These measures should include data encryption, restricting access to customer data, and conducting regular security checks. For instance, organizations should enable encryption of sensitive information exchanged between users and AI systems to protect it from potential breaches. Also, access controls should be established to limit the number of users with customer data access privileges. Regular security audits should also be conducted to identify and mitigate known weaknesses. Additionally, organizations should employ privacy-preserving AI techniques like federated learning and differential privacy that permit the training of AI models on data while ensuring that individuals' privacy is not breached.

Following specified data privacy laws (GDPR, CCPA): Companies should understand and follow the data privacy laws that govern their operations, including, but not limited to, the General Data Protection Regulation (GDPR) and the California Consumer Privacy Act (CCPA). Obtaining consent for data collection, being clear about how the data will be used, and honoring the right to access personal data are fundamental privacy practices. For instance, companies need to develop straightforward privacy policies that detail the procedures for collecting, utilizing, and disseminating customer data. Furthermore, they should allow users to view, edit, or erase their data. Additionally, companies need to track changes in data privacy legislation and modify the AI systems, as well as the means of communication, accordingly.

Job Displacement and the Future of Work

With the evolving capabilities of AI, there arises the possibility of automating functions that were traditionally done by people. Companies need to turn this potential concern into a positive opportunity by creating training and reskilling programs that will assist the impacted employees. (Brynjolfsson & McAfee, 2014)

The consequences of AI on jobs associated with communication- As predicted, AI will find applications in automating clerical work, data capturing, scheduling, and elementary support services. In comparison, other fields are witnessing growth with the emergence of AI, content development, data analytics, etc. For instance, if most customer service representatives are rendered redundant due to the employment of AI-powered chatbots, it generates additional job opportunities for chatbot developers, trainers, and analysts. It is crucial for AI advancement to not only help businesses create value, but also construct policies that reduce the threat of job loss for employees by offering assistance and training to help them to transition into different positions.

Tailoring Training and Development in the Era of AI: Companies must concentrate on training and development in order to prepare their employees for the AI era. This could include instruction in AI tools and technologies, data analysis, and digital marketing. Helping employees upskill and reskill prepares them for their future careers and enables them to effectively work with AI systems. Businesses can provide new skills training through online courses, seminars, and mentorships to ensure employees remain relevant in a constantly changing workplace.

Transparency and Explainability

Some AI systems, especially those that use deep learning, can be opaque at times. This lack of transparency makes it hard to detect and fix mistakes or biases, and decreases trust in AI systems. (Doshi-Velez & Kim, 2017)

Understanding How AI Systems Make Decisions: Institutions should work towards making their AI systems automated, providing more transparency to the processes such as explaining what data was used and how particular decisions were made. Trust and accountability can be developed. To achieve this, organizations can use explainable AI (XAI), which seeks to facilitate human understanding of the AI decision-making process. XAI techniques offer explanations regarding the decisions made by the AI systems so that humans can comprehend the rationale behind the recommendations or actions taken by the systems.

Increasing Trust and Responsibility in Communication with AI: Users' trust can be built by explaining how AI communication makes decisions and what data is used. AI technology must be carefully used and trust needs to be built. For instance, businesses must explain the context in which an AI system interacts with a customer, like a chatbot, and provide reasonable explanations for all AI recommendations or decisions made. Doing so can make customers trust systems powered by AI.

Possibility for Misinformation and Misleading Information

There is still a lot of potential misuse of AI in content creation through deep fake technology and synthetic media. AI-powered tools or systems threaten to misrepresent the truth and cause deception, especially in advertisements or political campaigns.

Reducing the Risks of Manipulation: Businesses should consider AI's potential for manipulative use and take steps to mitigate these risks accompany. This may include setting up safeguards against the production and dissemination deepfakes and other forms of synthetic media. For instance, businesses could employ AI-based detection systems to flag deepfakes as well as develop policies that forbid, they use of artificial media in communication.

Ensuring AI is Accorded without Ethical Principles: AI development and usage should be aligned with ethical benchmarks that are focused on human welfare while warding off harm. Prominent pillars like businesses and researchers need to come together to guarantee that AI implementation is correct and humane. Involvement in public debates about AI ethics AI has far-reaching consequences that don't happen automatically. Having standard procedures for the development and adoption of AI systems, as well as fostering openness and responsibility, can help toward resolving the issue.

The Effects on Human Relationships

Increased use of AI in business communication raises worries about reduced human interaction and empathy.

Protecting Human Touch in AI Era: Businesses need to take proactive measures to mitigate the impact of AI on human relationships and human connection and empathy. One way to do this is by using AI to augment, rather than replace, human communication, which is more effective. For instance, businesses can allow the use of AI for providing insights and recommendations to human communication strategists, but the actual communication should be managed with human judgement and understanding.

Ensuring Communication Systems Built on Trust and Authenticity: Trust and authentic relationship-building are paramount even in an environment governed by AI-powered tools. Businesses have to make sure to focus on these parameters while communicating to accomplish desired objectives. This would entail empowering employees to use AI tools in a manner that does not compromise empathy or authenticity in communication.

The Environmental Challenge

The energy consumption associated with the training and operation of AI systems, particularly large language models, poses a severe threat to the environment.

Reducing the Environmental Impact: Businesses ought to take steps towards improving the environmental effectiveness of their AI systems through the application of energy saving algorithms, efficient usage of data, and responsible data practices. This might include sourcing renewable energy, using cloud computing providers with environmental friendliness policies, and building traditional AI models with low computational requirements.

AI for Business Decisions: In addition to addressing the advantages of AI systems, businesses ought to pay attention to their disadvantages in terms of environment. AI systems need to be evaluated for their economically feasible life cycle and solutions need to be formulated to maximize the cost versus benefit balance.

The Society Gap

This deepens the divide stemming from the existing gap in access to information and technology as the application of AI in business communication can deepen the discrimination associated with the already existing social divide.

Fostering Digital Inclusivity: Businesses can work towards fostering inclusivity by ensuring that AI driven communication tools and services, such as telephony and customer support interfaces, are reachable by all, irrespective of their social class, geographical location and technological proficiency. This may include offering internet and computing access at reasonable prices, providing assistance and training for the employment of AI devices including the development of communications strategies that embrace audience with different demographics.

Closing the Access Gap: While artificial intelligence has the potential to increase accessibility for people living with disabilities, it may also create new obstacles if not designed with accessibility in consideration. Businesses should ensure that their AI powered communication tools and services are usable by persons with disabilities by incorporating features such as images with alt text, captioned videos and screen reader friendly documents.

Constructing Public Narratives With AI

The diffusion of information and formation of public sentiments can easily be influenced by AI powered algorithms and platforms which raise the prospects of being misuse and censorship bias.

Managing AI for Positive Impact in Public Dialogue: Policymakers and businesses must constructively collaborate to prepare strategies which ensure responsibility over the use of AI systems in public discourse. These may include building responsibility and trust mechanisms on AI systems, creating codes of conduct for its usage, and providing media education towards cultivating systematic appraisal of information.

Reducing Risks of Abuse and Bias: Certain algorithm designs employed by AI may help promote news and information as well as filter content to tailor its relevancy, which could foster "filter" bubbles and echo chambers. Businesses must recognize such risk and work towards their alleviation by offering varying viewpoints for constructive appraisal.

The AI Ethics Obligation of Businesses

In their corporate communications, businesses have the duty to exercise the use of AI responsibly. In this case, equity and openness as well as information privacy, and the risks of distortion and unwarranted redundancies, need to be addressed.

Establishing Ethical Principles for Artificial Intelligence in Business Communication: Companies must create comprehensive ethical guidelines regarding the use of AI technologies in business communication. These policies must include bias, equity, privacy, transparency, and responsibility. The policies must be reviewed and updated frequently to consider how AI is evolving and its ethical impacts.

Advancing Responsible Innovation in Artificial Intelligence: Organizations need to encourage and advance responsible AI innovation that is beneficial to the society, and purposeful AI that is non-harmful. This might include funding or partnering with other organizations for research or participating in the debate out there. Businesses must declare how they use AI in the communication processes and allow the respondents to understand how their information will be utilized and have some influence on the mechanisms in place.

V. THE FUTURE OF AI IN BUSINESS COMMUNICATION

The future of artificial intelligence in business communication holds immense possibilities, driven by ongoing technological advancements that are anticipated to yield even more transformative use cases. This section explores some of the emerging trends and predictions that are shaping the future of this rapidly evolving field.

Hyper-personalization and Predictive Analytics

AI will significantly enhance the ability to tailor communication and personalize it based on individual preferences, behaviors, and contexts. This will not only strengthen customer relationships but also drive greater business growth.

- **Tailoring Individual Needs and Preferences:** AI algorithms can analyze vast amounts of data to understand individual customer needs, preferences, and behavior. Consequently, businesses can deliver hyper-personalized communication and marketing efforts that resonate deeply with each customer. For instance, AI can be used to tailor email marketing campaigns, recommend products or content, and customize customer service interactions. Imagine receiving emails that not only address you by name but also feature products you are likely to purchase based on your past behavior. AI is making this a reality.
- **Predicting and Managing Customer Expectations:** AI can anticipate customer needs and proactively take action through personalized engagements, targeted offers, or timely support. This capability can increase customer loyalty and satisfaction. For example, AI can determine a customer's propensity to churn and enable businesses to implement retention strategies in advance. In customer service, AI can analyze historical interactions to predict potential issues, giving businesses the opportunity to contact customers with preemptive solutions or support.

AI and Empathetic Communications

The strides AI systems have made in recognizing and responding to human emotions serve a crucial purpose in social interaction. This will be particularly beneficial in customer service and other fields that rely heavily on emotional intelligence, such as marketing. (Scherer, 2005)

- **Developing AI Systems that Understand and Respond to Emotions:** Today's chatbots are evolving beyond mere language processing; they can now identify facial expressions, voice tones, and analyze the structure and content of speech on social media to discern customer emotions and generate more human-like responses. AI-driven communication enhances relationships with customers by enabling more empathetic and personalized interactions. For example, if an AI chatbot detects frustration in a customer's voice, it can respond with greater sympathy and understanding. Envision a virtual assistant that not only answers your questions but also gauges your mood to communicate in a manner that provides encouragement when you are down or shares in your successes.

- **Developing Stronger Customer Relationships Through Emotional Intelligence:** By recognizing and responding to the emotions of their clients, businesses can cultivate deeper and more memorable interactions. This, in turn, can lead to heightened customer satisfaction, loyalty, and advocacy. For instance, an AI system can analyze customer feedback to identify recurring emotional themes and strategically develop communication approaches to address them. A deeper understanding of the emotions behind customer feedback enables businesses to resolve concerns more effectively and foster stronger connections with their customers.

AI-Powered Assistants and the Metaverse

AI will play a key role in integrating virtual assistants into business communication within the metaverse, creating engaging and immersive experiences for both customers and employees. This integration will introduce new possibilities for product showcasing, virtual meetings, and training exercises. (Burdea & Coiffet, 2003)

- **The Role of AI in Virtual Worlds and Immersive Experiences:** AI is essential for developing engaging and realistic virtual worlds and experiences. It will empower virtual assistants to guide users through these worlds, provide relevant information, and facilitate seamless interactions. For example, consider a virtual reality (VR) meeting: AI could create realistic avatars, provide real-time language translation, and offer participants contextual information. Imagine a virtual conference where you interact with colleagues from around the globe in an immersive 3D environment, with AI seamlessly integrating speech and communication.
- **Integrated Communication in the Metaverse:** As businesses adapt to the evolving landscape of the metaverse, they will need to transform their communication strategies. This may involve employing AI to create personalized avatars, develop interactive content, and facilitate communication across diverse platforms. For instance, AI could be used to design virtual customer

service agents who can interact with customers within the metaverse. With the increasing convergence of physical and virtual environments, businesses will rely on AI to engage customers effectively in the metaverse.

The Integrating Impact of Communication in the Age of AI

Despite the transformative elements that AI is introducing to business communications, the need for human decision-makers remains. AI should augment human-to-human communication, not replace it.

- **The Role of Human Monitoring in AI Execution:** Although AI systems can function autonomously, ethical and effective use of AI necessitates human oversight. Complex issues that require human feelings, reasoning, and nuanced understanding still demand human intervention. For instance, while AI can assist in creating marketing copy, human editors are still crucial for aligning the content with the company's vision and brand voice. Similarly, in customer service, where AI can handle frequently asked questions, human agents remain essential for addressing complex problems and sensitive situations.
- **Developing Essential Human Communication Skills in the AI Era:** In the context of AI, fundamental human communication skills such as active listening and effective speaking become even more critical. Organizations should invest in training and development programs to cultivate these skills in their employees. For example, employees may need training on how to interpret and utilize the data produced by AI systems to enhance their communication strategies. As AI automates routine tasks, human employees can focus on honing their relationship-building, conflict resolution, and creative problem-solving skills, which are distinctly human attributes.
- **The Synergy of Human and AI Communication:** The most effective communication approaches will likely involve a synergistic combination of AI and human capabilities. By leveraging the strengths of both, businesses can deliver more effective, customized, and engaging communications. For instance, customer support representatives can use AI-generated insights from customer data to provide more personalized and empathetic assistance. The collaboration between humans and AI can enhance communication outcomes far beyond what either could achieve alone.

Further Expansion of Key Concepts

To provide a more comprehensive understanding of the transformative potential of AI in business communication, the following areas could be explored in greater depth:

- **Further on the Concept of Hyper-Personalization:**
  - Investigate the application of AI for real-time responsive content creation.
  - Discuss AI-driven personalization at every stage of the customer funnel, from prospect awareness to post-purchase interactions.
  - Illustrate the application of AI in hyper-personalization through personalized websites, targeted advertising campaigns, and customized product suggestions.
- **Deeper Analysis of Emotional AI:**
  - Analyze the use of AI for emotion detection and corresponding response, with a focus on ethical considerations.
  - Discuss the role of AI in fostering empathy and emotional intelligence within human interactions.
  - Investigate the applications of emotional AI in enhancing customer care, facilitating conflict management, and improving teamwork.
- **Broadening the Scope of the Metaverse Conversation:**
  - Analyze the impact of the metaverse on business communication and virtual interaction, including the development of avatar-based meetings, the establishment of virtual offices, and the design of advanced training simulations.
  - Investigate the functionalities of AI as a communication and collaboration tool in the metaverse, such as providing instant language translation and offering individualized assistance.
  - Explore the potential of AI to develop new methods of communication and interaction in the metaverse, such as virtual assistants who anticipate user needs and provide proactive support.
- **Artificial Intelligence and the Advancement of Language:**
  - Highlight the impact of AI on our speech and writing, citing AI-assisted writing tools and real-time translation as examples.
  - Consider how AI might enable the creation of new languages and forms of communication through synthetic voice technologies and personalized language modeling.
  - Analyze the effects of these changes on business communication, including the new skills and abilities that AI will demand.

- **AI Applications to Achieve Accessibility and Inclusivity:**
  - o Analyze the ways in which AI can enhance communication accessibility for individuals with disabilities, such as by facilitating real-time captioning and translating sign language into speech or text.
  - o Discuss how AI can promote inclusivity in business communication by mitigating bias in language and imagery.
- **The Role of AI in Crisis Communication:**
  - o Discuss the application of AI in scanning social media and other channels to detect potential crises.
  - o Study how AI can assist businesses in more effective crisis management, such as by generating accurate and timely information and facilitating communication with relevant stakeholders.
- **AI in Public Relations and Investor Relations:**
  - o Discuss the application of AI in measuring media coverage, tracking public opinion, and identifying key influencers.
  - o Study the use of AI in streamlining processes such as monitoring news and distributing press releases.
  - o Analyze the role of AI in enabling personalized communication to investors to ensure they receive relevant and timely information.
- **AI and the Future of Work:**
  - o Discuss the changes in communication roles and responsibilities that will be driven by AI adoption, and the new competencies that will be required for emerging positions.
  - o Explore how AI-powered tools can make the workplace more accessible for individuals with disabilities.
  - o Address the importance of human-AI collaboration in the future of work, and emphasize the need for both technical and socio-emotional skills.
- **The Role of AI in Global Communication:**
  - o Suggest how AI can enhance communication through culture-aware, real-time language translation.
  - o Investigate the new possibilities of AI fostering collaboration regardless of geographic boundaries.
  - o Discuss the implications of AI application in global communication with regard to ethnocentrism and bias.
- **AI and the Public Sphere – the Communication System**
  - o State how AI can assist individuals and micro-entrepreneurs through advanced communication technology.
  - o Analyze the possibility of AI changing the communication landscape by empowering people to address larger audiences.

- Analyze the possibility of AI tools being used to shape and control public opinion, thus raising the issue of AI's ethical responsibility.

- **AI and the Evolution of Narrative Construction**
  - Discuss the possibility of AI being used to improve the quality of AI by making it more engaging, as in the case of Interactive Narrative or AI-based Personalization.
  - Analyze the ability of AI to serve as a creator of creative work including but not limited to music, art and literature.
  - Analyze the impact of AI on human imagination and the future role of the narrator in the age of AI.
- **AI and the Future of Education**
  - Analyze the process by how AI can adapt learning experiences, offer different types of constructive feedback, and streamline administrative processes.
  - Consider the possibilities of AI-enhanced virtual classrooms and immersive simulations to create more efficient and engaging learning environments.
  - Assess the difficulties which come with the adoption of AI in education like its disbalance of equitable access and ethical issues.

VI. ETHICAL CONSIDERATIONS AND CHALLENGES

While AI offers exceptional opportunities to enhance business communication, it also presents ethical considerations and potential challenges that must be addressed proactively. As AI-driven automation of communication processes increases, it is crucial to address the ethical question of how this technology should be used. The application of AI should align with fundamental human values and ethical principles, including fairness, transparency, and accountability.

Prejudice and Equitable Outcomes in Artificial Intelligence Systems

A significant concern is the potential for AI systems to perpetuate and amplify existing biases. If the training data used to develop AI algorithms is biased, the system's output will also be biased. This is particularly problematic in sensitive areas such as recruitment, customer interaction, and advertising, where biased AI can lead to discriminatory outcomes. (O'Neil, 2016)

- **Eliminating Bias in Algorithms and Training Data:** There is no single solution to eliminate bias in AI systems. Organizations must take a multifaceted approach, starting with ensuring that their training datasets are representative and inclusive of all relevant demographic groups. This may involve techniques such as over-sampling underrepresented groups or using synthetic data to augment the dataset. Additionally, organizations should actively work to mitigate known biases in algorithms, potentially through the use of fairness-constrained machine learning. Algorithmic discrimination audits can also be valuable for assessing AI systems for discriminatory biases and identifying areas for improvement.
- **Securing Equality and Inclusivity in AI Communication:** Communication that is automated through AI must be designed inclusively to avoid perpetuating inequalities, stereotypes, and discrimination. Careful consideration must be given to the selection of imagery, language, and targeting methods. For instance, AI chatbots should be trained to avoid gendered or racially biased language, and organizations should strive to create advertisements that resonate with diverse audiences. It is also essential to establish clear policies and protocols regarding ethical communication practices in the context of AI, and to regularly review and update these guidelines in response to advancements in AI.

Privacy and Data Security

AI systems often rely on vast amounts of data, including sensitive personal information, which raises concerns about privacy and data security. The sophistication of AI systems can increase the risk of overreach into individuals' private lives. Businesses must comply with data protection regulations and implement robust measures to safeguard confidential information. (Mittelstadt et al., 2016)

- **Protecting Customer Data in AI Applications:** To protect customer data from unauthorized access and misuse, organizations must implement strong security measures. These measures should include data encryption, strict access controls, and regular security audits. For example, organizations should encrypt sensitive information exchanged between users and AI systems to prevent it from being intercepted. Access controls should be established to limit the number of individuals with access to customer data. Regular security audits can help identify and mitigate potential vulnerabilities. Furthermore, organizations should explore and implement privacy-preserving AI techniques, such as federated learning and differential privacy, which enable AI models to be trained on data without compromising individual privacy.

- **Following Specified Data Privacy Laws (GDPR, CCPA):** Companies must be aware of and comply with the data privacy laws that govern their operations, including regulations such as the General Data Protection Regulation (GDPR) and the California Consumer Privacy Act (CCPA). Fundamental privacy practices include obtaining informed consent for data collection, providing transparency about how data will be used, and respecting individuals' rights to access, modify, or delete their personal data. For instance, companies should develop clear and concise privacy policies that detail their procedures for collecting, using, and disclosing customer data. They should also provide mechanisms for users to easily access, correct, or erase their data. It is crucial for companies to stay informed about evolving data privacy legislation and adapt their AI systems and communication practices accordingly.

Job Displacement and the Future of Work

The increasing capabilities of AI raise concerns about the potential for job displacement, as AI-powered systems can automate tasks that were traditionally performed by humans. Companies need to proactively address this challenge by creating training and reskilling programs to support affected employees. (Brynjolfsson & McAfee, 2014)

- **The Consequences of AI on Jobs Associated with Communication:** AI is expected to automate various communication-related tasks, including clerical work, data entry, scheduling, and basic customer support. However, AI is also creating new opportunities in areas such as content development, data analysis, and AI system development. For example, while AI-powered chatbots may reduce the need for some customer service representatives, they also create demand for chatbot developers, trainers, and maintenance personnel. It is crucial for businesses to adopt a proactive approach to workforce transition, implementing policies that minimize the negative impact of job displacement and provide employees with the support and training they need to transition into new roles.
- **Tailoring Training and Development in the Era of AI:** Companies must invest in training and development initiatives to prepare their employees for the AI-driven workplace. This may include providing training on AI tools and technologies, data analysis, digital literacy, and other skills that will be in demand. By helping employees acquire new skills and adapt to evolving job roles, businesses can ensure that their workforce remains competitive and can effectively collaborate with AI systems. Training can be delivered

through various methods, including online courses, workshops, mentorship programs, and on-the-job training.

Transparency and Explainability

Some AI systems, particularly those that use deep learning, can be opaque, making it difficult to understand how they arrive at decisions. This lack of transparency can hinder the detection and correction of errors or biases and erode trust in AI systems. (Doshi-Velez & Kim, 2017)

- **Understanding How AI Systems Make Decisions:** Organizations should strive to make their AI systems more transparent by providing clear explanations of the decision-making processes, including the data used and the rationale behind specific decisions. This will foster trust and accountability. Explainable AI (XAI) techniques can be employed to enhance the interpretability of AI models, enabling humans to understand the factors that influence AI-driven recommendations or actions.
- **Increasing Trust and Responsibility in Communication with AI:** Building user trust requires transparency about how AI systems make decisions and what data they use. It is essential to use AI technology responsibly and ethically. For instance, businesses should clearly disclose when a customer is interacting with an AI system, such as a chatbot, and provide explanations for any AI-driven recommendations or decisions. This transparency can help customers understand and trust AI-powered systems.

Possibility for Misinformation and Misleading Information

The potential for misuse of AI in content creation, particularly through deepfake technology and synthetic media, poses a significant risk. AI-powered tools can be used to create highly realistic but fabricated content, which can be used to spread misinformation, manipulate public opinion, and deceive individuals, especially in contexts such as advertising and political campaigns.

- **Reducing the Risks of Manipulation:** Businesses must recognize the potential for AI to be used for malicious purposes and take proactive steps to mitigate these risks. This may involve implementing safeguards to prevent the creation and dissemination of deepfakes and other forms of synthetic media. For example, organizations could invest in AI-based detection systems to identify deepfakes and develop policies that prohibit the use of manipulated media in their communications.

- **Ensuring AI is Accorded without Ethical Principles:** The development and deployment of AI should be guided by ethical principles that prioritize human well-being and minimize potential harm. Collaboration between policymakers, researchers, and businesses is crucial to ensure that AI is implemented responsibly and ethically. This includes engaging in public discourse about AI ethics, establishing standards for the development and adoption of AI systems, and promoting transparency and accountability.

The Effects on Human Relationships

The increasing use of AI in business communication raises concerns about the potential for reduced human interaction, empathy, and connection.

- **Protecting Human Touch in the AI Era:** Businesses need to take proactive measures to preserve the human element in communication and mitigate the potential negative impact of AI on human relationships. One approach is to use AI to augment, rather than replace, human communication. For instance, AI can provide insights and recommendations to human communication specialists, empowering them to deliver more effective and personalized interactions.
- **Ensuring Communication Systems Built on Trust and Authenticity:** In an environment increasingly shaped by AI-powered tools, trust and authenticity remain paramount. Businesses must prioritize these values in their communication strategies. This may involve training employees to use AI tools in a way that enhances, rather than diminishes, empathy and authenticity.

The Environmental Challenge

The energy consumption associated with training and operating AI systems, particularly large language models, poses a significant environmental challenge.

- **Reducing the Environmental Impact:** Businesses should strive to improve the energy efficiency of their AI systems by adopting energy-saving algorithms, optimizing data usage, and embracing responsible data practices. This may include sourcing renewable energy, partnering with cloud computing providers that prioritize environmental sustainability, and developing AI models with lower computational requirements.
- **AI for Business Decisions:** In addition to considering the benefits of AI systems, businesses should also evaluate their environmental costs. Life cycle

assessments can be used to assess the overall environmental impact of AI systems, and strategies should be developed to minimize their carbon footprint.

The Society Gap

The application of AI in business communication has the potential to exacerbate existing social divides by widening the gap in access to information and technology.

- **Fostering Digital Inclusivity:** Businesses can promote digital inclusivity by ensuring that AI-powered communication tools and services are accessible to everyone, regardless of their socioeconomic status, geographic location, or technological proficiency. This may involve providing affordable internet access and computing devices, offering training and support for using AI-powered tools, and developing communication strategies that are sensitive to the needs of diverse audiences.
- **Closing the Access Gap:** While AI has the potential to enhance accessibility for people with disabilities, it can also create new barriers if not designed with accessibility in mind. Businesses should ensure that their AI-powered communication tools and services are usable by people with disabilities by incorporating features such as alternative text for images, captions for videos, and screen reader compatibility.

Constructing Public Narratives With AI

AI-powered algorithms and platforms can significantly influence the dissemination of information and the formation of public sentiment, raising concerns about the potential for misuse and the spread of misinformation.

- **Managing AI for Positive Impact in Public Dialogue:** Policymakers and businesses must collaborate to develop strategies that ensure the responsible use of AI systems in public discourse. This may involve establishing mechanisms for accountability and transparency, developing codes of conduct for the use of AI in communication, and promoting media literacy to empower individuals to critically evaluate information.
- **Reducing Risks of Abuse and Bias:** Certain AI algorithms can amplify biases and contribute to the formation of “filter bubbles” and echo chambers, where individuals are primarily exposed to information that confirms their existing beliefs. Businesses should be aware of these risks and take steps to mitigate them, such as by promoting diverse perspectives and designing algorithms that prioritize balanced and objective information.

The AI Ethics Obligation of Businesses

Businesses have an ethical obligation to use AI responsibly in their corporate communications. This includes addressing concerns related to bias, fairness, privacy, transparency, and the potential for manipulation and job displacement.

- **Establishing Ethical Principles for Artificial Intelligence in Business Communication:** Companies should develop comprehensive ethical guidelines that govern the use of AI technologies in their business communication practices. These guidelines should address key issues such as bias, fairness, privacy, transparency, and accountability. The guidelines should be regularly reviewed and updated to reflect the latest advancements in AI and their ethical implications.
- **Advancing Responsible Innovation in Artificial Intelligence:** Organizations should foster and promote responsible AI innovation that benefits society and minimizes potential harm. This may involve funding or partnering with research institutions, participating in public discourse on AI ethics, and prioritizing the development of AI systems that are aligned with human values. Businesses should also be transparent about how they use AI in their communication processes and empower stakeholders to understand how their data is being used and to have a voice in shaping AI policies.

VII. CONCLUSION

In today's interconnected and rapidly evolving business landscape, effective communication strategies are more critical than ever. The emergence of artificial intelligence (AI) has ushered in a paradigm shift in business communication. Organizations are increasingly leveraging AI-powered tools such as chatbots, email automation, social media listening and analysis platforms, and AI-driven content creation to enhance their communication efforts. AI offers unprecedented opportunities to improve efficiency, personalize interactions, and expand reach. By strategically implementing AI tools, businesses can optimize their communication strategies, enhance stakeholder engagement, and drive growth.

However, the adoption of any new technology comes with its own set of challenges, risks, and ethical considerations. Businesses must prioritize transparency, accuracy, and data security to mitigate the potential for unethical AI usage. Furthermore, organizations need to invest in training and development programs to equip their workforce with the skills needed to thrive in the AI-augmented communication landscape.

The future of AI in business communication is bright, with emerging trends such as hyper-personalization, emotional AI, and the metaverse promising to further transform how businesses connect with their stakeholders. As communication tools and technologies continue to evolve, AI-driven automation will play an increasingly important role in helping businesses meet the dynamic demands of the modern business world.

This chapter has provided an in-depth analysis of the transformative impact of AI on business communication. We have explored the fundamental concepts of AI, examined its core technologies, and analyzed its diverse applications across various communication functions. We have also addressed the ethical considerations and potential risks associated with AI adoption, emphasizing the importance of responsible and ethical AI implementation.

By acknowledging both the opportunities and challenges presented by AI, businesses can harness its power to drive positive change and achieve their communication objectives. It is crucial for organizations to stay informed about emerging AI trends and their potential impact on business communication. Embracing a proactive and adaptive approach to communication will be essential for navigating the evolving technological landscape and ensuring continued success in the years to come.

Provide an overview of the impacts that AI technology has created: I plan to discuss the multifaceted impact of AI on business communication, highlighting its key advantages, potential challenges, and transformative effects.

Point out the need for human and AI collaboration: I will emphasize the importance of human intelligence in conjunction with AI to develop optimal communication strategies.

Consider and give options for businesses: I will provide practical guidance for businesses on how to integrate AI into their communication practices in an ethical and responsible manner, including recommendations for employee training and development, and strategies for adapting to future changes.

Analyze the impact of AI on communication as a whole: I will broaden the discussion to explore the broader societal implications of AI in communication, including its potential effects on democracy, social relationships, and individual well-being.

Finish with a strong motivational speech: I will conclude by underscoring the importance of embracing AI as a powerful tool for enhancing business communication and driving positive change, while also acknowledging the need for careful consideration of its ethical and societal implications.

Focusing on the Necessity of Human-AI Cooperation

While AI technology offers immense potential for optimizing automation, data analysis, and personalization, it is crucial to remember that AI is not intended to completely replace human communicators. Instead, the most effective communication strategies are likely to emerge from a synergistic blend of human input and AI capabilities. By combining the unique strengths of both, organizations can develop communication systems that are both highly personalized and exceptionally efficient, while also leveraging human creativity and strategic thinking. AI excels at analyzing data, identifying patterns, and automating repetitive tasks, while humans possess superior emotional intelligence, relationship management skills, and the ability to adapt to complex and nuanced situations. By combining these complementary capabilities, businesses can overcome the limitations of each and develop communication approaches that are more effective and impactful than either could achieve alone. This collaborative approach will be essential for navigating the rapid changes and challenges of the evolving business communication landscape, ensuring that AI serves to augment, rather than hinder, meaningful human interaction.

REFERENCES

Adamopoulou, E., & Moussiades, L. (2020). Chatbots: History, technology, and applications. *Machine Learning with Applications*, *2*, 100007. DOI: 10.1016/j.mlwa.2020.100006

Brynjolfsson, E., & McAfee, A. (2014). *The second machine age: Work, progress, and prosperity in a time of brilliant technologies*. W. W. Norton & Company.

Burdea, G. C., & Coiffet, P. (2003). *Virtual reality technology*. John Wiley & Sons.

Chowdhary, K. R. (2020a). *Natural language processing*. Springer.

Chowdhary, K. R. (2020b). Natural language processing. Fundamentals of Artificial Intelligence, 603-649.

Doshi-Velez, F., & Kim, B. (2017). Towards a rigorous science of interpretable machine learning. *arXiv preprint arXiv:1702.08608*.

Dwivedi, Y. K., Hughes, L., Baabdullah, A. M., Ribeiro-Navarrete, S., Jain, P., & Tamilmani, K. (2023). Artificial Intelligence (AI): Multidisciplinary perspectives on emerging challenges, opportunities, and agenda for research, practice and policy. *International Journal of Information Management*, *68*, 102399.

Goodfellow, I., Bengio, Y., & Courville, A. (2016). *Deep learning*. MIT press.

IBM Cloud Education. (2022, December 21). *What is natural language generation?* Retrieved from https://www.ibm.com/cloud/learn/natural-language-processing

Kaplan, A., & Haenlein, M. (2019). Siri, Siri in my hand, who's the fairest in the land? On the interpretations, illustrations, and implications of artificial intelligence. *Business Horizons*, *62*(1), 15–25. DOI: 10.1016/j.bushor.2018.08.004

Kumar, V., Ayedh, A. H., Khan, I. A., & Jha, G. (2019). Artificial intelligence in marketing: A review and future research directions. *European Journal of Marketing*.

Kumar, V., Rajan, B., Venkatesan, R., & Lecinski, J. (2019). Understanding the role of artificial intelligence in personalized engagement marketing. *California Management Review*, *61*(4), 135–155. DOI: 10.1177/0008125619859317

Mitchell, T. M. (1997). *Machine learning*. McGraw-Hill.

Mittelstadt, B. D., Allo, P., Taddeo, M., Wachter, S., & Floridi, L. (2016). The ethics of algorithms: Mapping the debate. *Big Data & Society*, *3*(2). DOI: 10.1177/2053951716679679

O'Neil, C. (2016). *Weapons of math destruction: How big data increases inequality and threatens democracy*. Crown.

Pangun, G. (2019a). *Artificial intelligence (AI) system's key characteristics*. Towards Data Science.

Pangun, J. M. (2019b). *Artificial intelligence: Concepts, drivers, and business implications*. IGI Global.

Russell, S. J., & Norvig, P. (2003). *Artificial intelligence: A modern approach*. Pearson Education.

Scherer, K. R. (2005). What are emotions? And how can they be measured? *Social Sciences Information. Information Sur les Sciences Sociales*, *44*(4), 695–729. DOI: 10.1177/0539018405058216

Syed, M. (2023). *The role of AI in social media marketing*. Simplilearn.

KEY TERMS AND DEFINITIONS

Artificial Intelligence (AI): The branch of computer science concerning the creation of computing devices that are able to accomplish activities which need human reasoning.

Deep Learning (DL): An area of ML concerned with the use of artificial neural networks with more than one hidden layer for the purpose of data analysis and feature extraction.

General or Strong AI: The AI improves upon human-level or broad-level intelligence, allowing machines to understand and learn the processing of basic human actions like speech.

Machine Learning (ML): It allows automatic recognition of patterns and trends without requiring programmed instructions and algorithms to learn by interpreting data and subsequently identifying trends.

Narrow (or Weak) AI: This form of AI is specialized, designed to handle specific narrowly defined tasks like playing chess, product recommendation, or filtering emails for spam.

Natural Language Processing (NLP): NLP systems operate primarily through the application of artificial intelligence as well as through the interaction of the user and the machine, making it possible for computers to talk and converse with human operators.

Super AI: This speculative form of AI goes beyond human capabilities, claiming to take hold of advanced supercomputers and potential threats to humanity.

Chapter 6
Construction and Validation of the Perceptions of AI Usage Scale in a Foreign Language Learning Context

Selami Aydin
https://orcid.org/0000-0003-1614-874X
Istanbul Medeniyet University, Turkey

ABSTRACT

The potential benefits of AI usage in EFL learning are directly related to how learners perceive AI as a language learning tool and environment. However, no studies have focused on constructing and validating a scale that aims to measure language learners' perceptions of AI usage. The current study aims to develop a valid and reliable scale of learners' perceptions of AI usage in EFL learning. The sampling of the study consisted of 26 students in the interview group, eight in the piloting phase, 525 participants in the Exploratory Factor Analysis (EFA) stage, 383 in the Confirmatory Factor Analysis (CFA) group, and 86 students in the test-retest reliability group. The study concluded that the Perceptions of AI Usage Scale (PAS), consisting of 17 items, obtained a high level of reliability, a two-factor solution, and a high level of test-retest reliability.

DOI: 10.4018/979-8-3373-5681-5.ch006

INTRODUCTION

EFL learning is of vital importance since it provides opportunities for interaction and communication on a global scale. In other words, since English is the most common language used in fields such as education, science, technology, tourism, and aviation, knowing English gives a unique chance to find jobs in one's home country and abroad (Rumsey, 2024). Moreover, it is necessary to have basic language skills in English to find opportunities to study at schools and universities. As English is the most popular language regarding web content, representing 59% of all languages (Statista, 2024), it is necessary to know English to access information. Knowing English is also advantageous for following films, shows, and books within the scope of popular culture (Harmer, 2003). Second, from the learners' perspective, EFL learning offers certain benefits, such as providing opportunities for interaction and communication in diverse contexts (Verga & Kotz, 2013). Within this scope, it develops intercultural awareness (Byram, 2012), problem-solving and critical thinking skills (W. Liang & Fung, 2021), and increases cognitive and affective functions (Kennedy, 2006).

While there are certain benefits to being proficient in the target language, several potential problems exist during the EFL learning process. For instance, the lack of authentic and contextual materials and practice opportunities and overreliance on using their first language during the learning process are some of the factors that result in ineffective learning (Savran Çelik & Aydın, 2018). In this way, learners experience difficulties due to the lack of comprehensible input and output, ineffective grammar and vocabulary knowledge, and the lack of basic language skills (Krashen, 1982). Inevitably, these problems may be sources of certain affective problems such as amotivation, demotivation, anxiety, EFL learners, and low levels of self-confidence. From this psychological perspective, the process may result in negative perceptions of and attitudes toward learning the new language and failure (Author, 2020).

AI applications may bring potential solutions to the problems encountered in the EFL learning process (Sayici & Aydın, 2025). For instance, they can be used for translation from the native language to the target language or vice versa within the scope of cross-cultural learning (Shadiev et al., 2018) and for identifying and correcting mistakes in written and oral language (Kanero et al., 2018). Moreover, AI applications can be regarded as collaborative and autonomous learning tools and environments through which learners can interact and communicate in the target language (Aydın, 2024; Kannan & Munday, 2018). Learners can also access authentic and contextual materials to develop basic language skills and knowledge of grammar and vocabulary. Learners can experience adaptive and personalized learning based on their needs, expectations, performance, and proficiency levels

(Hartono et al., 2023). On the other hand, the efficient use of AI in the language learning process depends on how EFL learners perceive AI tools and environments. In other words, learners' perceptions of AI usage can profoundly affect achievement in the target language. From this point of view, two significant problems appear in the research context. First, there is a serious lack of research on learners' perceptions of using AI-based tools and environments in the EFL learning process, as clarified below. Second, the current literature does not have a scale for measuring EFL learners' perceptions of AI usage. Below, a research synthesis is provided after drawing a theoretical background regarding learners' perceptions of AI use in the EFL learning process.

Theoretical Background

AI, a multidisciplinary combination of computer science and linguistics, is able to perform multitasks, including understanding, learning, and acquiring knowledge (Aydın & Zeinolabedini, 2024). AI can use creative language within this scope by reactivating current knowledge (Cizrelioğlu & Aydin, 2024; Sarker, 2022). From this perspective, the usage of AI in the foreign language learning process is based on the *Activity Theory* that deals with the mental capabilities of the learner who is capable of using the cultural and technical aspects of human actions (Bertelsen & Bødker, 2003). AI may also provide self-regulated and self-directed learning within the scope of *autonomous learning* that depends on Bandura's (1986) Social Cognitive Theory, which is defined as an agentive activity of initiative, resourcefulness, and persistence in one's self-regulated and/or self-directed learning (Ponton & Rhea, 2006). *Learner-centeredness,* a process that requires involvement in activities and tasks (Dang, 2006), is also appropriate for AI usage, which may provide a learning environment within the scope of engagement and involvement. Moreover, AI tools may provide opportunities for *interaction* that is connected with technology (Anderson & Elloumi, 2004). In this way, learners can have comprehensible input and negotiation of meaning (Ellis, 1999). In addition, under the concept of *active learning* that is considered as a model for student-centered teaching (Meyers, 1993), *blended learning* that integrates technology and face-to-face components (Hockly, 2018), and *flipped learning* that includes interactive learning activities in traditional and technology-based environments (Ercan & Aydin, 2022; Romero et al., 2019) may constitute a theoretical background for the AI usage in the foreign language learning process. In addition, since *constructivism* establishes basic components for learning outputs (Wood et al., 1976), AI can be seen as the source of action-taking during activities within the scope of *scaffolding,* a process through which tasks and activities are organized in accordance with learners' intellectual readiness (Vygotsky, 1978).

Perception can be defined as the organization and interpretation of sensory information to understand the information in relation to the environment (Schacter et al., 2009) and shaped by the learner's attention, expectations, memory, and learning (Bernstein et al., 2008). According to the *Social Cognitive Theory,* which underlines that cognitive processes and environment affect human behaviors, agency is based on beliefs, attitudes, and perceptions that may directly affect human behaviors (Fishbein & Ajzen, 1975). From this constructive perspective, perception is the end product depending on the interaction between stimulus and the knowledge and expectations of the learner (Démuth, 2013). From a computational perspective, perception is operated by easy mechanical rules that can be applied to unconscious entities rather than conscious intentionality or motivation (Gregory, 2015). Within this scope, it can be inferred that perception may depend on algorithms that can be applied to apprehend human perception but not on conscious or alive senses (Démuth, 2013).

Research Results

In a general perspective, research shows conflicting results regarding the use of AI in the EFL learning process. For instance, AI tools provided opportunities for meaningful conversations and collaborative learning (Tafazoli et al., 2019). Moussalli and Cardoso (2020) found that AI usage was beneficial for comprehension in basic language skills, grammar, and vocabulary learning. Similar positive effects were reported regarding reading comprehension (Yılmaz & Aydın, 2025), speaking performance (Ballıdağ & Aydın, 2025; Yin et al., 2021), and writing quality (Berk & Aydın, 2025; Fitria, 2021). Liang et al. (2023) reported that AI utilization enhanced self-confidence and motivation and decreased anxiety. Bailey et al. (2021) also noted that AI integration into language learning caused an increase in motivation. On the other hand, research demonstrated certain negative conclusions. As an example, Wang et al. (Wang et al., 2024) found that learners had unsatisfactory experiences due to the lack of teachers' input and subject teaching (Alrajhi, 2023). Learners also found the feedback provided by AI tools too technical (Yu et al., 2022). Moreover, AI tools increased plagiarism within students' assignments, failed in complicated reasoning (Perkins, 2023), debilitated problem-solving and critical thinking skills in the writing context (Nguyen, 2023), and finally produced decontextualized content (Wilson et al., 2021).

While studies cited above mainly focus on AI-based experimental environments through which AI tools are mainly used to teach basic language skills and knowledge areas, research is insufficient to comprehensively describe how learners perceive AI-based language learning (An et al., 2023). In a recent study, An et al. (2023)

explored 524 high school learners' perceptions of AI-based language learning. After collecting data using a survey, they found that cultural interest, performance expectancy, and instrumental promotion could predict learners' behavioral intentions regarding using AI tools. In a study by Zou et al. (2020), university students' attitudes were investigated within the scope of the development of speaking skills using AI-assisted mobile applications. They found that students preferred AI tools due to the lack of limited teacher feedback. Regarding the study, it should be noted that the focus was not on learners' perceptions but on their attitudes and speaking skills rather than the overall language learning process. In another study by Persulessy et al. (2024), the focus was on engineering students' perceptions of AI usage in vocabulary learning. This descriptive research concluded that learners had positive perceptions of vocabulary learning using AI tools. In a mixed-method study, Phan (2023) examined 100 learners' perceptions of AI-powered writing tools and found that learners had positive perceptions concerning the simplicity, adaptability, and accessibility of AI tools in the EFL writing context. Considering that research was mainly confined to students' perspectives on using AI-based tools in school work and teachers' perspectives on plagiarism, Ibrahim et al. (2023) compared the performance of ChatGPT among students in 32 university-level courses using a global survey across five countries. They concluded that learners had a consensus regarding using the tool. On the other hand, it should be stated that the study focused on learners' perspectives and was not related to language learning. Similarly, Demir and Güraksın (2022) examined middle school students' perceptions of the concept of AL through metaphors in general but not specifically foreign language learning and found that learners had mainly positive perceptions. Among the studies that did not focus on foreign language learners, Al-Badi et al. (2022) also noted that both university students and teachers had positive perceptions of AI implementation in personalized learning.

In the current literature, no study has focused on constructing and validating a scale that aims to measure language learners' perceptions of AI usage. Moreover, few studies focusing on measuring perceptions have some potential problems. For instance, An et al. (2023) adapted the items in the questionnaire from the previous studies rather than developing a new scale. While the tool indicated a high level of internal consistency (Cronbach's alpha=.97) and validity (% of variance between 74 and 98), it included items about effort and performance expectancy, social influence, facilitating conditions, behavioral intention, motivation, learning experience, cultural interest, and instrumentality-promotion in the AI context rather than directly focusing on EFL learners' overall perceptions of AI usage in the EFL learning context. In the study by Ibrahim et al. (2023) that reported data on perceptions of conversational AI across university courses, no findings were reported regarding the validity and reliability of the data collection tools. Repeatedly, it should be noted that this study did not deal with learners' perceptions in the language learning context. In the previously cited study, while Persulessy et al. (2024) administered a six-item questionnaire to 29 engineering students' perceptions of vocabulary learning, they did not report data on the validity and reliability. Last, Wang et al. (2024) used an adapted version of the scale developed by Law et al. (2019), who measured student enrolment, learning motivation, social, teaching, and cognitive presence, and learning performance. In the adapted version of the scale, Wang et al. (2024) focused on social, cognitive, and teaching presence and enjoyment rather than learners' perceptions. While the scale had acceptable levels of internal consistency in Cronbach's alpha for social (.76), cognitive (.90), and teaching presence (.70), no data were reported regarding the overall scale. No data were also reported for % of variance the scale and variables measured in the study.

Overview of the Current Study

As emphasized above, EFL learning is of utmost importance due to providing opportunities for interaction and communication in the areas of education, science, technology, tourism, and aviation at a global scale. However, while learners need comprehensible input and output for developing basic language skills and knowledge areas, some potential problems in the EFL learning process exist, such as the lack of authentic and contextual materials and practice opportunities and overreliance on the use of the first language. From this perspective, AI-based tools, environments, and applications may have the potential to provide opportunities for authentic and contextual materials, practice, and mistake and error correction within collaborative, autonomous, adaptive, and personalized learning perspectives. Nevertheless, there is no consensus on AI usage in the EFL learning process since research shows positive and negative results regarding basic language skills and learning areas. Moreover, the results of a fairly limited number of studies show no consensus regarding how EFL learners perceive AI-based tools during the learning process. It should also be noted that the studies focusing on the perceptions deal with vocabulary learning and writing rather than EFL learning on a broader perspective, while some studies on learners' perceptions do not concentrate on language learning but the implementation of AI in general educational settings. The most dramatic point is that no study focuses on constructing and validating a scale that aims to measure language learners' perceptions of AI usage. While few studies use adapted and compiled measurement tools focusing on various aspects noted above and lacking evidence for reliability and validity, no original scale has been developed for measuring learners' perceptions of AI usage in EFL learning. With these concerns in mind, the current study aims to develop a valid and reliable scale of learners' perceptions of AI usage in EFL learning and seeks the answer to the following research question:

How valid and reliable is the Perceptions of AI-usage Scale?

METHOD

Research Context

Scale development and validation constitute a significant place in the research context due to the complex phenomena of the processes of teaching and learning a foreign language (Aydın et al., 2024) and include several steps. First, it is necessary to obtain item generation and content validity assessment. Next, the scale should involve construction in the order of piloting and pre-testing, reducing the number of items, and providing evidence for underlying factors. Finally, it seems necessary to find and test the number of dimensions and to obtain the values regarding the reliability and validity of the scale (Boateng et al., 2018). Considering the phases clarified, the current study follows the steps of (1) *substantive and content validity*, (2) *construct validity in EFA and reliability*, and (3) *construct validity in CFA, criterion validity, and reliability,* as shown in Figure 1.

Figure 1. Flowchart of the scale development process (Aydın et al., 2024)

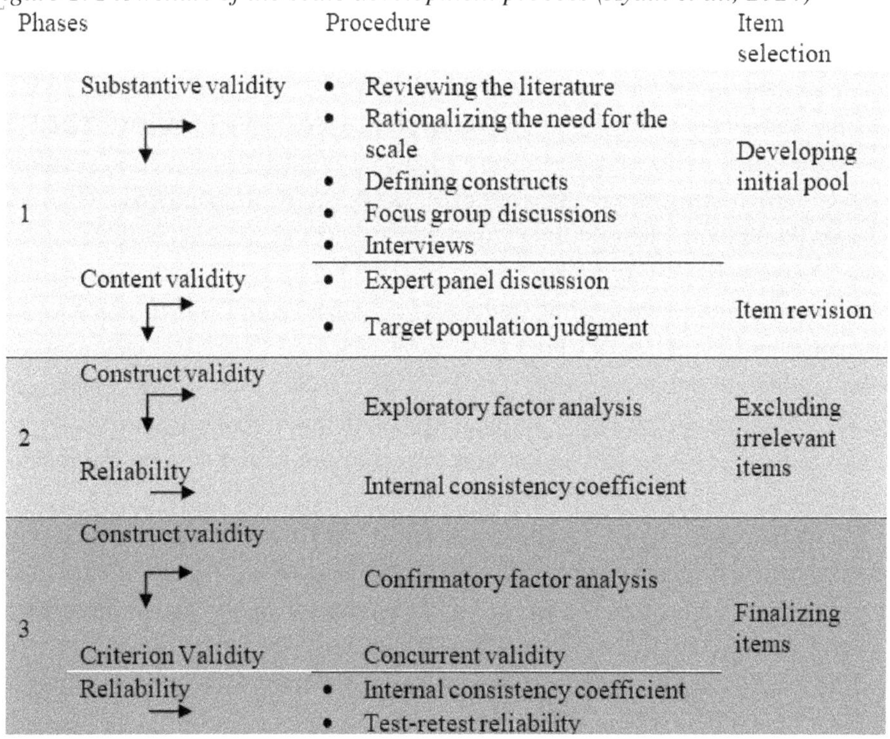

The study is designed following the psychological and educational testing *Standards* that are based on best practices in psychological and educational testing and measurements that include validity as a unitary concept as an indication of the contribution to construct validity (AERA et al., 2014; Messick, 1995). It should also be noted that validation of a scale includes *content, response processes, internal structure, relations to other factors,* and *consequences* that are determined for interpretation (Downing, 2003). In brief, the study aims to find evidence from the internal structure and relations to other variables at the item and scale levels; there is a strong necessity for following the procedure for test specifications, item development, reviewing, developing scoring procedures, and revision (AERA et al., 2014).

Participants

In the study, five groups were assigned to collect data. The first group included the participants in the interviews. The second group involved the ones in the piloting phase. Then, a third group of participants were used in the EFA group, whereas the fourth one consisted of the participants who were used in the CFA group. The last group included the students who participated in the test-retest step. The descriptives of each group of participants are provided below and shown in Table 1.

Nineteen students enrolled in the Department of English Language Teaching undergraduate program participated in the interviews. The group included 19 female (73.1%) and seven male (73.1%) participants. The mean score for their age was 22.04, within the range of 21 and 24 (SD=0.87). Of the participants, 12 were third-grade students (46.2%), while 14 were fourth-grade (35.8%). All of the students who participated in the interviews were advanced English learners (C1) according to the Common European Framework of Reference (CEFR) standards.

Eight participants in the piloting group were undergraduate and graduate students of the Department of English Language Teaching. The group included one male (12.5%) and seven female (87.5) students. The mean score for their age was 23.8 between 21 and 24 (SD=3.01). Four participants were fourth-grade students (50.0%) in the graduate program, whereas four students (50.0%) were in the department's graduate program. Regarding their language proficiency, four participants were at the advanced (C1) level (50.0%), while four students (50%) were at the mastery level (C2) according to the CEFR standards.

The explanatory sample group consisted of 525 participants enrolled in the Department of English Language Teaching undergraduate program. The group comprised 394 female (69.3%) and 161 (30.7%) male students. The mean score for their age was 21.15 between 18 and 29 (STD=1.95). The participants were first-, (n=180, 34.3%), second- (n=103, 19.6%), third- (n=98, 18.7%), and fourth-grade (n=144, 27.4%) students. All of the participants were advanced learners of English (C1) (n=525, 100.0%) learners of English according to the CEFR standards.

The sample group in the confirmatory group consisted of 383 participants. The group included 255 female (66.6%) and 128 (33.4%) male students. The mean score for age was found to be 21.03 (STD=2.65), within the range of 17 and 35. The participants were preparatory (n=70, 18.3%), first-, (n=92, 24.0%), second- (n=93, 24.3%), third- (n=59, 15.4%), and fourth-grade (n=69, 18.0%) students. They were intermediate (B1) (n=35, 9.1%), upper-intermediate (B2) (n=167, 43.6%), and advanced (C1) (n=181, 47.3%) learners of English according to the CEFR standards. Of the participants, 210 (54.8%) students enrolled in the Department of English Language Teaching, whereas 102 (26.6%) were from the Department of English Language and Literature. Finally, 71 (18.6) students enrolled in the Department of Translation and Interpretation (English).

The test-retest group in the study consisted of 86 participants. The mean score for their age was 18.51 (STD=.65) between 18 and 21. The group included 56 females (65.1%) and 30 males (34.9). The participants were preparation (n=35, 40.7%), first- (n=46, 53.5%), and second-grade (n=5, 5.8%) students. They were intermediate (B1) (n=9, 10.5%), upper-intermediate (B2) (n=35, 40.7%), and advanced (C1) (n=42, 48.8%) learners of English according to the CEFR standards. Finally, they studied in the Departments of English Language Teaching (n=40, 46.5), English Language and Literature (n=33, 38.4), and Translation and Interpretation (n=13, 15.1%).

Table 1. Descriptives for the participants

	Sample 1: Interview (n=26)		**Sample 2: Piloting (n=8)**		**Sample 3: EFA (n=525)**		**Sample 4: CFA (n=383)**		**Sample 5: Test-retest reliability (n=86)**	
	Mean	**Std. Dev.**	**Mean**	**Std. Dev.**	**Mean**	**Std. Dev.**	**Mean**	**Std. Dev.**	**Mean**	**Std. Dev.**
Age	22.04	0.87	23.75	3.01	21.15	1.95	21.03	2.65	18.51	.65
	N	%	N	%	N	%	N	%	N	%
Gender										
Female	19	73.1	7	87.5	161	30.7	255	66.6	56	65.1
Male	7	26.9	1	12.5	394	69.3	128	33.4	30	34.9
Grade										
Prep.							70	18.3	35	40.7
1					180	34.3	92	24.0	46	53.5
2					103	19.6	93	24.3	5	5.8
3	12	46.2			98	18.7	59	15.4		

continued on following page

Table 1. Continued

	Sample 1: Interview (n=26)		Sample 2: Piloting (n=8)		Sample 3: EFA (n=525)		Sample 4: CFA (n=383)		Sample 5: Test-retest reliability (n=86)	
	Mean	**Std. Dev.**	**Mean**	**Std. Dev.**	**Mean**	**Std. Dev.**	**Mean**	**Std. Dev.**	**Mean**	**Std. Dev.**
4	14	35.8	4	50.0	144	27.4	69	18.0		
MA			4	50.0						
Proficiency										
B1							35	9.1	9	10.5
B2							167	43.6	35	40.7
C1	26	100.0	4	50.0	525	100.0	181	47.3	42	48.8
C2			4	50.0						
Department										
English Language Teaching	26	100.0	8	100.0	525	100.0	210	54.8	40	46.5
English Language and Literature							102	26.6	33	38.4
Translation and Interpretation							71	18.6	13	15.1

Tools

The data collection tools consisted of a background questionnaire and the scale developed in the study. First, the background questionnaire was used to interrogate participants' ages, genders, grades, proficiency levels in the target language, and departments they enrolled. Second, the items developed through the study were used to measure participants' perceptions of AI usage in the foreign language learning process. The scale consisted of 46 items in the EFA process and 31 items in the CFA process. The items were presented on a 5-point Likert scale (1=strongly disagree, 2=disagree, 3=undecided, 4=agree, and 5=strongly agree).

Procedure

After obtaining approval from the ethics committee, the online versions of the research tools were prepared and shared via Google Forms. The participants invited were informed about the purpose of the study. They were also informed that the participation was voluntary. In addition, they were informed that the anonymity and confidentiality of the responses were ensured. Finally, the participants were invited to participate in the study using posts on Google Classroom. Each of the forms was kept online for around one month.

The items were generated from the interview group with the participants in the Department of English Language Teaching. Then, a literature review was performed for item generation. The researcher managed the interviews before the saturation and triangulation process of the data gathered. In the piloting stage, 65 items that developed independently were reduced to 46 items. The researchers and eight participants checked the items regarding syntactic, lexical, and semantic clarity and consistency. The whole process was performed in English.

The potential items were administered to the students in the exploratory group. After the statistical analysis in the exploratory study, the items were reduced to 31. Next, the factor structure and psychometric properties of the generated scale were assessed with the confirmatory group. Last, the scale was administered to the participants in the test-retest reliability group.

Data Analysis

IBM SPSS Version 21 and IBM SPSS Amos Version 22 were preferred for the analysis process. Before carrying out the analysis, sample size criterion, univariate and multivariate normality, univariate and multivariate outliers, multicollinearity assumptions, and linearity and homoscedasticity were checked (Tabachnick & Fidell, 2014). Then, the EFA, as a method used to uncover the underlying structure of the variables, was used to see the construct of the scale. The maximum likelihood extraction method was also preferred. The items with low factor loadings that are lower than .70 and communalities lower than .50 were removed from the scale. The remaining items were reevaluated through the EFA process. Last, Cronbach's Alpha coefficient was performed to measure internal consistency levels.

RESULTS

Explanatory Factor Analysis

Before analyzing the data, the assumptions of EFA were tested to check missing data, sample adequacy, and normality. The participant-to-item ratio was found to be 11.4:1 within 525 participants and 46 initial items. The ratio indicated that the group was adequate for the analysis (Hair et al., 1998). Then, the assumption of normality was tested using the skewness (> 2) and kurtosis (> 7) values within an acceptable range (Pallant, 2013). The values of the items fell within the acceptable range (minimum=-1.50, maximum=0.48 for *skewness*, and minimum=-1.15, maximum=5.97 for *kurtosis*). Bartlett's test of sphericity (p=.00) and the Kaiser-Meyer-Olkin KMO test (.93) were used to determine how suited the data was for factor analysis, indicated that the data was appropriate for the EFA, as shown in the following table.

After observing that the items in the scale worked best for the EFA, commonalities, and factors loading were performed. The items were removed sequentially considering the commonalities and factors loadings. Among 46 items, 15 items with communalities lower than .50 and factor analysis lower than .60 were removed from the scale (Hair et al., 1998). Then, the remaining 31 items were reexamined regarding Bartlett's test of sphericity and the Kaiser-Meyer-Olkin KMO test. According to Bartlett's test of sphericity (p=.00) and the Kaiser-Meyer-Olkin KMO test (.90), the data were found to be appropriate for the EFA, as shown in Table 2.

Table 2. Bartlett's test of sphericity and the Kaiser-Meyer-Olkin KMO test

		Initial Check (Item number=46)	**After-item-removing check (Item number=31)**
Kaiser-Meyer-Olkin Measure of Sampling Adequacy.		**.93**	**0.90**
Bartlett's Test of Sphericity	Approx. Chi-Square	13049.9	8376.1
	df	1035	465
	Sig.	.00	.00

For the remaining 31 items, 66.22% *of variance explained* by seven factors, as shown in Figure 2. Percentages of variance were 11.65 for the first factor, 23.25 for the second factor, 35.31 for the third factor, 44.61 for the fourth factor, 51.91 for the fifth factor, 59.85 for the sixth factor, and 66.22 for the last factor. *Parallel analysis* was carried out to examine the statistical simulation of the set of random data with the same participants and the number of factors (Watkins, 2018). The random data eigenvalues were found to be 1.0 for root, means, and *prcntyle*, indicating compatibility with the scree plot. The Cronbach's alpha internal consistency coefficient calculated over the 31 items was .90. Last, the inter-item correlation was between r = .068 to r =. 629. Finally, the values for *Cronbach's alpha if item deleted* was found between .894 and .904, as indicated in Table 3.

Table 3. Communalities, factor loadings, and item-total statistics of the items (n=525)

Items	Communalities	Factor Loadings							Corrected Item Total Correlations	Cronbach's Alpha If Item Deleted
		Factor 1	Factor 2	Factor 3	Factor 4	Factor 5	Factor 6	Factor 7		
Factor: Writing practice										
39. AI tools are useful for generating ideas.	.817	.638							.435	.897
40. AI tools are useful for planning.	.859	.713							.527	.896
41. AI tools are useful for outlining.	.770	.690							.509	.896
42. AI tools are useful for summarizing.	.766	.674							.438	.897
43. AI tools are useful for paraphrasing.	.826	.716							.451	.897
44. AI tools are useful for note-taking.	1.131	.683							.501	.896
45. AI tools are useful for proofreading.	1.012	.667							.571	.895
46. AI tools are useful for receiving feedback.	1.144	.618							.504	.896
Factor: Contributions to language learning										
4. AI-based environments provide equality in language learning opportunities.	1.071		.697						.404	.898
7. I believe that AI-supported learning is more effective than traditional methods.	1.451		.767						.503	.896
8. AI tools can enhance my communicative skills.	1.307		.752						.540	.895
9. The integration of AI tools into language classes contributes to autonomous learning.	.933		.746						.585	.895
10. The integration of AI tools in language classes contributes to personalized learning.	.937		.743						.567	.895
11. The integration of AI tools in language classes contributes to adaptive learning.	.879		.703						.602	.895
Factor: Pronunciation, listening, and speaking skills										
21. I find AI tools helpful in practicing my pronunciation skills.	1.813			1.187					.549	.895
22. AI tools enhance my listening comprehension.	1.736			1.133					.582	.894
27. I find that AI tools enhance my speaking performance.	1.579			.888					.605	.894
Factor: Concerns										
35. I think that AI tools produce unnatural language content.	1.274				.814				.140	.902
36. AI tools produce inappropriate language content.	1.461				.927				.171	.902
37. AI tools produce fake information.	1.326				.919				.068	.904
38. I encounter decontextualized content when I use AI tools.	1.220				.884				.231	.901
Factor: Reading and writing skills										
20. AI tools help to improve my reading skills.	1.383					.617			.629	.893
26. I think that AI tools positively impact my reading comprehension.	1.173					.618			.618	.894

continued on following page

Table 3. Continued

Items	Communalities	Factor Loadings							Corrected Item Total Correlations	Cronbach's Alpha If Item Deleted
		Factor 1	Factor 2	Factor 3	Factor 4	Factor 5	Factor 6	Factor 7		
28. I believe that AI tools can positively influence my writing skills.	1.141					.866			.502	.896
29. I believe that AI tools positively influence writing quality.	1.043					.758			.542	.895
Factor: Affect										
14. AI tools provide emotional support in language learning.	1.591						.979		.472	.897
15. AI tools help to reduce my anxiety level.	1.534						.985		.468	.897
30. My participation in classroom activities has increased after I started using AI tools.	1.581						.687		.587	.894
Factor: Awareness										
32. I am aware of the increase in plagiarism in my papers due to the use of AI tools.	1.563							1.002	.279	.900
33. I believe that overreliance on writing with AI tools debilitates my critical thinking skills.	1.148							.773	.267	.900
34. I think the use of AI debilitates my problem-solving abilities.	1.184							.725	.279	.900

Figure 2. Scree Plot

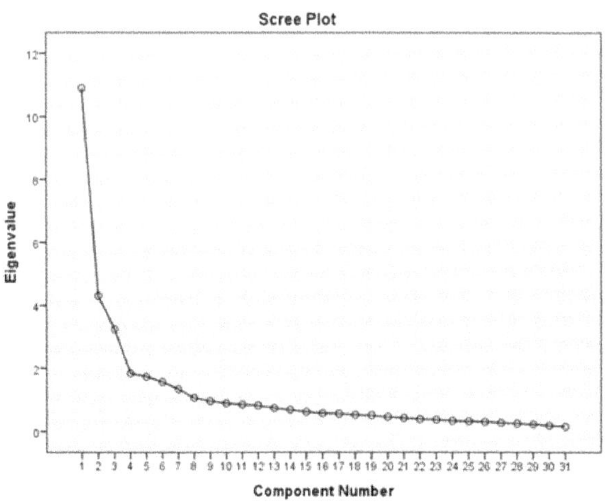

Confirmatory Factor Analysis

Before starting the CFA, the participant-to-item ratio and the assumption of normality, appropriateness, Mahalanobis distances, and the multicollinearity assumption were tested. First, the participant-to-item ratio was 12.4 within 383 participants and 31 items. This ratio was found to be adequate for the analysis (Hair et al., 1998). Second, the test for the assumption of normality indicated that the skewness (> 2) and kurtosis (> 7) values were within an acceptable range (Pallant, 2013). The values of the items fell within the acceptable range (minimum=-1.50, maximum=0.48 for *skewness*, and minimum=-1.15, maximum=5.97 for *kurtosis*). Third, the values for Bartlett's test of sphericity (p=.00) the Kaiser-Meyer-Olkin KMO test (.87), and Approx. Chi-Square (5284) showed that the data were appropriate for the analysis. Fourth, the Mahalanobis distances were computed and found to be .00, showing that the assumptions of the CFA were met in terms of the determination of the outliers (Mertler & Vannatta Reinhart, 2017; Tabachnick & Fidell, 2014). Last, according to the multicollinearity assumption statistics, the variance inflation factor (VIF) values were found to be less than 10 (minimum=1.46, maximum=3.17). In addition, the tolerance value (TV) was found to be higher than .10 (minimum=.34, maximum=.68) (Marcoulides & Raykov, 2019). The values showed that the multicollinearity assumption was met.

The CFA that used maximum likelihood was calculated to see the structure of the scale. For this purpose, the Chi-square test was performed to evaluate the model fit (χ^2 (122) = 248.61, p< .00). While the Chi-square test should show no significance, it should be stated that the test was sensitive to the sample size (Tabachnick & Fidell, 2014). The minimum discrepancy function by degrees of freedom divided (CMIN/DF) was found to be good since the values were 2.32 (good 3 > and 5 > acceptable) (Kyriazos, 2018). The measures of goodness of fit indexes were also calculated using the root mean square error of approximation (RMSEA), the comparative fit index (CFI), and the Tucker-Lewis Index (TLI). The values, which were .059 for RMSEA, .95 for CFI, and .94 for TLI, supported the model (Xia & Yang, 2019).

The factor loadings were between 1.23 and .57, indicating a two-factor solution, as shown in Figure 3. The internal consistency with Cronbach's alpha was .88, within the range of .87 and .88. Since no scale in the current literature might be associated with the scale developed in the current study, the concurrent validity could not be carried out. On the other hand, the rest-retest validity of the scale was checked regarding the data collected in one-month intervals. The correlation coefficient was found to be .82 (p=.00). This value demonstrated a good level of test-retest reliability.

Figure 3. Factor loadings as a result of CFA

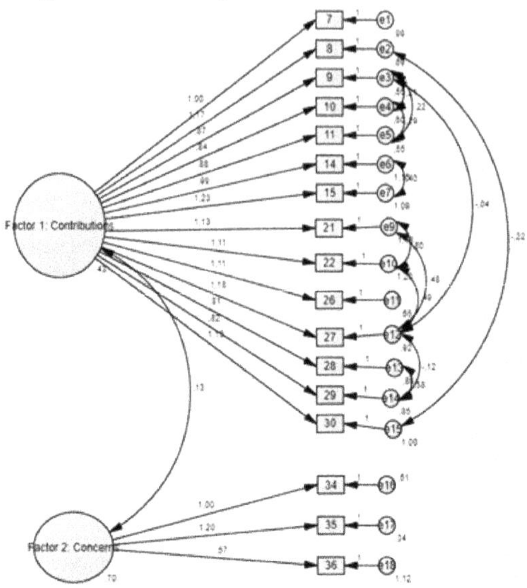

CONCLUSIONS AND DISCUSSION

According to the results obtained in the study that aims to develop a reliable and valid scale for the measurement of learners' perceptions of AI usage in the foreign language learning context, one conclusion was reached. The conclusion is that the PAS comprising 17 items shows a high level of internal consistency and an accepted level of variance explained by a two-factor solution as AI contributes *to foreign language learning* and *concerns with AI usage* when the CFA results are considered (see Appendix A). In other words, the scale indicates two-factor dimensionality and a high level of internal consistency coefficient. To this end, it can be stated that the PAS developed in the current study is a valid and reliable tool for measuring how foreign language learners perceive AI usage in their learning process.

This study seems significant for several reasons. First, since current literature indicates conflicting results regarding collaborative learning (Tafazoli et al., 2019), basic language skills, grammar and vocabulary learning (Fitria, 2021; Moussalli & Cardoso, 2020; Yin et al., 2021), self-confidence, motivation, and anxiety (Bailey et al., 2021; J. Liang et al., 2023), teachers' input and feedback (Wang et al., 2024; Yu et al., 2022), reasoning (Perkins, 2023), problem-solving and critical thinking skills (Nguyen, 2023) and decontextualized content (Wilson et al., 2021), the scale developed will contribute to clarifying the conflicting areas in the research context. Second, studies mostly focus on AI-based experimental environments through which AI tools are mainly used for teaching basic language skills and knowledge areas (Al-Badi et al., 2022; An et al., 2023; Demir & Güraksın, 2022; Ibrahim et al., 2023; Persulessy et al., 2024; Phan, 2023; Zou et al., 2020), the findings of the current study directly relate to how learners perceive AI in foreign language learning. Finally, no prior studies aim to construct and validate a scale that aims to measure language learners' perceptions of AI usage in the current literature, while several studies focus on measuring perceptions of conversational AI across university courses (Ibrahim et al., 2023), perceptions of vocabulary learning (Persulessy et al., 2024), student enrolment, learning motivation (An et al., 2023), social, teaching and cognitive presence, and learning performance (Wang et al., 2024), the current study directly focuses on learners' overall perceptions of AI usage in foreign language learning rather than specific areas. In conclusion, the study is the first attempt to measure learners' perceptions of AI usage in foreign language learning.

The study is not without limitations. First, the study is limited to the data collected from Turkish EFL learners who have similar educational and target language proficiency levels since they enrolled in the Departments of English Language Teaching, English Language and Literature, and Translation and Interpretation. Second, the statistical procedure of the study is confined to EFA, CFA, and test-retest reliability. In addition, the procedure lacks criterion validity since no prior study exists to compare it. Third, according to the Standards for Psychological and Educational Testing, the data collected is limited to internal structure and relations to other factors at a scale and item level (AERA et al., 2014). Finally, multiple models were not used in the study since the factor structure in the study was compatible with the results provided by EFA and CFA analyses.

Several recommendations for further research can also be noted. First, there is a strong need to test the validity and reliability of the scale in various language cultures and contexts using larger and heterogeneous sample groups. Second, further research should focus on multiple models in different structures to compare CFA and EFA structures using the sources of evidence for validity according to the Standards for Educational and Psychological Testing that were suggested by AERA et al. (2014). Finally, the Differential Item Functioning (DIF) for measuring different aspects in separate subgroups (Holland & Wainer, 1993) and the measurement invariance as an indication of the constructs should tested across specified groups (Vandenberg & Lance, 2000).

REFERENCES

AERA, APA, & NCME. (2014). Standards for educational and psychological testing. In *American Educational Research Association, American Psychological Association, & National Council on Measurement in Education*. American Educational Research Association.

Al-Badi, A., Khan, A., & Eid-Alotaibi, . (2022). Perceptions of learners and instructors towards artificial intelligence in personalized learning. *Procedia Computer Science*, *201*, 445–451. DOI: 10.1016/j.procs.2022.03.058

Alrajhi, A. S. (2023). Genre effect on Google Translate–assisted L2 writing output quality. *ReCALL*, *35*(3), 305–320. DOI: 10.1017/S0958344022000143

An, X., Chai, C., Li, Y., Zhou, Y., & Yang, B. (2023). Modeling students' perceptions of artificial intelligence assisted language learning. *Computer Assisted Language Learning*, 1–22. DOI: 10.1080/09588221.2023.2246519

Anderson, T., & Elloumi, F. (2004). *Theory and practice of online learning*. Athabasca University.

Aydın, S. (2024). Using ChatGPT in foreign language research: An overview. *Innovational Research in ELT*, *5*(1), 20–26. DOI: 10.29329/irelt.2024.1045.2

Aydın, S., Tekin, I., & Akkaş, F. (2024). Construction and validation of the foreign language learning enjoyment scale. *Psychology in the Schools*, *61*(2), 657–670. DOI: 10.1002/pits.23076

Aydın, S., & Zeinolabedini, M. (2024). Integrating artificial intelligence into foreign language learning: Learners' perspectives. *11th EJER Congress*.

Bailey, D., Southam, A., & Costley, J. (2021). Digital storytelling with chatbots: Mapping L2 participation and perception patterns. *Interactive Technology and Smart Education*, *18*(1), 85–103. DOI: 10.1108/ITSE-08-2020-0170

Ballıdağ, M., & Aydın, S. (2025). *A comparison of the effects of AI-based chatbots and peer interactions on speaking anxiety among EFL learners*. Future in Educational Research., DOI: 10.1002/fer3.70005

Bandura, A. (1986). *Social foundations of thought and action: A social cognitive theory*. Prentice Hall.

Berk, E. H., & Aydın, S. (2025). The impact of artificial intelligence-powered writing assistance systems on metacognitive writing strategies. In *Transformations in Digital Learning and Educational Technologies* (pp. 241–274). IGI Global., DOI: 10.4018/979-8-3373-3678-7.ch011

Bernstein, D., Nash, P., Clarke-Stewart, A., Penner, L., & Roy, E. (2008). *Essentials of psychology* (4th ed.). Houghton Mifflin Company.

Bertelsen, O., & Bødker, S. (2003). Activity Theory. In Carroll, C. (Ed.), *HCI models, theories, and frameworks: Toward a multidisciplinary science* (pp. 291–324). Elsevier., DOI: 10.1016/B978-155860808-5/50011-3

Boateng, G., Neilands, T., Frongillo, E., Melgar-Quiñonez, H., & Young, S. (2018). Best practices for developing and validating scales for health, social, and behavioral research: A primer. *Frontiers in Public Health*, *6*, 149. Advance online publication. DOI: 10.3389/fpubh.2018.00149 PMID: 29942800

Byram, M. (2012). Language awareness and (critical) cultural awareness – relationships, comparisons and contrasts. *Language Awareness*, *21*(1–2), 5–13. DOI: 10.1080/09658416.2011.639887

Cizrelioğlu, İ., & Aydin, S. (2024). Using artificial intelligence in EFL learning among multilingual young learners. In Z. Sanmugam, M. Edwards, B. Barkhaya, N. Khlaif (Ed.), *Fostering Inclusive Education With AI and Emerging Technologies* (pp. 303–322). IGI Global. DOI: 10.4018/979-8-3693-7255-5.ch013

Dang, H. (2006). Learner-centeredness and EFL instruction in Vietnam: A case study. *International Education Journal*, *7*(4), 598–610.

Demir, K., & Güraksın, G. (2022). Determining middle school students' perceptions of the concept of artificial intelligence: A metaphor analysis. *Participatory Educational Research*, *9*(2), 297–312. DOI: 10.17275/per.22.41.9.2

Démuth, A. (2013). *Perception theories*. Trnava University.

Downing, S. (2003). Validity: On the meaningful interpretation of assessment data. *Medical Education*, *37*(9), 830–837. DOI: 10.1046/j.1365-2923.2003.01594.x PMID: 14506816

Ellis, R. (1999). *Learning a second language through interaction*. John Benjamins Publishing. DOI: 10.1075/sibil.17

Ercan, G., & Aydin, S. (2022). Teachers' and learners' perceptions of flipped learning in a foreign language context. *FIRE: Futuristic Implementations of Research in Education*, *3*(2), 111–128.

Fishbein, M., & Ajzen, I. (1975). *Belief, attitude, intention, and behavior: An introduction to theory and research*. Addison-Wesley Publishing Company.

Fitria, T. (2021). Grammarly as AI-powered English writing assistant: Students' alternative for writing English. *Metathesis: Journal of English Language, Literature, and Teaching*, *5*(1), 65–78. DOI: 10.31002/metathesis.v5i1.3519

Gregory, R. (2015). *Eye and brain: The psychology of seeing*. Princeton University Press. DOI: 10.2307/j.ctvc77h66

Hair, J., Black, W., Babin, B., Anderson, R., & Tatham, R. (1998). *Multivariate data analysis*. Pearson.

Harmer, J. (2003). Popular culture, methods, and context. *ELT Journal*, *57*(3), 288–294. DOI: 10.1093/elt/57.3.288

Hartono, W., Nurfitri, N., Ridwan, R., Kase, E., Lake, F., & Zebua, R. (2023). Artificial intelligence (AI) solutions in English language teaching: Teachers-students perceptions And experiences. *Journal of Education*, *6*(1), 1452–1461. DOI: 10.31004/joe.v6i1.3101

Hockly, N. (2018). Blended learning. *ELT Journal*, *72*(1), 97–101. DOI: 10.1093/elt/ccx058

Holland, P., & Wainer, H. (1993). *Differential item functioning*. Psychology Press.

Ibrahim, H., Liu, F., Asim, R., Battu, B., Benabderrahmane, S., Alhafni, B., Adnan, W., Alhanai, T., AlShebli, B., Baghdadi, R., Bélanger, J., Beretta, E., Celik, K., Chaqfeh, M., Daqaq, M., Bernoussi, Z., Fougnie, D., Garcia de Soto, B., Gandolfi, A., & Zaki, Y. (2023). Perception, performance, and detectability of conversational artificial intelligence across 32 university courses. *Scientific Reports*, *13*(1), 1–13. DOI: 10.1038/s41598-023-38964-3 PMID: 36593249

Kanero, J., Geçkin, V., Oranç, C., Mamus, E., Küntay, A., & Göksun, T. (2018). Social robots for early language learning: Current evidence and future directions. *Child Development Perspectives*, *12*(3), 146–151. DOI: 10.1111/cdep.12277

Kannan, J., & Munday, P. (2018). New trends in second language learning and teaching through the lens of ICT, networked learning, and artificial intelligence. *Círculo de Lingüística Aplicada a la Comunicación*, *76*, 13–30. DOI: 10.5209/CLAC.62495

Kennedy, T. (2006). Language learning and its impact on the brain: Connecting language learning with the mind through content-based instruction. *Foreign Language Annals*, *39*(3), 471–486. DOI: 10.1111/j.1944-9720.2006.tb02900.x

Krashen, S. D. (1982). *Principles and practice in second language acquisition.* Pergamon Press.

Kyriazos, T. (2018). Applied psychometrics: Sample size and sample power considerations in factor analysis (EFA, CFA) and SEM in general. *Psychology (Irvine, Calif.)*, *09*(08), 2207–2230. DOI: 10.4236/psych.2018.98126

Law, K., Geng, S., & Li, T. (2019). Student enrollment, motivation and learning performance in a blended learning environment: The mediating effects of social, teaching, and cognitive presence. *Computers & Education*, *136*, 1–12. DOI: 10.1016/j.compedu.2019.02.021

Liang, J., Hwang, G., Chen, M., & Darmawansah, D. (2023). Roles and research foci of artificial intelligence in language education: An integrated bibliographic analysis and systematic review approach. *Interactive Learning Environments*, *31*(7), 4270–4296. DOI: 10.1080/10494820.2021.1958348

Liang, W., & Fung, D. (2021). Fostering critical thinking in English-as-a-second-language classrooms: Challenges and opportunities. *Thinking Skills and Creativity*, *39*, 1–12. DOI: 10.1016/j.tsc.2020.100769

Marcoulides, K., & Raykov, T. (2019). Evaluation of variance inflation factors in regression models using latent variable modeling methods. *Educational and Psychological Measurement*, *79*(5), 874–882. DOI: 10.1177/0013164418817803 PMID: 31488917

Mertler, C., & Vannatta Reinhart, R. (2017). *Advanced and multivariate statistical methods: Practical application and interpretation.* Routledge.

Messick, S. (1995). Validity of psychological assessment: Validation of inferences from persons' responses and performances as scientific inquiry into score meaning. *The American Psychologist*, *50*(9), 741–749. DOI: 10.1037/0003-066X.50.9.741

Meyers, M. (1993). *Teaching to diversity: Teaching and learning in the multi-ethnic classroom.* Addison-Wesley Publishing Company.

Moussalli, S., & Cardoso, W. (2020). Intelligent personal assistants: Can they understand and be understood by accented L2 learners? *Computer Assisted Language Learning*, *33*(8), 865–890. DOI: 10.1080/09588221.2019.1595664

Nguyen, T. (2023). EFL teachers' perspectives toward the use of ChatGPT in writing classes: A case study at Van Lang University. *International Journal of Language Instruction*, *2*(3), 1–47. DOI: 10.54855/ijli.23231

Pallant, J. (2013). *SPSS survival manual.* McGraw-Hill Education.

Perkins, M. (2023). Academic integrity considerations of AI Large Language Models in the post-pandemic era: ChatGPT and beyond. *Journal of University Teaching & Learning Practice, 20*(2). Advance online publication. DOI: 10.53761/1.20.02.07

Persulessy, S., Nikijuluw, R., & Jakob, J. C. (2024). Utilizing artificial intelligence in language learning: What about engineering students' perception? *Journal of English Education Program, 5*(1), 48–58. DOI: 10.26418/jeep.v5i1.71159

Phan, T. (2023). Students' perceptions of the AI technology application in English writing classes. *Proceedings of the AsiaCALL International Conference, 4*, 45–62. DOI: 10.54855/paic.2344

Ponton, M., & Rhea, N. (2006). Autonomous Learning from a Social Cognitive Perspective. *New Horizons in Adult Education and Human Resource Development, 20*(2), 38–49. DOI: 10.1002/nha3.10250

Romero, M., Buzón-García, O., & Touron, J. (2019). The flipped learning model in online based education for secondary teachers. *Journal of Technology and Science Education, 9*(2), 109. DOI: 10.3926/jotse.435

Rumsey, C. (2024). *Why it's important to learn English.* Studio Cambridge. https://www.studiocambridge.co.uk/why-it-is-important-to-learn-english/

Sarker, I. (2022). AI-based modeling: Techniques, applications and research issues towards automation, intelligent and smart systems. *SN Computer Science, 3*(2), 1–20. DOI: 10.1007/s42979-022-01043-x PMID: 35194580

Savran Çelik, Ş., & Aydın, S. (2018). A review of research on the use of native language in EFL classes. *The Literacy Trek, 4*(2), 1–14.

Sayici, S., & Aydın, S. (2025). Using artificial intelligence in foreign language teaching: Teachers' perspectives. *Proceedings of The World Conference on Education and Teaching, 4*(1), 1–10. DOI: 10.33422/etconf.v4i1.1016

Schacter, D., Gilbert, D., & Wegner, D. (2009). *Introducing psychology*. Macmillan.

Shadiev, R., Wu, T., Sun, A., & Huang, Y. (2018). Applications of speech-to-text recognition and computer-aided translation for facilitating cross-cultural learning through a learning activity: Issues and their solutions. *Educational Technology Research and Development, 66*(1), 191–214. DOI: 10.1007/s11423-017-9556-8

Statista. (2024). *Languages most frequently used for web content as of January 2024, by share of websites.* https://www.statista.com/statistics/262946/most-common-languages-on-the-internet/

Tabachnick, B., & Fidell, L. (2014). *Using multivariate statistics.* Pearson.

Tafazoli, D., María, E., & Abril, C. (2019). Intelligent language tutoring system. *International Journal of Information and Communication Technology Education, 15*(3), 60–74. DOI: 10.4018/IJICTE.2019070105

Vandenberg, R., & Lance, C. (2000). A review and synthesis of the measurement invariance literature: Suggestions, practices, and recommendations for organizational research. *Organizational Research Methods, 3*(1), 4–70. DOI: 10.1177/109442810031002

Verga, L., & Kotz, S. (2013). How relevant is social interaction in second language learning? *Frontiers in Human Neuroscience, 7*, 1–7. DOI: 10.3389/fnhum.2013.00550 PMID: 24027521

Vygotsky, L. (1978). Interaction between learning and development. In Gauvain, M., & Cole, M. (Eds.), *Readings on the development of children* (pp. 34–40). Scientific American Books.

Wang, X., Pang, H., Wallace, M., Wang, Q., & Chen, W. (2024). Learners' perceived AI presences in AI-supported language learning: A study of AI as a humanized agent from community of inquiry. *Computer Assisted Language Learning, 37*(4), 814–840. DOI: 10.1080/09588221.2022.2056203

Watkins, M. (2018). Exploratory factor analysis: A guide to best practice. *The Journal of Black Psychology, 44*(3), 219–246. DOI: 10.1177/0095798418771807

Wilson, J., Ahrendt, C., Fudge, E., Raiche, A., Beard, G., & MacArthur, C. (2021). Elementary teachers' perceptions of automated feedback and automated scoring: Transforming the teaching and learning of writing using automated writing evaluation. *Computers & Education, 168*, 104208. DOI: 10.1016/j.compedu.2021.104208

Wood, D., Bruner, J., & Ross, G. (1976). The role of tutoring in problem solving. *Journal of Child Psychology and Psychiatry, and Allied Disciplines, 17*(2), 89–100. DOI: 10.1111/j.1469-7610.1976.tb00381.x PMID: 932126

Xia, Y., & Yang, Y. (2019). RMSEA, CFI, and TLI in structural equation modeling with ordered categorical data: The story they tell depends on the estimation methods. *Behavior Research Methods, 51*(1), 409–428. DOI: 10.3758/s13428-018-1055-2 PMID: 29869222

Yılmaz, Ö. K., & Aydın, S. (2025). The impact of the use of artificial intelligence-generated materials on reading motivation among EFL learners. *Reading Research Quarterly, 60*(3), e70016. DOI: 10.1002/rrq.70016

Yin, J., Goh, T., Yang, B., & Xiaobin, Y. (2021). Conversation technology with micro-learning: The impact of chatbot-based learning on students' learning motivation and performance. *Journal of Educational Computing Research*, *59*(1), 154–177. DOI: 10.1177/0735633120952067

Yu, D., Zhou, Y., Li, Y., Shen, X., Tian, M., Yang, B., Su, J., & Sun, Y. (2022). A survey of English learning softwares based on TPACK framework. *The 17th Academic Annual Conference of the Information Technology Education Professional Committee of China Educational Technology Association*, 1–9.

Zou, B., Liviero, S., Hao, M., & Wei, C. (2020). Artificial intelligence technology for EAP speaking skills: Student perceptions of opportunities and challenges. In N. Freiermuth, M., Zarrinabadi (Ed.), *Technology and the Psychology of Second Language Learners and Users. New Language Learning and Teaching Environments* (pp. 433–463). Palgrave Macmillan. DOI: 10.1007/978-3-030-34212-8_17

ADDITIONAL READING

Ahmadi Fatalaki, J., Saeedi, Z., Sheikhzadeh Marand, E., & Nasiri Firuz, A. R. (2025). Artificial intelligence in education and EFL teachers' attitudes: Scale development and validation. *Innovation in Language Learning and Teaching*, 1–17. DOI: 10.1080/17501229.2025.2494823

An, X., Chai, C. S., Li, Y., Zhou, Y., & Yang, B. (2023). Modeling students' perceptions of artificial intelligence assisted language learning. *Computer Assisted Language Learning*, 1–22. DOI: 10.1080/09588221.2023.2246519

Kurni, M., & Mohammed, M. S. (2023). *A beginner's guide to introduce artificial intelligence in teaching and learning*. Springer Nature.

Last, R. W. (1989). *Artificial intelligence techniques in language learning*. Halsted Press.

Slamet, J. (2024). Potential of ChatGPT as a digital language learning assistant: EFL teachers' and students' perceptions. *Discover Artificial Intelligence*, *4*(1), 46. Advance online publication. DOI: 10.1007/s44163-024-00143-2

Üzüm, B., Elçiçek, M., & Pesen, A. (2025). Development of teachers' perception scale regarding artificial intelligence use in education: Validity and reliability study. *International Journal of Human-Computer Interaction*, *41*(5), 2776–2787. DOI: 10.1080/10447318.2024.2385518

Vo, A., & Nguyen, H. (2024). Generative artificial intelligence and ChatGPT in language learning: EFL students' perceptions of technology acceptance. *Journal of University Teaching & Learning Practice*, *21*(6), 199–218. DOI: 10.53761/fr1rkj58

Wang, X., Pang, H., Wallace, M. P., Wang, Q., & Chen, W. (2024). Learners' perceived AI presences in AI-supported language learning: A study of AI as a humanized agent from community of inquiry. *Computer Assisted Language Learning*, *37*(4), 814–840. DOI: 10.1080/09588221.2022.2056203

KEY TERMS AND DEFINITIONS

Artificial Intelligence: A field of computer science focused on creating machines and software capable of performing tasks that typically require human intelligence.

English as a Foreign Language: Refers to the teaching and learning of English in contexts where it is not the primary language of communication. Learners typically learn English in formal educational settings for academic, professional, or personal purposes.

Perceptions: Refers to subjective beliefs, attitudes, and interpretations that individuals hold regarding a phenomenon.

Reliability: The consistency and stability of measurement results across different occasions or samples. In this context, reliability was assessed through internal consistency and test-retest methods to confirm the precision of the scale over time.

Scale: A psychometric instrument designed to measure specific constructs or variables through a series of items.

Validity: The degree to which a scale or instrument measures what it claims to measure. This study examines content, construct, and criterion-related validity to ensure the appropriateness of the scale.

APPENDIX

Table 4. The factors and items in the PAS

Items	Completely Disagree (1)	Disagree (2)	Undecided (3)	Agree (4)	Completely Agree (5)
Factor: Contributions to foreign language learning					
I believe that AI-supported learning is more effective than traditional methods.	(1)	(2)	(3)	(4)	(5)
AI tools can enhance my communicative skills.	(1)	(2)	(3)	(4)	(5)
The integration of AI tools into language classes contributes to autonomous learning.	(1)	(2)	(3)	(4)	(5)
The integration of AI tools in language classes contributes to personalized learning.	(1)	(2)	(3)	(4)	(5)
The integration of AI tools in language classes contributes to adaptive learning.	(1)	(2)	(3)	(4)	(5)
AI tools provide emotional support in language learning.	(1)	(2)	(3)	(4)	(5)
AI tools help to reduce my anxiety level.	(1)	(2)	(3)	(4)	(5)
I find AI tools helpful in practicing my pronunciation skills.	(1)	(2)	(3)	(4)	(5)
AI tools enhance my listening comprehension.	(1)	(2)	(3)	(4)	(5)
I think that AI tools positively impact my reading comprehension.	(1)	(2)	(3)	(4)	(5)
I find that AI tools enhance my speaking performance.	(1)	(2)	(3)	(4)	(5)
I believe that AI tools can positively influence my writing skills.	(1)	(2)	(3)	(4)	(5)
I believe that AI tools positively influence writing quality.	(1)	(2)	(3)	(4)	(5)
My participation in classroom activities has increased after I started using AI tools.	(1)	(2)	(3)	(4)	(5)
Factor: Concerns					
I believe that overreliance on writing with AI tools debilitates my critical thinking skills.	(1)	(2)	(3)	(4)	(5)
I think the use of AI debilitates my problem-solving abilities.	(1)	(2)	(3)	(4)	(5)
AI tools produce inappropriate language content.	(1)	(2)	(3)	(4)	(5)

Chapter 7
Echoes of AI:
Revolutionizing English Communication

Papi Naidu Mavidi
https://orcid.org/0000-0003-0706-8094
Aditya Institute of Technology and Management, India

ABSTRACT

The integration of Artificial Intelligence (AI) into the realm of language learning and communication has ushered in a revolutionary era, reshaping the ways English is taught, learned, and used globally. This chapter explores the profound impact of AI on English language acquisition, examining how cutting-edge technologies such as natural language processing (NLP), machine learning, and AI-powered platforms are redefining linguistic engagement. The narrative delves into the role of AI in fostering autonomy, enhancing learner motivation, and personalizing the learning journey to suit diverse needs. Furthermore, it addresses challenges such as ethical considerations, accessibility disparities, and the future trajectory of AI in communication. By weaving research insights, case studies, and practical applications, this work illuminates the transformative potential of AI in bridging cultural and linguistic divides, ultimately revolutionizing global communication.

1. THE DAWN OF A NEW ERA IN LANGUAGE LEARNING

Language is the bedrock of human communication, being a means of talking, articulation, and information sharing. Of the numerous languages spoken around the world, English has evolved as a lingua franca, bridging people from diverse cultures, occupations, and fields of study. Effective expression in English is an asset, which oftentimes influences career, studies, and international interaction.

DOI: 10.4018/979-8-3373-5681-5.ch007

But learning English as a second or foreign language has always been a difficult endeavor, limited by conventional teaching practices that are not personalized and lack relevance to everyday life.

The emergence of Artificial Intelligence (AI) heralds the beginning of a new era in language acquisition. AI-based tools are revolutionizing traditional methods, rendering learning more engaging, responsive, and inclusive. In contrast to the traditional classroom environment, which is based on fixed curricula and universal instruction, AI-enabled apps read individual learner requirements, offering personalized feedback and individualized exercises that address individual linguistic strengths and weaknesses? These innovations are shattering boundaries by providing learners with independence, motivation, and a more engaging means of developing their English language skills.

One of the biggest limitations of the old way of language learning has been its universality. Teaching in the classroom cannot cater to various learning styles, and therefore some students fall behind while others progress faster. AI addresses this problem by individualizing the learning process. Machine learning algorithms review user progress, determine areas where users are falling behind, and make adjustments in lesson plans accordingly. For example, a platform that utilizes AI can identify pronunciation mistakes in spoken English and give instant feedback, allowing students to improve their speech with accuracy. Likewise, writing assistants powered by automation can identify grammatical mistakes and propose corrections, and students can hone their writing abilities.

Another significant advantage of AI in language learning is its ability to create immersive experiences. Traditional methods often rely on textbooks and rote memorization, which may not prepare learners for real-world communication. AI-powered applications integrate voice recognition, natural language processing (NLP), and interactive simulations to mimic authentic conversations. Virtual tutors and chatbots enable learners to practice speaking and listening skills in a low-pressure environment, fostering confidence and fluency. Additionally, AI-driven speech synthesis allows users to listen to diverse accents and dialects, improving their comprehension and adaptability in real-life scenarios.

Moreover, AI facilitates accessibility in language learning. Students who lack access to native-speaking teachers or structured courses can benefit from AI-driven resources that provide high-quality instruction at their convenience. Mobile applications, online platforms, and virtual assistants enable learners to practice anytime and anywhere, making English learning more inclusive and flexible. This is particularly beneficial for professionals, students, and non-traditional learners who may have time constraints or geographical limitations.

As AI continues to evolve, its impact on language learning will only expand. Future developments may include AI-powered tutors with enhanced emotional intelligence, virtual reality (VR) environments for immersive learning, and real-time translation tools that break language barriers. These advancements signify a paradigm shift in how English is learned and taught, paving the way for a more dynamic, efficient, and personalized approach to communication.

This book, *Echoes of AI: Revolutionizing English Communication*, explores the transformative role of AI in English language learning, delving into its impact on listening, speaking, reading, and writing (LSRW) skills. By embracing AI-driven methodologies, learners can navigate the complexities of English with greater ease and confidence, ultimately enhancing their linguistic competence and global communication abilities.

2. UNDERSTANDING AI IN THE CONTEXT OF LANGUAGE LEARNING

Artificial Intelligence (AI) is revolutionizing the field of language learning by simulating human intelligence and automating various linguistic processes. AI encompasses technologies such as machine learning, natural language processing (NLP), speech recognition, and adaptive learning systems. These innovations provide learners with personalized instruction, immediate feedback, and engaging learning experiences, ultimately enhancing their English language proficiency.

One of the most significant contributions of AI to language learning is its ability to analyze vast amounts of linguistic data. Traditional learning methods rely on static lesson plans, whereas AI-powered systems continuously adapt based on individual learner performance. These adaptive learning models assess strengths and weaknesses, customizing exercises to address specific linguistic gaps. For instance, an AI-driven language application can track a learner's pronunciation accuracy and suggest corrective measures tailored to their accent and fluency level.

AI also enhances interaction and engagement in language learning. Chatbots and virtual tutors, powered by NLP, provide real-time conversational practice, helping learners develop fluency and confidence in spoken English. These AI-driven interfaces simulate human-like interactions, allowing learners to practice dialogues, receive feedback on pronunciation, and correct grammatical errors in an interactive environment. Unlike human instructors, AI tutors are available 24/7, offering learners the flexibility to practice at their convenience.

Another groundbreaking aspect of AI in language learning is its role in automated assessment and feedback. Traditionally, students rely on teachers for evaluation, which can be time-consuming and subjective. AI-powered tools such as automated essay scoring systems analyze writing samples based on coherence, grammar, vocabulary usage, and structure. These tools provide instant feedback, enabling learners to refine their writing skills through iterative practice. Additionally, AI-powered speech recognition tools assess spoken language proficiency, analyzing factors such as intonation, pronunciation, and fluency, thereby offering a comprehensive evaluation of linguistic performance.

AI is also bridging gaps in accessibility and inclusivity. Language learning has historically been constrained by geographical and economic barriers, making high-quality instruction accessible only to a privileged few. AI-powered language platforms democratize learning by offering free or affordable courses, personalized coaching, and multilingual support. For instance, mobile applications equipped with AI-driven translation and speech synthesis tools enable non-native English speakers to access educational content in their preferred language, facilitating seamless learning experiences.

Furthermore, AI is fostering immersive learning environments through the integration of Virtual Reality (VR) and Augmented Reality (AR). These technologies allow learners to engage in real-world scenarios, such as ordering food in a restaurant or attending a business meeting, within a simulated environment. Such immersive experiences reinforce language retention and comprehension by contextualizing learning in a practical setting.

While AI presents numerous advantages, it is not without challenges. Ethical concerns such as data privacy, bias in AI algorithms, and over-reliance on automation must be addressed to ensure equitable and effective learning experiences. Nevertheless, AI's potential in language learning is undeniable, paving the way for more efficient, interactive, and personalized education.

3. THE EVOLUTION OF ENGLISH LANGUAGE LEARNING: FROM TRADITIONAL TO AI-DRIVEN METHODS

The evolution of English language learning has been marked by a transition from rigid, teacher-centered approaches to dynamic, technology-driven methods. Historically, language learning relied heavily on grammar-translation techniques, which emphasized rote memorization and written translations rather than practical communication. While this method provided a strong foundation in grammatical accuracy, it often failed to develop conversational fluency.

The emergence of the communicative approach in the 20th century shifted focus to real-world language use. This methodology prioritized interaction, dialogue, and listening comprehension, making language learning more practical. However, it was still largely dependent on instructor availability and classroom settings, limiting accessibility and personalized learning opportunities.

With the rise of digital education in the 21st century, language learning expanded beyond traditional classrooms. Online courses, language apps, and virtual learning platforms provided learners with more flexible and self-paced options. AI further revolutionized this landscape by introducing personalized learning experiences, real-time feedback, and immersive simulations. AI-powered tools, such as speech recognition software and virtual tutors, enable learners to practice pronunciation, receive instant corrections, and engage in realistic conversations.

Today, AI-driven methodologies continue to enhance accessibility, engagement, and efficiency in language learning. Intelligent tutoring systems, adaptive learning models, and virtual reality experiences offer learners a customized and interactive way to master English, making language acquisition more effective than ever before.

4. AI-POWERED TOOLS AND THEIR IMPACT ON LSRW SKILLS

The four essential language skills—Listening, Speaking, Reading, and Writing—are the pillars of effective communication. AI enhances each of these skills in distinct ways:

Listening: AI-driven platforms such as speech recognition software and AI-generated podcasts offer learners exposure to diverse accents, speech patterns, and real-life conversations. Personalized listening exercises help learners improve comprehension, pronunciation, and contextual understanding.

Speaking: AI-powered chatbots and virtual assistants provide an interactive environment for learners to practice speaking. These tools use NLP algorithms to analyze pronunciation, intonation, and fluency, offering corrective feedback in real time. Voice recognition software also assists in accent neutralization and confidence building.

Reading: AI-enabled reading assistants analyze comprehension skills by providing interactive reading materials, contextual definitions, and instant translations. Adaptive learning systems adjust the difficulty level based on the learner's proficiency, ensuring gradual improvement.

Writing: AI-driven writing assistants, such as Grammarly and Quillbot, help learners enhance grammar, coherence, and vocabulary usage. Automated essay scoring systems provide structured feedback, enabling learners to refine their writing skills through iterative practice.

5. AI AND LEARNER AUTONOMY: A PARADIGM SHIFT

One of the most significant advantages of AI in language learning is its ability to foster learner autonomy. Traditional classroom settings often rely on instructor-led approaches, limiting students' ability to take control of their learning. AI-driven platforms empower learners to set their own pace, track their progress, and focus on areas that require improvement. This shift towards self-directed learning encourages intrinsic motivation, making language acquisition a more engaging and rewarding experience.

Moreover, AI-based recommendation systems curate personalized learning materials tailored to individual needs. Whether a learner struggles with pronunciation, grammar, or vocabulary, AI ensures that resources are aligned with their specific challenges, maximizing learning efficiency. This personalized approach not only enhances retention but also cultivates a deeper connection with the language.

6. CHALLENGES AND ETHICAL CONSIDERATIONS IN AI-ENHANCED LANGUAGE LEARNING

While AI presents revolutionary opportunities in language learning, it also brings forth significant challenges and ethical considerations. These issues range from data privacy concerns to potential biases in AI models and the long-term implications of automation replacing human-led instruction. Addressing these challenges is crucial to ensuring that AI-driven education remains effective, equitable, and ethically sound.

6.1 Data Privacy and Security

One of the primary concerns in AI-driven language learning is the handling of user data. AI-powered tools collect vast amounts of information, including voice recordings, written responses, and personal learning progress. While this data is essential for personalization, it also raises questions about privacy and security. If not properly managed, sensitive learner information could be vulnerable to breaches, unauthorized use, or exploitation. Ensuring that AI language learning platforms comply with stringent data protection laws, such as the General Data Protection Regulation (GDPR), is essential for safeguarding user privacy.

6.2 Bias and Fairness in AI Algorithms

AI models are only as unbiased as the data they are trained on. If training datasets are not diverse enough, AI language learning systems can unintentionally reinforce linguistic biases. For example, AI-powered speech recognition tools may struggle to accurately transcribe accents that were underrepresented in training data, disadvantaging certain learners. Similarly, grammar correction tools may favor specific writing styles, marginalizing those that do not conform to traditional norms. Developers must ensure that AI training datasets are diverse, inclusive, and representative of different linguistic backgrounds to avoid perpetuating bias in language education.

6.3 The Risk of Over-Reliance on AI

While AI-driven tools offer efficiency and scalability, over-reliance on automation could diminish the role of human educators. Language learning is not solely about grammar and vocabulary—it also involves cultural nuances, emotional intelligence, and social interaction. AI, despite its advancements, still struggles to replicate the depth of human communication, particularly in areas such as humor, empathy, and contextual understanding. Therefore, AI should be seen as a complement rather than a replacement for human instructors, ensuring that learners receive a balanced approach that combines technological efficiency with human intuition.

6.4 The Ethical Use of AI in Assessments

AI is increasingly being used for automated grading and language proficiency assessments. While this approach offers speed and consistency, it may lack the nuanced understanding of human evaluators. AI-driven assessment tools may not accurately gauge creativity, tone, or intent in writing, potentially leading to unfair evaluations. Moreover, automated speech recognition tools may misinterpret spoken responses due to background noise, pronunciation variations, or technical limitations. To ensure fair assessments, AI evaluation systems must be regularly updated, validated by human educators, and supplemented with human oversight where necessary.

6.5 Digital Divide and Accessibility

Despite AI's potential to democratize education, not all learners have equal access to AI-powered tools. Socioeconomic disparities, lack of technological infrastructure, and language barriers can prevent individuals from benefiting from AI-driven language learning resources. Efforts must be made to bridge this digital divide by providing affordable and accessible AI tools, offering multilingual support, and promoting inclusive learning initiatives. Governments, educators, and technology developers must work collaboratively to ensure that AI-enhanced education reaches learners from diverse backgrounds.

Conclusion

The integration of AI into language learning is a double-edged sword—it holds immense potential to enhance accessibility, engagement, and efficiency, but also presents challenges that must be carefully managed. Ethical AI development, transparency in data usage, and the balanced integration of human-led instruction are essential in ensuring that AI-enhanced language learning remains fair, effective, and inclusive. As AI technology continues to evolve, ongoing discussions on ethical best practices and equitable implementation will be key in shaping the future of AI-driven education.

7. THE FUTURE OF AI IN ENGLISH COMMUNICATION

The future of AI in English communication holds immense promise, transforming the way individuals acquire, refine, and utilize language skills. AI will continue to evolve, making English learning more personalized, interactive, and inclusive. Advances in natural language processing (NLP) and machine learning will enhance AI's ability to understand and generate human-like conversations, facilitating seamless communication between speakers of different linguistic backgrounds.

AI-driven chatbots and virtual assistants will become even more sophisticated, capable of engaging in meaningful and contextually aware dialogues. These systems will provide real-time conversational feedback, helping learners improve fluency, pronunciation, and comprehension with greater accuracy. Additionally, AI-powered translation tools will bridge linguistic gaps, making cross-cultural communication more efficient and accessible.

Moreover, the integration of AI with Virtual Reality (VR) and Augmented Reality (AR) will create immersive language-learning environments. Learners will experience real-world scenarios, such as business meetings or social interactions, in a simulated setting, fostering practical language acquisition. These innovations will make learning more engaging, reducing the intimidation of real-life communication.

Ethical considerations, including data privacy and bias in AI models, will need to be addressed to ensure equitable language education. However, as AI continues to advance, it will play an instrumental role in shaping the future of English communication, enabling learners to master the language with unprecedented ease and efficiency.

Conclusion

Echoes of AI: Revolutionizing English Communication aims to provide an in-depth exploration of how AI is reshaping the landscape of English language learning. By harnessing the power of AI, learners can overcome traditional barriers, personalize their learning experiences, and develop proficiency in a more engaging and efficient manner. As we embark on this journey, it is crucial to embrace the potential of AI while addressing ethical concerns and maintaining a human-centric approach to language education. The echoes of AI in language learning are not just a technological advancement—they represent a paradigm shift that will redefine the way we communicate, connect, and learn in the years to come.

2. LITERATURE REVIEW

The role of AI in English language learning has been widely discussed in academic and professional circles, with numerous studies exploring its effectiveness in improving learners' linguistic competencies. This literature review examines key contributions from researchers and educators in the field, highlighting the impact of AI on listening, speaking, reading, and writing (LSRW) skills, as well as its role in fostering learner autonomy, engagement, and motivation.

2.1 Theoretical Foundations of AI in Language Learning

Several scholars have explored AI's integration into language learning through the lens of cognitive and constructivist learning theories. According to Vygotsky's (1978) theory of social constructivism, learners develop language skills through social interactions. AI-powered chatbots and virtual tutors facilitate this process by providing real-time conversational practice. Additionally, Skinner's (1957) behaviorist theory supports AI-driven personalized learning, where adaptive algorithms reinforce positive learning behaviors through instant feedback and customized exercises. Piaget's (1980) cognitive development theory also aligns with AI applications in language learning, suggesting that learners progress through stages of cognitive development, and AI tools can be tailored to match their proficiency levels and learning needs.

2.2 AI-Powered Tools in LSRW Skill Development

Numerous studies have investigated how AI-driven tools enhance language proficiency. Speech recognition software, such as Google's Speech-to-Text and Duolingo's AI-based pronunciation feedback, has been found effective in improving speaking and listening skills (Li & Lalani, 2022). AI-powered grammar checkers like Grammarly and Hemingway Editor contribute to better writing skills by offering contextual corrections and style recommendations (Matsuda & Silva, 2021). Additionally, Natural Language Processing (NLP)-based reading assistants, such as AI-driven summarization tools, support comprehension and reading fluency (Jones, 2020). Research by Crossley (2018) also highlights that AI-enhanced text analysis tools can help learners develop critical reading skills by identifying patterns, themes, and complex sentence structures in texts, making comprehension more intuitive.

2.3 AI and Learner Autonomy

Research suggests that AI fosters learner autonomy by providing self-paced and personalized learning environments. Studies by Benson (2011) indicate that autonomous learners are more motivated and achieve higher proficiency levels. AI platforms like Rosetta Stone and ELSA Speak enable learners to track their progress, set goals, and receive adaptive learning suggestions, aligning with Holec's (1981) concept of self-directed learning. Moreover, Reinders and White (2016) argue that AI-enhanced learning environments encourage metacognitive awareness, allowing learners to reflect on their language use and adjust their strategies accordingly. AI-driven analytics also support autonomy by providing learners with insights into their performance trends, strengths, and weaknesses, helping them make informed decisions about their learning paths.

2.4 Engagement and Motivation in AI-Enhanced Learning

Gamification elements embedded in AI-powered applications have been identified as key drivers of student engagement. Deterding et al. (2011) found that AI-integrated gamification, such as Duolingo's reward-based system, increases motivation and retention rates. Studies by Ryan and Deci (2000) on self-determination theory highlight how AI-driven personalized learning experiences enhance intrinsic motivation, making language acquisition more enjoyable and effective. Furthermore, research by Wang and Tahir (2020) indicates that AI-generated adaptive challenges and real-world simulations increase student interest and persistence in language learning. AI's ability to create interactive, immersive experiences through Virtual Reality

(VR) and Augmented Reality (AR) also contributes to engagement, as learners can practice English in realistic scenarios, such as virtual interviews or travel simulations.

2.5 Ethical and Pedagogical Considerations

While AI offers numerous advantages, concerns related to data privacy, algorithmic bias, and over-reliance on technology have been raised by scholars like Selwyn (2019). Ethical considerations in AI-enhanced education necessitate a balanced approach, where AI serves as a supplementary tool rather than a replacement for human instruction. Further research by Smith and Gray (2021) highlights issues of equity in AI-driven language learning, as access to advanced AI tools may be limited for learners from disadvantaged backgrounds. Additionally, transparency in AI algorithms and data usage remains a pressing issue, with educators advocating for clearer ethical guidelines and regulatory frameworks to ensure fairness and accountability in AI-enhanced learning environments.

2.6 AI in Assessment and Feedback Mechanisms

Recent literature explores AI's role in language assessment and feedback mechanisms, emphasizing the accuracy and efficiency of automated grading systems. Studies by Attali and Burstein (2006) on AI-assisted essay scoring suggest that AI tools can provide objective, detailed, and immediate feedback, reducing the workload on educators while offering learners valuable insights into their writing proficiency. Similarly, automated speech evaluation tools, such as SpeechRater by ETS, have been shown to accurately assess pronunciation, fluency, and coherence (Zechner et al., 2019). However, researchers caution against over-reliance on AI grading systems, arguing that human evaluators are still necessary for assessing creativity, nuance, and contextual appropriateness in language use.

2.7 The Future of AI in Language Learning Research

As AI continues to evolve, researchers predict further advancements in AI-driven language learning. Emerging trends include the integration of AI with blockchain technology to enhance credentialing and verification of language proficiency (Chen et al., 2021), as well as the use of deep learning algorithms to create more nuanced and human-like conversational AI tutors. Additionally, studies by Kumar and Sharma (2022) suggest that AI-driven cultural adaptation tools may soon enable learners to practice language in culturally specific contexts, further enhancing their communicative competence. Future research should focus on refining AI-driven methodologies to ensure equitable and effective learning experiences for diverse learners.

Conclusion

The literature reviewed indicates that AI has a transformative impact on English language learning by enhancing LSRW skills, promoting learner autonomy, and increasing motivation through personalized and interactive learning experiences. Theoretical perspectives support AI's role in facilitating language acquisition through adaptive learning and social interaction. Empirical studies highlight AI's effectiveness in improving engagement, assessment, and feedback mechanisms. However, ethical concerns and pedagogical challenges require further exploration to optimize AI's role in language education. Future research should address the need for ethical AI practices, accessibility, and the integration of AI with emerging technologies to create more inclusive and effective language learning experiences.

3.OBJECTIVES OF THE RESEARCH

1. **To analyze the impact of AI on English language learning** – Examining how AI-driven tools enhance listening, speaking, reading, and writing (LSRW) skills.
2. **To explore AI-powered applications in communication development** – Investigating the role of chatbots, virtual tutors, speech recognition, and other AI-driven technologies in improving English proficiency.
3. **To assess learner autonomy and engagement through AI-enhanced methodologies** – Understanding how AI fosters self-directed learning, motivation, and active participation in language acquisition.
4. **To evaluate the effectiveness of AI-based feedback mechanisms** – Studying how real-time feedback from AI tools helps in refining pronunciation, grammar, vocabulary, and overall fluency.
5. **To investigate the role of AI in personalized learning experiences** – Analyzing how adaptive learning platforms cater to individual learning styles and proficiency levels.
6. **To identify challenges and ethical considerations in AI-driven language education** – Addressing concerns related to AI dependency, data privacy, and potential biases in language models.
7. **To propose a framework for integrating AI into English communication training** – Developing strategies for educators and institutions to incorporate AI effectively in English language teaching.

4. RESEARCH METHODOLOGY

The research will follow a **mixed-methods approach**, integrating both qualitative and quantitative methods to comprehensively analyze the impact of AI in English communication.

1. Research Design

The study will adopt an **exploratory and descriptive** research design to assess the effectiveness of AI-driven tools in enhancing English communication skills (LSRW - Listening, Speaking, Reading, and Writing).

2. Data Collection Methods

a. Primary Data Collection

1. **Surveys & Questionnaires**
   - o Designed for students, educators, and language learners to gather insights on AI-based tools in English learning.
   - o Questions will focus on engagement, motivation, perceived effectiveness, and challenges.
2. **Experimental Study (Pre-test & Post-test Analysis)**
   - o Participants will be divided into two groups:
     - ▪ **Control Group**: Learners using traditional methods.
     - ▪ **Experimental Group**: Learners using AI-enhanced tools (chatbots, speech recognition, grammar correction, etc.).
   - o Performance in LSRW skills will be measured before and after AI intervention.
3. **Interviews & Focus Group Discussions**
   - o Conducted with students and teachers to explore experiences, attitudes, and expectations regarding AI-driven language learning.

b. Secondary Data Collection

1. **Literature Review**
   - o Analyzing existing studies, articles, and reports on AI applications in English communication.
2. **Case Studies of AI Integration**
   - o Examining successful implementations of AI in English language learning.

3. Data Analysis Methods

1. **Quantitative Analysis** (for surveys, pre-test & post-test results)
   - o **Statistical tools (SPSS, Excel, or Python)** will be used to analyze numerical data.
   - o Descriptive statistics, t-tests, and ANOVA will be applied to compare performance differences.
2. **Qualitative Analysis** (for interviews & focus groups)
   - o **Thematic Analysis** will be used to identify patterns in perceptions, challenges, and advantages of AI in communication.

4. Ethical Considerations

- **Informed Consent**: Participants will be briefed about the research objectives and their rights.
- **Data Privacy**: Confidentiality of personal responses and AI-generated learning data will be ensured.
- **Bias Reduction**: AI tools from diverse sources will be evaluated to avoid algorithmic bias.

5. Expected Outcome

- Establishing the effectiveness of AI in improving English communication skills.
- Understanding learners' adaptability to AI-driven learning.
- Providing recommendations for AI integration in English language education.

5.FINDINGS AND DISCUSSION

Figure 1.

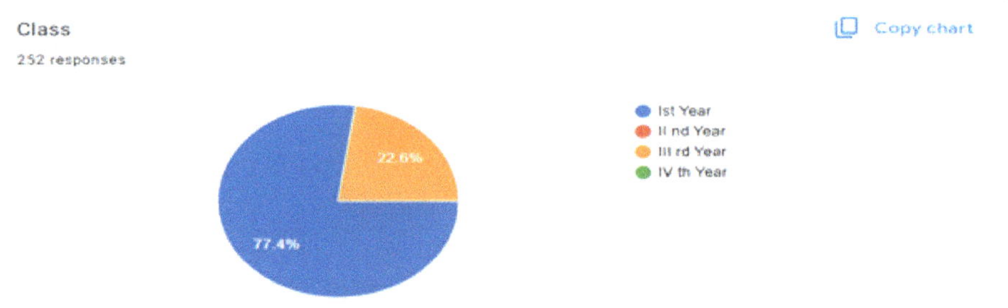

Participants from the different years of their study

The pie chart represents responses from 252 students regarding their class year distribution. Here are the key observations:

1. Majority Representation:
   - o 1st Year students (represented in blue) make up the largest portion, 77.4% of the total responses.
   - o This indicates that most of the respondents are freshmen.
2. Smaller Representation:
   - o 2nd Year students (represented in orange) constitute 22.6% of the total.
   - o There is no visible data for 3rd Year and 4th Year students, suggesting that either they did not respond or were excluded.
3. Data Implications:
   - o The data suggests a strong engagement from 1st-year students, while upper-year students have either lower participation or were not included in the survey.
   - o If the survey was open to all students, efforts may be needed to encourage higher participation from 2nd, 3rd, and 4th-year students.
   - o Alternatively, if the survey was primarily targeted at 1st and 2nd-year students, then the response rate is balanced between these groups.

Figure 2. Participants from the different branches of their study

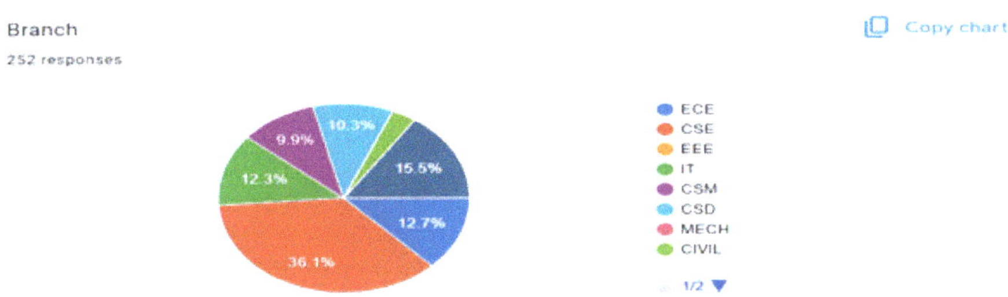

The pie chart represents the distribution of students across different branches based on 252 responses. Here are the key observations:

Major Branch Representation:

1. CSE (Computer Science and Engineering) has the highest number of students, making up 36.1% of the total responses.

  - This suggests a strong preference for CSE among students.
2. ECE (Electronics and Communication Engineering) follows with 15.5% of the total responses.
3. CSD (Computer Science and Design) accounts for 12.7% of the responses.

Moderate Branch Representation:

4. IT (Information Technology) comprises 12.3% of students, showing a balanced interest in this field.
5. CSM (Computer Science and Mathematics) holds 9.9% of the total responses.

Lower Representation:

6. EEE (Electrical and Electronics Engineering) has 10.3% of students.
7. MECH (Mechanical Engineering) and CIVIL have the least representation, each below 10%.
   - This indicates a declining preference for traditional engineering fields like Mechanical and Civil.

Insights and Implications:

- Technology-oriented branches (CSE, IT, CSD, and CSM) dominate, indicating students' increasing interest in computer science-related fields.
- ECE and EEE still hold a significant share, showing continued interest in electronics-based disciplines.
- Mechanical and Civil Engineering have lower representation, which aligns with current trends where software and IT-related fields are more in demand.

Figure 3.

The pie chart represents responses from 252 students regarding the duration of their English learning experience. Here's an analysis:

Key Observations:

1. Majority have extensive English learning experience:
   - o 34.9% of students have been learning English for more than 6 years, indicating a strong background in the language.
2. Moderate experience:
   - o 25% of students have been learning English for 4–6 years, suggesting they are at an intermediate level.
3. Shorter learning duration:
   - o 24.2% of students have been learning English for less than a year, which indicates a significant portion of beginners.
   - o 15.9% of students have been learning for 1–3 years, placing them in an early learning stage.

Insights and Implications:

- Since nearly 60% of respondents (4+ years learners) have been learning English for a long time, their proficiency might be moderate to high.
- The 24.2% beginners (less than a year) may require foundational support and tailored instruction.
- The mix of learners with varying experience levels suggests that English teaching strategies should accommodate both beginners and advanced learners, possibly through differentiated instruction.

Figure 4.

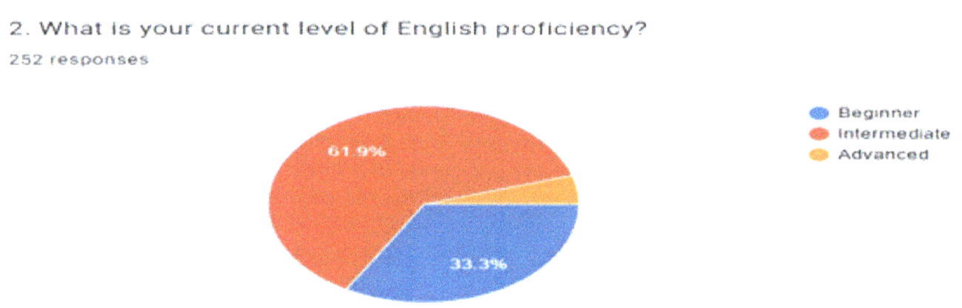

The pie chart represents responses from 252 students regarding their current level of English proficiency. Here's an analysis:

Key Observations:

1. Majority at the Intermediate Level:
   - o 61.9% of respondents classify themselves as Intermediate learners, indicating a solid foundation in English but still needing improvement in fluency and advanced skills.
2. Significant Beginner Population:
   - o 33.3% of respondents identify as Beginners, suggesting they require fundamental language support, including grammar, vocabulary, and basic communication skills.
3. Minimal Advanced Proficiency:
   - o Only a small fraction of students fall into the Advanced category, showing that very few have near-native proficiency or high-level fluency in English.

Insights and Implications:

- Teaching Strategies Should Target Intermediate Learners: Since most students are at an intermediate level, lessons should focus on improving fluency, writing skills, and comprehension rather than just basic grammar.
- Support for Beginners: With over 33% beginners, foundational courses should be included to help them build essential skills before progressing to more complex language structures.
- Encouraging Advanced Learning: Since very few students consider themselves advanced, there may be a need for more exposure to advanced English training, such as academic writing, public speaking, or business English.

Figure 5.

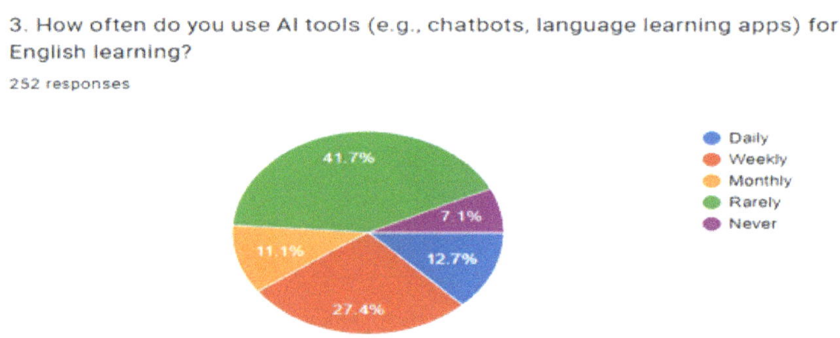

The pie chart represents responses from 252 students regarding their frequency of using AI tools (e.g., chatbots, language learning apps) for English learning. Here's a breakdown of the data:

Key Observations:

1. Largest Group Uses AI Tools Rarely (41.7%)
    - o A significant percentage of students (41.7%) reported using AI tools rarely for English learning.
    - o This suggests that while they may be aware of these tools, they do not actively integrate them into their learning routine.
2. Moderate Weekly Usage (27.4%)
    - o 27.4% of students use AI tools weekly, indicating a structured yet non-daily approach to AI-enhanced learning.
3. Low Daily Usage (12.7%)
    - o Only 12.7% of students use AI tools daily, which suggests limited adoption of AI as a regular learning resource.
4. Limited Monthly Use (11.1%)
    - o 11.1% of students reported using AI tools monthly, meaning they engage with AI learning sporadically.
5. Minimal "Never" Usage (7.1%)
    - o Only 7.1% of students reported never using AI tools, indicating general awareness of AI-based learning tools but a reluctance or lack of necessity to use them.

Insights and Implications:

- Underutilization of AI for English Learning: With nearly 50% (Rarely + Never) of students not using AI tools regularly, there is a need to promote the benefits of AI-enhanced language learning.
- Potential to Increase Daily Use: Given that only 12.7% of students use AI tools daily, educators can encourage more consistent use of chatbots, apps, and AI-driven platforms to support English proficiency.
- AI Tools as a Supplementary Resource: The weekly and monthly usage patterns suggest that while students recognize AI tools as helpful, they do not rely on them as their primary learning method.

Figure 6.

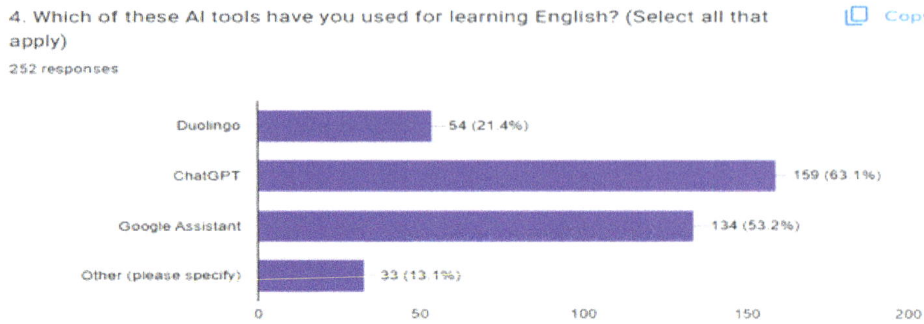

The bar chart represents responses from 252 students regarding their usage of different AI tools for learning English. Since multiple selections were allowed, percentages exceed 100%.

Key Observations:

1. ChatGPT is the Most Popular AI Tool (63.1%)
   - o 159 students (63.1%) reported using ChatGPT for English learning, making it the most widely used tool.
   - o This suggests that students prefer AI-driven conversational tools for improving their English skills, possibly for grammar correction, vocabulary expansion, or practice-based learning.
2. Google Assistant is Also Commonly Used (53.2%)
   - o 134 students (53.2%) have used Google Assistant, indicating that voice-based AI assistants are a popular method for language practice, possibly for pronunciation and quick translations.
3. Duolingo Has Lower Adoption (21.4%)
   - o 54 students (21.4%) use Duolingo, which is a structured language-learning app.
   - o This suggests that gamified learning is less preferred compared to AI chatbots and assistants, possibly due to its structured nature or limited conversational practice.
4. Other AI Tools (13.1%)
   - o 33 students (13.1%) reported using other AI tools, which might include platforms like Grammarly, Microsoft Copilot, or AI-powered translation tools.

Insights and Implications:

- Conversational AI is Preferred Over Structured Learning: The higher adoption of ChatGPT and Google Assistant suggests that students find interactive and conversational AI more useful than structured apps like Duolingo.
- Opportunities for AI Integration in Teaching: Since more than 60% of students already use AI tools, incorporating them into English learning activities (e.g., chatbot-based assignments or voice-based practice) could enhance engagement.
- Need to Promote Varied AI Tools: The lower usage of Duolingo and other AI tools suggests a gap in awareness or preference. Encouraging diverse AI-based learning methods could cater to different learning styles.

Figure 7.

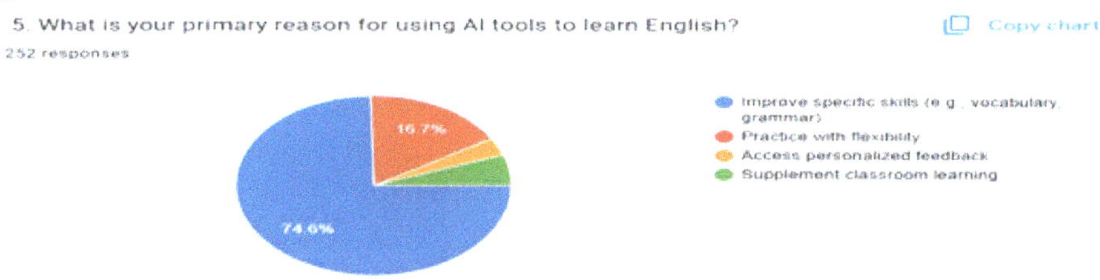

The pie chart represents the primary reasons why students use AI tools for learning English, based on 252 responses.

Key Observations:

1. Majority Focus on Skill Improvement (74.6%)
   - o Three-fourths of students (74.6%) use AI tools primarily to improve specific skills like vocabulary and grammar.
   - o This suggests that students see AI as a tool for enhancing language fundamentals rather than just practice or feedback.
2. Flexible Practice (16.7%)
   - o 16.7% of students value AI tools for practicing with flexibility (e.g., using them anytime, anywhere).
   - o This highlights the convenience and accessibility of AI-driven learning compared to traditional methods.
3. Personalized Feedback (Small Percentage)
   - o A very small fraction of students use AI for personalized feedback or as a classroom supplement, indicating that AI-driven assessment tools may not be widely recognized or used yet.

Insights and Implications:

- Skill-focused Learning Dominates: AI is mainly seen as a self-improvement tool rather than for real-time practice or personalized learning.
- Potential for More Personalized AI Use: Since very few students use AI for feedback or classroom integration, educators can introduce AI-driven feedback tools like Grammarly, ChatGPT corrections, or AI-powered quizzes to enhance engagement.
- AI's Role in Self-Learning: The data shows that students are independent learners using AI primarily for individual skill enhancement rather than structured classroom assistance.

Figure 8.

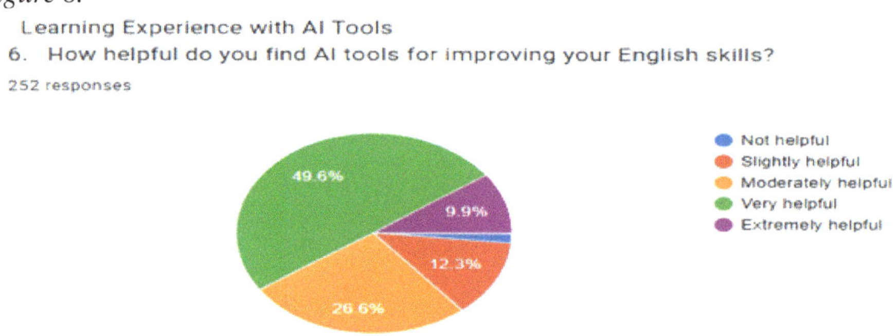

The pie chart represents students' perception of AI tools' effectiveness in improving their English skills, based on 252 responses.

Key Observations:

1. Nearly Half of Respondents Find AI Tools Very Helpful (49.6%)
   - The largest portion (49.6%) rates AI tools as very helpful in improving their English.
   - This indicates a strong positive perception of AI tools for language learning.
2. Moderate Helpfulness (26.6%)
   - 26.6% of students consider AI tools to be moderately helpful, suggesting they provide some benefits but may have limitations.
3. Extremely Helpful (9.9%)

- o A small percentage (9.9%) finds AI tools to be extremely effective, indicating high satisfaction among a few students.

4. Limited Effectiveness (12.3%)
   - o 12.3% of students think AI tools are only slightly helpful, meaning they may not meet their learning needs effectively.
5. No Help (Negligible Percentage)
   - o A very small percentage (almost negligible) finds AI not helpful, suggesting that most students do see some benefits.

Insights & Implications:

- High Satisfaction Overall: More than 85% of students (combining "very helpful," "extremely helpful," and "moderately helpful") have a positive experience with AI tools for learning English.
- Room for Improvement: Since around 12.3% find AI slightly helpful, it suggests that AI tools may not fully address all learning needs (e.g., speaking practice, personalized guidance).
- Potential for Greater AI Integration: Educators can explore ways to increase engagement with AI tools by incorporating interactive AI-based activities, adaptive learning strategies, or AI-driven conversational practice.

Figure 9.

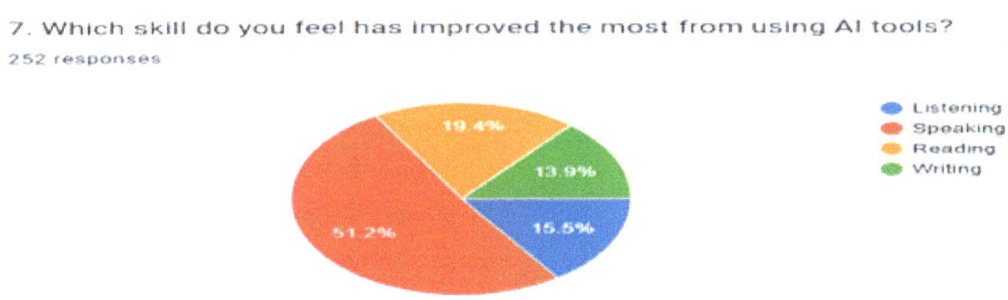

The pie chart represents students' perception of which English skill has improved the most through AI tools, based on 252 responses.

Key Observations:

1. Speaking Improvement is Most Notable (51.2%)
   - o More than half of respondents (51.2%) believe their speaking skills have improved the most.

    o This suggests that AI tools such as chatbots, pronunciation guides, and conversation simulators are effectively helping students enhance their spoken English.

2. Reading Improvement (19.4%)
    o 19.4% of students feel their reading skills have benefited the most.
    o AI-based text analyzers, reading comprehension apps, and interactive exercises likely contribute to this improvement.
3. Listening Improvement (15.5%)
    o Listening skills saw noticeable improvement for 15.5% of students.
    o This aligns with the use of AI-powered speech recognition, podcasts, and interactive listening tools that provide feedback.
4. Writing Improvement (13.9%)
    o The least improved skill (13.9%) is writing.
    o AI-based grammar checkers, writing assistants, and automated feedback tools might not be fully addressing advanced writing needs like coherence, creativity, or structuring arguments.

Insights & Implications:

- AI is Highly Effective for Speaking Skills: Tools like ChatGPT, speech recognition software, and pronunciation trainers are boosting confidence in spoken English.
- Writing Needs More AI Support: Since writing skills show the least improvement, AI tools may need enhancements in areas like essay structuring, critical thinking, and detailed feedback.
- Balanced AI Integration is Needed: While speaking and reading benefit the most, educators could integrate AI writing tutors or interactive listening exercises to support holistic skill development.

Figure 10.

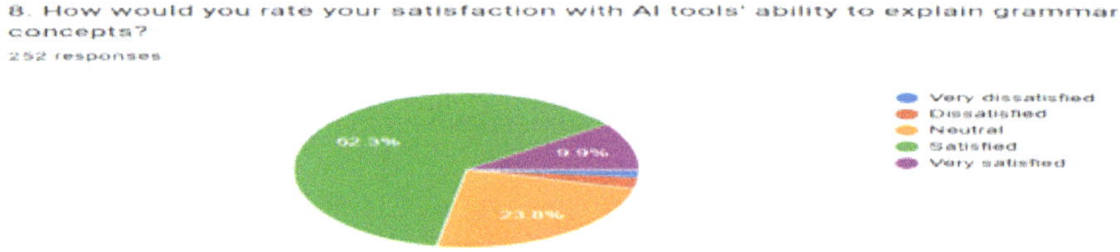

This pie chart represents students' satisfaction levels regarding AI tools' ability to explain grammar concepts, based on 252 responses.

Key Observations:

1. High Satisfaction (62.3%)
   - o A majority (62.3%) of students are satisfied with how AI tools explain grammar.
   - o This indicates that AI-powered grammar checkers and tutoring tools are effectively helping learners understand grammar rules.
2. Neutral Responses (23.8%)
   - o Nearly one-fourth (23.8%) of respondents feel neutral about AI tools' grammar explanations.
   - o This suggests that while AI provides basic explanations, it may not be as engaging or clear for complex grammar topics.
3. Low Satisfaction (9.9%)
   - o A small portion (9.9%) of students are dissatisfied or very dissatisfied.
   - o This could be due to confusing explanations, lack of contextual examples, or limited interactive learning features.

Insights & Recommendations:

- AI Tools Are Mostly Effective: The high satisfaction rate (62.3%) shows that students find AI tools useful for grammar learning.
- Enhancing Clarity for Complex Topics: AI tools might need to simplify explanations, provide more examples, or offer interactive exercises to engage learners better.
- Addressing Neutral & Dissatisfied Users: Features like step-by-step breakdowns, visual aids, and personalized feedback could increase satisfaction.

Figure 11.

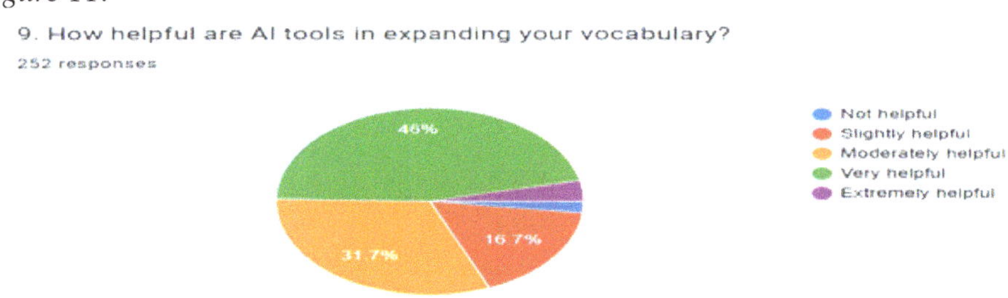

This pie chart represents students' perceptions of AI tools' effectiveness in expanding their vocabulary, based on 252 responses.

Key Observations:

1. Very Helpful (46%)
   - o Almost half (46%) of respondents find AI tools very helpful for vocabulary expansion.
   - o This suggests that AI-powered language tools (e.g., ChatGPT, Duolingo, and Google Assistant) are effectively introducing new words and their meanings.
2. Moderately Helpful (31.7%)
   - o A significant portion (31.7%) believes AI tools provide a moderate level of vocabulary improvement.
   - o These students might be benefiting from word suggestions and contextual usage but may not find AI tools as engaging or structured as traditional methods.
3. Slightly Helpful (16.7%)
   - o Some users (16.7%) feel AI tools are only slightly helpful, implying that the vocabulary learning experience might be too passive, repetitive, or lacking deeper contextual examples.
4. Minimal Dissatisfaction (Small Purple & Blue Sections)
   - o Only a small fraction of students (less than 10%) find AI tools not helpful or extremely helpful, indicating that most learners recognize some level of benefit.

Insights & Recommendations:

- AI Tools Are Beneficial for Vocabulary Growth:
  The high approval rate (46% "very helpful") confirms that AI tools successfully assist in learning new words and meanings.
- Enhancing Personalization for Better Learning:
  AI tools could be more effective if they adapt to users' proficiency levels and provide interactive learning features like gamification or contextual sentence-building activities.
- Encouraging Practical Usage:
  AI-driven conversation simulations or flashcard-based revision techniques could reinforce vocabulary retention.

Figure 12.

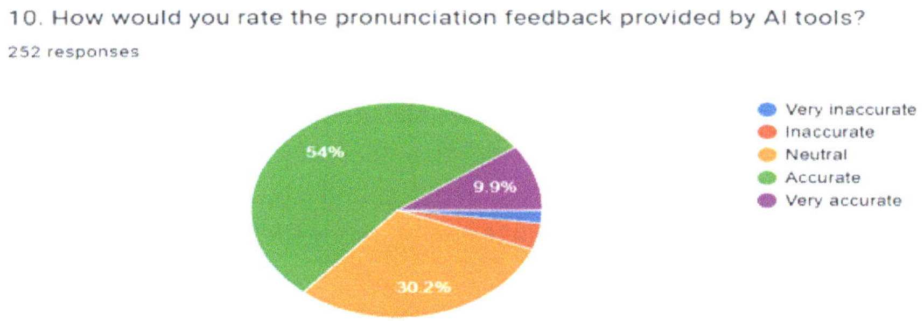

Analysis of Pronunciation Feedback from AI Tools

This chart represents users' ratings on the accuracy of pronunciation feedback provided by AI tools, based on 252 responses.

Key Findings:

1. Majority Find AI Pronunciation Feedback Accurate (54%)
    - o A significant 54% of respondents rated AI pronunciation feedback as accurate.
    - o This suggests that AI tools like Google Assistant, Duolingo, and ChatGPT offer reasonably effective pronunciation evaluation.
2. Neutral Perception (30.2%)
    - o About 30.2% of users rated the feedback as neutral, indicating they found AI pronunciation assistance somewhat helpful but not highly reliable.
    - o This may be due to a lack of detailed phonetic breakdowns, intonation guidance, or real-time corrective feedback.
3. Very Accurate (9.9%)
    - o A small percentage (9.9%) believe AI pronunciation feedback is very accurate, suggesting that some users find AI highly effective for pronunciation training.
4. Minimal Dissatisfaction (Tiny Red & Blue Sections)
    - o Only a very small portion of users rated AI pronunciation feedback as inaccurate or very inaccurate, which means most users at least acknowledge some benefit.

Insights & Recommendations:

- AI Is Helpful for Pronunciation but Could Improve Further

- o While most users find AI pronunciation feedback useful (54% accuracy rating), many still feel it's not perfect.
  - o AI tools could enhance pronunciation evaluation by offering clearer phonetic breakdowns, speech rhythm analysis, and tone correction.
- Need for Real-Time & Interactive Pronunciation Training
  - o Current AI tools may lack real-time feedback mechanisms like intonation analysis, syllable stress correction, and conversation-based practice.
  - o Incorporating AI-driven speech simulations and live interaction feedback could boost effectiveness.
- AI Could Offer More Personalized Feedback
  - o Pronunciation feedback could be more personalized, providing individualized improvement tips based on the user's native language interference and accent issues.

Figure 13.

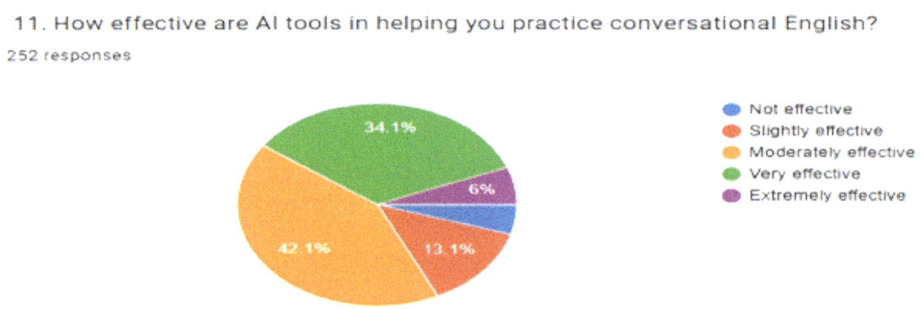

Analysis of AI Tools for Conversational English Practice

This chart represents user feedback on how effective AI tools are in helping with conversational English, based on 252 responses.

Key Findings:

1. Majority Find AI Moderately Effective (42.1%)
   - o The largest segment (42.1%) rated AI tools as moderately effective, suggesting they provide some help but have limitations.
   - o This could be because most AI tools lack natural conversation flow or human-like interaction.
2. A Significant Portion Finds AI Very Effective (34.1%)
   - o 34.1% of users find AI tools very effective for conversational English.

- o This indicates that AI-powered platforms like ChatGPT, Duolingo, and Elsa Speak provide valuable speaking practice.

3. Smaller Percentage Sees AI as Extremely Effective (6%)
   - o Only 6% of users feel AI is extremely effective in improving spoken English.
   - o This suggests that AI still needs to improve fluency-building, real-time interaction, and contextual understanding.
4. Some Users Find AI Slightly Effective or Not Effective (13.1% & 6%)
   - o 13.1% rate AI as slightly effective, indicating some difficulty in real-time conversation practice.
   - o 6% find AI not effective, possibly due to monotone responses, lack of emotional expression, or improper contextual adaptation.

Insights & Recommendations:

- AI Can Improve Conversational Practice but Has Limitations
  - o While AI tools provide a good starting point for conversation practice, they lack spontaneity, cultural context, and interactive depth.
  - o Adding speech recognition, real-time dialogue correction, and AI avatars for immersive roleplay could enhance effectiveness.
- Integrate AI with Human Interaction
  - o AI-based learning should be combined with human interaction, such as live tutoring, peer conversations, or AI-assisted debate sessions.
- Develop More Advanced AI Features for Spoken English
  - o AI tools should focus on intonation training, emotion recognition, and context-based responses to simulate real-life conversations better.

Figure 14.

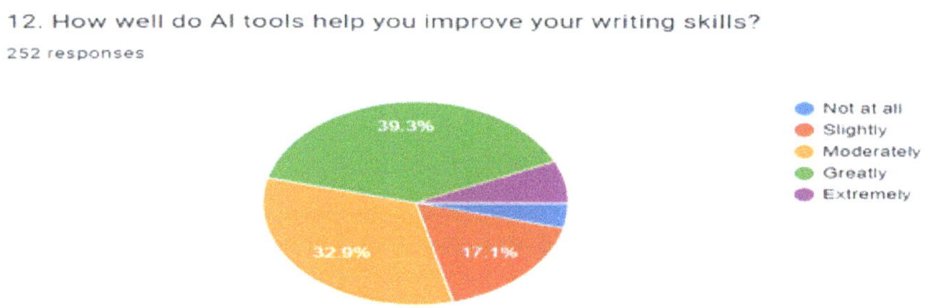

Analysis of AI Tools in Improving Writing Skills

This chart illustrates how well AI tools help users enhance their writing skills, based on 252 responses.

Key Findings:

1. Most Users Find AI Tools Highly Beneficial for Writing (39.3%)
    - 39.3% of respondents stated that AI tools help them greatly in improving writing skills.
    - This suggests that AI-powered writing assistants like Grammarly, ChatGPT, QuillBot, and Hemingway Editor are effectively enhancing grammar, structure, and clarity.
2. A Significant Portion Finds AI Moderately Helpful (32.9%)
    - 32.9% of users find AI moderately helpful, implying that while AI assists with grammar and structure, it may lack creativity, depth, or contextual understanding.
3. Some Users Feel AI Helps Slightly or Not at All (17.1% & Small Percentage in Blue)
    - 17.1% rate AI as slightly helpful, indicating that AI may not address complex writing issues, advanced vocabulary usage, or coherence.
    - A small portion finds AI not useful at all, possibly due to over-reliance on automation or lack of personalized writing guidance.
4. Only a Small Percentage Find AI Extremely Effective (Purple Section)
    - Few respondents rate AI as extremely effective, suggesting that while AI tools can help correct errors and provide feedback, they lack human creativity and nuanced writing improvement.

Insights & Recommendations:

- AI Tools Are Effective for Grammar and Structure but Not Creativity
    - AI writing tools are great at correcting mistakes, improving readability, and enhancing fluency.
    - However, they may not fully develop creativity, critical thinking, or nuanced expression.
- Combine AI Assistance with Human Feedback
    - AI-generated suggestions should be reviewed by educators or mentors to refine writing style, argumentation, and coherence.
- Use AI for Drafting and Editing, Not Solely for Writing
    - Students should leverage AI for structuring ideas, checking grammar, and revising drafts rather than relying on AI-generated content entirely.

Figure 15.

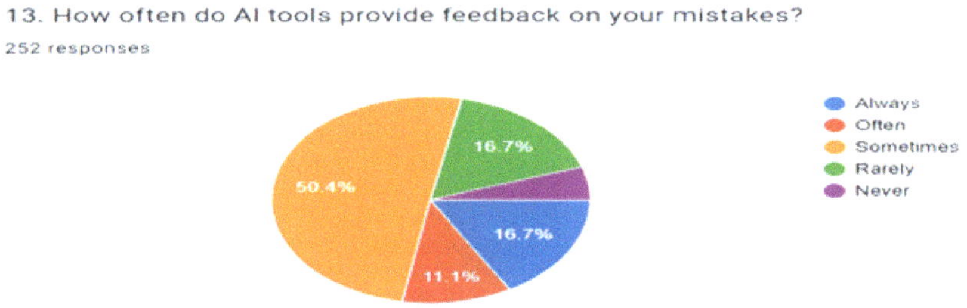

Analysis of AI Tools' Feedback on Mistakes

This pie chart displays how often AI tools provide feedback on users' mistakes, based on 252 responses.

Key Findings:

1. AI Tools Often Provide Feedback (50.4%)
   - o Half of the respondents (50.4%) say AI tools often give feedback on their mistakes.
   - o This suggests AI tools are consistently identifying and correcting errors, particularly in grammar, spelling, and structure.
2. AI Always Provides Feedback for Some Users (16.7%)
   - o 16.7% report that AI always provides feedback, which means these users rely on AI tools that actively detect and suggest corrections in real-time.
3. AI Sometimes Provides Feedback (16.7%)
   - o Another 16.7% feel AI only sometimes provides feedback, possibly due to limitations in context recognition, advanced writing analysis, or lack of detailed explanations.
4. Limited Feedback for a Few Users (11.1% Rarely & Small Percentage in Purple for Never)
   - o 11.1% report that AI rarely provides feedback, and a small percentage feel AI never helps.
   - o This could be due to AI's inability to recognize deeper language mistakes, poor input quality, or limited tool capabilities.

Insights & Recommendations:

- AI Tools Are Helpful but Not Perfect

- AI tools are effective in detecting grammatical and structural errors, but they might miss nuanced mistakes in content coherence, logic, or advanced language use.

- Users Should Complement AI Feedback with Human Review
    - While AI is useful for quick corrections, teachers or language experts should review complex errors for clarity and depth.
- Choosing the Right AI Tool Matters
    - Some AI tools, such as Grammarly, ProWritingAid, and ChatGPT, provide detailed explanations, while others may only highlight basic errors.

Figure 16.

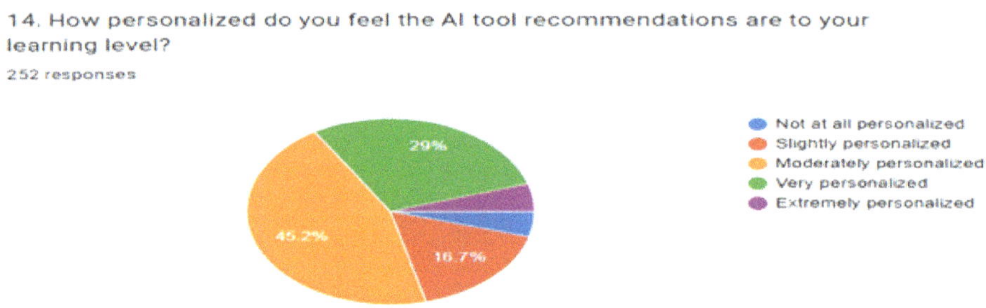

Analysis of AI Tool Personalization for Learning Levels

This pie chart shows how 252 respondents feel about the personalization of AI tool recommendations to their learning levels.

Key Findings:

1. Moderate Personalization is Most Common (45.2%)
    - Nearly half (45.2%) of the respondents believe AI tools provide moderate personalization.
    - This suggests that AI tools partially adjust recommendations based on individual needs but may not be fully adaptive.
2. Highly Personalized for Some Users (29%)
    - 29% of users feel AI recommendations are very personalized.
    - This indicates that some AI tools effectively adapt to different proficiency levels.
3. Limited Personalization for a Significant Percentage (16.7% Slightly Personalized, Small Percentage in Blue for Not Personalized at All)
    - 16.7% feel AI recommendations are only slightly personalized.

- o A small number of users believe AI tools are not personalized at all, which may indicate that some platforms offer generic suggestions rather than tailored content.

4. Extremely Personalized for a Few Users
   - o A small percentage (purple segment) found AI recommendations extremely personalized, meaning that some advanced AI tools do provide highly customized learning paths.

Insights & Recommendations:

- AI Personalization Needs Improvement
  - o While AI tools show some adaptability, they may not fully analyze user progress or customize learning paths effectively.
- Adaptive Learning AI Could Be More Effective
  - o AI tools should incorporate more adaptive learning features, such as progress tracking, real-time assessments, and dynamic difficulty adjustment.
- Users Should Choose AI Tools with Customization Features
  - o Platforms like Duolingo, Grammarly, and ChatGPT allow some personalization.
  - o More advanced AI-powered tools with machine learning adaptation might be needed for highly personalized learning experiences.

Figure 17. Analysis of AI Translation and Vocabulary Explanation Accuracy

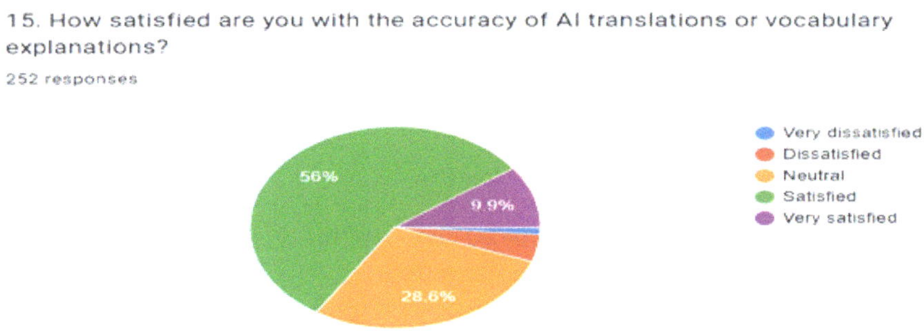

This pie chart represents the satisfaction levels of 252 respondents regarding the accuracy of AI-powered translations and vocabulary explanations.

Key Findings:

1. Majority of Respondents Are Satisfied (56%)
   - o A majority (56%) of respondents feel satisfied with AI translations and vocabulary explanations.
   - o This suggests that AI tools are generally effective in providing accurate translations and word meanings.
2. Moderate Neutrality (28.6%)
   - o About 28.6% of respondents remain neutral, meaning that while AI tools are useful, they may still require improvements in precision or contextual accuracy.
3. Very Satisfied Users (9.9%)
   - o A small percentage (9.9%) find AI translations extremely reliable, indicating that some users experience highly accurate and contextually appropriate results.
4. Dissatisfaction Is Minimal
   - o Very few users report dissatisfaction (small red and blue segments).
   - o This implies that AI-powered language tools rarely provide completely inaccurate translations, though occasional errors may occur.

Insights & Recommendations:

- AI Translation Tools Are Largely Effective
  - o Popular AI tools like Google Translate, DeepL, and ChatGPT appear to provide mostly accurate translations and vocabulary explanations.
- Contextual Understanding Needs Refinement
  - o AI tools may struggle with idioms, slang, or domain-specific vocabulary, which could explain the neutral and dissatisfied responses.
  - o AI should integrate deeper contextual learning to improve language nuances.
- Users Should Rely on Multiple Tools for Best Accuracy
  - o Combining AI tools (e.g., using Google Translate for word-to-word accuracy and ChatGPT for contextual understanding) can enhance results.
  - o Cross-referencing different AI tools ensures higher accuracy in meaning and translation.

Figure 18.

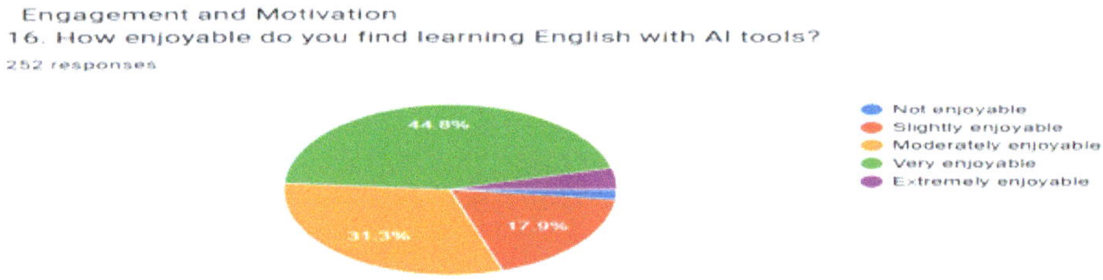

The pie chart presents data on the enjoyment levels of students learning English with AI tools. Here's an analysis:

1. Overall Positive Response:
   - o A significant portion of respondents (44.8%) found learning with AI tools very enjoyable (green).
   - o Another 31.3% found it moderately enjoyable (orange).
   - o A smaller but notable 5% (approx.) found it extremely enjoyable (purple).
   - o This means nearly 81% of students had a positive experience using AI tools for learning English.
2. Mixed to Negative Response:
   - o 17.9% of respondents found AI-assisted learning only slightly enjoyable (red).
   - o A very small proportion (blue section), likely under 5%, found it not enjoyable at all.
   - o This suggests that while a minority may struggle or find AI tools ineffective, the overall perception remains positive.
3. Implications for AI in English Learning:
   - o The high percentage of "very enjoyable" and "moderately enjoyable" responses suggests that AI tools can be engaging and effective for language learning.
   - o The small group that found it not enjoyable or slightly enjoyable may require better personalization or training to maximize AI tool benefits.
   - o Educators might consider integrating more interactive AI-based exercises to increase engagement for those with a lower enjoyment level.

Conclusion:

AI-enhanced English learning appears to be largely well-received, with over three-fourths of students reporting positive experiences. Future studies could explore how different AI tools contribute to motivation, personalization, and learning effectiveness.

Figure 19.

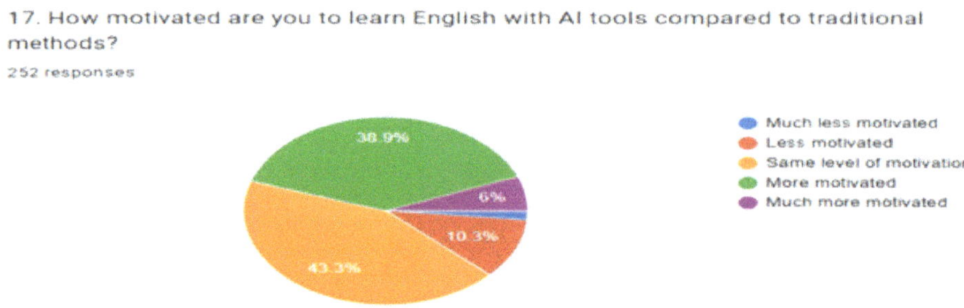

The pie chart presents data on students' motivation levels when learning English with AI tools compared to traditional methods. Here's an analysis:

Key Findings:

1. Higher Motivation with AI Tools:
   - 38.9% of respondents feel more motivated (green) when using AI tools.
   - 6% feel much more motivated (purple).
   - Together, this means nearly 45% of students feel AI tools increase their motivation to learn English.
2. Moderate Motivation Levels:
   - The largest segment (43.3%, orange) reports having the same level of motivation as with traditional methods.
   - This suggests that while AI tools enhance engagement for some, they do not drastically change motivation levels for a significant portion.
3. Lower Motivation with AI Tools:
   - 10.3% of students feel less motivated (red).
   - The portion for "much less motivated" (blue section) is either negligible or absent in the chart.
   - This indicates that only a small fraction of students perceive AI-based learning as demotivating.

Implications for AI-Enhanced Learning:

- Since nearly half of the students feel more motivated, AI tools seem to have a positive impact on engagement.
- However, the large proportion reporting the same level of motivation (43.3%) suggests that AI tools may not be inherently better at increasing motivation compared to traditional methods—rather, their effectiveness might depend on how they are implemented.
- The 10.3% who feel less motivated may require more personalized AI learning experiences or additional support to make AI-assisted learning more engaging.

Conclusion:

The data suggests that AI tools are generally effective in enhancing motivation, with nearly half the students feeling more motivated than with traditional methods. However, educators should explore tailored AI-driven learning experiences to ensure that all students benefit equally and to address the small group that finds AI learning less motivating.

Figure 20.

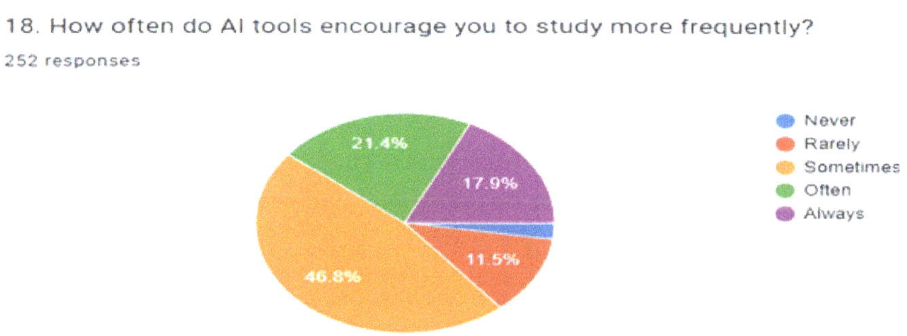

The pie chart provides insights into how often AI tools encourage students to study more frequently. Here's a detailed analysis:

Key Findings:

1. Moderate to High Encouragement by AI Tools:
   - o 46.8% of respondents say AI tools encourage them to study sometimes (orange).
   - o 21.4% report that AI tools encourage them to study often (green).
   - o 17.9% say AI tools always encourage them to study (purple).

- o Together, this means over 86% of students experience at least some level of encouragement from AI tools.

2. Limited Encouragement:
   - o 11.5% of students feel AI tools rarely encourage them to study (red).
   - o A very small portion (blue section, likely below 5%) indicates that AI tools never encourage them to study.
   - o This suggests that while a small minority does not find AI motivating, most students still experience some level of study encouragement.

Implications for AI in Learning:

- Since nearly 40% of students (combining "often" and "always") feel highly encouraged by AI tools, these tools appear to have a strong impact on study frequency.
- The largest group (46.8%) falls into the "sometimes" category, which suggests that while AI tools are helpful, they may not be consistently motivating for all students.
- The small percentage (rarely or never) might indicate a need for more engaging AI-driven learning methods or better personalization.

Conclusion:

AI tools generally encourage students to study more frequently, with a majority (86%+) experiencing at least some level of encouragement. However, more research is needed to understand how AI can be improved to consistently motivate students and cater to those who currently feel less encouraged.

Figure 21.

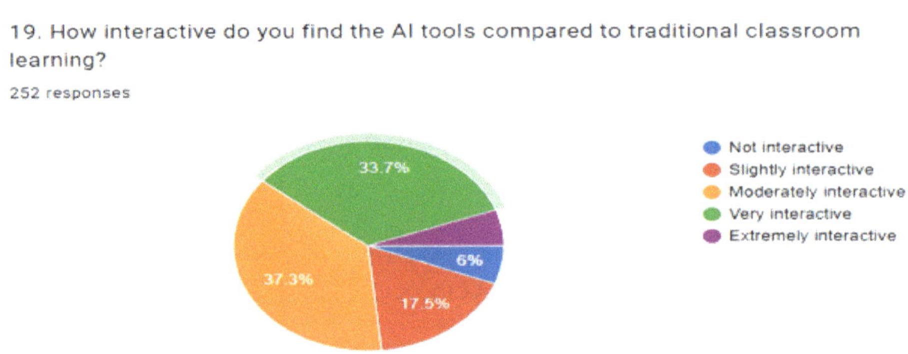

The pie chart presents students' perceptions of how interactive AI tools are compared to traditional classroom learning. Here's an analysis:

Key Findings:

1. Moderate to High Interactivity:
    - o 37.3% of students rated AI tools as moderately interactive (orange).
    - o 33.7% found them very interactive (green).
    - o A smaller but notable 6% found them extremely interactive (purple).
    - o This means nearly 77% of students view AI tools as interactive to some extent.
2. Lower Interactivity Ratings:
    - o 17.5% of students found AI tools slightly interactive (red).
    - o Only 6% felt AI tools were not interactive at all (blue).
    - o This suggests that a minority of students perceive AI tools as lacking interactivity, but the majority still find them engaging.

Implications for AI in Learning:

- Since over 70% of students perceive AI as interactive, this indicates that AI tools are effective in engaging learners, though they may not yet fully replicate traditional classroom interactivity.
- The large "moderately interactive" group (37.3%) suggests that AI tools could benefit from additional features like real-time feedback, adaptive learning paths, and gamification to increase engagement.
- The small proportion (6%) who found AI tools "not interactive" may have experienced tools with limited engagement features or may prefer human interaction over AI-based learning.

Conclusion:

AI tools are largely seen as interactive, with a strong majority (77%) acknowledging at least a moderate level of interactivity. However, further improvements in personalization, real-time feedback, and interactive elements could help make AI-assisted learning even more engaging and comparable to traditional classrooms.

Figure 22.

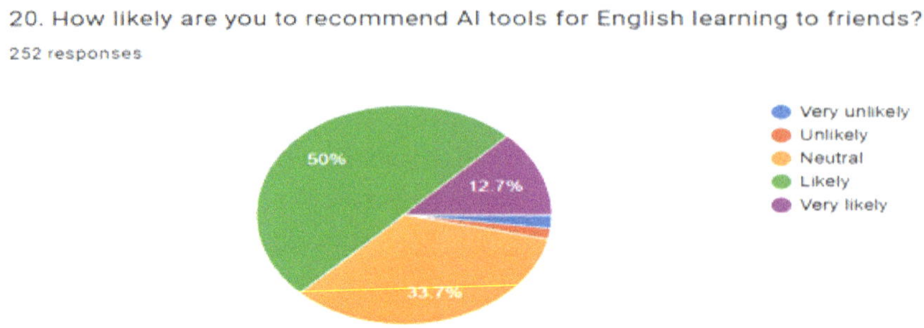

The pie chart presents students' likelihood of recommending AI tools for English learning to their friends. Here's an analysis:

Key Findings:

1. Strong Positive Recommendation:
   - 50% of respondents (green) are likely to recommend AI tools for English learning.
   - 12.7% (purple) are very likely to recommend them.
   - This means over 62% of students would recommend AI tools, suggesting a generally favorable perception.
2. Neutral Opinions:
   - 33.7% of students (orange) are neutral, meaning they neither strongly endorse nor reject AI tools.
   - This could indicate that while they find AI tools useful, they may not see them as significantly better than traditional learning methods.
3. Low Negative Sentiment:
   - The unlikeable (red) and very unlikely (blue) segments are either negligible or absent, meaning very few students would discourage others from using AI tools.
   - This suggests that negative experiences with AI tools are minimal.

Implications for AI in Learning:

- Since over 60% of students are willing to recommend AI tools, this highlights their perceived effectiveness in language learning.

- The large neutral group (33.7%) suggests that some students may not have experienced AI tools deeply enough to form a strong opinion or that AI tools need to offer more compelling benefits.
- The lack of strong negative responses indicates that AI tools are generally well-accepted, though improvements in personalization and engagement could further increase positive recommendations.

Conclusion:

AI tools for English learning enjoy a high level of recommendation, with a majority (62%+) actively supporting them and only a minimal number of students expressing negative views. However, addressing the neutral segment (33.7%) with more engaging features could further increase overall satisfaction and advocacy for AI-driven learning.

Figure 23.

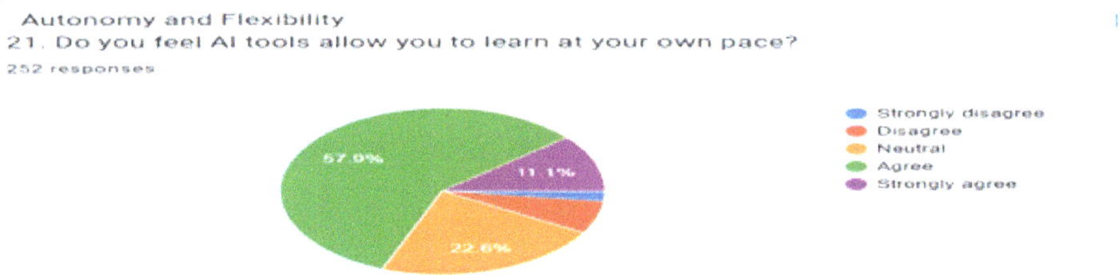

The pie chart analyzes students' perceptions of autonomy and flexibility when using AI tools for learning. Specifically, it addresses whether AI tools allow students to learn at their own pace.

Key Findings:

1. Strong Agreement on Learning Flexibility:
   - o 57.9% (green) agree that AI tools allow them to learn at their own pace.
   - o 11.1% (purple) strongly agree with this statement.
   - o This means nearly 69% of students feel AI tools provide learning autonomy, indicating that AI-driven platforms successfully cater to individual learning speeds.
2. Neutral Perspective:
   - o 22.6% (yellow) remain neutral, meaning they neither agree nor disagree.
   - o This group may not have fully explored AI's adaptability or may feel it depends on the specific tool used.
3. Low Disagreement Rate:

- o A small percentage (red and blue) disagrees with the statement, though the exact values are low.
- o This suggests that very few students feel restricted by AI tools.

Implications for AI in Learning:

- AI tools appear highly effective in allowing learners to study at their own pace, as nearly 70% of users confirm this benefit.
- The neutral group (22.6%) might indicate that some AI tools lack customizable pacing options, or students may not be fully utilizing available self-paced features.
- The minimal disagreement rate highlights that most students find AI tools more flexible compared to traditional learning methods.

Conclusion:

AI-powered learning tools are widely recognized for their autonomy and flexibility, with close to 70% of students confirming their effectiveness in self-paced learning. Future improvements in adaptive learning paths and personalized recommendations could help address the neutral segment and make AI tools even more effective for self-directed learning.

Figure 24.

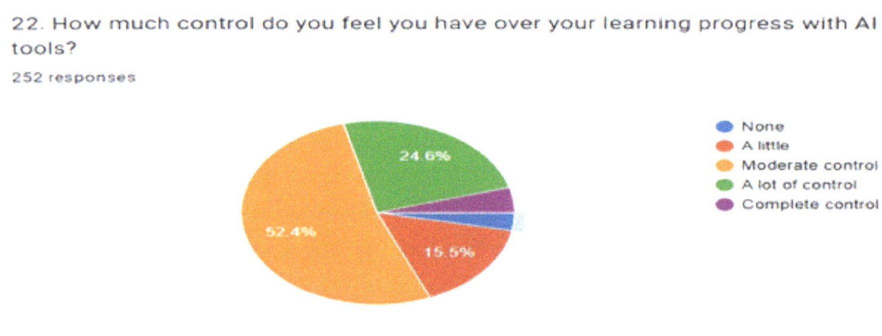

The pie chart presents data on students' perceptions of how much control they feel they have over their learning progress when using AI tools.

Key Observations:

1. Moderate to High Control:

- o 52.4% (orange) feel they have moderate control over their learning progress.
- o 24.6% (green) believe they have a lot of control.
- o A smaller group (purple, ~5%) feels they have complete control.
- o Together, about 82% of students believe AI tools offer at least moderate control over their learning progress, indicating that AI tools provide structure while allowing customization.

2. Lower Control Perception:
   - o 15.5% (red) feel they have only a little control.
   - o A very small percentage (blue, almost negligible) report having no control at all over their learning progress.

Implications for AI in Learning:

- Most students feel empowered by AI tools, as over 80% perceive some level of control over their learning progress.
- The 15.5% who feel they have little control might be struggling with AI-driven content personalization, indicating a need for more user-driven learning options or better guidance on how to navigate AI-based learning platforms.
- The small group that feels they have no control suggests that some students might find AI-driven learning too rigid or non-customizable.

Conclusion:

AI tools appear to be successful in offering learners control over their study progress, with the majority experiencing moderate to high autonomy. However, further enhancements in customization, adaptive learning paths, and learner-driven settings could improve engagement for those who feel restricted.

Figure 25.

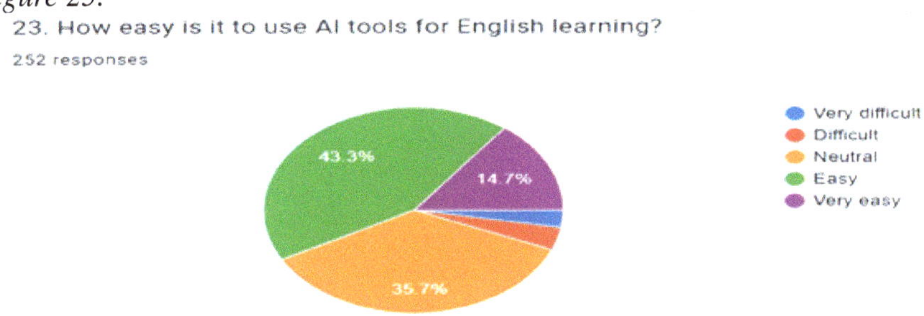

The pie chart provides insights into students' perceptions of the ease of using AI tools for English learning.

Key Observations:

1. Majority Find AI Tools Easy to Use:
   - o 43.3% (green) say AI tools are easy to use.
   - o 14.7% (purple) find them very easy.
   - o Together, 58% of students find AI tools user-friendly, indicating that most learners adapt well to AI-based learning platforms.
2. Neutral Response:
   - o 35.7% (orange) hold a neutral stance, suggesting they might have mixed experiences with AI tools.
   - o This group might find some AI tools accessible but struggle with others due to usability, complexity, or lack of familiarity.
3. Challenges in Using AI Tools:
   - o A small percentage (red & blue, combined less than 10%) find AI tools either difficult or very difficult to use.
   - o This suggests that some learners may face barriers such as a lack of digital literacy, complicated interfaces, or insufficient guidance.

Implications for AI in Learning:

- Most learners (over half) find AI tools easy to use, making them an accessible option for English learning.
- A significant neutral group (35.7%) suggests that some improvements in AI tool design, tutorials, and user support could help ease adoption.
- A small group struggles with AI tools, highlighting a need for simpler interfaces, better onboarding, and user-friendly experiences.

Conclusion:

AI tools are generally well-received in terms of usability, but further refinements in interface design, user experience, and guidance could enhance accessibility, especially for those who find them challenging.

Figure 26.

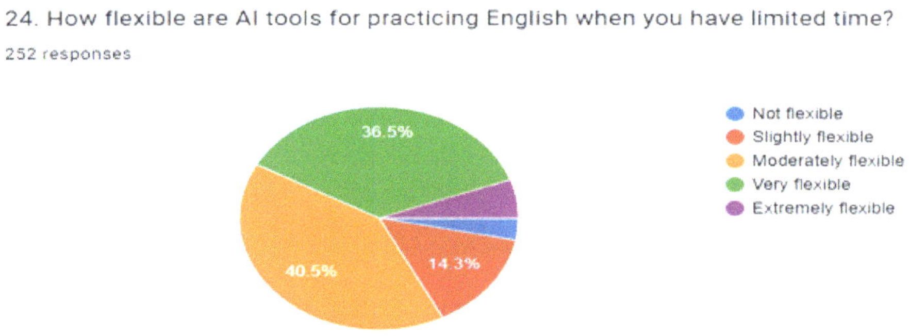

This pie chart illustrates students' perceptions of the flexibility of AI tools for practicing English when they have limited time.

Key Observations:

1. AI Tools Are Considered Flexible by Most Students:
    - o 36.5% (green) find AI tools very flexible.
    - o 40.5% (orange) consider them moderately flexible.
    - o Together, 77% of respondents acknowledge AI tools as at least moderately flexible, showing that these tools effectively adapt to students' schedules.
2. Limited but Present Challenges:
    - o 14.3% (red) perceive AI tools as slightly flexible, indicating that some learners may struggle to integrate AI learning into their busy schedules.
    - o A small fraction (blue and purple, combined less than 10%) feel AI tools are either not flexible or extremely flexible, suggesting a more polarized experience among a few students.

Implications for AI-Driven English Learning:

- AI tools offer a high degree of flexibility, making them suitable for learners with time constraints.
- Some learners still face barriers in using AI tools effectively when pressed for time, possibly due to:
    - o Rigid AI tool structures.
    - o Insufficient personalization.
    - o The need for self-discipline in using AI for learning.

- Future improvements should focus on adaptive learning features, quick-access lessons, and personalized schedules to enhance flexibility for all learners.

Conclusion:

AI tools are widely perceived as flexible, making them a valuable resource for busy learners. However, refinements in AI-driven personalization and time-efficient learning modules could further improve user experience and accessibility.

Figure 27.

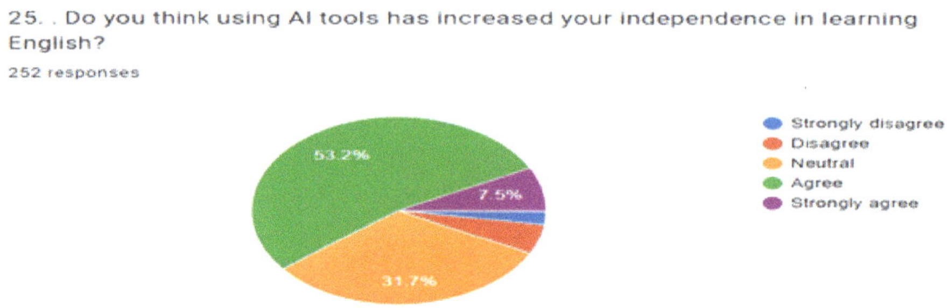

This pie chart represents students' perceptions of whether AI tools have increased their independence in learning English.

Key Observations:

1. AI Tools Promote Independence for Most Students:
   - 53.2% (green) agree that AI tools have increased their independence.
   - 7.5% (purple) strongly agree, indicating a high level of self-reliance fostered by AI.
   - Together, 60.7% of students feel that AI tools make them more independent learners.
2. Moderate Views:
   - 31.7% (yellow) remain neutral, meaning they have not noticed a significant impact on their independence.
   - These students may still rely on traditional classroom methods or require additional guidance while using AI tools.
3. Skepticism Exists:
   - A small portion (blue and red, less than 10%) either disagree or strongly disagree that AI tools have increased their independence.

- This suggests that for some students, AI tools may lack sufficient guidance, personalized feedback, or engaging methodologies to encourage self-learning.

Implications for AI-Based English Learning:

- AI tools are effective in fostering independent learning, as a majority (over 60%) believe they have become more self-reliant.
- Some students remain uncertain, highlighting the need for better self-paced learning features and personalized AI feedback to improve their confidence.
- A small percentage struggles with AI-based independence, possibly due to:
  - Lack of structured guidance.
  - Difficulty adapting to AI-driven learning.
  - Preference for teacher-led instruction.

Conclusion:

AI tools significantly enhance learner independence, but further improvements in personalized learning experiences and adaptive support can help make AI-based education even more effective for all students.

Figure 28.

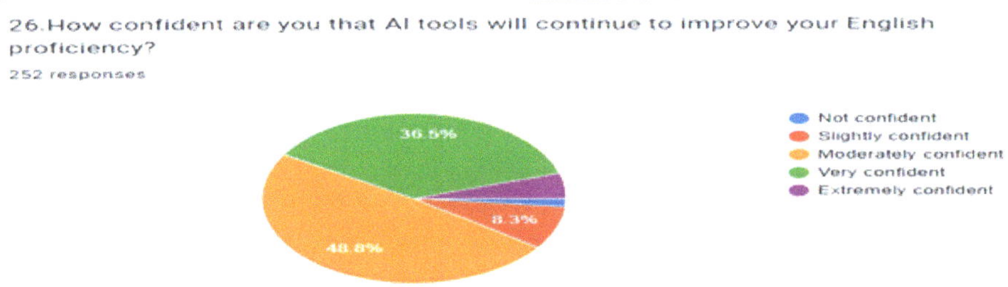

This pie chart illustrates students' confidence in AI tools' ability to improve their English proficiency.

Key Observations:

1. Overall Confidence in AI for English Improvement:
   - 36.5% (green) are very confident, showing strong belief in AI's effectiveness.
   - 48.8% (orange) are moderately confident, suggesting they recognize AI's potential but may have some reservations.

- o Together, 85.3% of respondents express at least moderate confidence in AI tools improving their English proficiency.

2. Lower Confidence Levels:
   - o 8.3% (red) are slightly confident, indicating some skepticism or dissatisfaction.
   - o A very small portion (purple) are extremely confident, possibly due to personal success with AI-driven learning.
3. Minimal Lack of Confidence:
   - o The absence of a "Not Confident" (blue) section suggests that nearly all respondents believe AI tools provide at least some benefits for English learning.

Implications for AI-Based English Learning:

- The majority of students (85.3%) believe AI will continue enhancing their proficiency, showing strong trust in AI-assisted learning.
- The 8.3% slight-confidence group might need more interactive, personalized, or engaging AI features to build trust.
- The low presence of extreme confidence suggests that while AI is helpful, students may still rely on traditional learning methods or human interaction for better fluency.

Conclusion:

AI tools are widely perceived as useful and effective in improving English proficiency, but there is room for enhanced adaptability, interactivity, and advanced learning features to boost user confidence further.

Figure 29.

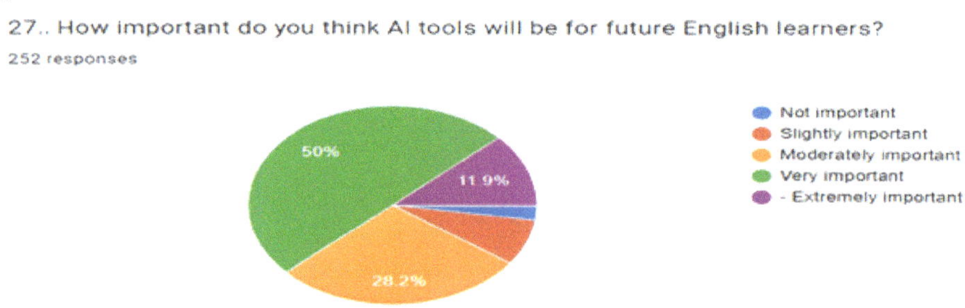

This pie chart presents data on the perceived importance of AI tools for future English learners.

Key Observations:

1. Strong Belief in AI's Importance:
   - o 50% (green) believe AI tools will be very important for future English learners.
   - o 28.2% (orange) see them as moderately important.
   - o Together, 78.2% of respondents recognize AI's role in future English learning.
2. Higher Confidence Levels:
   - o 11.9% (purple) consider AI tools extremely important, showing enthusiasm for AI's potential.
   - o Only a small portion of respondents consider AI slightly important (red), suggesting some uncertainty.
3. Minimal Opposition:
   - o The absence of "Not Important" (blue) responses indicates that nearly all participants acknowledge AI's relevance in language learning.

Implications for AI in Language Learning:

- The overwhelming support (78.2%) suggests that AI will play a crucial role in shaping future language learning methods.
- The 11.9% extreme-confidence group may already see AI as transformative, possibly due to its ability to provide personalized learning experiences.
- A small fraction remains skeptical, highlighting the need for improvements in AI-driven learning tools to address various learner needs.

Conclusion:

AI is widely regarded as an essential tool for future English learning, with most respondents expecting it to play a major role. Future improvements in AI's adaptability and interactivity can further solidify its importance in education.

Figure 30.

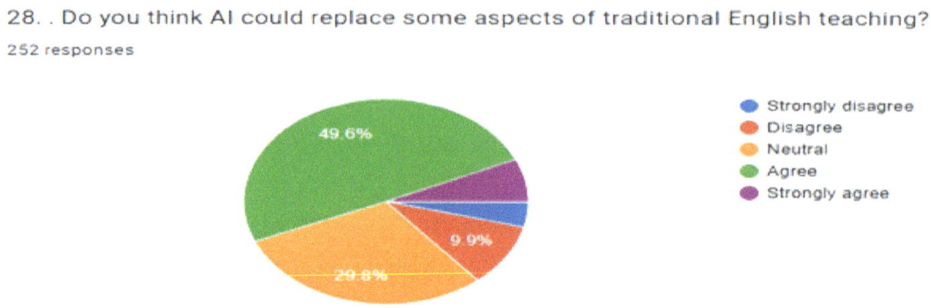

This pie chart presents responses to whether AI could replace some aspects of traditional English teaching.

Key Observations:

1. Strong Agreement with AI's Role:
   - o 49.6% (green) agree that AI could replace certain aspects of traditional English teaching.
   - o 9.9% (purple) strongly agree, reinforcing the belief that AI has significant potential in education.
2. Neutral Stance:
   - o 29.8% (orange) are neutral, indicating that while they see AI's potential, they are not fully convinced it can replace traditional teaching.
3. Skepticism Exists:
   - o A small percentage (red and blue) disagrees or strongly disagrees, meaning they believe AI cannot fully replace human-led teaching methods.

Implications for AI in English Teaching:

- Over 59% of respondents acknowledge AI's capability to handle some aspects of teaching, which could mean tasks like grammar correction, vocabulary building, and personalized feedback.
- The neutral group (29.8%) may need further evidence or experience with AI-assisted learning before forming a strong opinion.
- Traditional teaching remains valuable, as a portion of respondents still disagrees with AI's potential to replace certain aspects.

Conclusion:

AI is widely seen as a valuable supplement rather than a full replacement for traditional English teaching. While it can handle some learning tasks efficiently, human educators remain essential for aspects like critical thinking, creativity, and personalized mentoring.

Figure 31.

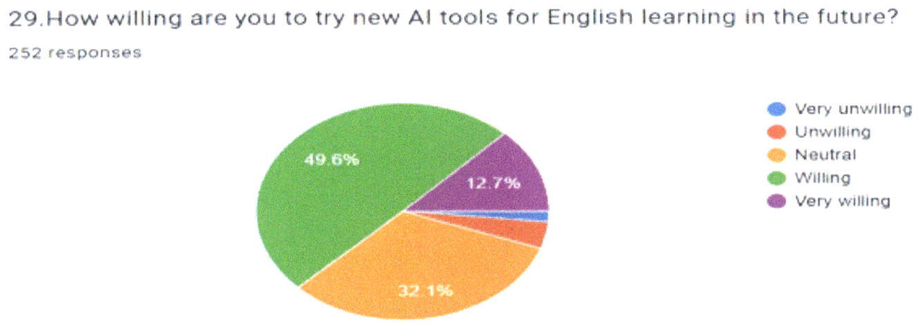

This pie chart presents responses to the question of willingness to try new AI tools for English learning in the future.

Key Observations:

1. Strong Willingness to Try AI Tools:
   - o 49.6% (green) are willing to try new AI tools.
   - o 12.7% (purple) are very willing, showing a positive outlook toward AI in language learning.
2. Neutral Attitude:
   - o 32.1% (orange) remain neutral, meaning they may need more information or positive experiences to make a decision.
3. Minimal Resistance:
   - o The unwilling category is very small, with only a small fraction of respondents indicating reluctance.

Implications for AI Adoption in English Learning:

- Over 62% are open to trying AI tools, indicating a favorable trend toward AI-driven learning solutions.
- The neutral group (32.1%) represents a potential area for awareness and training programs to boost AI adoption.

- Very few are unwilling, meaning there is no major resistance to AI tools in English learning.

Conclusion:

AI tools have strong potential for adoption in English learning, with a majority of users showing interest. Future efforts should focus on educating the neutral group about the benefits of AI in language learning.

Figure 32.

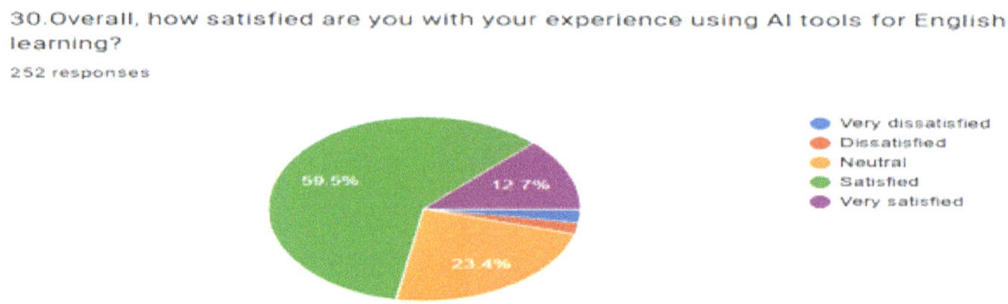

This pie chart represents respondents' satisfaction levels with their experience using AI tools for English learning.

Key Observations:

1. High Satisfaction Levels:
   - o 59.5% (green) are satisfied with their experience.
   - o 12.7% (purple) are very satisfied, reinforcing a strong positive response.
   - o Total positive feedback: 72.2%, indicating that most users find AI tools beneficial.
2. Neutral Response:
   - o 23.4% (orange) are neutral, meaning they neither had a positive nor negative experience. They might require further engagement or improvements in AI tools.
3. Minimal Dissatisfaction:
   - o A very small percentage is dissatisfied, with hardly any respondents being very dissatisfied.
   - o This suggests that negative experiences with AI tools are rare.

Implications for AI in English Learning:

- Strong user satisfaction (72.2%) indicates AI tools are effective and appreciated.
- The neutral group (23.4%) presents an opportunity for further enhancement of AI tools, possibly through better personalization or training.
- Very low dissatisfaction rates suggest that AI tools are generally well-received, with room for refinement rather than major overhauls.

Conclusion:

AI tools for English learning are widely accepted and effective, with a majority of users satisfied with their experience. To improve adoption further, engaging the neutral group and addressing minor concerns could enhance overall satisfaction levels.

LIMITATIONS OF AI

1. The Teacher's Role in an AI-Augmented Classroom

Despite the growing integration of AI tools into educational environments, **teachers remain irreplaceable as facilitators, mentors, and cultural mediators**. In AI-enhanced language learning, the teacher's role evolves rather than diminishes. They:

- **Guide personalized learning pathways**, interpreting AI feedback and adapting it to student needs.
- **Support emotional and social learning**, which AI tools currently cannot replicate effectively.
- **Contextualize content** to ensure relevance, cultural appropriateness, and alignment with curriculum goals.
- **Bridge the gap between human nuance and machine output**, helping learners critically assess and refine AI-generated content.
- **Promote ethical AI usage**, including issues of plagiarism, privacy, and data consent.

Far from being displaced, educators become **orchestrators of a human-AI symphony**, ensuring that technological integration remains purposeful, pedagogically sound, and student-centered.

2. Limitations of AI in Education

While AI offers tremendous capabilities in automating feedback, adaptive learning, and instant translation, it is **far from infallible**:

- **Contextual Misunderstanding**: AI struggles with idiomatic expressions, sarcasm, and cultural subtext—crucial aspects of authentic communication.
- **Bias and Inaccuracy**: AI models trained on large datasets may reflect **biases** or produce inaccurate or inappropriate suggestions without context awareness.
- **Lack of Emotional Intelligence**: AI cannot fully grasp or respond to students' emotional states, motivational levels, or mental health concerns.
- **Ethical Ambiguity**: Questions around data privacy, surveillance, and algorithmic decision-making remain unresolved.

Hence, AI should be treated not as a replacement for educators but as a **complementary tool that requires human oversight**.

3. The Digital Divide: A Barrier to Equitable Access

AI-enhanced education depends on **infrastructure, digital literacy, and socioeconomic status**—factors that create a sharp digital divide:

- **Device and Connectivity Inequity**: Rural or underprivileged students often lack access to the necessary hardware, software, or reliable internet.
- **Language and Interface Accessibility**: Many AI tools are optimized for major world languages and may exclude vernacular or indigenous language speakers.
- **Digital Literacy Gaps**: Both students and teachers may struggle with unfamiliar interfaces, limiting the tool's effectiveness.

Bridging the digital divide demands **policy interventions**, **inclusive design**, and **localized support systems** to ensure AI benefits do not widen existing inequalities.

4. Cross-Culturally Shifted Communication: Globalization Meets AI

AI-mediated communication tends to reflect the dominant cultural norms embedded in its training data—often **Western-centric, urban, and monolingual**. This poses risks in diverse classrooms:

- **Cultural Erasure or Misrepresentation**: Local idioms, rituals, and linguistic variations may be undervalued or misinterpreted.
- **Accent and Pronunciation Bias**: Some AI speech recognition tools perform poorly with non-native accents, reinforcing linguistic hierarchies.

- **Homogenization of Language Use**: Students may emulate AI-suggested responses that conform to global norms, eroding local linguistic identity.

Thus, educators must foster critical media literacy, helping students analyze and question AI-mediated communication while celebrating linguistic and cultural diversity.

CONCLUSION

As we navigate the dynamic intersection of artificial intelligence and English communication, it becomes increasingly evident that AI is not merely an accessory but a transformative force. From personalized language learning platforms to real-time translation tools and intelligent writing assistants, AI is reshaping how we read, write, speak, and listen in English.

"Echoes of AI" reflects the growing harmony between human expression and machine intelligence. This revolution empowers learners, educators, and professionals alike to break linguistic barriers, enhance fluency, and cultivate global communication skills with greater efficiency and confidence. However, as we embrace AI, it is vital to balance technological innovation with human insight, ensuring that communication remains authentic, empathetic, and culturally nuanced.

In essence, the echoes of AI are not replacing the human voice — they are amplifying it. By leveraging the potential of AI thoughtfully, we can usher in a new era of inclusive, accessible, and effective English communication for all.

REFERENCES

Attali, Y., & Burstein, J. (2006). Automated essay scoring with e-rater® V.2. *The Journal of Technology, Learning, and Assessment*, *4*(3), 1–30.

Benson, P. (2011). *Teaching and researching autonomy in language learning*. Routledge.

Chen, X., Wang, X., & Li, Y. (2021). Blockchain for language education: Enhancing authentication and credibility in AI-assisted learning. *Journal of Educational Technology & Society*, *24*(2), 45–58.

Crossley, S. A. (2018). Natural language processing applications for second language learners. *Language Learning & Technology*, *22*(2), 1–8.

Deterding, S., Dixon, D., Khaled, R., & Nacke, L. (2011). Gamification: Toward a definition. *Proceedings of CHI 2011*, 12-15.

Holec, H. (1981). *Autonomy and foreign language learning*. Pergamon Press.

Jones, R. (2020). The impact of NLP on reading comprehension: An empirical study. *Applied Linguistics Review*, *11*(1), 56–79.

Kumar, P., & Sharma, R. (2022). AI-driven cultural adaptation tools for language learning: A future perspective. *International Journal of Applied Linguistics*, *32*(4), 87–102.

Li, J., & Lalani, F. (2022). AI-assisted speech recognition for ESL learners: A comparative study. *Computer Assisted Language Learning*, *35*(3), 212–230.

Matsuda, P. K., & Silva, T. (2021). AI-based writing feedback: Implications for second language writing instruction. *Journal of Second Language Writing*, *51*, 100775.

Piaget, J. (1980). *Experiments in child language and thought*. Routledge.

Reinders, H., & White, C. (2016). 20 years of autonomy and technology: How far have we come and where to next? *Language Learning & Technology*, *20*(2), 143–154.

Ryan, R. M., & Deci, E. L. (2000). Self-determination theory and the facilitation of intrinsic motivation. *The American Psychologist*, *55*(1), 68–78. DOI: 10.1037/0003-066X.55.1.68 PMID: 11392867

Selwyn, N. (2019). Should robots replace teachers? AI and the future of education. *Learning, Media and Technology*, *44*(1), 1–7.

Skinner, B. F. (1957). *Verbal behavior.* Appleton-Century-Crofts. DOI: 10.1037/11256-000

Smith, J., & Gray, P. (2021). AI in language education: Issues of accessibility and equity. *Educational Review*, *73*(4), 522–540.

Vygotsky, L. S. (1978). *Mind in society: The development of higher psychological processes*. Harvard University Press.

Wang, H., & Tahir, R. (2020). Gamification and AI: Enhancing motivation in second language acquisition. *Interactive Learning Environments*, *28*(3), 456–470.

Zechner, K., Evanini, K., & Yoon, S. Y. (2019). Automated speech assessment: Current trends and future directions. *Language Testing*, *36*(1), 39–62.

Chapter 8
AI-Powered Language Instruction in the Culinary Arts

Manan Chakraborty
https://orcid.org/0000-0002-1793-9992
G.D. Goenka University, Gurgaon, India

Nagendra Yadav
https://orcid.org/0009-0008-9743-9250
Welcomgroup Graduate School of Hotel Administration, Manipal Academy of Higher Education, India

ABSTRACT

AI language is increasingly being integrated into culinary arts teaching, enhancing both the learning experience and the creativity involved in cooking. Various systems leverage artificial intelligence to provide personalized guidance, recipe generation, and meal analysis, thereby transforming traditional culinary education. Artificial Intelligence (AI) is the process of creating a machine that can think and act like a person. With the advancement of science and technology, teachers' tasks, including correction, student attendance, daily assessments, knowledge explanation, administrative report creation, and other systemic tasks, can be delegated to technological devices for completion. A golden generation with greater character and quality and natural intelligence—something that robots cannot do—can be created by teachers using less energy and concentrating more on non-systemic tasks.

DOI: 10.4018/979-8-3373-5681-5.ch008

INTRODUCTION

In the rapidly changing discipline of current technology, artificial intelligence (AI) has become a disruptive force that is altering several industries. AI is basically a machine learning technique that can perform tasks that often require human intelligence. AI is already a part of our daily life, assisting us with anything from natural language interpretation to learning and problem-solving. Because AI can handle vast volumes of data at previously unachievable speeds, it also has the potential to increase productivity, foster creativity, and enhance decision-making. Despite the fact it was once thought to be inconceivable, AI integration is rapidly expanding across several sectors, including banking, healthcare, entertainment, and manufacturing. One of the many industries that specifically benefit from AI's capabilities is the combination of technology and gastronomy. Through process optimization, raising overall quality and safety standards, and producing cutting-edge culinary items, artificial intelligence has been at the forefront of the food industry's change. (Jadhav et al., 2024).

The traditional educational system has several challenges, such as packed classrooms, a lack of individualized attention for each student, different learning styles and speeds, and difficulty keeping up with the rapid advancements in knowledge and technology. Artificial intelligence (AI)-powered chatbots are becoming a viable way to successfully solve some of these challenges as the educational landscape changes. While some educational institutions are more conservative and are not rushing to embrace AI-powered chatbots in contemporary educational settings, others are rapidly embracing them as they see their value.

Language researchers are now concentrating an immense amount of emphasis on the use of information technology in language learning and instruction. (Lai et al., 2022; Lei et al., 2022; Soleimani et al., 2022; Shadiev et al., 2023). Leveraging information technology in language education can enhance the learning experience for learners by enabling personalized, interactive, and communicative learning processes (Shatri, 2020; Rahimi and Fathi, 2022). Information technology is being used by language teachers to create virtual learning environments that actively engage students and speed up language acquisition. (Fathi and Rahimi, 2022; Loncar et al., 2023; Nguyen and Le, 2023).

Artificial intelligence (AI) has grown into a possible approach in information technology programs that can be used to enhance language learning and teaching outcomes. (Huang et al., 2023).

AI is transforming language instruction at a rapid pace, bringing with it both new opportunities and difficulties. This suggests that the way language education and learning are currently approached has undergone a substantial change. Traditional approaches to teaching and learning languages are being transformed by AI. This change makes it possible for learning experiences to be more engaging, flexible, and tailored to the requirements and preferences of each individual student. Some AI-based applications that can assist students' learning process are Intelligent tutoring systems that give students individualized feedback and assistance. Chatbots facilitate conversational practice and can simulate real-life interactions. Speech Recognition helps learners improve their pronunciation and speaking skills. Natural language processing improves learning experiences by facilitating a deeper comprehension and production of human language.\

As artificial intelligence (AI) develops increasingly prevalent in education, it becomes essential for teachers to figure out how AI can assist students whose first language is not English to learn and understand English. Therefore, for the purpose of assisting the academic and practitioner community in understanding how AI is helping English language instructors and learners, a review of existing research is necessary. This is echoed by scholars (e.g., Sharadgah & Sa'di, 2022; Yang & Kyun, 2022) who called for an up-to-date systematic review of AI in English language education. Recent systematic reviews have examined AI in education but have not focused on English language education (viz., Crompton et al., 2022; Zawacki-Richter et al., 2019). Those targeting English language education have often focused on a single type of AI (e.g., Baranwal, 2022) or examined studies learning a language in general without a focus on English (e.g., Yang & Kyun, 2022).

Machines can learn and comprehend logic just like humans thanks to a technology known as artificial intelligence, or AI. It is said that this technology can assist in making complicated human life easier (Fitria, 2021a).

Artificial Intelligence (AI) technology is becoming more and more apparent in several fields, including education. The curriculum has changed because of AI technology, particularly in the areas of technology, science, math, and engineering. However, AI will also transform the entire field of education. Artificial Intelligence (AI) is a new technology that has drawn interest. Numerous work activities, particularly those in the field of education, are made easier by this technology. Common language assistants include Google Home Assistant, Microsoft Cortina, Samsung Bixby, Apple Siri, and Amazon Alexa. In addition, intelligent tutors can be found in an extensive variety of programs and are perceived by the user as text prompts, voice-over help, or even visual aids in addition to voice (Vuong et al., 2023). AI can be applied in the field of education as well. Instructors and lecturers can more easily and fully understand the demands of their students (Fitria, 2021b). Students are also able to learn in line with their needs without experiencing any obstacles.

AI has transformed several industries in recent years, including hotels and restaurants, transportation, and healthcare. Its impact can equally be seen in the cooking and culinary arts industries. In educational contexts, the use of AI in the kitchen is growing in popularity as it develops. Innovation in the culinary arts and the promotion of culinary creativity are being greatly aided by AI. Chefs and other culinary experts can push the limits of conventional culinary techniques, experiment with novel combinations, and discover new flavors by utilizing AI technologies. The presence of AI in the culinary industry can be seen in several ways, including menu planning, recipe development, food waste reduction, and kitchen management. Advanced algorithms and machine learning capabilities enable AI apps to examine data and use patterns and trends to generate predictions or recommendations that support and boost the industry.

The antecedents of technology acceptance and adoption, particularly about artificial intelligence (AI) devices and related technological devices, have been shown to be complex despite previous experiences demonstrating that customer willingness is a strong predictor of actual behavior.

AI gadgets and associated technologies by contrasting them with the services that human workers are probably going to provide. Consequently, several elements, including hedonic motives, social influence, and prior experiences, are anticipated to have a greater impact on the process of evaluating the relative advantages of AI in comparison to comparable technologies than other elements. Traditional education techniques are changing because of the quick advancement of technology. Among these developments, artificial intelligence (AI) has become a potent instrument with important ramifications for teaching. AI technologies offer special chances to improve several teaching-related areas. This covers immediate feedback, adaptive learning, and individualized training.

AI creates new opportunities for innovation, increasing the impact, efficiency, and personalization of education. It can give tailored learning pathways, pinpoint areas for development, and offer focused practice to assist students become more proficient in the language. The goal of pedagogical integration initiatives should be to create AI-enhanced learning environments that enhance conventional teaching methods and enable educators to fully utilize AI. More inclusive, efficient, and fair language learning experiences can result from the incorporation of AI by taking these issues and concerns into account.

AI is the process by which computer systems mimic human intelligence.

These systems can carry out operations like learning, reasoning, problem-solving, perception, and language comprehension that normally demand human intellect. AI systems frequently outperform humans in particular disciplines due to their capacity to analyze vast datasets, identify patterns, generate predictions, and modify their behavior in response to new information.

To fully understand AI's significance, one must understand how it relates to the culinary arts. The creation of computer systems that can carry out operations that normally call for human intelligence is referred to as artificial intelligence (AI). This technology can evaluate data, identify trends, and make judgments that are comparable to those made by a professional chef in the food industry. Culinary education is changing dramatically because of utilizing AI, providing students with cutting-edge and engaging educational experiences.

Similar AI challenges to Annamalai were reported by other scholars (e.g., Wang et al., 2023), that found that AI was behaving passively and mechanically. While AI has many advanced capabilities, problems with technical issues, such as programs breaking or not functioning correctly, have been reported (eg, Ericsson et al., 2023).

The use of AI in dining experiences provides special potential and challenges in creating elaborate recipes, local variations, and diverse flavor profiles. The custom of matching wine and food, which has become more and more popular as its culinary culture becomes more globally integrated, necessitates a thorough comprehension of the sensory experiences connected to each component. AI offers a unique method for becoming proficient in this art because of its capacity to examine enormous datasets and spot patterns that are beyond human perception. Sommeliers and culinary professionals can use machine learning algorithms to forecast combinations that improve the dining experience by combining the ideal wine pairings with the robust flavors of cuisines.

In a nation that is both a large producer and consumer of food, streamlining these processes is essential. AI technologies can simplify processes, such as recipe preparation and inventory management development, and quality assurance, guaranteeing effectiveness, durability, and uniformity. Better demand forecasting, waste reduction, and better supply chain responsiveness to market fluctuations are all made possible by predictive analytics. AI has enormous potential to improve customer experience, which is a crucial component of the food sector. Machine learning algorithms that examine customer data can be used to create individualized eating experiences that cater to each customer's tastes and dietary needs. Predictive analytics is another area where this personalization is present, providing suggestions that improve customer experience from menu selection to post-dinner interactions. The integration of AI into Indian culinary practices is not without its challenges. Concerning data privacy, the digital divide, and the preservation of traditional culinary knowledge in the face of technological advancement are pertinent. Addressing these challenges requires a balanced approach, one that respects and integrates traditional knowledge with innovative technologies. The tourism industry has been transformed by digital innovation and artificial intelligence (AI), and the culinary sector is no exception. These technologies have created new opportunities for local dining experiences that benefit both travelers and businesses. AI and digital innovation are improving culinary tourism in a few ways, with an emphasis on regional culinary experiences.

ONLINE PLATFORMS AND FOOD APPS

Digital platforms and food apps allow simple access to information about local culinary experiences. These websites allow travelers to discover local cuisines, identify real restaurants, and read reviews and recommendations from other travelers. They give a straightforward way to find and arrange food-focused itineraries, so visitors can immerse themselves in local cuisine culture.

AI-POWERED RECOMMENDATION SYSTEMS

AI algorithms may assess user preferences, location data, and previous interactions to deliver personalized suggestions for local culinary experiences. These recommendation systems might propose popular local meals, hidden treasures, or eateries that correspond with specific dietary restrictions or tastes. This lets travelers discover unique gastronomic experiences tailored to their tastes.

VIRTUAL REALITY (VR) AND AUGMENTED REALITY (AR)

VR and AR technologies enable immersive experiences that promote gastronomic tourism. For example, virtual food tours can allow passengers to digitally explore local food markets, engage with vendors, and learn about traditional culinary techniques. AR apps can deliver real-time information and data about dishes while scanning menus or food items, improving the eating experience with educational and interactive components.

AI-DRIVEN MENU OPTIMIZATION

Restaurants can employ AI to optimize their menus based on client preferences and trends. By evaluating client data and feedback, AI systems can suggest menu adjustments, recommend new dishes, or uncover chances to include local products or flavors. This ensures that businesses may change their products to meet the increasing expectations of travelers seeking local dining experiences.

VIRTUAL ASSISTANTS AND CHAT BOATS

Chatbots and virtual assistants can be connected to websites, applications, or messaging systems to provide speedy support and information about local dining experiences. They can answer frequently asked questions, set appointments, provide advice, and offer real-time support. Chatbots equipped with natural language processing capabilities can interpret and reply to requests in many languages, facilitating engagement with foreign passengers.

DATA ANALYTICS AND INSIGHTS

Digital innovation helps organizations collect and analyze data about customer preferences, behavior, and feedback. By employing AI-driven data analytics, gastronomy tourism operators can acquire insights into customer preferences, identify upcoming food trends, and make data-driven decisions. This enables businesses to customize their offerings and marketing methods to attract food connoisseurs seeking authentic local experiences.

SOCIAL MEDIA INFLUENCE

Social media platforms play a key role in promoting local cuisine experiences. Travelers share their culinary trips through images, reviews, and suggestions on platforms like Instagram, Facebook, and Twitter.

These platforms can be used by gastronomy providers to advertise their special offerings, interact with customers, and create excitement about regional cuisine. Influencer partnerships can also increase these events' visibility and influence. The gastronomy tourism sector is undergoing a transformation due to the greater accessibility, personalization, and immersive nature of local culinary experiences brought about by digital innovation and artificial intelligence. With the use of these technologies, companies can design fantastic gourmet experiences for their clients, and visitors may discover and enjoy a region's unique culinary traditions.

REVIEW OF LITERATURE

The theoretical basis of this research is based on Vygotsky's (1984) major contributions to social constructivist learning theories. The development of social constructivism, which emphasizes the significance of social interactions, collaborative learning experiences, and cognitive development, was made possible by Vygotsky's work. Based on this viewpoint, students who are less proficient engage in collaborative learning activities with greater competent individuals, such as teachers or computer programs within contemporary environments. These transactions beneficial effects less skilled students in gaining and expanding their knowledge by acting as cognitive scaffolding.

This study acknowledges the revolutionary impact of technology on instruction in languages and integrates current theories about artificial intelligence and computer-assisted learning in line with Vygotsky's ideas. The incorporation of AI technology provides additional dimensions of cooperative education. (Zheng et al., 2021; Weng and Chiu, 2023), where learners interact with AI-assisted language learning tools to regulate their language learning experiences and advance toward their ZPD. These interactions, which parallel the core principles of Vygotsky's social constructivist theory, emphasize the role of technology as a collaborative partner in the language learning process.

Within the context of AI-mediated instruction and learning, it is also important to note that collaboration capabilities emerge as an essential component that significantly impacts the effectiveness of AI-based technology for education. (Akata et al., 2020; Chen et al., 2022).

The willingness of learners to communicate effectively with classmates, teachers, or AI systems with the objective of improving learning outcomes and collectively improving learning skills can be defined as collaborative abilities. These competencies encompass an array of tactics and abilities used by students to communicate well in AI-mediated settings.

In addition, the dynamics of AI-assisted learning of a new language are significantly shaped by collaborative skills (Fitria, 2023). Strong collaborative learners are skilled at using AI technologies to have important discussions, ask questions, and jointly create knowledge. Additionally, the use of feedback mechanisms in AI systems is directly linked to collaboration skills (Hsu et al., 2023). Learners' ability to work together to successfully evaluate and apply feedback to their language learning practices determines the caliber and impact of the feedback they get. Overall, by combining modern theories in artificial intelligence and computer-assisted learning with Vygotsky's fundamental ideas, this study aims to investigate the changing dynamics of language learning in. The time of digitalization. A deeper understanding of language learning achievement, motivation, and self-regulated learning in the context of AI-mediated language instruction may result from the cooperative interactions between students and AI technology, which may represent a convergence of established educational theories and new technological paradigms.

ARTIFICIAL INTELLIGENCE

The introduction of AI-based applications in culinary labs and classrooms is one of the most significant advances AI has brought about in the field of culinary education. With the help of these resources, students can practice and hone their culinary abilities in a virtual setting while engaging in immersive and interactive learning experiences. AI applications provide real-time feedback and direction for everything from creating recipes to presenting food, which improves learning and fosters creativity.

Personalized learning in culinary education is also made possible by AI. With the capacity to examine unique learning preferences and styles, AI algorithms can customize instructional materials to each student's unique requirements. A deeper understanding of trade is fostered, and culinary ideas are better understood by students thanks to this individualized approach. The rapid advancement of AI has revolutionized various domains, including education, with profound implications for teaching and learning practices (Chen et al., 2020).

As a branch of computer science, artificial intelligence (AI) enables robots to mimic human intelligence, learn from errors, and carry out positions that usually require human cognitive abilities. AI technologies possess the potential to revolutionize traditional teaching methods in educational institutions by offering individualized learning experiences that cater to each student's requirements and preferences (Hwang et al., 2020).

Researchers, educators, and legislators from all over the world have recently been paying close attention to the use of AI in education, from adaptive learning platforms to intelligent tutoring systems and language learning programs. (Chen et al., 2022; Huang and Tan, 2023).

According to Aldosari (2020), AI is referred to as an intelligent program that can do a variety of activities. For example, people can use AI-powered tools to help them with their academic research, and these tools quickly give them the knowledge they need. AI can be used in educational settings to make intelligent decisions that are comparable to those made by humans. AI is also frequently used in language learning to improve students' language proficiency and related abilities.

AI can be described as a program with intelligence that can do an array of activities. People can, for example, ask AI-powered tools for help with their academic studies, and these tools quickly deliver the knowledge they need. AI is utilized in educational settings, where it may make wise decisions that are like those made by humans. Additionally, a lot of language learning uses AI to enhance students' language and sub-skills. (Zhang and Zou, 2020; Xia et al., 2022a).

Language learners may benefit from a variety of AI-assisted language learning materials which are accessible through computers and mobile devices. These materials provide helpful assistance to improve a variety of language learning abilities. An AI-assisted tool named ChatGPT, for example, might be used in language learning environments to assist students in honing their language learning abilities and subskills. (Fang et al., 2023; Fitria, 2023; Kim, 2023; Schmidt-Fajlik, 2023; Su et al., 2023; Yan, 2023).

To support language learners' general language achievement, ChatGPT could provide the necessary input and comments on various language learning skills and sub-skills concerns. The capacity of ChatGPT to generate properly formed phrases can assist students in creating messages that are well-structured. Additionally, this AI-powered language learning tool can comprehend human questions and offer the most appropriate responses.

(Huang and Tan, 2023). A substantial body of studies has been carried out examining the effects of AI-assisted language learning tools on English language learners' language achievement (Suryana et al., 2020; Divekar et al., 2022; Fitria, 2023).

An AI-powered language learning tool that utilized speech recognition improved students' language learning performance and maintained their interest in interactive exercises. Ebadi and Amini (2022) investigated how AI-assisted language learning impacted the engagement of EFL learners.

Questionnaires on human likeness, social presence, and motivation were utilized for gathering the data, in addition to recordings of the EFL students' interactions with the AI tool. The results showed that the AI tool significantly affected the learners' motivation as well as participation in their education. Parallel to this, Carpio Cañada et al. (2015) explored how language learners' motivation and academic performance were affected by an AI-powered language learning strategy.

The results of this study showed that the AI-assisted technique for language learning enhanced the learners' motivation to learn the language. The participants' enhanced academic achievement was also a result of their motivation in language learning activities. In a similar vein, Ali et al. (2023) investigated how an AI tool, ChatGPT, affects the motivation of English language learners and teachers. Results showed that the AI-assisted language learning tool significantly improved the learners' writing and reading abilities while having little effect on their speaking or listening abilities. Accordingly, Schmidt-Fajlik (2023) examined the distinctions between ChatGPT, Grammarly, and ProWritingAid programs for evaluating, understanding, and enhancing the English grammar of EFL learners.

Hsu et al. (2023), for example, examined the impact of AI-assisted picture recognition technologies on the vocabulary knowledge, anxiety, and self-regulation of EFL learners with respect to language learning principles. By using an experimental research design, the experimental group's learners utilized AI-assisted image recognition technologies to increase their vocabulary by showing them images and the associated terminology. The results demonstrated that the experimental students reduced their anxiety regarding language acquisition while also improving their vocabulary and self-regulation. Only in vocabulary knowledge did the experimental learners overcome their control counterparts.

In addition, the experimental and control groups' levels of self-regulation and anxiety associated with language acquisition did not differ considerably. Kim (2019) also investigated how AI-assisted language learning training affected the grammar proficiency of EFL university students. An experimental study looked at was used, with one set of students obtaining the AI tool and the other group receiving traditional grammatical instruction. The findings demonstrated that experimental students who got AI-based education fared better than those who did not, indicating that the student's improvement of their grammatical skills was greatly aided by the AI-assisted language learning instruction.

Addressing language learning abilities, Yan (2023), for example, investigated how an AI-assisted language learning tool affected the writing skills of EFL students. The outcomes showed that the EFL learners' writing skills improved simultaneously with the AI-assisted language learning tool. Yan further asserted that the AI-assisted language learning tool allowed EFL students to complete their writing assignments faster than ever before. These results tapped into the effectiveness of the AI-assisted language learning tool for writing assignments. The effect of AI-powered language acquisition on the academic research writing of three Indonesian EFL learners was also examined by Utami et al. (2023).

Lee et al. (2023) also explored the effects of an AI-assisted language learning tool on EFL learners' reading enjoyment. A group of EFL learners received the AI tool to generate reading topics for the learners based on their interests, while the other group was engaged in conventional reading comprehension activities.

El Shazly (2021) examined how speaking performance and foreign language anxiety were impacted by AI-powered language learning resources for Egyptian EFL learners. A questionnaire was used to evaluate the learners' foreign language anxiety while roleplaying exercises and an IELTS speaking test were used to assess their ability to speak. According to the results, learners' concern about foreign languages was not reduced by using AI-assisted language applications during speaking exercises. The use of AI-assisted language learning resources, however, was found to improve students' interactive speaking exercises and speaking abilities

The effect of AI-assisted language learning tools on the speaking skills of EFL learners was also examined by Junaidi (2020). The speaking abilities of the experimental and control groups, including fluency, grammar, vocabulary, and pronunciation, were evaluated using pre- and post-tests within the framework of a quasi-experimental research design. This enabled the comparison of the experimental and control groups' speaking abilities as well as the assessment of the learners' progress in speaking. The results demonstrated while both groups' speaking abilities improved, the experimental learners' speaking abilities proved superior to those of their control counterparts, confirming the important contributions of AI-powered language learning resources to the speaking skill development of EFL learners.

The study highlights the potential of AI-assisted language learning tools to improve vocabulary knowledge, grammar proficiency, writing skills, reading enjoyment, speaking performance, as well as learners' motivation and engagement. It also sheds light on the multifaceted effects of these tools on a variety of language skills and sub-skills. Even though earlier studies have examined how AI affects various aspects of language acquisition, there is a notable lack of study on how AI affects language accomplishment, especially when it comes to EFL instruction for Chinese learners.

These evident gaps in the literature provide the stage for the current investigation, which aims to determine whether the observed variations between AI and conventional teaching environments are due to pedagogical innovation or technological creativity. Therefore, the goal of this research is to shed light on AI's ability to change language learning paradigms while also developing an expanded understanding of technology-driven language instruction and its intricate consequences.

AI is revolutionizing the creative and innovative aspects of cooking. With the help of technology, cooks may create and alter recipes by suggesting tasty and inventive component combinations and cooking methods. Artificial intelligence (AI) algorithms may also evaluate flavor profiles and food pairing, allowing chefs to try out novel and intriguing flavor combinations that might not have been found otherwise.

AI has the potential to enhance the effectiveness, affordability, and accessibility of education.

AI is being utilized for administrative work automation, student support, and learning personalization. Moreover, AI is being utilized to advance research and develop fresh educational alternatives. The demand for data security and privacy, the possibility of prejudice, and the requirement that teachers receive appropriate AI training are some of the difficulties related to AI in education (Crompton & Burke, 2023)

AI chatbots serve as virtual assistants, carrying out the tasks and obligations of teachers. AI chatbots promote teachers' efficacy and efficiency, thereby raising the standard of instruction. AI chatbots help students study more effectively and improve their academic performance (Chen et al., 2020).

AI transforms the teaching strategies utilized by teachers and the methods in which pupils learn. The development of teaching and learning programs arises from the incorporation of AI into educational systems. Despite it is acknowledged that AI will not entirely replace the traditional educational system, it has brought about significant changes in the sphere of education (Krstić et al., 2022).

AI in education provides a wealth of chances for educators and learners to utilize and reap its benefits. In industrialized countries, AI is already being used in several fields, including education. Adopting AI in education has several obstacles, such as organizational worries about the possible displacement of humans by AI, technological issues including data ownership and utilization, and ethical issues (Tahiru, 2021). AI is transforming culinary operations outside of the creative sphere. AI-powered automated baking and culinary systems are simplifying the cooking process, guaranteeing reliable outcomes, and lowering human error. Additionally, AI is being used in quality control and food safety, keeping an eye on variables like temperature and ingredient freshness to uphold strict food safety regulations. AI is also revolutionizing supply chain and inventory management, lowering waste and optimizing stock levels.

Even though artificial intelligence (AI) has a huge impact on school culinary arts, its use presents both potential and obstacles. The skill gap and workforce adaptability are important factors to consider because the arrival of AI necessitates that chefs and other culinary experts learn new technology skills. In addition, to fully utilize AI's potential in kitchen operations and culinary instruction, infrastructure and technologies must be invested in. Additionally, ethical and cultural issues come up because using AI in cooking calls into question authenticity and the preservation of culinary traditions.

AI is completely changing the way that student's study, practice, and hone their culinary abilities in the realm of culinary education. AI technology integration is making culinary instruction more efficient, individualized, and interactive. A dynamic and engaging learning environment is being created in culinary labs and classrooms with the integration of AI. Artificial intelligence (AI)--powered virtual reality (VR) and augmented reality (AR) technologies let students experience authentic culinary situations without the need for tangible ingredients or equipment. Students can practice culinary skills, try out flavors, and get real-time performance feedback through virtual simulations. By doing this, skill development is improved, and the expense and waste of conventional hands-on training are decreased.

Applications based on artificial intelligence are being created especially to aid with culinary education. Numerous features are available in these apps, including recipe databases, cooking lessons, and suggestions for item substitutions. Large volumes of culinary data are analyzed by AI algorithms to give students thorough resources and direction. These resources can give students detailed instructions, improve their comprehension of culinary concepts, and give them immediate feedback on how they're doing. Culinary educators can improve the quality of their learning and give students useful resources for their culinary journeys by utilizing AI-based teaching. Complex interactions between chemicals, scents, and textures make the science of flavor. AI's ability to discover and forecast taste characteristics by analyzing large datasets adds a new degree of comprehension to this complex dance. By pushing the limits of culinary imagination, this aptitude enables cooks to produce dishes with complex and nuanced flavors. AI's capacity to understand taste chemistry creates new pairings that satisfy a range of palates. Beyond just creating recipes, AI is also making inroads into the culinary arts. It can modify recipes according to dietary guidelines, personal tastes, and nutritional needs. AI can create recipes that meet the demands of those who are following a certain diet, controlling allergies, or working toward health objectives. The increasing need for healthier, more individualized food selections is met by this personality, which also improves the dining experience.

In the field of cooking, the incorporation of AI into smart kitchen appliances is a big step toward smooth human-machine cooperation. These days, cooking appliances, smart ovens, and even robotic kitchen helpers can follow recipes created by artificial intelligence. Precision and uniformity are ensured by this equipment's ability to adjust to changing cooking circumstances. A new era of intelligent cooking is promised by the resulting combination of technical efficiency and human intuition. AI makes it possible for culinary education to be individualized. Through the analysis of unique learning preferences, styles, and ability levels, artificial intelligence algorithms are able to customize instructional materials to each student's unique requirements. Students' learning potential is maximized through targeted education and assistance thanks to this individualized approach. AI can create personalized challenges to keep students interested and motivated, modify the speed of education, and provide extra resources based on each student's strengths and shortcomings. AI-powered personalized learning helps students grasp culinary topics more deeply and lets them go at their own speed.

The use of AI in the culinary arts has much greater potential for the future. Virtual kitchen assistants powered by AI, augmented reality eating experiences, and chef-AI collaboration to expand culinary research are examples of emerging trends. As technology develops further, the combination of human creativity and artificial intelligence has the potential to completely transform the culinary industry. In culinary education, AI technologies enable worldwide learning opportunities and collaboration. Online platforms and AI-powered communication technologies allow international culinary students to interact, exchange stories, and work together on culinary projects. Geographical boundaries can be broken down and diversity in culinary education can be promoted by using AI algorithms to translate languages, exchange cultures, and share expertise. In addition to exposing students to other culinary traditions, this global perspective enhances their culinary knowledge and promotes a sense of camaraderie within the culinary business.

AI-MEDIATED LANGUAGE LEARNING PLATFORM

The experimental group obtained individualized and interactive English language training using the AI-mediated language learning website Duolingo. Due to its widely recognized ability to deliver engaging and responsive instruction in languages, Duolingo is an appropriate platform for this research. The experimental set of learners had access to an assortment of interactive exercises, language games, online assessments, and real-time feedback based on how well they performed on the platform. Textbooks, lectures, and classroom exercises were among the conventional teaching resources used to provide the control group with traditional language learning. To help the control group learn the language, the curriculum included teacher-led talks, grammatical drills, reading passages, and writing assignments.

INTRINSIC MOTIVATION AND ACTIVE ENGAGEMENT

Students' intrinsic need and active engagement with the English language were significantly boosted by the AI-mediated training. Participants spoke of an increased level of enthusiasm and interest outside of the classroom. Many of them actively sought out more language resources and practice opportunities. By encouraging a genuine interest in English, the AI platform sparked a desire for continuous study and discovery.

This motivation can be seen by the participants' commitment to consistent language practice and their readiness to put in more work during their language learning process. One participant said, "I was motivated by the AI platform. I truly wanted to get better at the language and learn more about it, not simply because I had to.

EMPOWERMENT IN SELF-REGULATED LEARNING

Owing to the AI platform's instruction, participants reported a noticeable sense of empowerment in their self-regulated learning operations. They highlighted how the platform helped them employ a variety of self-regulation techniques, including establishing specific learning objectives, scheduling study periods, and constantly evaluating their progress. The AI platform served as a trustworthy partner, providing participants with the tools and structure they needed to confidently navigate their learning paths.

Testimonials of the participants demonstrated how the AI platform's direction helped them become more independent learners. One student said, "I learned how to effectively manage my learning time and set specific goals with the AI platform." I felt more in charge of my growth. "The AI platform helped me become a more independent learner," wrote another student. I figured out how to take ownership of my education and set goals as a result.

FACTORS THAT INFLUENCE ATTITUDE TOWARD AI IN HIGHER EDUCATION

Attitude is one of the major concerns to adapt to any technology or system. The literature, as stated by Al Darayseh (2023), identified the significant impact of AI in education on the attitude of learners. It is identified that conducive technical advancement and allied infrastructure support the implementation of the new system (Pedral Sampaio et al., 2023). The sense of facility condition in an organization controls the behavioral intention of the workforce (Venkatesh et al.,2012). A study conducted by van Twillert et al. (2020) emphasized the role of facilities and infrastructure that influenced faculties' attitudes toward adopting Web 2.0 technologies in higher education.

APPLICATIONS FOR AI IN HIGHER EDUCATION

Higher education saw a transformation with the adoption of a digital learning strategy (Khoza & Mpungose, 2022). In research published in 2022, Carvalho et al. investigated how society will predict the future of education using a collaborative approach involving students, educators, and artificial intelligence. Improving students' learning experiences is one of the main uses of AI in higher education (Ge & Hu, 2020). Furthermore, (Chang et al., 2022; Kelly et al., 2023) noted how the introduction of AI has altered how society views schooling. According to Chang et al. (2022), research has expressed legitimate concerns regarding the use of AI in education by highlighting its effects on the demographic, cultural, and behavioral characteristics of users and learners.

APPLICATIONS OF AI AND FACULTIES WORK ENGAGEMENT

In higher education, artificial intelligence can completely change how instructors interact with students and carry out their duties. To participate in learning activities more effectively, many institutions have implemented AI technologies (Cui et al., 2019). Users' opinions toward implementing AI for course design, grading and assessment, student support, and individualized professional development were highlighted in the studies (Franzoni et al., 2020; Rahimi & Tafazoli, 2022). Recently, research has examined how teachers behave and think when using AI-integrated CRM systems, as well as how their digital skills improve work engagement (Chatterjee et al., 2021; Ng et al., 2023). Furthermore, the positive feelings and attitudes of academic staff members toward ICT-related elements that increase their work engagement were investigated by Moreira-Fontán et al. (2019). These results indicate the connection between users' opinions and actions regarding. Based on these findings, the relationship between users' attitudes and behaviors towards AI on work engagement is inevitable. Motivation and excitement are significantly linked to work engagements (De Simone et al., 2016). Teachers who are highly engaged are more likely to be receptive to new ideas and digital teaching methods (Scherer et al., 2019). Several studies have found that when it comes to digital innovation in higher education, work engagement is strongly correlated with a higher degree of flexibility and resilience (Al-Takhayneh et al., 2022; Antonietti et al., 2022). According to a study cited by AlAjmi (2022), the use of digital technology has also improved teachers' job satisfaction in higher education. The relationship between work engagement and the use of cutting-edge technology in higher education is highlighted by all these findings.

Potential Application of Digital Innovations and AI in Gastronomy, Tourism, and Local Food Experiences

Metaverse gastronomy may seem contradictory given how much of it is focused on tangible, sensory experiences. Because it fails to properly utilize the senses that are essential to the tasting, smelling, and enjoyment of food and wine, the use of non-fungible tokens (NFTs) to open a store on the metaverse is frequently perceived as a marketing ploy for wineries or restaurants. But food and wine are about more than just eating; they are about establishing connections with people, cultures, and far-off places. The hospitality sector faced an unforeseen hurdle because of the recent COVID-19 epidemic. Social and health distancing measures caused the closure of numerous hotels, cafés, vineyards, and pubs. The financial difficulties brought on by containment measures have prompted numerous international hospitality companies to shut down their operations permanently. Therefore, it is essential to give innovation top priority while seeking out innovative solutions for hospitality and culinary industries. Physical food, as it is commonly called, is a food innovation that incorporates both the digital and physical aspects of the eating experience. Through immersive activities like gamifying the dining room, gastronomy in the metaverse must enhance dining experiences in addition to flavor. Projects like virtual wine tastings, virtual tours of cellars and vineyards, and ghost, cloud, and dark kitchens were among the projects that highlighted the significance of virtual technology during the outbreak. (Yung et al., 2020; Buonincontri et al., 2022). Traveling to new areas became crucial for gastronomic tourism, as sharing experiences with friends, family, followers, and peers became essential. Wine and gastronomy in the Metaverse offer new chances, such as visiting farms, breweries, or manufacturing facilities across states or nations and meeting with influencers and chefs (Kumar.S, 2018). Since 2022, businesses have been experimenting with real-world eating experiences. They have constructed virtual restaurants in which users can place orders using virtual reality goggles and have meals delivered right to their homes. It is difficult to foresee if physical-gastronomic sensations will be displaced by virtual ones. However, there are various chances for advertising places through VR, AR, MR, and the metaverse. They can erase physical borders for those who are unable to travel; yet, at initially, only a certain consumer base may be able to take advantage of these experiences. They can erase physical borders for those who are unable to travel; yet, at initially, only a certain consumer base may be able to take advantage of this situation. Despite criticism that metaverse tourism encourages a sedentary lifestyle, immersion virtual experiences can lessen the perceived risks associated with intangible services, allowing visitors to make educated decisions and have acceptable expectations for their actual visits. People increasingly prioritize their health and safety in the post-COVID-19 environment, even if it means modifying their travel plans to take advantage of virtual opportunities.

Finally, the usage of artificial intelligence (AI) capabilities can further tailor each traveler's experience. Griffin and colleagues (2017), Klein and colleagues (2003), Gursoy and colleagues (2022), Suanpang and colleagues (2022), and Corbisiero and colleagues (2021) While there are numerous potential advantages to incorporating digital technology and AI into culinary tourism, there are also certain difficulties that must be overcome. To guarantee that these improvements benefit the tourism sector and the local inhabitants, it is vital to underline the value of safeguarding cultural heritage and fostering sustainable practices.

The Role of Digital Innovations and Artificial Intelligence in Gastronomy and Tourism

Digital innovations and artificial intelligence (AI) have significantly transformed various industries, including gastronomy and tourism. Gastronomy tourism refers to travel experiences centered around food and culinary exploration. Here are some key roles that digital innovations and AI play in enhancing gastronomy and tourism:

- Travelers can receive individualized restaurant and food recommendations from AI-driven algorithms that analyze a vast amount of data, including dietary restrictions, prior dining experiences, and personal preferences. This guarantees that travelers may have the greatest culinary experiences based on their preferences and areas of interest.

- Virtual experiences and excursions: Thanks to technological advancements, travelers can take advantage of virtual gastronomic journeys before they even travel to a region, thanks to virtual reality (VR) and augmented reality (AR). With the aid of technological exploration, they can organize their excursions and foster excitement by learning about local markets, food festivals, and cooking classes. • Language Translation: AI-driven language translation systems help travelers communicate with locals, comprehend menus, and participate in culinary classes by removing language obstacles. This promotes cross-cultural dialogue and enhances the whole culinary tourist experience.
- Food safety and quality may be monitored throughout the supply chain using sensors and analytics powered by artificial intelligence. This is crucial for gastronomy tourism since tourists frequently seek authentic and secure dining experiences, and AI can assist in making sure that food complies with safety and health standards.
- Intelligent Restaurant Management: AI and digital innovations can expedite restaurant operations, including inventory control and reservation systems. Due to its efficiency, wait times are reduced, and the whole dining experience is enhanced for both patrons and restaurateurs.
- Food and Recipe Suggestions: AI-powered platforms can evaluate regional ingredients, culinary customs, and worldwide food trends in order to provide innovative and unique recipes. This inspires travelers to experiment with new flavors and culinary techniques.
- Customer Reviews and Feedback: By analyzing customer evaluations and feedback, AI-powered sentiment analysis may determine areas for development and overall satisfaction, allowing gastronomy businesses to improve their offerings and better meet the expectations of tourists.
- Sustainability and Food Sourcing: By providing information about locally sourced, in-season, and environmentally favorable food sources, digital innovations and artificial intelligence (AI) can help encourage sustainable behaviors. This encourages responsible culinary tourism, which is becoming more essential for tourists who are worried about how their travels may affect the environment. Improved Food and Beverage Pairings: AI can suggest the best food and drink pairings depending on the ingredients, flavors, and local preferences. This would enhance the eating experience and introduce visitors to new flavors.
- Food Innovation and Creativity: Artificial Intelligence (AI) can be applied to culinary research and development, leading to innovative food creations, fresh cooking methods, and thrilling culinary encounters that draw travel-

ers seeking new culinary experiences. In summary, digital advances and AI are changing gastronomy tourism by providing individualized experiences, boosting cultural exchange, ensuring food safety, supporting sustainability, and driving culinary creativity. As these technologies continue to evolve, they will further enrich the entire travel experience of culinary travelers globally

The culinary tourism industry has seen a significant transformation due to digital advancements and artificial intelligence (AI), which offer several opportunities to improve visitors' experiences with local cuisine. Robotics, chatbots, kiosks, smartphone apps, and artificial intelligence (AI) have already shown promise in automating restaurant operations and improving the guest experience. These technologies function as significant value generators, offering enormous potential for process innovation and transforming conventional service delivery methods. Nevertheless, there are barriers that prevent enterprises from fully utilizing new technologies, even with their alluring promises. Many businesses still lack the necessary knowledge of AI and robots, and some still struggle to generate profits from these developments.

The transition from manual labor to technological systems presents a challenge for restaurant management, particularly considering personnel shortages and concerns about job replacements. The literature review emphasizes the need to strike a balance between the cooperation of artificial intelligence and humans to provide innovative customer experiences inside restaurant ecosystems. In the service industry, customer involvement is essential, and social and emotional intelligence are necessary to achieve excellence in hospitality, customer satisfaction, and customer loyalty. Furthermore, even in situations where travel is prohibited, the post-COVID-19 era has highlighted the value of virtual technologies, such as immersive dining experiences and virtual food tours, to promote regional culinary cultures and engage with communities. These technological advancements enhance the entire culinary tourism experience by providing real-time language translation, personalized suggestions, food safety monitoring, and sustainability promotion.

In culinary tourism, integrating digital technology and artificial intelligence (AI) has many potential advantages, but there are drawbacks as well, such as concerns over cultural appropriation, data privacy, and technological accessibility. Collaborative partnerships, cultural education, and ethical values are necessary to guarantee responsible AI development and a sustainable approach. Future studies and advancements can concentrate on AI-powered culinary innovation, certified sustainable gastronomy, and cooperative projects to strengthen local economies and preserve culinary traditions. In addition to providing visitors with more genuine and meaningful experiences, the culinary tourism industry may enhance the welfare of the communities it interacts with by carefully implementing these technological advancements.

CONCLUSION

To conclude AI has the potential to revolutionize language instruction, but to fully reap its rewards, it is imperative that the related issues be resolved, in the field of culinary education by proposing an innovative AI-assisted cooking tutorial app that addresses existing limitations, enhances user interaction, and provides a more personalized learning experience. Artificial intelligence is becoming a powerful force in the dynamic field of culinary arts, adding new levels of creativity, accuracy, and customization. AI is improving the depth of taste profiling and motivating cooks with innovative recipes, but it is not taking the place of human interaction in the kitchen. AI is transforming culinary education through the development of interactive learning environments, AI-based teaching resources, individualized learning opportunities, adaptive evaluations and feedback, and the promotion of international cooperation. As artificial intelligence develops, culinary education will become more efficient, interesting, and accessible, educating future chefs and culinary professionals about the opportunities and challenges of the always-changing culinary industry. The system effectively improves the teaching experience by providing users with accurate menu knowledge and skills. The research highlights the potential for AI technology to drive sustainability in the food industry. By encouraging healthier eating habits and providing easy access to recipes, the system can contribute to more sustainable food practices and better public health outcomes. The paper underscores the transformative potential of culinary teaching in enhancing culinary experiences, promoting healthy eating, ensuring accessibility, and contributing to sustainability in the food industry. Digital innovations and artificial intelligence (AI) have revolutionized the gastronomy tourist industry by enhancing local cuisine experiences and automating restaurant operations. Concerns about job displacement, a shortage of labor, and a lack of experience with AI and robotics are some of the remaining problems. To provide innovative customer experiences, human-AI cooperation needs to be balanced. Virtual technologies are essential for connecting with communities and developing local culinary cultures. Virtual culinary tours and immersive dining experiences are two examples of this technology. The challenges include issues with technology accessibility, data privacy, and cultural appropriation. Future research should focus on culinary innovation powered by AI, sustainable gastronomy certification systems, and initiatives that preserve culinary heritage and uplift local communities. Addressing privacy and safety concerns is a major obstacle in the application of AI. It's critical to make sure that personal information shared by students using online learning platforms is secure and private. The establishment of explicit norms and standards for the creation and application of AI-powered tools in higher education is therefore necessary. These standards should cover topics like data protection, security, and ethical considerations. Universities and other institutions must set aside funds to support and train teachers so they can acquire the skills and knowledge necessary to successfully integrate AI-powered tools into their learning systems, as the research's findings indicate that awareness and performance expectations are crucial for implementing AI in educational settings.

REFERENCES

Akata, Z., Balliet, D., De Rijke, M., Dignum, F., Dignum, V., Eiben, G., Fokkens, A., Grossi, D., Hindriks, K., Hoos, H., Hung, H., Jonker, C., Monz, C., Neerincx, M., Oliehoek, F., Prakken, H., Schlobach, S., van der Gaag, L., van Harmelen, F., & Welling, M. (2020). A research agenda for hybrid intelligence: Augmenting human intellect with collaborative, adaptive, responsible, and explainable artificial intelligence. *Computer*, *53*(8), 18–28. DOI: 10.1109/MC.2020.2996587

Al-Takhayneh, S. K., Karaki, W., Hasan, R. A., Chang, B.-L., Shaikh, J. M., & Kanwal, W. (2022). Teachers' psychological resistance to digital innovation in Jordanian entrepreneurship and business schools: Moderation of teachers' psychology and attitude toward educational technologies. *Frontiers in Psychology*, *13*, 1004078. DOI: 10.3389/fpsyg.2022.1004078 PMID: 36225699

Aldosari, S. A. M. (2020). The future of higher education in the light of artificial intelligence transformations. *International Journal of Higher Education*, *9*(3), 145–151. DOI: 10.5430/ijhe.v9n3p145

Antonietti, C., Cattaneo, A., & Amenduni, F. (2022). Can teachers' digital competence influence technology acceptance in vocational education? Computers inhuman. *Behaviour*, *132*, 10726.

Baranwal, D. (2022). A systematic review of exploring the potential of teachable agents in English learning. *Pedagogical Research*, *7*(1), em0117. Advance online publication. DOI: 10.29333/pr/11553

Chang, Y., Lee, S., Wong, S. F., & Jeong, S.-P. (2022). AI-powered learning application use and gratification: An integrative model. *Information Technology & People*, *35*(7), 2115–2139. DOI: 10.1108/ITP-09-2020-0632

Chen, X., Xie, H., Zou, D., & Hwang, G. J. (2020). Application and theory gaps during the rise of artificial intelligence in education. *Comput. Educ. Artif. Intell.*, *1*, 100002. DOI: 10.1016/j.caeai.2020.100002

Chen, X., Zou, D., Xie, H., Cheng, G., & Liu, C. (2022). Two decades of artificial intelligence in education: Contributors, collaborations, research topics, challenges, and future directions. *Journal of Educational Technology & Society*, *28*, 1323–1358. DOI: 10.1007/s10639-022-11209-y

Chen, Y.-L., Hsu, C.-C., Lin, C.-Y., & Hsu, H.-H. (2022). Robot-assisted language learning: Integrating artificial intelligence and virtual reality into English tour guide practice. Education Sciences, 12, 437.

Crompton, H., & Burke, D. (2020). Mobile learning and pedagogical opportunities: A configurative systematic review of PreK-12 research using the SAMR framework. Computers & Education, 156, 103945.

Crompton, H., & Burke, D. (2023). Artificial intelligence in higher education: The State of the field. *International Journal of Educational Technology in Higher Education*, *20*(1), 22. DOI: 10.1186/s41239-023-00392-8

De Simone, S., Cicotto, G., Pinna, R., & Giustiniano, L. (2016). Engaging public servants. Management Decision, 54(7), 1569–1594. DOI: 10.1108/MD-02-2016-0072

Ebadi, S., & Amini, A. (2022). Examining the roles of social presence and human-likeness on Iranian EFL learners' motivation using artificial intelligence technology: A case of CSIEC chatbot. *Interactive Learning Environments*, *2022*, 1–19. DOI: 10.1080/10494820.2022.2096638

Ericsson, E., Hashemi, S. S., & Lundin, J. (2023). Fun and frustrating: Pupils' perspectives on practising speaking English with virtual humans. Cogent Education, 10, 2170088.

Fang, T., Yang, S., Lan, K., Wong, D. F., Hu, J., & Chao, L. S. (2023). Is chatgpt a highly fluent grammatical error correction system? A comprehensive evaluation. / arXiv.2304.01746DOI: 10.48550

Fathi, J., & Rahimi, M. (2022). Electronic writing portfolio in a collaborative writing environment: Its impact on EFL students' writing performance. *Computer Assisted Language Learning*, *2022*, 1–39. DOI: 10.1080/09588221.2022.2097697

Fitria, T. N. (2021a). Grammarly as AI-powered English Writing Assistant: Students' Alternative for Writing English. Metathesis. *Journal of English Language, Literature, and Teaching*, *5*(1), 65–78. DOI: 10.31002/metathesis.v5i1.3519

Fitria, T. N. (2021b). QuillBot as an online tool: Students' alternative in paraphrasing and rewriting of English writing. Englisia. *Journal of Language, Education, and Humanities*, *9*(1), 183–196. DOI: 10.22373/ej.v9i1.10233

Fitria, T. N. (2023). Artificial intelligence (AI) technology in Open AI Chat GPT application: A review of Chat GPT in writing English essay. *ELT J. English Lang. Teach.*, *12*(1), 44–58. DOI: 10.15294/elt.v12i1.64069

Franzoni, V., Milani, A., Mengoni, P., & Piccinato, F. (2020). Artificial intelligence visual metaphors in e-learning interfaces for learning analytics. *Applied Sciences (Basel, Switzerland)*, *10*(20), 1–25. DOI: 10.3390/app10207195

Ge, Z., & Hu, Y. (2020) Innovative application of artificial intelligence (AI) in the Management of higher edu-cation and teaching. In *2020 International Conference on Artificial Intelligence and Information Technology, ICAIIT 2020*. Institute of Physics Publishing.

Hsu, T. C., Chang, C., & Jen, T. H. (2023). Artificial intelligence image recognition using self-regulation learning strategies: Effects on vocabulary acquisition, learning anxiety, and learning behaviours of English language learners. *Interactive Learning Environments*, 1–19. DOI: 10.1080/10494820.2023.2165508

Huang, J., & Tan, M. (2023). The role of Chat GPT in scientific communication: Writing better scientific review articles. *American Journal of Cancer Research, 13*, 1148–1154. PMID: 37168339

Huang, X., Zou, D., Cheng, G., Chen, X., & Xie, H. (2023). Trends, research issues and applications of artificial intelligence in language education. *Journal of Educational Technology & Society*, *26*, 112–131.

Hwang, G. J., Xie, H., Wah, B. W., & Gašević, D. (2020). Vision, challenges, roles and research issues of artificial intelligence in education. *Computers & Education*, *1*, 100001. DOI: 10.1016/j.caeai.2020.100001

Junaidi, J. (2020). Artificial intelligence in EFL context: Rising students' speaking performance with Lyra virtual assistance. *Int. J. Adv. Sci. Technol. Rehabil.*, *29*, 6735–6741.

Khoza, S. B., & Mpungose, C. B. (2022). Digitalised curri-culum to the rescue of a higher education institution. *African Identities*, *20*(4), 310–330. DOI: 10.1080/14725843.2020.1815517

Kim, N. Y. (2019). A study on the use of artificial intelligence Chatbots for improving English grammar skills. *J. Digital Converg.*, *17*, 89–110.

Krstić, L., Aleksić, V., & Krstić, M. (2022). Artificial intelligence in education. *RE:view*.

Lai, Y., Saab, N., & Admiraal, W. (2022). University students' use of mobile technology in self-directed language learning: Using the integrative model of behavior prediction. *Computers & Education*, *179*, 104413. DOI: 10.1016/j.compedu.2021.104413

Lee, J. H., Shin, D., & Noh, W. (2023). Artificial intelligence-based content generator technology for young English-as-a-foreign-language learners' reading enjoyment. *RELC Journal*, *54*(2), 508–516. DOI: 10.1177/00336882231165060

Loncar, M., Schams, W., & Liang, J. S. (2023). Multiple technologies, multiple sources: Trends and analyses of the literature on technology-mediated feedback for L2 English writing published from 2015-2019. *Computer Assisted Language Learning*, *36*(4), 722–784. DOI: 10.1080/09588221.2021.1943452

Moreira-Fontán, E., García-Señorán, M., Conde-Rodríguez, Á., & González, A. (2019). Teachers' ICT-related self-efficacy, job resources, and positive emotions: Their structural relations with autonomous motivation and work engagement. *Computers & Education*, *134*, 63–77. DOI: 10.1016/j.compedu.2019.02.007

Nguyen, L. Q., & Le, H. V. (2023). Enhancing L2 learners' lexical gains via Quizlet learning tool: The role of individual differences. *Education and Information Technologies*, *28*(9), 12143–12167. DOI: 10.1007/s10639-023-11673-0

Scherer, R., Siddiq, F., & Tondeur, J. (2019). The technology acceptance model (TAM): A meta-analytic structural equation modeling approach to explaining teachers 'adoption of digital technology in education. *Computers & Education*, *128*, 13–35. DOI: 10.1016/j.compedu.2018.09.009

Shadiev, R., Wen, Y., Uosaki, N., & Song, Y. (2023). Future language learning with emerging technologies. *Journal of Computers in Education*, *10*(3), 463–467. DOI: 10.1007/s40692-023-00285-9

Sharadgah, T. A., & Sa'di, R. A. (2022). A systematic review of research on the use of artificial intelligence in English language teaching and learning (2015-2021): What are the current effects? *Journal of Information Technology Education*, *21*, 337–377. DOI: 10.28945/4999

Tahiru, F. (2021). AI in education: A systematic literature review. *Journal of Cases on Information Technology*, *23*(1), 1–20. DOI: 10.4018/JCIT.2021010101

Utami, S. P. T., Andayani, A., Winarni, R., & Sumarwati, S. (2023). Utilization of artificial intelligence technology in an academic writing class: How do Indonesian students perceive? *Contemporary Educational Technology*, *15*(4), ep450. DOI: 10.30935/cedtech/13419

Vuong, Q.-H., La, V.-P., Nguyen, M.-H., Jin, R., La, M.-K., & Le, T.-T. (2023). AI's humanoid appearance can affect human perceptions of its emotional capability: Evidence form self-reported data in the U.S. International Journal of Human-Computer Interaction, 1–12.

Weng, X., & Chiu, T. K. (2023). Instructional design and learning outcomes of intelligent computer assisted language learning: Systematic review in the field. *Comput. Educ. Artif. Intell.*, *4*, 100117. DOI: 10.1016/j.caeai.2022.100117

Xia, Q., Chiu, T. K., & Chai, C. S. (2022). The moderating effects of gender and need satisfaction on self-regulated learning through artificial intelligence (AI). *Education and Information Technologies*, *28*(7), 8691–8713. DOI: 10.1007/s10639-022-11547-x

Yan, D. (2023). Impact of Chat GPT on learners in a L2 writing practicum: an exploratory investigation. Educ. Inf. Technol., 1–25. DOI: 10.1007/s10639-023-11742-4

Zawacki-Richter, O., Marín, V. I., Bond, M., & Gouverneur, F. (2019). Systematic review of research on artificial intelligence applications in higher education—Where are the educators? *International Journal of Educational Technology in Higher Education*, *16*(1), 1–27. DOI: 10.1186/s41239-019-0171-0

Zhang, R., & Zou, D. (2020). Types, purposes, and effectiveness of state-of-the-art technologies for second and foreign language learning. *Computer Assisted Language Learning*, *35*(4), 696–742. DOI: 10.1080/09588221.2020.1744666

Compilation of References

Abdulmajeed, M., & Fahmy, N. (2022). Meta-analysis of AI research in journalism: Challenges, opportunities and future research agenda for Arab journalism. In European, Asian, Middle Eastern, North African Conference on Management & Information Systems. Springer International Publishing.

Acemoglu, D., & Restrepo, P. (2017). Robots and jobs: Evidence from US labor markets. *NBER Working Paper Series*, No. 23285.

Adamopoulou, E., & Moussiades, L. (2020). Chatbots: History, technology, and applications. *Machine Learning with Applications*, *2*, 100007. DOI: 10.1016/j.mlwa.2020.100006

Adams, P. (2006). Exploring social constructivism: Theories and practicalities. *Education 3-13, 34*(3), 243–257. DOI: 10.1080/03004270600898893

AERA, APA, & NCME. (2014). Standards for educational and psychological testing. In *American Educational Research Association, American Psychological Association, & National Council on Measurement in Education*. American Educational Research Association.

Akata, Z., Balliet, D., De Rijke, M., Dignum, F., Dignum, V., Eiben, G., Fokkens, A., Grossi, D., Hindriks, K., Hoos, H., Hung, H., Jonker, C., Monz, C., Neerincx, M., Oliehoek, F., Prakken, H., Schlobach, S., van der Gaag, L., van Harmelen, F., & Welling, M. (2020). A research agenda for hybrid intelligence: Augmenting human intellect with collaborative, adaptive, responsible, and explainable artificial intelligence. *Computer*, *53*(8), 18–28. DOI: 10.1109/MC.2020.2996587

Al-Abdullatif, A. M., Al-Dokhny, A. A., & Drwish, A. M. (2023). Implementing the Bashayer chatbot in Saudi higher education: Measuring the influence on students' motivation and learning strategies. *Frontiers in Psychology*, *14*, 1129070. Advance online publication. DOI: 10.3389/fpsyg.2023.1129070 PMID: 37255522

Alamdari, E. F., & Bozorgian, H. (2021). Gender, metacognitive intervention, and dialogic interaction: EFL multimedia listening. *System*, *104*, 102709. DOI: 10.1016/j.system.2021.102709

Al-Badi, A., Khan, A., & Eid-Alotaibi, . (2022). Perceptions of learners and instructors towards artificial intelligence in personalized learning. *Procedia Computer Science*, *201*, 445–451. DOI: 10.1016/j.procs.2022.03.058

Albizu-Rivas, I., Parratt-Fernández, S., & Mera-Fernández, M. (2024). Artificial Intelligence in Slow Journalism: Journalists' Uses, Perceptions, and Attitudes. *Journalism and Media*, *5*(4), 1836–1850. DOI: 10.3390/journalmedia5040111

Aldosari, S. A. M. (2020). The future of higher education in the light of artificial intelligence transformations. *International Journal of Higher Education*, *9*(3), 145–151. DOI: 10.5430/ijhe.v9n3p145

Aldridge, I. (2013). *High-frequency trading: A practical guide to algorithmic strategies and trading systems*. John Wiley & Sons.

Ali, J. K. M., Shamsan, M. A. A., Hezam, T. A., & Mohammed, A. A. Q. (2023). Impact of ChatGPT on learning motivation: Teachers and students' voices. *Journal of English Studies in Arabia Felix*, *2*(1), 41–49. DOI: 10.56540/jesaf.v2i1.51

Alpert, R., & Haber, R. N. (1960). Anxiety in academic achievement situations. *Journal of Abnormal and Social Psychology*, *61*(2), 207–215. DOI: 10.1037/h0045464 PMID: 13682679

Alrajhi, A. S. (2023). Genre effect on Google Translate–assisted L2 writing output quality. *ReCALL*, *35*(3), 305–320. DOI: 10.1017/S0958344022000143

Alrasheedi, S. (2024). The effect of using AI applications to develop EFL listening comprehension skills among university students. *Conhecimento & Diversidade*, *16*(44), 601–637. DOI: 10.18316/rcd.v16i44.12346

Al-Takhayneh, S. K., Karaki, W., Hasan, R. A., Chang, B.-L., Shaikh, J. M., & Kanwal, W. (2022). Teachers' psychological resistance to digital innovation in Jordanian entrepreneurship and business schools: Moderation of teachers' psychology and attitude toward educational technologies. *Frontiers in Psychology*, *13*, 1004078. DOI: 10.3389/fpsyg.2022.1004078 PMID: 36225699

Altınay, G., & Aydın, S. (2024). Automated feedback and writing achievement in a foreign language context. *1st International Literature,Language and Educational Research Symposium*, 246–260.

Anderson, T., & Elloumi, F. (2004). *Theory and practice of online learning*. Athabasca University.

Antonietti, C., Cattaneo, A., & Amenduni, F. (2022). Can teachers' digital competence influence technology acceptance in vocational education? Computers inhuman. *Behaviour*, *132*, 10726.

An, X., Chai, C., Li, Y., Zhou, Y., & Yang, B. (2023). Modeling students' perceptions of artificial intelligence assisted language learning. *Computer Assisted Language Learning*, ●●●, 1–22. DOI: 10.1080/09588221.2023.2246519

Arkin, R. C. (2009). *Governing lethal behavior in autonomous robots*. CRC Press. DOI: 10.1201/9781420085952

Aryadoust, V., & Luo, L. (2022). The typology of second language listening constructs: A systematic review. *Language Testing*, *40*(2), 375–409. DOI: 10.1177/02655322221126604

Assiri, M. (2014). Metacognitive and cognitive strategy use and performance on a reading test with multiple-format tasks. *Arab World English Journal*, *5*(4), 187–202.

Attali, Y., & Burstein, J. (2006). Automated essay scoring with e-rater® V.2. *The Journal of Technology, Learning, and Assessment*, *4*(3), 1–30.

Aula Blasco, J. (2016). The relationship between writing anxiety, writing self-efficacy, and Spanish EFL students' use of metacognitive writing strategies: A case study. *Journal of English Studies*, *14*, 7–45. DOI: 10.18172/jes.3069

Aydın, S. (2024). Using ChatGPT in foreign language research: An overview. *Innovational Research in ELT*, *5*(1), 20–26. DOI: 10.29329/irelt.2024.1045.2

Aydın, S., Tekin, I., & Akkaş, F. (2024). Construction and validation of the foreign language learning enjoyment scale. *Psychology in the Schools*, *61*(2), 657–670. DOI: 10.1002/pits.23076

Aydın, S., & Zeinolabedini, M. (2024). Integrating artificial intelligence into foreign language learning: Learners' perspectives. *11th EJER Congress*.

Baesens, B., Van Gestel, T., Viaene, S., Stepanova, M., Suykens, J., & Vanthienen, J. (2003). Benchmarking state-of-the-art classification algorithms for credit scoring. *The Journal of the Operational Research Society*, *54*(6), 627–635. DOI: 10.1057/palgrave.jors.2601545

Bai, L., & Hu, G. (2017). In the face of fallible AWE feedback: How do students respond? *Educational Psychology*, *37*(1), 67–81. DOI: 10.1080/01443410.2016.1223275

Bailey, D., Southam, A., & Costley, J. (2021). Digital storytelling with chatbots: Mapping L2 participation and perception patterns. *Interactive Technology and Smart Education, 18*(1), 85–103. DOI: 10.1108/ITSE-08-2020-0170

Ballıdağ, M., & Aydın, S. (2025). *A comparison of the effects of AI-based chatbots and peer interactions on speaking anxiety among EFL learners*. Future in Educational Research., DOI: 10.1002/fer3.70005

Bandura, A. (1986). *Social foundations of thought and action: A social cognitive theory*. Prentice Hall.

Baranwal, D. (2022). A systematic review of exploring the potential of teachable agents in English learning. *Pedagogical Research, 7*(1), em0117. Advance online publication. DOI: 10.29333/pr/11553

Benali, A. (2021). The impact of using automated writing feedback in ESL/EFL classroom contexts. *English Language Teaching, 14*(12), 189. DOI: 10.5539/elt.v14n12p189

Benson, P. (2011). *Teaching and researching autonomy in language learning*. Routledge.

Berk, E. H., & Aydın, S. (2025). The impact of artificial intelligence-powered writing assistance systems on metacognitive writing strategies. In *Transformations in Digital Learning and Educational Technologies* (pp. 241–274). IGI Global., DOI: 10.4018/979-8-3373-3678-7.ch011

Bernstein, D., Nash, P., Clarke-Stewart, A., Penner, L., & Roy, E. (2008). *Essentials of psychology* (4th ed.). Houghton Mifflin Company.

Bertelsen, O., & Bødker, S. (2003). Activity Theory. In Carroll, C. (Ed.), *HCI models, theories, and frameworks: Toward a multidisciplinary science* (pp. 291–324). Elsevier., DOI: 10.1016/B978-155860808-5/50011-3

Boateng, G., Neilands, T., Frongillo, E., Melgar-Quiñonez, H., & Young, S. (2018). Best practices for developing and validating scales for health, social, and behavioral research: A primer. *Frontiers in Public Health, 6*, 149. Advance online publication. DOI: 10.3389/fpubh.2018.00149 PMID: 29942800

Bolton, R. J., & Hand, D. J. (2002). Statistical fraud detection: A review. *Statistical Science, 17*(3), 235–255. DOI: 10.1214/ss/1042727940

Bozkurt, A., Xiao, J., Farrow, R., Bai, J. Y. H., Nerantzi, C., Moore, S., Dron, J., Stracke, C. M., Singh, L., Crompton, H., Koutropoulos, A., Terentev, E., Pazurek, A., Nichols, M., Sidorkin, A. M., Costello, E., Watson, S., Mulligan, D., Honeychurch, S., & Asino, T. I. (2024). The manifesto for teaching and learning in a time of generative AI: A critical collective stance to better navigate the future. *Open Praxis*, *16*(4), 487–513. DOI: 10.55982/openpraxis.16.4.777

Brookhart, S. M. (2017). *How to give feedback to your students* (2nd ed.). ASCD.

Brown, H. D., & Yule, G. (1983). *Teaching the spoken language: An approach based on the analysis of conversational speech*. Longman.

Brynjolfsson, E., & McAfee, A. (2014). *The second machine age: Work, progress, and prosperity in a time of brilliant technologies*. W. W. Norton & Company.

Bryson, J. J., & Winfield, A. F. (2017). Standardizing ethical design for artificial intelligence and autonomous systems. *Computer*, *50*(5), 116–119. DOI: 10.1109/MC.2017.154

Bsharat-Maalouf, D., & Karawani, H. (2022). Learning and bilingualism in challenging listening conditions: How challenging can it be? *Cognition*, *222*, 105018. DOI: 10.1016/j.cognition.2022.105018 PMID: 35032867

Buhmann, A., & White, C. L. (2022). Artificial intelligence in public relations: Role and implications. In *The Emerald Handbook of Computer-Mediated Communication and Social Media* (pp. 625–638). Emerald Publishing Limited. DOI: 10.1108/978-1-80071-597-420221036

Bulut, S. E. (2019). *The effects of automated writing evaluation on EFL students' writing achievement and motivation towards writing* [Master's Thesis]. Istanbul University.

Buolamwini, J., & Gebru, T. (2018). Gender shades: Intersectional accuracy disparities in commercial gender classification. *Conference on Fairness, Accountability and Transparency*, 77-91.

Burdea, G. C., & Coiffet, P. (2003). *Virtual reality technology*. John Wiley & Sons.

Byram, M. (2012). Language awareness and (critical) cultural awareness – relationships, comparisons and contrasts. *Language Awareness*, *21*(1–2), 5–13. DOI: 10.1080/09658416.2011.639887

Cahyono, B. Y., Astuti, U. P., & Suryati, N. (2023). Online writing class: EFL university students' perception of teachers' strategies in alleviating their writing anxiety. *Computer Assisted Language Learning*, *42*(1), 1–24.

Cahyono, B. Y., & Rahayu, T. (2020). EFL students' motivation in writing, writing proficiency and gender. *TEFLIN Journal*, *31*(2), 162. DOI: 10.15639/teflinjournal.v31i2/162-180

Çakır, İ. (2010). Yazma becerisinin kazanılması yabancı dil öğretiminde neden zordur? [Why is it difficult to acquire writing skills in foreign language teaching?]. *Erciyes University Journal of Social Sciences Institute*, *1*(28), 1–12.

Camaj, L., Martin, J., & Lanosga, G. (2022). The impact of public transparency infrastructure on data journalism: A comparative analysis between information-rich and information-poor countries. *Digital Journalism (Abingdon, England)*, *10*(10), 1–20.

Carless, D. (2006). Differing perceptions in the feedback process. *Studies in Higher Education*, *31*(2), 219–233. DOI: 10.1080/03075070600572132

Carrell, P. L. (1989). Metacognitive awareness and second language reading. *Modern Language Journal*, *73*(2), 121–134. DOI: 10.1111/j.1540-4781.1989.tb02534.x

Cartner, H., & Cameron, D. (2023). Investigating metacognitive strategy awareness for multimodal listening. *E-Learning and Digital Media*, *20*(5), 424–441. DOI: 10.1177/20427530221108014

Celce-Murcia, M., Brinton, D. M., & Snow, M. A. (Eds.). (2014). *Teaching English as a second or foreign language* (4th ed.). National Geographic Learning/Cengage.

Chang, Y., Lee, S., Wong, S. F., & Jeong, S.-P. (2022). AI-powered learning application use and gratification: An integrative model. *Information Technology & People*, *35*(7), 2115–2139. DOI: 10.1108/ITP-09-2020-0632

Chastain, K. (1975). Affective and ability factors in second language acquisition. *Language Learning*, *25*(1), 153–161. DOI: 10.1111/j.1467-1770.1975.tb00115.x

Chen, Y.-L., Hsu, C.-C., Lin, C.-Y., & Hsu, H.-H. (2022). Robot-assisted language learning: Integrating artificial intelligence and virtual reality into English tour guide practice. Education Sciences, 12, 437.

Cheng, Y. S. (2004a). A measure of second language writing anxiety: Scale development and preliminary validation. *Journal of Second Language Writing*, *13*(4), 313–335. DOI: 10.1016/j.jslw.2004.07.001

Cheng, Y. S. (2004b). EFL students' writing anxiety: Sources and implications. *English Teaching & Learning*, *29*(2), 41–62.

Chen, X., Wang, X., & Li, Y. (2021). Blockchain for language education: Enhancing authentication and credibility in AI-assisted learning. *Journal of Educational Technology & Society*, *24*(2), 45–58.

Chen, X., Xie, H., Zou, D., & Hwang, G. J. (2020). Application and theory gaps during the rise of artificial intelligence in education. *Comput. Educ. Artif. Intell.*, *1*, 100002. DOI: 10.1016/j.caeai.2020.100002

Chen, X., Zou, D., Xie, H., Cheng, G., & Liu, C. (2022). Two decades of artificial intelligence in education: Contributors, collaborations, research topics, challenges, and future directions. *Journal of Educational Technology & Society*, *28*, 1323–1358. DOI: 10.1007/s10639-022-11209-y

Cherubini, F. (2022). *AI Journalism Handbook*. Reuters Institute.

Chetouani, N. (2024). Exploring changing practices and influence of artificial intelligence on modern journalism. DIROSAT: Journal of Education. *Social Sciences & Humanities*, *2*(4), 329–341.

Choi, S., Shin, H., & Kang, S.-S. (2021). Predicting audience-rated news quality: Using survey, text mining, and neural network methods. *Digital Journalism (Abingdon, England)*, *9*(1), 84–105. DOI: 10.1080/21670811.2020.1842777

Choi, Y., & Zhang, D. (2018). The relative role of vocabulary and grammatical knowledge in L2 reading comprehension: A systematic review of literature. *IRAL -. International Review of Applied Linguistics in Language Teaching*, *59*(1), 1–30. DOI: 10.1515/iral-2017-0033

Chou, M.-H. (2017). A task-based language teaching approach to developing metacognitive strategies for listening comprehension. *International Journal of Listening*, *31*(1), 51–70. DOI: 10.1080/10904018.2015.1098542

Chowdhary, K. R. (2020b). Natural language processing. Fundamentals of Artificial Intelligence, 603-649.

Chowdhary, K. R. (2020a). *Natural language processing*. Springer.

Chung, K. H., & Tseng, S. P. (2020). An empirical study on the factors influencing the effectiveness of customer service chatbots. *Journal of Management and Marketing Research*, *24*, 1–16.

Chung, Y. B., & Yuen, M. (2011). The role of feedback in enhancing students' self-regulation in inviting schools. *Journal of Invitational Theory and Practice*, *17*, 22–27. DOI: 10.26522/jitp.v17i.3777

Cizrelioğlu, İ., & Aydin, S. (2024). Using artificial intelligence in EFL learning among multilingual young learners. In Z. Sanmugam, M. Edwards, B. Barkhaya, N. Khlaif (Ed.), *Fostering Inclusive Education With AI and Emerging Technologies* (pp. 303–322). IGI Global. DOI: 10.4018/979-8-3693-7255-5.ch013

Clariana, R. B. (1999, February). Differential memory effects for immediate and delayed feedback: A delta rule explanation of feedback timing effects. *Association for Educational Communications and Technology Annual Convention.*

Creswell, J. W. (2014). *Research design: Qualitative, quantitative, and mixed methods approaches* (4th ed.). SAGE Publications.

Crompton, H., & Burke, D. (2020). Mobile learning and pedagogical opportunities: A configurative systematic review of PreK-12 research using the SAMR framework. Computers & Education, 156, 103945.

Crompton, H., & Burke, D. (2023). Artificial intelligence in higher education: The State of the field. *International Journal of Educational Technology in Higher Education, 20*(1), 22. DOI: 10.1186/s41239-023-00392-8

Crossley, S. A. (2018). Natural language processing applications for second language learners. *Language Learning & Technology*, *22*(2), 1–8.

Dalman, M., & Plonsky, L. (2022). The effectiveness of second-language listening strategy instruction: A meta-analysis. *Language Teaching Research.* Advance online publication. DOI: 10.1177/13621688221140003

Daly, J. A., & Miller, M. D. (1975). Apprehension of writing as a predictor of message intensity. *The Journal of Psychology*, *89*(2), 175–177. DOI: 10.1080/00223980.1975.9915748 PMID: 28135469

Daly, J. A., & Shamo, W. (1976). Writing apprehension and occupational choice. *Journal of Occupational Psychology*, *49*(1), 55–56. DOI: 10.1111/j.2044-8325.1976.tb00329.x

Dang, H. (2006). Learner-centeredness and EFL instruction in Vietnam: A case study. *International Education Journal*, *7*(4), 598–610.

Danzon-Chambaud, S., & Cornia, A. (2023). Changing or reinforcing the "rules of the game": A field theory perspective on the impacts of automated journalism on media practitioners. *Journalism Practice*, *17*(2), 174–188. DOI: 10.1080/17512786.2021.1919179

De Simone, S., Cicotto, G., Pinna, R., & Giustiniano, L. (2016). Engaging public servants. Management Decision, 54(7), 1569–1594. DOI: 10.1108/MD-02-2016-0072

Deci, E., & Ryan, R. (2012). Self-determination theory. In Van Lange, P. A. M., Kruglanski, A. W., & Higgins, T. E. (Eds.), *Handbook of Theories of Social Psychology* (1st ed., Vol. 1, pp. 416–437). SAGE Publications. DOI: 10.4135/9781446249215.n21

Demir, K., & Güraksın, G. (2022). Determining middle school students' perceptions of the concept of artificial intelligence: A metaphor analysis. *Participatory Educational Research*, *9*(2), 297–312. DOI: 10.17275/per.22.41.9.2

Démuth, A. (2013). *Perception theories*. Trnava University.

Deterding, S., Dixon, D., Khaled, R., & Nacke, L. (2011). Gamification: Toward a definition. *Proceedings of CHI 2011*, 12-15.

Devitt, S. (1997). Reading and writing one's way into language awareness. *Language Awareness*, *6*(2-3), 119–135. DOI: 10.1080/09658416.1997.9959922

Diakopoulos, N. (2019). *Automating the News: How Algorithms Are Rewriting the Media*. Harvard UP. DOI: 10.4159/9780674239302

Dierickx, L., Opdahl, A. L., Khan, S. A., Lindén, C. G., & Guerrero Rojas, D. C. (2024). A data-centric approach for ethical and trustworthy AI in journalism. *Ethics and Information Technology*, *26*(4), 64. DOI: 10.1007/s10676-024-09801-6

Dikli, S. (2010). The nature of automated essay scoring feedback. *CALICO Journal*, *28*(1), 99–134. DOI: 10.11139/cj.28.1.99-134

Dimitrov, D. V. (2016). Medical internet of things and big data in healthcare. *Healthcare Informatics Research*, *22*(3), 156–163. DOI: 10.4258/hir.2016.22.3.156 PMID: 27525156

Dizon, G., & Gold, J. (2023). Exploring the effects of Grammarly on EFL students' foreign language anxiety and learner autonomy. *The JALT CALL Journal*, *19*(3), 299–316. DOI: 10.29140/jaltcall.v19n3.1049

Do, H. M., & Phan, H. L. T. (2021). Metacognitive awareness of reading strategies on second language Vietnamese undergraduates. *Arab World English Journal*, *12*(1), 90–112. DOI: 10.24093/awej/vol12no1.7

Domingos, P. (2015). *The master algorithm: How the quest for the ultimate learning machine will remake our world*. Basic Books.

Dörnyei, Z. (1998). Motivation in second and foreign language learning. *Language Teaching*, *31*(3), 117–135. DOI: 10.1017/S026144480001315X

Dörnyei, Z., & Ryan, S. (2015). *The psychology of the language learner revisited*. Routledge. DOI: 10.4324/9781315779553

Doshi-Velez, F., & Kim, B. (2017). Towards a rigorous science of interpretable machine learning. *arXiv preprint arXiv:1702.08608*.

Downing, S. (2003). Validity: On the meaningful interpretation of assessment data. *Medical Education*, *37*(9), 830–837. DOI: 10.1046/j.1365-2923.2003.01594.x PMID: 14506816

Drigas, A. S., & Ioannidou, R.-E. (2012). Artificial intelligence in special education: A decade review. *International Journal of Engineering Education*, *28*(6), 1366–1372.

Dulay, H., Burt, M., & Krashen, S. (1982). *Language two*. Oxford University Press.

Dwivedi, Y. K., Hughes, L., Baabdullah, A. M., Ribeiro-Navarrete, S., Jain, P., & Tamilmani, K. (2023). Artificial Intelligence (AI): Multidisciplinary perspectives on emerging challenges, opportunities, and agenda for research, practice and policy. *International Journal of Information Management*, *68*, 102399.

Dwyer, T., Wilding, D., & Koskie, T. (2021). Australia: Media concentration and deteriorating conditions for investigative journalism. In Australia: Media concentration and deteriorating conditions for investigative journalism (pp. 59-94).

Ebadi, S., & Amini, A. (2022). Examining the roles of social presence and human-likeness on Iranian EFL learners' motivation using artificial intelligence technology: A case of CSIEC chatbot. *Interactive Learning Environments*, *2022*, 1–19. DOI: 10.1080/10494820.2022.2096638

Ekmekçi, E. (2018). Exploring Turkish EFL students' writing anxiety. *The Reading Matrix: An International Online Journal*, *18*(1), 158–175.

El Ebyary, K., & Windeatt, S. (2010). The impact of computer-based feedback on students' written work. *The International Journal of Educational Spectrum*, *10*(2), 121–142. www.um.es/ijes. DOI: 10.6018/ijes/2010/2/119231

El Shazly, R. (2021). Effects of artificial intelligence on English speaking anxiety and speaking performance: A case study. *Expert Systems: International Journal of Knowledge Engineering and Neural Networks*, *38*(3), e12667. Advance online publication. DOI: 10.1111/exsy.12667

Ellis, R. (1999). *Learning a second language through interaction*. John Benjamins Publishing. DOI: 10.1075/sibil.17

Ellis, R. (2009). Corrective feedback and teacher development. *Journal of Linguistics and Language Teaching*, *1*(1), 3–18. DOI: 10.5070/L2.V1I1.9054

Ellis, R. (2015). *Understanding second language acquisition* (Ellis, R., Ed.; 2nd ed.). Oxford University Press.

Ercan, G., & Aydin, S. (2022). Teachers' and learners' perceptions of flipped learning in a foreign language context. *FIRE: Futuristic Implementations of Research in Education*, *3*(2), 111–128.

Ericsson, E., Hashemi, S. S., & Lundin, J. (2023). Fun and frustrating: Pupils' perspectives on practising speaking English with virtual humans. Cogent Education, 10, 2170088.

Esteva, A., Kuprel, B., Novoa, R. A., Ko, J., Swetter, S. M., Blau, H. M., & Thrun, S. (2017). Dermatologist-level classification of skin cancer with deep neural networks. *Nature*, *542*(7639), 115–118. DOI: 10.1038/nature21056 PMID: 28117445

Fang, T., Yang, S., Lan, K., Wong, D. F., Hu, J., & Chao, L. S. (2023). Is chatgpt a highly fluent grammatical error correction system? A comprehensive evaluation. / arXiv.2304.01746DOI: 10.48550

Fareed, M., Khan, I., & Akhtar, H. (2021). The causes of English writing anxiety among Pakistani ESL students: Perceptions of teachers and students. *Pakistan Journal of Humanities and Social Sciences*, *9*(1), 21–27. DOI: 10.52131/pjhss.2021.0901.0109

Fathi, J., Derakhshan, A., & Torabi, S. (2020). The effect of listening strategy instruction on second language listening anxiety and self-efficacy of Iranian EFL learners. *SAGE Open*, *10*(2), 1–13. DOI: 10.1177/2158244020933878

Fathi, J., & Rahimi, M. (2022). Electronic writing portfolio in a collaborative writing environment: Its impact on EFL students' writing performance. *Computer Assisted Language Learning*, *2022*, 1–39. DOI: 10.1080/09588221.2022.2097697

Ferris, D. (1999). The case for grammar correction in L2 writing classes: A response to Truscott (1996). *Journal of Second Language Writing*, *8*(1), 1–11. DOI: 10.1016/S1060-3743(99)80110-6

Field, J. (2008). *Listening in the language classroom*. Cambridge University Press.

Fishbein, M., & Ajzen, I. (1975). *Belief, attitude, intention, and behavior: An introduction to theory and research*. Addison-Wesley Publishing Company.

Fitria, T. (2021). Grammarly as AI-powered English writing assistant: Students' alternative for writing English. *Metathesis: Journal of English Language, Literature, and Teaching*, *5*(1), 65–78. DOI: 10.31002/metathesis.v5i1.3519

Fitria, T. N. (2021b). QuillBot as an online tool: Students' alternative in paraphrasing and rewriting of English writing. Englisia. *Journal of Language, Education, and Humanities*, *9*(1), 183–196. DOI: 10.22373/ej.v9i1.10233

Fitria, T. N. (2023). Artificial intelligence (AI) technology in Open AI Chat GPT application: A review of Chat GPT in writing English essay. *ELT J. English Lang. Teach.*, *12*(1), 44–58. DOI: 10.15294/elt.v12i1.64069

Floridi, L., Cowls, J., Beltramini, M., Chatila, R., Chazerand, P., Dignum, V., & Vayena, E. (2018). AI4People—an ethical framework for a good AI society: Opportunities, risks, principles, and recommendations. *Minds and Machines*, *28*(4), 689–707. DOI: 10.1007/s11023-018-9482-5 PMID: 30930541

Flower, L., & Hayes, J. R. (1981). A cognitive process theory of writing. *College Composition and Communication*, *32*(4), 365–387. DOI: 10.58680/ccc198115885

Franzoni, V., Milani, A., Mengoni, P., & Piccinato, F. (2020). Artificial intelligence visual metaphors in e-learning interfaces for learning analytics. *Applied Sciences (Basel, Switzerland)*, *10*(20), 1–25. DOI: 10.3390/app10207195

Frey, C. B., & Osborne, M. A. (2017). The future of employment: How susceptible are jobs to computerisation? *Technological Forecasting and Social Change*, *114*, 254–280. DOI: 10.1016/j.techfore.2016.08.019

Fridman, M., Krøvel, R., & Palumbo, F. (2023). How (not to) run an AI project in investigative journalism. *Journalism Practice*, 1–18.

Gardner, R. C. (1985). *Social psychology and second language learning: The role of attitudes and motivation* (H. Giles, Ed.; 1st ed., Issue 4). Edward Arnold. DOI: 10.1037/h0083787

Ge, Z., & Hu, Y. (2020) Innovative application of artificial intelligence (AI) in the Management of higher edu-cation and teaching. In *2020 International Conference on Artificial Intelligence and Information Technology, ICAIIT 2020*. Institute of Physics Publishing.

Goh, C. C. (2000). A cognitive perspective on language learners' listening comprehension problems. *System*, *28*(1), 55–75. DOI: 10.1016/S0346-251X(99)00060-3

Goh, C. C. M., & Hu, G. (2014). Exploring the relationship between metacognitive awareness and listening performance with questionnaire data. *Language Awareness*, *23*(3), 255–274. DOI: 10.1080/09658416.2013.769558

Goodfellow, I., Bengio, Y., & Courville, A. (2016). *Deep learning*. MIT press.

Grabe, W. (2009). *Reading in a second language: Moving from theory to practice*. Cambridge University Press.

Grabe, W., & Kaplan, R. B. (1996). *Theory and practice of writing: An applied linguistic perspective* (1st ed.). Routledge. https://www.routledge.com/Theory-and-Practice-of-Writing-An-Applied-Linguistic-Perspective/Grabe-Kaplan/p/book/9780582553835

Graham, S., & Santos, D. (2015). *Strategies for second language listening comprehension.* Oxford University Press.

Gregory, R. (2015). *Eye and brain: The psychology of seeing*. Princeton University Press. DOI: 10.2307/j.ctvc77h66

Griffiths, L., & Nicolls, B. (2010). e-Support4U: An evaluation of academic writing skills support in practice. *Nurse Education in Practice*, *10*(6), 341–348. DOI: 10.1016/j.nepr.2010.02.005 PMID: 20471319

Guichon, N., & McLornan, S. (2008). The effects of multimodality on L2 learners: Implications for CALL resource design. *System*, *36*(1), 85–93. DOI: 10.1016/j.system.2007.11.005

Hair, J., Black, W., Babin, B., Anderson, R., & Tatham, R. (1998). *Multivariate data analysis*. Pearson.

Hamidun, N., Hashim, S. H. M., & Othman, N. F. (2012). Enhancing students' motivation by providing feedback on writing: The case of international students from Thailand. *International Journal of Social Science and Humanity*, *2*(6), 591–594. DOI: 10.7763/IJSSH.2012.V2.179

Hamp-Lyons, L., & Heasley, B. (2006). *Study writing: A course in written English for academic purposes*. Cambridge University Press.

Han, J., Yoo, H., Kim, Y., Myung, J., Kim, M., Lim, H., Kim, J., Lee, T. Y., Hong, H., Ahn, S. Y., & Oh, A. (2023). RECIPE: How to Integrate ChatGPT into EFL Writing Education. *L@S 2023 - Proceedings of the 10th ACM Conference on Learning @ Scale*, 416–420. DOI: 10.1145/3573051.3596200

Harmer, J. (2003). Popular culture, methods, and context. *ELT Journal*, *57*(3), 288–294. DOI: 10.1093/elt/57.3.288

Harmer, J. (2004). *How to teach writing*. Pearson/Longman.

Hartono, W., Nurfitri, N., Ridwan, R., Kase, E., Lake, F., & Zebua, R. (2023). Artificial intelligence (AI) solutions in English language teaching: Teachers-students perceptions And experiences. *Journal of Education*, *6*(1), 1452–1461. DOI: 10.31004/joe.v6i1.3101

Hassan, B. A. (2001). *The relationship of writing apprehension and self-esteem to the writing quality and quantity of EFL university students.*

Hattie, J., & Timperley, H. (2007). The power of feedback. *Review of Educational Research, 77*(1), 81–112. DOI: 10.3102/003465430298487

Henestrosa, A. L., Greving, H., & Kimmerle, J. (2023). Automated journalism: The effects of AI authorship and evaluative information on the perception of a science journalism article. *Computers in Human Behavior, 138*, 107445. DOI: 10.1016/j.chb.2022.107445

He, X. (2024). Enhancing reading comprehension with AI-generated adaptive texts. *International Journal of New Developments in Education, 6*(7), 46–52. DOI: 10.25236/IJNDE.2024.060708

Hilgard, E. E., Atkinson, R. C., & Atkinson, R. L. (1971). *Introduction to psychology*. Harcourt Brace and Company.

Hockly, N. (2018). Blended learning. *ELT Journal, 72*(1), 97–101. DOI: 10.1093/elt/ccx058

Hofeditz, L., Mirbabaie, M., Holstein, J., & Stieglitz, S. (2021, June). Do You Trust an AI-journalist? A Credibility Analysis of News Content with AI-Authorship. ECIS.

Holec, H. (1981). *Autonomy and foreign language learning*. Pergamon Press.

Holland, P., & Wainer, H. (1993). *Differential item functioning*. Psychology Press.

Horwitz, E. (2001). Language anxiety and achievement. *Annual Review of Applied Linguistics, 21*, 112–126. DOI: 10.1017/S0267190501000071

Horwitz, E., Horwitz, M., & Cope, J. (1986). Foreign language classroom anxiety. *Modern Language Journal, 70*(2), 125–132. DOI: 10.1111/j.1540-4781.1986.tb05256.x

Hsu, T. C., Chang, C., & Jen, T. H. (2023). Artificial intelligence image recognition using self-regulation learning strategies: Effects on vocabulary acquisition, learning anxiety, and learning behaviours of English language learners. *Interactive Learning Environments*, 1–19. DOI: 10.1080/10494820.2023.2165508

Huang, J., & Tan, M. (2023). The role of Chat GPT in scientific communication: Writing better scientific review articles. *American Journal of Cancer Research, 13*, 1148–1154. PMID: 37168339

Huang, X., Zou, D., Cheng, G., Chen, X., & Xie, H. (2023). Trends, research issues and applications of artificial intelligence in language education. *Journal of Educational Technology & Society*, *26*, 112–131.

Hu, N. (2025). English listening and speaking ability improvement strategy from artificial intelligence wireless network. *Wireless Networks*, *31*(2), 1071–1080. DOI: 10.1007/s11276-024-03812-3

Hwang, G. J., Xie, H., Wah, B. W., & Gašević, D. (2020). Vision, challenges, roles and research issues of artificial intelligence in education. *Computers & Education*, *1*, 100001. DOI: 10.1016/j.caeai.2020.100001

Hyland, K. (2022). *The Routledge handbook of second language acquisition and writing* (Manchón, R. M., & Polio, C., Eds.; 2nd ed.). Routledge.

Hyland, K., & Hyland, F. (2006). *Feedback in second language writing*. Cambridge University Press., DOI: 10.1017/CBO9781139524742

IBM Cloud Education. (2022, December 21). *What is natural language generation?* Retrieved from https://www.ibm.com/cloud/learn/natural-language-processing

Ibrahim, H., Liu, F., Asim, R., Battu, B., Benabderrahmane, S., Alhafni, B., Adnan, W., Alhanai, T., AlShebli, B., Baghdadi, R., Bélanger, J., Beretta, E., Celik, K., Chaqfeh, M., Daqaq, M., Bernoussi, Z., Fougnie, D., Garcia de Soto, B., Gandolfi, A., & Zaki, Y. (2023). Perception, performance, and detectability of conversational artificial intelligence across 32 university courses. *Scientific Reports*, *13*(1), 1–13. DOI: 10.1038/s41598-023-38964-3 PMID: 36593249

Januarty, R., & Nima, H. N. A. (2018). Energizing students' reading comprehension through multimodal texts. *International Journal of Language Education*, *2*(2), 14–22. DOI: 10.26858/ijole.v2i2.4347

Jiang, L., & Yu, S. (2022). Appropriating automated feedback in L2 writing: Experiences of Chinese EFL student writers. *Computer Assisted Language Learning*, *35*(7), 1329–1353. DOI: 10.1080/09588221.2020.1799824

Johari, S. K. (2008). Building vocabulary and improving writing while developing a tourist brochure. *English Teaching Forum, 46*(2), 38–42.

Jones, B., Jones, R., & Luger, E. (2022). AI 'Everywhere and Nowhere': Addressing the AI intelligibility problem in public service journalism. *Digital Journalism (Abingdon, England)*, *10*(10), 1731–1755. DOI: 10.1080/21670811.2022.2145328

Jones, R. (2020). The impact of NLP on reading comprehension: An empirical study. *Applied Linguistics Review*, *11*(1), 56–79.

Jou, Y.-J. (2015). Investigation of technological university students' use of metacognitive reading strategies in first and second languages. *English Language Teaching*, *8*(1), 180–188. DOI: 10.5539/elt.v8n1p180

Junaidi, J. (2020). Artificial intelligence in EFL context: Rising students' speaking performance with Lyra virtual assistance. *Int. J. Adv. Sci. Technol. Rehabil.*, *29*, 6735–6741.

Jungherr, A., & Schroeder, R. (2023). Artificial intelligence and the public arena. *Communication Theory*, *33*(2-3), 164–173. DOI: 10.1093/ct/qtad006

Jurafsky, D., & Martin, J. H. (2023). *Speech and Language Processing* (3rd ed.). Pearson.

Kamberi, L. (2013). The significance of teacher feedback in EFL writing for tertiary level foreign language learners. *Procedia: Social and Behavioral Sciences*, *70*, 1686–1690. DOI: 10.1016/j.sbspro.2013.01.241

Kanero, J., Geçkin, V., Oranç, C., Mamus, E., Küntay, A., & Göksun, T. (2018). Social robots for early language learning: Current evidence and future directions. *Child Development Perspectives*, *12*(3), 146–151. DOI: 10.1111/cdep.12277

Kannan, J., & Munday, P. (2018). New trends in second language learning and teaching through the lens of ICT, networked learning, and artificial intelligence. *Círculo de Lingüística Aplicada a la Comunicación*, *76*, 13–30. DOI: 10.5209/CLAC.62495

Kaplan, A., & Haenlein, M. (2019). Siri, Siri in my hand, who's the fairest in the land? On the interpretations, illustrations, and implications of artificial intelligence. *Business Horizons*, *62*(1), 15–25. DOI: 10.1016/j.bushor.2018.08.004

Kennedy, T. (2006). Language learning and its impact on the brain: Connecting language learning with the mind through content-based instruction. *Foreign Language Annals*, *39*(3), 471–486. DOI: 10.1111/j.1944-9720.2006.tb02900.x

Khoza, S. B., & Mpungose, C. B. (2022). Digitalised curri-culum to the rescue of a higher education institution. *African Identities*, *20*(4), 310–330. DOI: 10.1080/14725843.2020.1815517

Kim, N. Y. (2018). A study on chatbots for developing Korean college students' English listening and reading skills. *Journal of Digital Convergence*, *16*(8), 19–26. DOI: 10.14400/JDC.2018.16.8.019

Kim, N. Y. (2019). A study on the use of artificial intelligence Chatbots for improving English grammar skills. *J. Digital Converg.*, *17*, 89–110.

Klimovich, M., & Richter, T. (2024). Metacognitive training can reduce mindless reading. *Journal of Educational Psychology, 116*(5), 836–852. DOI: 10.1037/edu0000884

Krashen, S. (1982). *Principles and practice in second language acquisition.* Pergamon Press.

Krashen, S. (1985). *The input hypothesis: Issues and implications* (1st ed.). Longman.

Krashen, S. D. (1982). *Principles and Practice in Second Language Acquisition.* Pergamon Press.

Krstić, L., Aleksić, V., & Krstić, M. (2022). Artificial intelligence in education. *RE:view.*

Kulhavy, R. W. (1977). Feedback in written instruction. *Review of Educational Research, 47*(2), 211–232. DOI: 10.3102/00346543047002211

Kumar, P., & Sharma, R. (2022). AI-driven cultural adaptation tools for language learning: A future perspective. *International Journal of Applied Linguistics, 32*(4), 87–102.

Kumar, V., Ayedh, A. H., Khan, I. A., & Jha, G. (2019). Artificial intelligence in marketing: A review and future research directions. *European Journal of Marketing.*

Kumar, V., Rajan, B., Venkatesan, R., & Lecinski, J. (2019). Understanding the role of artificial intelligence in personalized engagement marketing. *California Management Review, 61*(4), 135–155. DOI: 10.1177/0008125619859317

Kusumaningputri, R., Ningsih, T. A., & Wisasongko, W. (2018). Second language writing anxiety of Indonesian EFL students. *Lingua Cultura, 12*(4), 357. DOI: 10.21512/lc.v12i4.4268

Kyriazos, T. (2018). Applied psychometrics: Sample size and sample power considerations in factor analysis (EFA, CFA) and SEM in general. *Psychology (Irvine, Calif.), 09*(08), 2207–2230. DOI: 10.4236/psych.2018.98126

Lai, Y., Saab, N., & Admiraal, W. (2022). University students' use of mobile technology in self-directed language learning: Using the integrative model of behavior prediction. *Computers & Education, 179*, 104413. DOI: 10.1016/j.compedu.2021.104413

Lantolf, J. P., & Pavlenko, A. (1995). Sociocultural theory and second language acquisition. *Annual Review of Applied Linguistics, 15*, 108–124. DOI: 10.1017/S0267190500002646

Laufer, B., & Ravenhorst-Kalovski, G. C. (2010). Lexical threshold revisited: Lexical text coverage, learners' vocabulary size and reading comprehension. *Reading in a Foreign Language*, *22*(1), 15–30.

Law, K., Geng, S., & Li, T. (2019). Student enrollment, motivation and learning performance in a blended learning environment: The mediating effects of social, teaching, and cognitive presence. *Computers & Education*, *136*, 1–12. DOI: 10.1016/j.compedu.2019.02.021

Lee, I. (2014). Revisiting teacher feedback in EFL writing from sociocultural perspectives. *TESOL Quarterly*, *48*(1), 201–213. DOI: 10.1002/tesq.153

Lee, I., Yu, S., & Liu, Y. (2018). Hong Kong secondary students' motivation in EFL writing: A survey study. *TESOL Quarterly*, *52*(1), 176–187. DOI: 10.1002/tesq.364

Lee, J. H., Shin, D., & Noh, W. (2023). Artificial intelligence-based content generator technology for young English-as-a-foreign-language learners' reading enjoyment. *RELC Journal*, *54*(2), 508–516. DOI: 10.1177/00336882231165060

Levak, N., & Son, J. (2016). Facilitating second language learners' listening comprehension with Second Life and Skype. *ReCALL*, *29*(2), 200–218. DOI: 10.1017/S0958344016000215

Liang, J., Hwang, G., Chen, M., & Darmawansah, D. (2023). Roles and research foci of artificial intelligence in language education: An integrated bibliographic analysis and systematic review approach. *Interactive Learning Environments*, *31*(7), 4270–4296. DOI: 10.1080/10494820.2021.1958348

Liang, W., & Fung, D. (2021). Fostering critical thinking in English-as-a-second-language classrooms: Challenges and opportunities. *Thinking Skills and Creativity*, *39*, 1–12. DOI: 10.1016/j.tsc.2020.100769

Li, H., Gunnell, E., & Sun, Y. (2021). An intelligent system to improve vocabulary and reading comprehension using eye tracking and artificial intelligence. In Wyld, D. C. (Eds.), *Proceedings of the 2021 CS & IT Conference* (pp. 27–36). AIRCC Publishing. https://doi.org/DOI: 10.5121/csit.2021.111703

Li, J., & Lalani, F. (2022). AI-assisted speech recognition for ESL learners: A comparative study. *Computer Assisted Language Learning*, *35*(3), 212–230.

Li, J., Link, S., & Hegelheimer, V. (2015). Rethinking the role of automated writing evaluation (AWE) feedback in ESL writing instruction. *Journal of Second Language Writing*, *27*, 1–18. DOI: 10.1016/j.jslw.2014.10.004

Lobo Paes, J. (2024). *Artificial Intelligence And News Consumption: A Study Of Trust*. Credibility And Transparency In Automated Journalism.

Loncar, M., Schams, W., & Liang, J. S. (2023). Multiple technologies, multiple sources: Trends and analyses of the literature on technology-mediated feedback for L2 English writing published from 2015-2019. *Computer Assisted Language Learning*, *36*(4), 722–784. DOI: 10.1080/09588221.2021.1943452

MacCutcheon, D., Hurtig, A., Pausch, F., Hygge, S., Fels, J., & Ljung, R. (2019). Second language vocabulary level is related to benefits for second language listening comprehension under lower reverberation time conditions. *Journal of Cognitive Psychology*, *31*(2), 175–185. DOI: 10.1080/20445911.2019.1575387

MacIntyre, P. D. (1999). Language anxiety: A review of the research for language teachers. In Young, D. J. (Ed.), *Affect in foreign language and second language: A practical guide to creating a low-anxiety classroom atmosphere* (pp. 34–70). McGraw-Hill.

MacKey, A. (2006). Feedback, noticing and instructed second language learning. *Applied Linguistics*, *27*(3), 405–430. DOI: 10.1093/applin/ami051

Mahapatra, S. (2024). Impact of ChatGPT on ESL students' academic writing skills: A mixed methods intervention study. *Smart Learning Environments*, *11*(1), 9. DOI: 10.1186/s40561-024-00295-9

Mahmoodi-Shahrebabaki, M., & Oslund, E. (2025). The relationships between reading attitude, metacognitive awareness of reading strategies and reading motivation of L2 learners: A mediational analysis. *Journal of Interdisciplinary Studies in Education*, *14*(1), 1–19. DOI: 10.32674/q5c82955

Manning, C. D., & Schütze, H. (1999). *Foundations of statistical natural language processing*. MIT press.

Marcoulides, K., & Raykov, T. (2019). Evaluation of variance inflation factors in regression models using latent variable modeling methods. *Educational and Psychological Measurement*, *79*(5), 874–882. DOI: 10.1177/0013164418817803 PMID: 31488917

Matsuda, P. K., & Silva, T. (2021). AI-based writing feedback: Implications for second language writing instruction. *Journal of Second Language Writing*, *51*, 100775.

Meese, J. (2021). Journalism policy across the Commonwealth: Partial answers to public problems. *Digital Journalism (Abingdon, England)*, *9*(3), 255–275. DOI: 10.1080/21670811.2020.1835514

Mehta, S. R., & Al-Mahrooqi, R. (2015). Can thinking be taught? Linking critical thinking and writing in an EFL context. *RELC Journal*, *46*(1), 23–36. DOI: 10.1177/0033688214555356

Mertler, C., & Vannatta Reinhart, R. (2017). *Advanced and multivariate statistical methods: Practical application and interpretation*. Routledge.

Messick, S. (1995). Validity of psychological assessment: Validation of inferences from persons' responses and performances as scientific inquiry into score meaning. *The American Psychologist*, *50*(9), 741–749. DOI: 10.1037/0003-066X.50.9.741

Meyers, M. (1993). *Teaching to diversity: Teaching and learning in the multi-ethnic classroom*. Addison-Wesley Publishing Company.

Miranty, D., & Widiati, U. (2021). Automated writing evaluation (AWE) in higher education: Indonesian EFL students' perceptions about Grammarly use across student cohorts. *Egitim ve Ögretim*, *11*(4), 126–137. DOI: 10.47750/pegegog.11.04.12

Mitchell, T. M. (1997). *Machine learning*. McGraw-Hill.

Mittelstadt, B. D., Allo, P., Taddeo, M., Wachter, S., & Floridi, L. (2016). The ethics of algorithms: Mapping the debate. *Big Data & Society*, *3*(2). DOI: 10.1177/2053951716679679

Mohammadi Golchi, M. (2012). Listening anxiety and its relationship with listening strategy use and listening comprehension among Iranian IELTS learners. *International Journal of English Linguistics*, *2*(4), 115–128. DOI: 10.5539/ijel.v2n4p115

Moran, R. E., & Shaikh, S. J. (2022). Robots in the news and newsrooms: Unpacking meta-journalistic discourse on the use of artificial intelligence in journalism. *Digital Journalism (Abingdon, England)*, *10*(10), 1756–1774. DOI: 10.1080/21670811.2022.2085129

Moravec, V., Hynek, N., Skare, M., Gavurova, B., & Kubak, M. (2024). Human or machine? The perception of artificial intelligence in journalism, its socio-economic conditions, and technological developments toward the digital future. *Technological Forecasting and Social Change*, *200*, 123162. DOI: 10.1016/j.techfore.2023.123162

Moreira-Fontán, E., García-Señorán, M., Conde-Rodríguez, Á., & González, A. (2019). Teachers' ICT-related self-efficacy, job resources, and positive emotions: Their structural relations with autonomous motivation and work engagement. *Computers & Education*, *134*, 63–77. DOI: 10.1016/j.compedu.2019.02.007

Moussalli, S., & Cardoso, W. (2020). Intelligent personal assistants: Can they understand and be understood by accented L2 learners? *Computer Assisted Language Learning*, *33*(8), 865–890. DOI: 10.1080/09588221.2019.1595664

Moybeka, A. M. S., Syariatin, N., Tatipang, D. P., Mushthoza, D. A., Dewi, N. P. J. L., & Tineh, S. (2023). Artificial intelligence and English classroom: The implications of AI toward EFL students' motivation. *Edumaspul - Jurnal Pendidikan,* *7*(2), 2444–2454.

Muche, T., Simegn, B., & Shiferie, K. (2024). Self-efficacy and metacognitive strategy use in reading comprehension: EFL learners' perspectives. *The Asia-Pacific Education Researcher*, *33*(1), 219–227. DOI: 10.1007/s40299-023-00721-5

Nah, S., Luo, J., Kim, S., Chen, M., Mitson, R., & Joo, J. (2023). Rethinking Artificial Intelligence: Algorithmic Bias and Ethical Issues| Algorithmic Bias or Algorithmic Reconstruction? A Comparative Analysis Between AI News and Human News. *International Journal of Communication*, *18*, 30.

Nakanishi, T. (2014). A meta-analysis of extensive reading research. *TESOL Quarterly*, *49*(1), 6–37. DOI: 10.1002/tesq.157

Nassaji, H. (2016). Anniversary article interactional feedback in second language teaching and learning: A synthesis and analysis of current research. *Language Teaching Research*, *20*(4), 535–562. DOI: 10.1177/1362168816644940

Newton, J. M., & Nation, I. S. P. (2021). *Teaching ESL/EFL listening and speaking* (2nd ed.). Routledge.

Nguyen, L. Q., & Le, H. V. (2023). Enhancing L2 learners' lexical gains via Quizlet learning tool: The role of individual differences. *Education and Information Technologies*, *28*(9), 12143–12167. DOI: 10.1007/s10639-023-11673-0

Nguyen, T. (2023). EFL teachers' perspectives toward the use of ChatGPT in writing classes: A case study at Van Lang University. *International Journal of Language Instruction*, *2*(3), 1–47. DOI: 10.54855/ijli.23231

Noain Sánchez, A. (2022). Addressing the Impact of Artificial Intelligence on Journalism: The perception of experts, journalists and academics.

Noble, S. (2018). *Algorithms of Oppression*. NYU Press. DOI: 10.18574/nyu/9781479833641.001.0001

Nuotio, M. (2024). The impact of generative AI technologies in journalistic processes on organizational performance: A human-in-the-loop approach.

O'Neil, C. (2016). *Weapons of math destruction: How big data increases inequality and threatens democracy*. Crown.

Oreoluwa, P. A. (2024). Online harassment of female journalists in Lagos State. Polit Journal Scientific Journal of Politics, 4(3), 162-174.

Oroujlou, N., & Vahedi, M. (2011). Motivation, attitude, and language learning. *Procedia: Social and Behavioral Sciences*, *29*, 994–1000. DOI: 10.1016/j.sbspro.2011.11.333

Oshima, S. (2024). Effectiveness of a multimodal approach during online reading strategy instruction. *Reading in a Foreign Language*, *36*(1), 1–20. https://nflrc.hawaii.edu/rfl

Pallant, J. (2013). *SPSS survival manual*. McGraw-Hill Education.

Pangun, G. (2019a). *Artificial intelligence (AI) system's key characteristics*. Towards Data Science.

Pangun, J. M. (2019b). *Artificial intelligence: Concepts, drivers, and business implications*. IGI Global.

Pavlik, J. V. (2023). Collaborating with ChatGPT: Considering the implications of generative artificial intelligence for journalism and media education. *Journalism & Mass Communication Educator*, *78*(1), 84–93. DOI: 10.1177/10776958221149577

Payne, A. R. (2012). *Development of the academic writing motivation questionnaire* [Master's Thesis]. University of Georgia.

Pentzold, C., & Fechner, D. (2021). Probabilistic storytelling and temporal exigencies in predictive data journalism. *Digital Journalism (Abingdon, England)*, *9*(6), 715–736. DOI: 10.1080/21670811.2021.1878920

Perkins, M. (2023). Academic integrity considerations of AI Large Language Models in the post-pandemic era: ChatGPT and beyond. *Journal of University Teaching & Learning Practice*, *20*(2). Advance online publication. DOI: 10.53761/1.20.02.07

Persulessy, S., Nikijuluw, R., & Jakob, J. C. (2024). Utilizing artificial intelligence in language learning: What about engineering students' perception? *Journal of English Education Program*, *5*(1), 48–58. DOI: 10.26418/jeep.v5i1.71159

Phan, T. (2023). Students' perceptions of the AI technology application in English writing classes. *Proceedings of the AsiaCALL International Conference*, *4*, 45–62. DOI: 10.54855/paic.2344

Piaget, J. (1980). *Experiments in child language and thought*. Routledge.

Ponton, M., & Rhea, N. (2006). Autonomous Learning from a Social Cognitive Perspective. *New Horizons in Adult Education and Human Resource Development, 20*(2), 38–49. DOI: 10.1002/nha3.10250

Postman, N. (2000). *The Humanism of Media Ecology*. Hampton Press.

Rahimi, M. (2024). Effects of integrating motivational instructional strategies into a process-genre writing instructional approach on students' engagement and argumentative writing. *System, 121*, 103261. Advance online publication. DOI: 10.1016/j.system.2024.103261

Rahimirad, M., & Moini, M. R. (2015). The challenges of listening to academic lectures for EAP learners and the impact of metacognition on academic lecture listening comprehension. *SAGE Open, 5*(2), 1–9. DOI: 10.1177/2158244015590609

Ramage, K. (1990). Motivational factors and persistence in foreign language study. *Language Learning, 40*(2), 189–219. DOI: 10.1111/j.1467-1770.1990.tb01333.x

Rasool, U., Qian, J., & Aslam, M. Z. (2023). An investigation of foreign language writing anxiety and its reasons among pre-service EFL teachers in Pakistan. *Frontiers in Psychology, 13*, 1–13. DOI: 10.3389/fpsyg.2022.947867 PMID: 36687864

Reinders, H., & White, C. (2016). 20 years of autonomy and technology: How far have we come and where to next? *Language Learning & Technology, 20*(2), 143–154.

Rezaei, M., & Jafari, M. (2014). Investigating the levels, types, and causes of writing anxiety among Iranian EFL students: A mixed method design. *Procedia: Social and Behavioral Sciences, 98*, 1545–1554. DOI: 10.1016/j.sbspro.2014.03.577

Ribeiro, M. T., Singh, S., & Guestrin, C. (2016). "Why should I trust you?" Explaining the predictions of any classifier. *Proceedings of the 22nd ACM SIGKDD International Conference on Knowledge Discovery and Data Mining*, 1135-1144.

Ricci, F., Rokach, L., Shapira, B., & Kantor, P. B. (Eds.). (2011). *Recommender systems handbook*. Springer. DOI: 10.1007/978-0-387-85820-3

Richards, J. C., & Rodgers, T. S. (2014). *Approaches and methods in language teaching* (3rd ed.). Cambridge University Press. DOI: 10.1017/9781009024532

Romero, M., Buzón-García, O., & Touron, J. (2019). The flipped learning model in online based education for secondary teachers. *Journal of Technology and Science Education, 9*(2), 109. DOI: 10.3926/jotse.435

Rukthong, A., & Brunfaut, T. (2019). Is anybody listening? The nature of second language listening in integrated listening-to-summarize tasks. *Language Testing, 37*(1), 26–52. DOI: 10.1177/0265532219871470

Rumsey, C. (2024). *Why it's important to learn English.* Studio Cambridge. https://www.studiocambridge.co.uk/why-it-is-important-to-learn-english/

Russell, S. J., & Norvig, P. (2020). *Artificial intelligence: A modern approach* (4th ed.). Pearson.

Russell, S., & Norvig, P. (2021). *Artificial Intelligence: A Modern Approach* (4th ed.). Pearson.

Ryan, R. M., & Deci, E. L. (2000). Self-determination theory and the facilitation of intrinsic motivation. *The American Psychologist, 55*(1), 68–78. DOI: 10.1037/0003-066X.55.1.68 PMID: 11392867

Ryan, R., & Deci, E. (2000). Intrinsic and extrinsic motivations: Classic definitions and new directions. *Contemporary Educational Psychology, 25*(1), 54–67. DOI: 10.1006/ceps.1999.1020 PMID: 10620381

Sabti, A. A., Md Rashid, S., Nimehchisalem, V., & Darmi, R. (2019). The impact of writing anxiety, writing achievement motivation, and writing self-efficacy on writing performance: A correlational study of Iraqi tertiary EFL learners. *SAGE Open, 9*(4), 1–13. DOI: 10.1177/2158244019894289

Salmani, S., & Rahimi, M. (2024). Does multimodality add to the value of L2 listening homework? A mixed-methods study of comprehension and cognitive load. *English Teaching & Learning*. 1-28. https://doi.org/DOI: 10.1007/s42321-024-00181-0

Sari, E., & Han, T. (2024). The impact of automated writing evaluation on English as a foreign language learners' writing self-efficacy, self-regulation, anxiety, and performance. *Journal of Computer Assisted Learning, 40*(5), 2065–2080. DOI: 10.1111/jcal.13004

Sarker, I. (2022). AI-based modeling: Techniques, applications and research issues towards automation, intelligent and smart systems. *SN Computer Science, 3*(2), 1–20. DOI: 10.1007/s42979-022-01043-x PMID: 35194580

Savran Çelik, Ş., & Aydın, S. (2018). A review of research on the use of native language in EFL classes. *The Literacy Trek, 4*(2), 1–14.

Sayici, S., & Aydın, S. (2025). Using artificial intelligence in foreign language teaching: Teachers' perspectives. *Proceedings of The World Conference on Education and Teaching, 4*(1), 1–10. DOI: 10.33422/etconf.v4i1.1016

Schacter, D., Gilbert, D., & Wegner, D. (2009). *Introducing psychology*. Macmillan.

Scherer, K. R. (2005). What are emotions? And how can they be measured? *Social Sciences Information. Information Sur les Sciences Sociales*, *44*(4), 695–729. DOI: 10.1177/0539018405058216

Scherer, R., Siddiq, F., & Tondeur, J. (2019). The technology acceptance model (TAM): A meta-analytic structural equation modeling approach to explaining teachers 'adoption of digital technology in education. *Computers & Education*, *128*, 13–35. DOI: 10.1016/j.compedu.2018.09.009

Schmidt, R. (2012). Attention, awareness, and individual differences in language learning. In Chan, W. M., Nyet Chin, K., Bhatt, S. K., & Walker, I. (Eds.), *Perspectives on individual characteristics and foreign language education* (pp. 6–27). De Gruyter Mouton., DOI: 10.1515/9781614510932.27

Schork, N. J. (2015). Personalized medicine: Time for one-person trials. *Nature*, *520*(7549), 609–611. DOI: 10.1038/520609a PMID: 25925459

Selwyn, N. (2019). Should robots replace teachers? AI and the future of education. *Learning, Media and Technology*, *44*(1), 1–7.

Shadiev, R., Wen, Y., Uosaki, N., & Song, Y. (2023). Future language learning with emerging technologies. *Journal of Computers in Education*, *10*(3), 463–467. DOI: 10.1007/s40692-023-00285-9

Shadiev, R., Wu, T., Sun, A., & Huang, Y. (2018). Applications of speech-to-text recognition and computer-aided translation for facilitating cross-cultural learning through a learning activity: Issues and their solutions. *Educational Technology Research and Development*, *66*(1), 191–214. DOI: 10.1007/s11423-017-9556-8

Shadish, W. R., Cook, T. D., & Campbell, D. T. (2002). *Experimental and quasi-experimental designs for generalized causal inference* (3rd ed., Vol. 1195). Houghton Mifflin.

Shafiee Rad, H. (2025). Reinforcing L2 reading comprehension through artificial intelligence intervention: Refining engagement to foster self-regulated learning. *Smart Learning Environments*, *12*(23), 23. Advance online publication. DOI: 10.1186/s40561-025-00377-2

Sharadgah, T. A., & Sa'di, R. A. (2022). A systematic review of research on the use of artificial intelligence in English language teaching and learning (2015-2021): What are the current effects? *Journal of Information Technology Education*, *21*, 337–377. DOI: 10.28945/4999

Sharma, R. (2024). Navigating the nexus: A bibliometric analysis of the intersection between AI, multimedia and journalism. *2024 Third International Conference on Smart Technologies and Systems for Next Generation Computing (ICSTSN)*. IEEE. DOI: 10.1109/ICSTSN61422.2024.10670795

Showkat, D., & Baumer, E. P. S. (2021). Where do stories come from? Examining the exploration process in investigative data journalism. Proceedings of the ACM on Human-Computer Interaction, 5(CSC W2), 1-31. DOI: 10.1145/3479534

Sivaji, V., Prabhavathy, P., Brinda Shree, V., Varadharajan, T. S., Angelin, S. Y. R., & Pradeepa, M. (2024, November 15–16). Leveraging advanced AI-driven pedagogical strategies to enhance English listening skills. *2024 Second International Conference on Computational and Characterization Techniques in Engineering & Sciences (IC3TES)*. https://doi.org/DOI: 10.1109/IC3TES62412.2024.10877491

Skinner, B. F. (1957). *Verbal behavior*. Appleton-Century-Crofts. DOI: 10.1037/11256-000

Smith, J., & Gray, P. (2021). AI in language education: Issues of accessibility and equity. *Educational Review*, *73*(4), 522–540.

Spielberger, C. D. (1983). *State-trait anxiety inventory for adults* (1st ed.). Consulting Psychologists Press.

Statista. (2024). *Languages most frequently used for web content as of January 2024, by share of websites*. https://www.statista.com/statistics/262946/most-common-languages-on-the-internet/

Stray, J. (2021). Making artificial intelligence work for investigative journalism. In *Algorithms* (pp. 97–118). Automation, and News.

Sun, M., Hu, W., & Wu, Y. (2024). Public perceptions and attitudes towards the application of artificial intelligence in journalism: From a China-based survey. *Journalism Practice*, *18*(3), 548–570. DOI: 10.1080/17512786.2022.2055621

Swain, M. (1985). Communicative competence: Some roles of comprehensible input and comprehensible output in its development. In *Input in second language acquisition* (pp. 165–179). Heinle & Heinle.

Sweeney, L. (2002). k-anonymity: A model for protecting privacy. *International Journal of Uncertainty, Fuzziness and Knowledge-based Systems*, *10*(05), 557–570. DOI: 10.1142/S0218488502001648

Syed, M. (2023). *The role of AI in social media marketing*. Simplilearn.

Syrewicz, C. C. (2023). The motivations that improve the creative writing process: What they might be and why we should study them. *New Writing*, *20*(2), 178–200. DOI: 10.1080/14790726.2022.2051563

Szeliski, R. (2010). *Computer vision: Algorithms and applications*. Springer.

Tabachnick, B., & Fidell, L. (2014). *Using multivariate statistics*. Pearson.

Tafazoli, D., María, E., & Abril, C. (2019). Intelligent language tutoring system. *International Journal of Information and Communication Technology Education*, *15*(3), 60–74. DOI: 10.4018/IJICTE.2019070105

Tahiru, F. (2021). AI in education: A systematic literature review. *Journal of Cases on Information Technology*, *23*(1), 1–20. DOI: 10.4018/JCIT.2021010101

Taskiran, A., Yazici, M., & Erdem Aydin, I. (2024). Contribution of automated feedback to the English writing competence of distance foreign language learners. *E-Learning and Digital Media*, *21*(1), 24–41. DOI: 10.1177/20427530221139579

Teng, M. F., & Zhang, L. J. (2021). Development of children's metacognitive knowledge, reading, and writing in English as a foreign language: Evidence from longitudinal data using multilevel models. *The British Journal of Educational Psychology*, *91*(4), 1202–1230. DOI: 10.1111/bjep.12413 PMID: 33694166

Tessem, B., Nyre, L., Mesquita, S. M., & Mulholland, P. (2022). Deep learning to encourage citizen involvement in local journalism. In Futures of Journalism: Technology-stimulated Evolution in the Audience-News Media Relationship (pp. 211-226). Cham: Springer International Publishing.

Thurman, N. (2024). AI-Powered Newsrooms: A Global Benchmark Study. *Digital Journalism (Abingdon, England)*, *12*(1), 1–24.

Tobias, S. (1979). Anxiety research in educational psychology. *Journal of Educational Psychology*, *71*(5), 573–582. DOI: 10.1037/0022-0663.71.5.573 PMID: 41010

Tran, L. T. (2007). Learners' motivation and identity in the Vietnamese EFL writing classroom. *English Teaching*, *6*(1), 151–163. https://education.waikato.ac.nz/research/files/etpc/2007v6n1art8.pdfpp.151-163

Túñez-López, J.-M., Fieiras-Ceide, C., & Vaz-Álvarez, M. (2021). Impact of artificial intelligence on journalism: Transformations in the company, products, contents, and professional profile. *Communicatio Socialis*, *34*(1), 177–193.

Utami, S. P. T., Andayani, A., Winarni, R., & Sumarwati, S. (2023). Utilization of artificial intelligence technology in an academic writing class: How do Indonesian students perceive? *Contemporary Educational Technology*, *15*(4), ep450. DOI: 10.30935/cedtech/13419

Valizadeh, M. R., & Alavinia, P. (2013). Listening comprehension performance viewed in the light of emotional intelligence and foreign language listening anxiety. *English Language Teaching*, *6*(12), 11–26. DOI: 10.5539/elt.v6n12p11

Vamathevan, J., Clark, D., Czodrowski, P., Dunham, I., Ferran, E., Lee, G., Li, B., Madabhushi, A., Shah, P., Spitzer, M., & Zhao, S. (2019). Applications of machine learning in drug discovery and development. *Nature Reviews. Drug Discovery*, *18*(6), 463–477. DOI: 10.1038/s41573-019-0024-5 PMID: 30976107

Vandenberg, R., & Lance, C. (2000). A review and synthesis of the measurement invariance literature: Suggestions, practices, and recommendations for organizational research. *Organizational Research Methods*, *3*(1), 4–70. DOI: 10.1177/109442810031002

Vandergrift, L. (1999). Facilitating second language listening comprehension: Acquiring successful strategies. *ELT Journal*, *53*(3), 168–176. DOI: 10.1093/elt/53.3.168

Vandergrift, L. (2004). Listening to learn or learning to listen? *Annual Review of Applied Linguistics*, *24*, 3–25. DOI: 10.1017/S0267190504000017

Vandergrift, L. (2007). *Teaching and learning in a second language: Listening, speaking, reading, and writing*. Pearson Longman.

Vandergrift, L., & Baker, S. (2015). Learner variables in second language listening comprehension: An exploratory path analysis. *Language Learning*, *65*(2), 390–416. DOI: 10.1111/lang.12105

Vandergrift, L., & Tafaghodtari, M. H. (2010). Teaching L2 learners how to listen does make a difference: An empirical study. *Language Learning*, *60*(2), 470–497. DOI: 10.1111/j.1467-9922.2009.00559.x

Varaporn, S., & Sitthitikul, P. (2019). Effects of multimodal tasks on students' critical reading ability and perceptions. *Reading in a Foreign Language*, *31*(1), 81–108. https://nflrc.hawaii.edu/rfl

Verga, L., & Kotz, S. (2013). How relevant is social interaction in second language learning? *Frontiers in Human Neuroscience*, *7*, 1–7. DOI: 10.3389/fnhum.2013.00550 PMID: 24027521

Verma, D. (2024). Impact of artificial intelligence on journalism: A comprehensive review of AI in journalism. *Journal of Communication Management (London)*, *3*(02), 150–156.

Vuong, Q.-H., La, V.-P., Nguyen, M.-H., Jin, R., La, M.-K., & Le, T.-T. (2023). AI's humanoid appearance can affect human perceptions of its emotional capability: Evidence form self-reported data in the U.S. International Journal of Human-Computer Interaction, 1–12.

Vygotsky, L. (1978). Interaction between learning and development. In Gauvain, M., & Cole, M. (Eds.), *Readings on the development of children* (pp. 34–40). Scientific American Books.

Vygotsky, L. S. (1978). *Mind in society: The development of higher psychological processes (M. Cole, V. John-Steiner* (Scribner, S., & Souberman, E., Eds.; 1st ed.). Harvard University Press.

Vygotsky, L. S. (1978). *Mind in society: The development of higher psychological processes*. Harvard University Press.

Waer, H. (2023). The effect of integrating automated writing evaluation on EFL writing apprehension and grammatical knowledge. *Innovation in Language Learning and Teaching*, *17*(1), 47–71. DOI: 10.1080/17501229.2021.1914062

Wale, B. D., & Kassahun, Y. F. (2024). The transformative power of AI writing technologies: Enhancing EFL writing instruction through the integrative use of Writerly and Google Docs. *Human Behavior and Emerging Technologies*, *2024*, 1–15. DOI: 10.1155/2024/9221377

Wallace, M. P., & Lee, K. (2020). Examining second language listening, vocabulary, and executive functioning. *Frontiers in Psychology*, *11*, 1122. Advance online publication. DOI: 10.3389/fpsyg.2020.01122 PMID: 32581951

Wang, H., & Tahir, R. (2020). Gamification and AI: Enhancing motivation in second language acquisition. *Interactive Learning Environments*, *28*(3), 456–470.

Wang, L., & MacIntyre, P. (2021). Second language listening comprehension: The role of anxiety and enjoyment in listening metacognitive awareness. *Studies in Second Language Learning and Teaching*, *11*(4), 491–515. DOI: 10.14746/ssllt.2021.11.4.2

Wang, X., Pang, H., Wallace, M., Wang, Q., & Chen, W. (2024). Learners' perceived AI presences in AI-supported language learning: A study of AI as a humanized agent from community of inquiry. *Computer Assisted Language Learning*, *37*(4), 814–840. DOI: 10.1080/09588221.2022.2056203

Watkins, M. (2018). Exploratory factor analysis: A guide to best practice. *The Journal of Black Psychology*, *44*(3), 219–246. DOI: 10.1177/0095798418771807

Watson, J. (2001). Social constructivism in the classroom. *Support for Learning*, *16*(3), 140–147. DOI: 10.1111/1467-9604.00206

Weiner, B. (1972). Attribution theory, achievement motivation, and the educational process. *Review of Educational Research*, *42*(2), 203–215. DOI: 10.3102/00346543042002203

Weng, X., & Chiu, T. K. (2023). Instructional design and learning outcomes of intelligent computer assisted language learning: Systematic review in the field. *Comput. Educ. Artif. Intell.*, *4*, 100117. DOI: 10.1016/j.caeai.2022.100117

Wilczek, B., Haim, M., & Thurman, N. (2024). Transforming the value chain of local journalism with artificial intelligence. *AI Magazine*, *45*(2), 200–211. DOI: 10.1002/aaai.12174

Wilson, J., Ahrendt, C., Fudge, E., Raiche, A., Beard, G., & MacArthur, C. (2021). Elementary teachers' perceptions of automated feedback and automated scoring: Transforming the teaching and learning of writing using automated writing evaluation. *Computers & Education*, *168*, 104208. DOI: 10.1016/j.compedu.2021.104208

Wilson, J., & Czik, A. (2016). Automated essay evaluation software in English language arts classrooms: Effects on teacher feedback, student motivation, and writing quality. *Computers & Education*, *100*, 94–109. DOI: 10.1016/j.compedu.2016.05.004

Wood, D., Bruner, J., & Ross, G. (1976). The role of tutoring in problem solving. *Journal of Child Psychology and Psychiatry, and Allied Disciplines*, *17*(2), 89–100. DOI: 10.1111/j.1469-7610.1976.tb00381.x PMID: 932126

Xiao, Y. (2025). The impact of AI-driven speech recognition on EFL listening comprehension, flow experience, and anxiety: A randomized controlled trial. *Humanities & Social Sciences Communications*, *12*(1), 425. Advance online publication. DOI: 10.1057/s41599-025-04672-8

Xia, Q., Chiu, T. K., & Chai, C. S. (2022). The moderating effects of gender and need satisfaction on self-regulated learning through artificial intelligence (AI). *Education and Information Technologies*, *28*(7), 8691–8713. DOI: 10.1007/s10639-022-11547-x

Xia, Y., & Yang, Y. (2019). RMSEA, CFI, and TLI in structural equation modeling with ordered categorical data: The story they tell depends on the estimation methods. *Behavior Research Methods*, *51*(1), 409–428. DOI: 10.3758/s13428-018-1055-2 PMID: 29869222

Xu, X. (2011). The relationship between language learning motivation and the choice of language learning strategies among Chinese graduates. *International Journal of English Linguistics*, *1*(2), 203–212. DOI: 10.5539/ijel.v1n2p203

Xu, Y., Aubele, J., Vigil, V., Bustamante, A. S., Kim, Y.-S., & Warschauer, M. (2022). Dialogue with a conversational agent promotes children's story comprehension via enhancing engagement. *Child Development*, *93*(2), e149–e167. DOI: 10.1111/cdev.13708 PMID: 34748214

Xu, Y., Wang, D., Collins, P., Lee, H., & Warschauer, M. (2021). Same benefits, different communication patterns: Comparing children's reading with a conversational agent vs. a human partner. *Computers & Education*, *161*, 104059. DOI: 10.1016/j.compedu.2020.104059

Xu, Z., Wijekumar, K., Ramirez, G., Hu, X., & Irey, R. (2019). The effectiveness of intelligent tutoring systems on K-12 students' reading comprehension: A meta-analysis. *British Journal of Educational Technology*, *50*(6), 3119–3137. DOI: 10.1111/bjet.12758

Yan, D. (2023). Impact of Chat GPT on learners in a L2 writing practicum: an exploratory investigation. Educ. Inf. Technol., 1–25. DOI: 10.1007/s10639-023-11742-4

Yaylı, D., & Genç, E. (2019). The second language writing anxiety: The perceived sources and consequences. *Pamukkale University Journal of Education*, *45*(45), 235–251. DOI: 10.9779/PUJE.2018.231

Yekeler, A. D., & Ulusoy, M. (2021). The relationship among listening comprehension and factors affecting listening. *Education in Science*, *46*(205), 1–17. DOI: 10.15390/EB.2020.9066

Yeung, M. (2016). Exploring the construct of learner autonomy in writing: The roles of motivation and the teacher. *English Language Teaching*, *9*(8), 122–139. DOI: 10.5539/elt.v9n8p122

Yılmaz, Ö. K., & Aydın, S. (2025). The impact of the use of artificial intelligence-generated materials on reading motivation among EFL learners. *Reading Research Quarterly*, *60*(3), e70016. DOI: 10.1002/rrq.70016

Yin, J., Goh, T., Yang, B., & Xiaobin, Y. (2021). Conversation technology with micro-learning: The impact of chatbot-based learning on students' learning motivation and performance. *Journal of Educational Computing Research*, *59*(1), 154–177. DOI: 10.1177/0735633120952067

Yu, D., Zhou, Y., Li, Y., Shen, X., Tian, M., Yang, B., Su, J., & Sun, Y. (2022). A survey of English learning softwares based on TPACK framework. *The 17th Academic Annual Conference of the Information Technology Education Professional Committee of China Educational Technology Association*, 1–9.

Zaman, M., & Kalam, A. (2012). Feedback in EFL writing at tertiary level: Teachers' and learners' perceptions. *ASA University Review, 6*(1).

Zarei, M., Ahour, T., & Seifoori, Z. (2020). Impacts of implicit, explicit, and emergent feedback strategies on EFL learners' motivation, attitude and perception. *Cogent Education, 7*(1), 1727130. Advance online publication. DOI: 10.1080/2331186X.2020.1727130

Zawacki-Richter, O., Marín, V. I., Bond, M., & Gouverneur, F. (2019). Systematic review of research on artificial intelligence applications in higher education—Where are the educators? *International Journal of Educational Technology in Higher Education, 16*(1), 1–27. DOI: 10.1186/s41239-019-0171-0

Zechner, K., Evanini, K., & Yoon, S. Y. (2019). Automated speech assessment: Current trends and future directions. *Language Testing, 36*(1), 39–62.

Zhang, L. J. (2001). Awareness in reading: EFL students' metacognitive knowledge of reading strategies in an acquisition-poor environment. *Language Awareness, 10*(4), 268–288. DOI: 10.1080/09658410108667039

Zhang, R., & Zou, D. (2020). Types, purposes, and effectiveness of state-of-the-art technologies for second and foreign language learning. *Computer Assisted Language Learning, 35*(4), 696–742. DOI: 10.1080/09588221.2020.1744666

Zhang, S., & Zhang, X. (2020). The relationship between vocabulary knowledge and L2 reading/listening comprehension: A meta-analysis. *Language Teaching Research, 24*(5), 577–612. DOI: 10.1177/1362168820913998

Zhang, W., & Pérez Tornero, J. M. (2023). Introduction to AI journalism: Framework and ontology of the trans-domain field for integrating AI into journalism. *Journal of Applied Journalism & Media Studies, 12*(3), 333–353. DOI: 10.1386/ajms_00063_1

Zhao, A., Guo, Y., & Dynia, J. (2013). Foreign language reading anxiety: Chinese as a foreign language in the United States. *Modern Language Journal, 97*(3), 764–778. DOI: 10.1111/j.1540-4781.2013.12032.x

Zimmerman, B. J. (2000). Motivational sources and outcomes of self-regulated learning and performance. In Zimmerman, B. J., & Schunk, D. H. (Eds.), *Handbook of self-regulation* (pp. 13–39). Elsevier. DOI: 10.1016/B978-012109890-2/50031-7

Zou, B., Liviero, S., Hao, M., & Wei, C. (2020). Artificial intelligence technology for EAP speaking skills: Student perceptions of opportunities and challenges. In N. Freiermuth, M., Zarrinabadi (Ed.), *Technology and the Psychology of Second Language Learners and Users. New Language Learning and Teaching Environments* (pp. 433–463). Palgrave Macmillan. DOI: 10.1007/978-3-030-34212-8_17

About The Contributors

Ankit Shukla is an accomplished educator and researcher with a robust background in the hospitality and tourism industry. His career spans various roles, from frontline food and beverage service to academic leadership and extensive research contributions. Ankit's journey exemplifies a blend of practical experience, academic acumen, and a passion for advancing knowledge in his field. Early Career and Industry Experience Ankit's career in the hospitality industry began at the Hyatt Regency Chandigarh in September 2015, where he worked in the Food & Beverage Service department. His responsibilities included taking room service orders, managing point-of-sale systems, and setting up banquets for events. This role provided Ankit with hands-on experience in the operational aspects of the hospitality industry. Following his time at the Hyatt Regency, Ankit transitioned into academia, joining Kumaun University Nainital as a teaching personnel in September 2016. He took on multiple responsibilities, including lecturing MBA Tourism students, overseeing practical training, and designing course curricula. This marked the beginning of his journey in education, where he contributed to shaping the next generation of hospitality professionals. Academic Leadership and Teaching Ankit's academic career continued to flourish as he assumed the role of Assistant Professor at SIHMCT & AN Tehri Garhwal in July 2017. He became the head of the Food & Beverage Service department, where he coordinated events, designed course curricula, and managed the department's overall functioning. From February 2018 to April 2022, Ankit served as an Assistant Professor at Shoolini University Solan. Here, he expanded his responsibilities to include training and placement coordination, NAAC coordination for the Hospitality Management department, and handling operations of a hotel with eight rooms. His leadership skills and ability to manage complex tasks were instrumental in the smooth functioning of the university's hospitality department. Contributions to Research and Academia Ankit's passion for research is evident through his significant contributions to academic literature. He has presented research papers at various international conferences, focusing on topics such as ecology, local and regional food in destination marketing, and the influence of technological amenities on hotel guest satisfaction. His research has been published in reputable journals, with manuscripts addressing safety and security measures in hotels, tobacco consumption in India, and the role of Indian spices in Indian history. In addition to his research publications, Ankit has filed 40 patents, copyrights, and utility applications, with several already granted. His commitment to innovation and intellectual property rights underscores his dedication to advancing knowledge in his field. Current Role and Future Endeavors As of July 2023, Ankit is a lecturer at Raja Mangala University of Technology Thanyaburi in Thailand. In this role, he continues to inspire and educate students in the field of hospitality while pursuing his research interests. Ankit's extensive experience in both industry and academia, coupled with his passion for teaching and research, positions him as a key figure in the ongoing development of the hospitality and tourism sector. Ankit Shukla's journey from industry practitioner to esteemed academic is a testament to his dedication, expertise, and unwavering commitment to excellence in hospitality and education.

Benjaporn Meeprom is a seasoned educator and researcher specializing in Computer-Assisted Language Learning (CALL), digital game-based language learning, and English for Specific Purposes (ESP). With a Ph.D. from the University of Newcastle, Australia, her expertise lies in integrating technology into language education to foster learner autonomy and enhance curriculum design. She has led innovative projects such as the Erasmus Plus "GreenEdAsia" initiative and spearheaded the development of online language assessment systems. As an award-winning faculty supervisor and curriculum innovator at Rajamangala University of Technology Thanyaburi (RMUTT), Dr. Meeprom has transformed English language programs by incorporating AI-driven tools and methodologies. Her research on digital learning tools and strategies for TOEIC and IELTS preparation has contributed to bridging gaps in English language proficiency among Thai learners. A prolific conference speaker and workshop facilitator, she advocates for leveraging AI to personalize learning experiences and improve teaching effectiveness. Friendly and approachable, Dr. Meeprom's work inspires educators to embrace cutting-edge technologies in empowering students to thrive in global communication. Dr. Meeprom's contribution in this book reflects her lifelong commitment to advancing English language teaching through AI innovation, underscoring her passion for creating meaningful, tech-enabled educational experience.

Kongkiat Khunasathitchai is a lecturer at Rajamangala University of Technology Thanyaburi, Thailand. His interests cover ESP courses related to hotel and tourism. He also specializes in teaching English as a foreign language.

Nagendra Yadav is an 11th-year academia professional with a master's degree in hotel management from Kurukshetra University. With a passion for culinary arts and management, Nagendra has dedicated his career to enhancing guests' culinary dining and hospitality experience worldwide. His expertise spans various facets of hotel operations, including culinary innovation, guest services, and management practices. As an educator, Nagendra shares his knowledge and experience with the next generation of hospitality professionals, inspiring them to pursue excellence and creativity in their careers. He continues to explore new trends and innovations in the industry, aiming to elevate the standards of hospitality and enrich the experiences of guests and clients. He extensively researched promoting local and authentic culinary offerings in destinations. His work has contributed to a broader understanding of how culinary experiences can drive tourism and support local economies.

***

Gülnihan Altınay is a research assistant at Istanbul Kültür University. Her work focuses on foreign language teaching and the integration of artificial intelligence.

Selami Aydin is a full professor in the Department of English Language Teaching at Istanbul Medeniyet University, Istanbul, Turkey. He researches on EFL writing, testing, affective states, technology use and social media effects on language learning and teaching processes. Currently, he teaches ELT related courses at BA and MA programs.

Susanta Das is a seasoned educator with a proven record of teaching and mentoring diverse students, working at multiple institutions, and providing service to the various initiatives of organizations. He received his Ph.D. & M.A. degrees from Western Michigan University, USA, and M.Sc. degree from Banaras Hindu University, India all in Physics. He continued his research as a Marie-Curie post-doctoral fellow at Stockholm University, Sweden, at the IISER-Kolkata, India as a Project Scientist-B & at the University of Electro-Communications, Tokyo, Japan as a Post-doctoral fellow. Dr. Das worked and collaborated with many researchers, Ph.D., master, and visiting students from different countries. He further visited many countries to discuss research and an international conference participant. He worked at several institutions before assuming his current role at Ajeenkya D Y Patil University.

Gökhan Hiniz is an English Language Teaching (ELT) instructor with a PhD in ELT. He has extensive experience in teaching, curriculum and material development, testing, departmental leadership, and coordinating professional development events at universities in Türkiye. He is currently working in the foreign languages department at Çanakkale Onsekiz Mart University. His research focuses on student engagement, teacher professional development and using technology within the field of ELT.

Abhishek Tiwari is an accomplished academic with More than five years of teaching experience in Thailand as a university lecturer. His dedication to education and research is evident through his extensive work in various academic fields. Abhishek has published numerous research papers in prestigious Scopus-indexed and international journals, contributing significantly to his areas of expertise. In addition to his research, Abhishek has actively participated in and presented at several international conferences, showcasing his commitment to sharing knowledge and fostering academic discussions. His academic journey is further enriched by his participation in numerous Faculty Development Programs (FDPs), where he has both gained and imparted knowledge, enhancing the educational experience for himself and his peers. Beyond the classroom and research, Abhishek has also organized various community service projects, demonstrating his dedication to giving back to society. His efforts in arranging industrial visits have provided students with valuable practical insights, bridging the gap between theoretical knowledge and real-world applications.

Samina Firoz Waglawala is a distinguished scholar in English Literature, holding a Doctor of Philosophy (Ph.D.) degree. Her groundbreaking doctoral thesis, "A Discourse on the Depiction of Female Protagonists by Male American Writers in Selected Novels," explores the nuanced portrayal of women through the lens of male authors, offering critical insights into gender representation in literature. Currently serving as an Assistant Professor at Ajeenkya DY Patil University, Pune, Dr. Waglawala brings a wealth of expertise and a passion for literature to her teaching. Her dynamic approach fosters a deeper understanding of literary theories and cultural narratives among her students. Known for her analytical rigor and exceptional command of English literature, she has also impressed peers and academics, including Dr. Surendra Sinh Gohil, who praised her during her Ph.D. viva defense. Dr. Waglawala continues to inspire and contribute to the literary academic community.

Index

A

B

C

D

E

J

L

M

N

P

R

S

www.ingramcontent.com/pod-product-compliance
Ingram Content Group UK Ltd.
Pitfield, Milton Keynes, MK11 3LW, UK
UKHW050844101026
15624UKWH00018B/547

9 798337 356815